This Little Piggy Stayed Home

Other Books by Stephan Pastis

Pearls Before Swine: BLTs Taste So Darn Good

This Little Piggy Stayed Home

Pearls Before Swine

by Stephan Pastis

**Andrews McMeel
Publishing**

Kansas City

Pearls Before Swine is distributed internationally by United Feature Syndicate.

This Little Piggy Stayed Home copyright © 2004 by Stephan Pastis. All rights reserved. Printed in the United States of America. No part of this book may be used or reproduced in any manner whatsoever without written permission except in the case of reprints in the context of reviews. For information, write Andrews McMeel Publishing, an Andrews McMeel Universal company, 4520 Main Street, Kansas City, Missouri 64111.

04 05 06 07 08 BBG 10 9 8 7 6 5 4 3 2 1

ISBN: 0-7407-3813-5

Library of Congress Control Number: 2003113030

Pearls Before Swine can be viewed on the Internet at

www.comics.com/comics/pearls.

These strips appeared in newspapers from October 7, 2002 to July 13, 2003.

Front cover colored by Paige Braddock of *Jane's World* fame.

──── **ATTENTION: SCHOOLS AND BUSINESSES** ────

Andrews McMeel books are available at quantity discounts with bulk purchase for educational, business, or sales promotional use. For information, please write to: Special Sales Department, Andrews McMeel Publishing, 4520 Main Street, Kansas City, Missouri 64111.

For Tom and Julia

Introduction

The question I get the most from *Pearls* readers is, "Where do you get your ideas?"

And the truth is I don't know.

What I do know is that most of the better ones seem to quite literally pop into my head, with most of the dialogue already written. A good example of this is one of the more popular daily strips, where Rat asks Pig, "If you could have a conversation with one person, living or dead, who would it be?" and Pig answers, "The living one." I don't think I spent more than a minute writing it. It was just there. The good ones always seem to be more "found" than "created."

I also know that the ideas seem to come in bunches. If there's one good idea, there's usually a few more behind it. For example, the Farina series (Rat's Bubble Girl girlfriend), which appears in the first *Pearls* book, consists of ten strips that were all written in the space of thirty minutes. It's an unbelievable feeling when that's happening. It's like all you have to do is keep the pen moving.

But the converse of this is also true. When there's nothing there, there's nothing there. I've had days where I've written for ten straight hours, not eating and not leaving my room, and I have not come up with a single idea. Those are the days that usually end with my breaking a set of pencils or a trash can or, when it's really bad, a chair.

While the thought process remains more or less a mystery, I have learned that there are certain circumstances that seem to be more conducive to creativity than others. For me, the key is total isolation, loud music, and coffee. Every time I explain what I do to achieve this in interviews, I look unbelievably strange. But it's the truth, and I am strange, so here goes.

First, I lock myself in a spare bedroom in our house. I remove the phone. I close the blinds. I even put a folding chair in front of the door, in case the lock doesn't work. I also turn off the lights, leaving only the minimal amount of sunlight that comes in through the closed blinds to show me where the notepad is.

Second, I turn on loud music. I have about a dozen compilation CDs that I've made, filled with what I think are great, soaring, more or less spiritual songs in which you can lose yourself. There tends to be a lot of U2, Peter Gabriel, Radiohead, Pink Floyd, and Counting Crows in the mix. I put three CDs in the player, hit the "shuffle" and "repeat" features, and put on the headphones. The volume is such that if I were to leave the room, and walk to the kitchen (about forty feet away), I could still hear the music coming out of the headphones.

Third, I drink a lot of coffee . . . two large cups. For the first hour, I just drink the coffee and walk back and forth with my headphones on, head nodding up and down to the music, occasionally playing the air guitar, and air drums and dancing. As I'm usually wearing only my boxers, you now have a good visual of how strange this really is.

To make matters even stranger, I periodically go to my bookshelf and read the same sections of the same books over and over. They are: 1) the end of F. Scott Fitzgerald's *The Great Gatsby*; 2) the beginning of Hunter Thompson's *Fear and Loathing in Las Vegas*; and 3) Ernest Hemingway's short story "A Clean, Well-Lighted Place."

By the second hour of this, the ideas will usually start coming, and I'll lie on my stomach on the floor and write them all down in a spiral notepad. I don't draw at all. I only write. After about eight hours of this, I'll usually have a week's worth of strips written. Which means I can put on my pants and get dinner . . . hopefully in that order.

So what does all this ugliness mean?

It means that the process of humor writing is most akin to what they say about sausage: It tastes great, but you probably don't want to see how it's made.

Enjoy your sausage.

Stephan Pastis

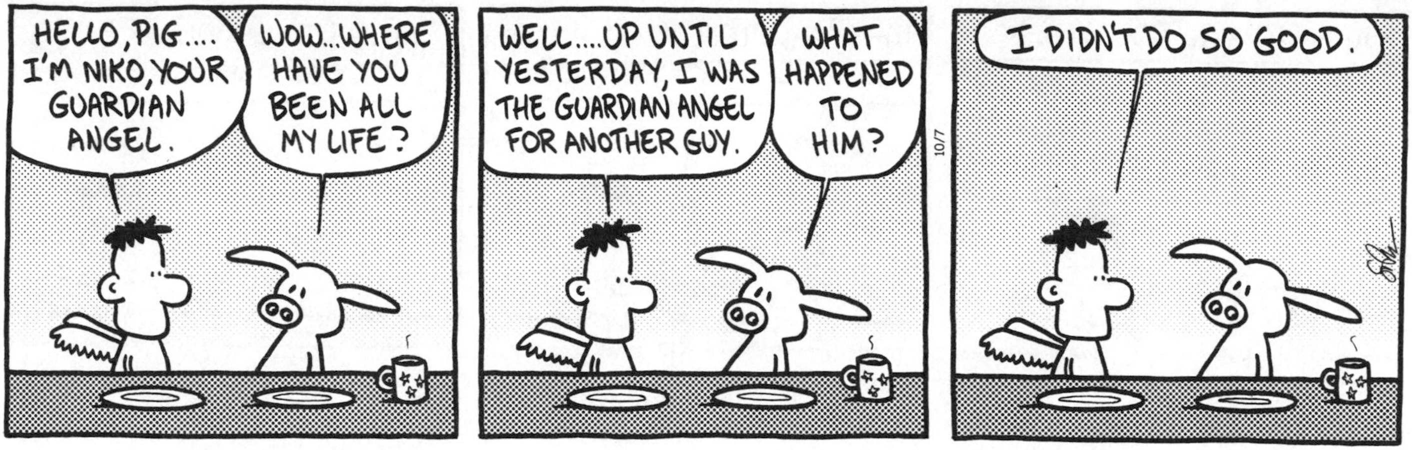
HELLO, PIG.... I'M NIKO, YOUR GUARDIAN ANGEL.
WOW...WHERE HAVE YOU BEEN ALL MY LIFE?
WELL....UP UNTIL YESTERDAY, I WAS THE GUARDIAN ANGEL FOR ANOTHER GUY.
WHAT HAPPENED TO HIM?
10/7
I DIDN'T DO SO GOOD.

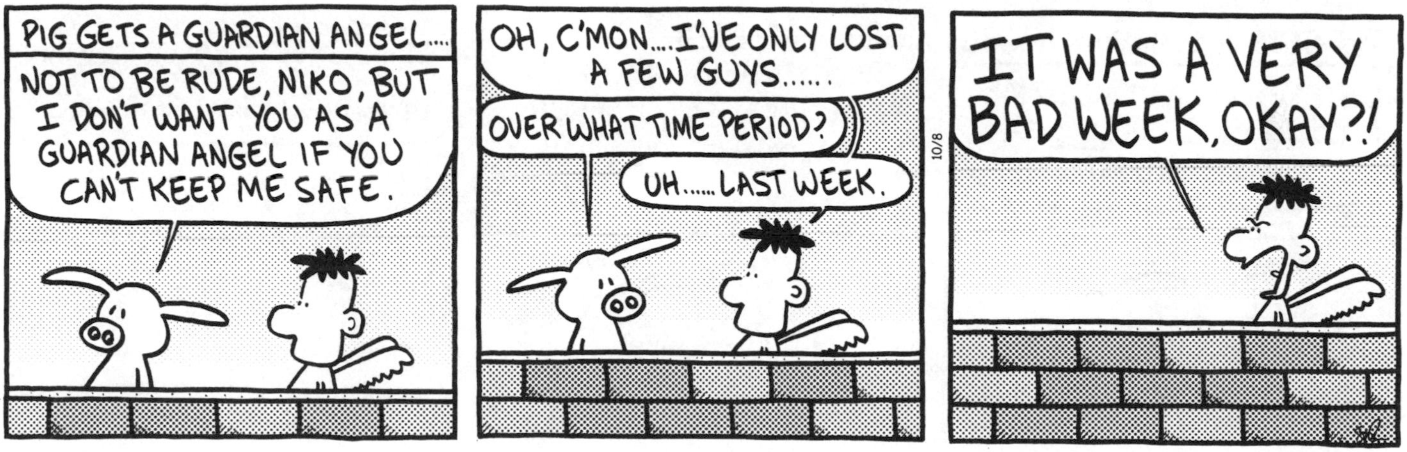
PIG GETS A GUARDIAN ANGEL....
NOT TO BE RUDE, NIKO, BUT I DON'T WANT YOU AS A GUARDIAN ANGEL IF YOU CAN'T KEEP ME SAFE.
OH, C'MON....I'VE ONLY LOST A FEW GUYS......
OVER WHAT TIME PERIOD?
UH......LAST WEEK.
10/8
IT WAS A VERY BAD WEEK, OKAY?!

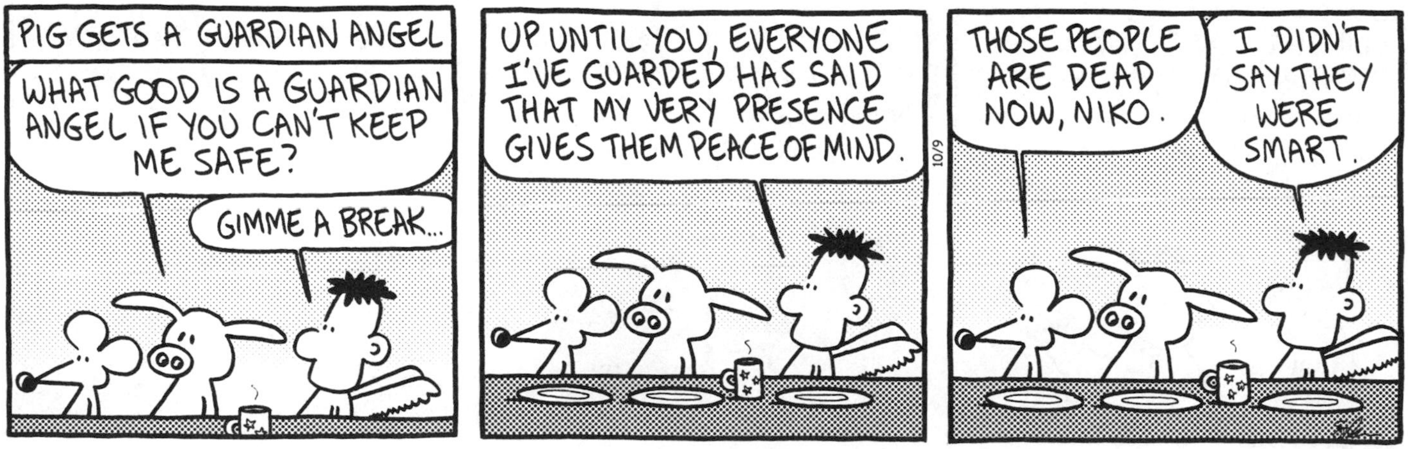
PIG GETS A GUARDIAN ANGEL
WHAT GOOD IS A GUARDIAN ANGEL IF YOU CAN'T KEEP ME SAFE?
GIMME A BREAK...
UP UNTIL YOU, EVERYONE I'VE GUARDED HAS SAID THAT MY VERY PRESENCE GIVES THEM PEACE OF MIND.
10/9
THOSE PEOPLE ARE DEAD NOW, NIKO.
I DIDN'T SAY THEY WERE SMART.

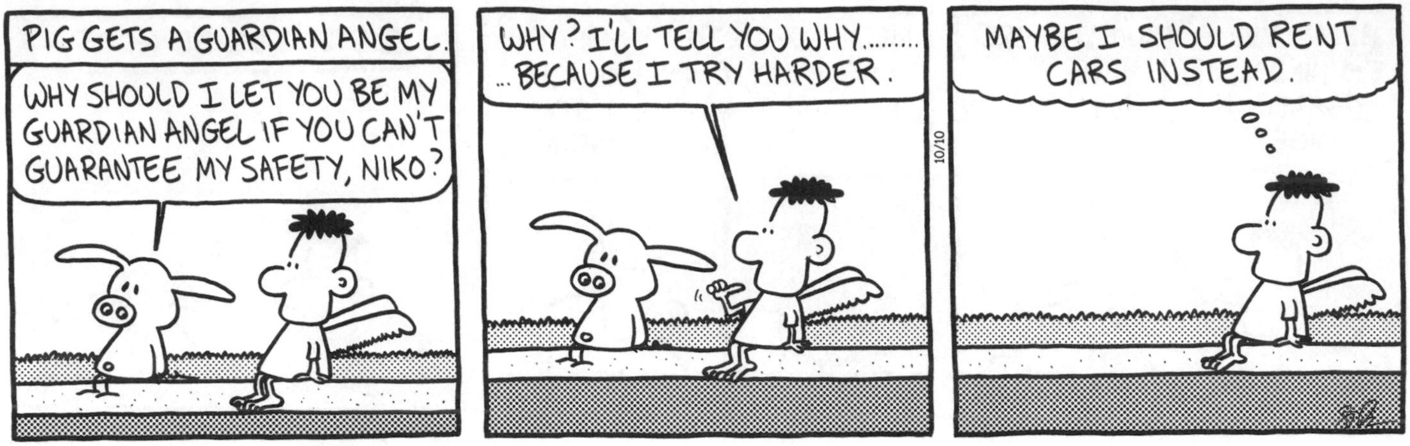
PIG GETS A GUARDIAN ANGEL.
WHY SHOULD I LET YOU BE MY GUARDIAN ANGEL IF YOU CAN'T GUARANTEE MY SAFETY, NIKO?
WHY? I'LL TELL YOU WHY.........
...BECAUSE I TRY HARDER.
10/10
MAYBE I SHOULD RENT CARS INSTEAD.

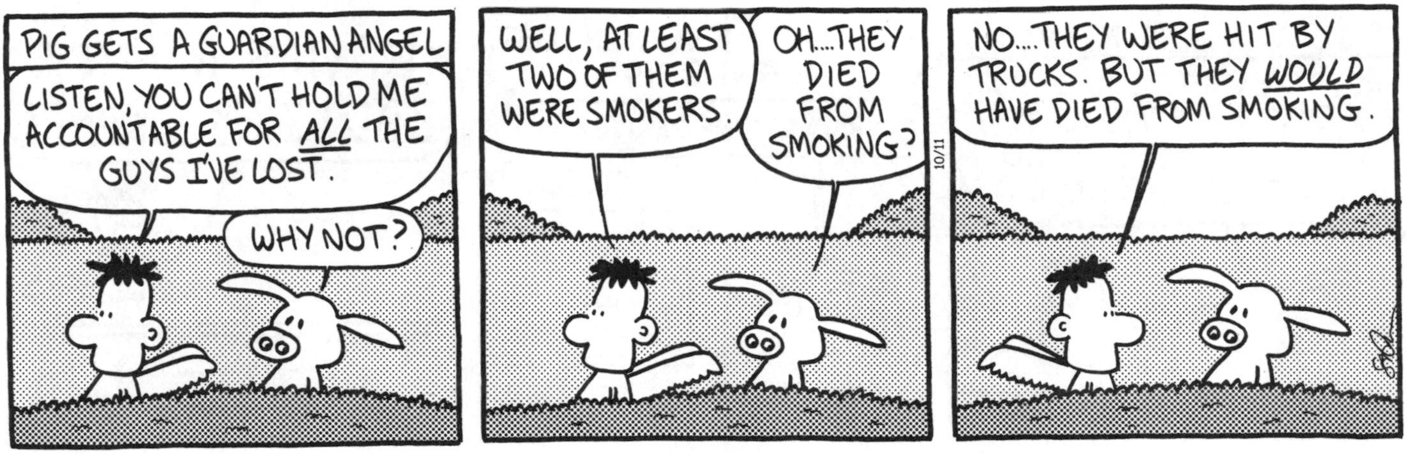
PIG GETS A GUARDIAN ANGEL
LISTEN, YOU CAN'T HOLD ME ACCOUNTABLE FOR ALL THE GUYS I'VE LOST.
WHY NOT?
WELL, AT LEAST TWO OF THEM WERE SMOKERS.
OH....THEY DIED FROM SMOKING?
10/11
NO....THEY WERE HIT BY TRUCKS. BUT THEY WOULD HAVE DIED FROM SMOKING.

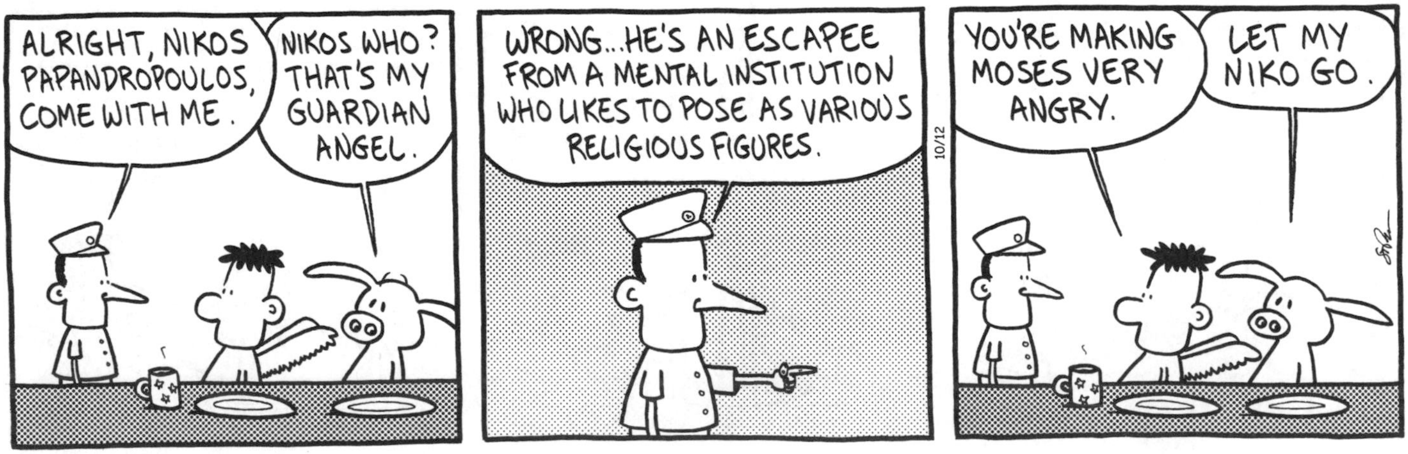
ALRIGHT, NIKOS PAPANDROPOULOS, COME WITH ME.
NIKOS WHO? THAT'S MY GUARDIAN ANGEL.
WRONG...HE'S AN ESCAPEE FROM A MENTAL INSTITUTION WHO LIKES TO POSE AS VARIOUS RELIGIOUS FIGURES.
10/12
YOU'RE MAKING MOSES VERY ANGRY.
LET MY NIKO GO.

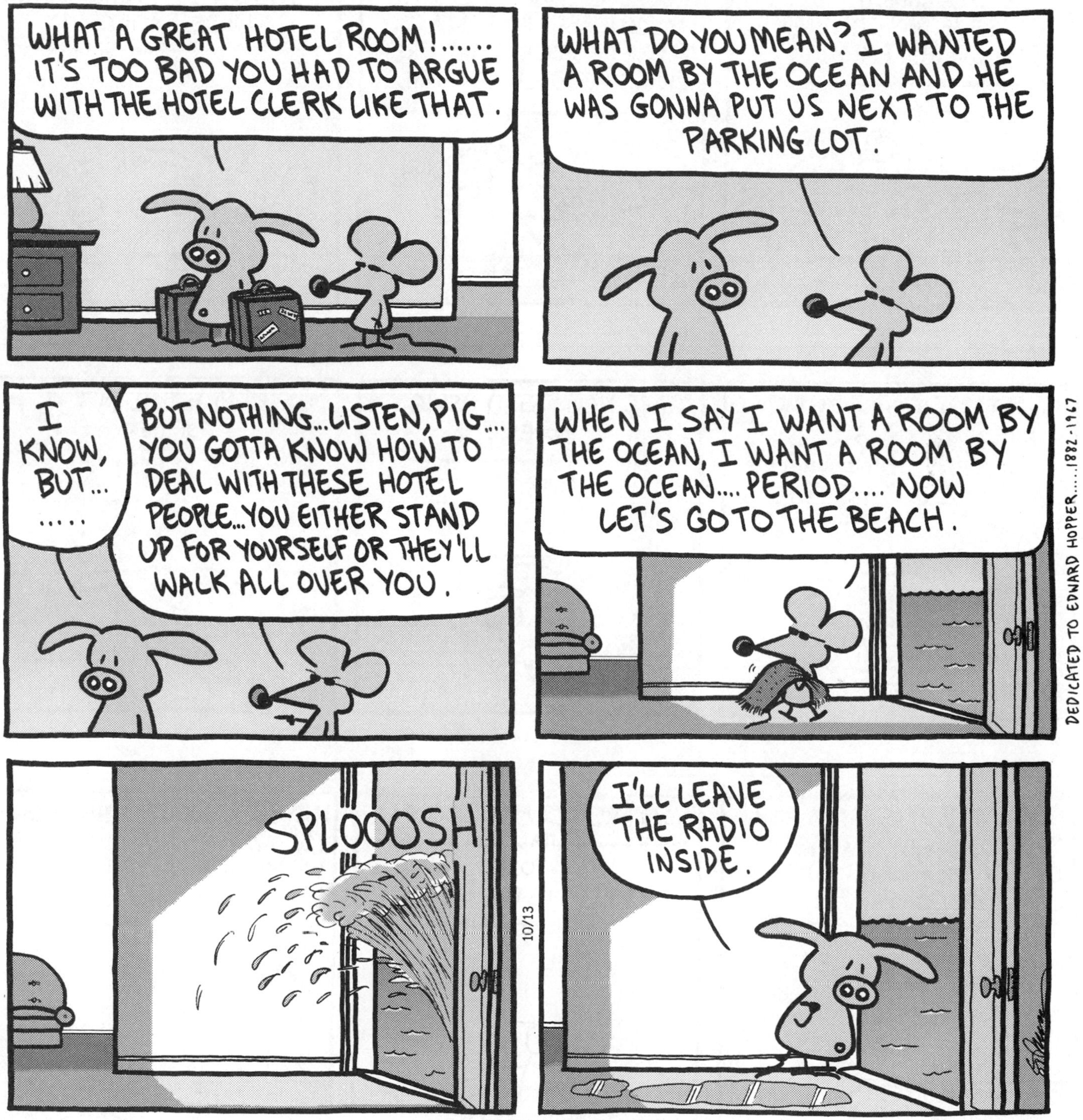
WHAT A GREAT HOTEL ROOM!...... IT'S TOO BAD YOU HAD TO ARGUE WITH THE HOTEL CLERK LIKE THAT.
WHAT DO YOU MEAN? I WANTED A ROOM BY THE OCEAN AND HE WAS GONNA PUT US NEXT TO THE PARKING LOT.
I KNOW, BUT... .....
BUT NOTHING...LISTEN, PIG.... YOU GOTTA KNOW HOW TO DEAL WITH THESE HOTEL PEOPLE...YOU EITHER STAND UP FOR YOURSELF OR THEY'LL WALK ALL OVER YOU.
WHEN I SAY I WANT A ROOM BY THE OCEAN, I WANT A ROOM BY THE OCEAN.... PERIOD.... NOW LET'S GO TO THE BEACH.
DEDICATED TO EDWARD HOPPER.....1882-1967
SPLOOOSH
10/13
I'LL LEAVE THE RADIO INSIDE.

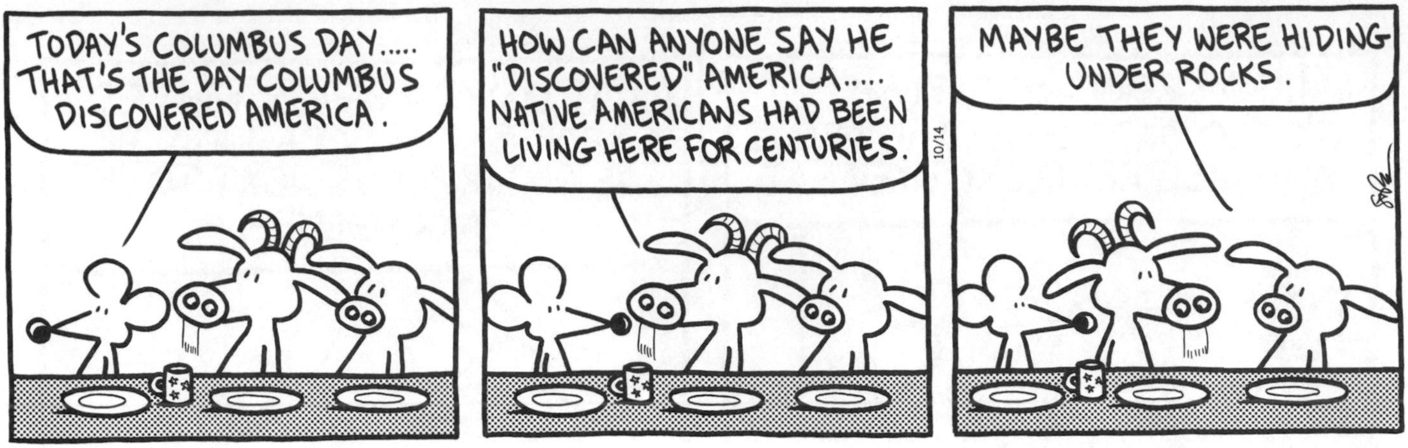
TODAY'S COLUMBUS DAY..... THAT'S THE DAY COLUMBUS DISCOVERED AMERICA.
HOW CAN ANYONE SAY HE "DISCOVERED" AMERICA..... NATIVE AMERICANS HAD BEEN LIVING HERE FOR CENTURIES.
10/14
MAYBE THEY WERE HIDING UNDER ROCKS.

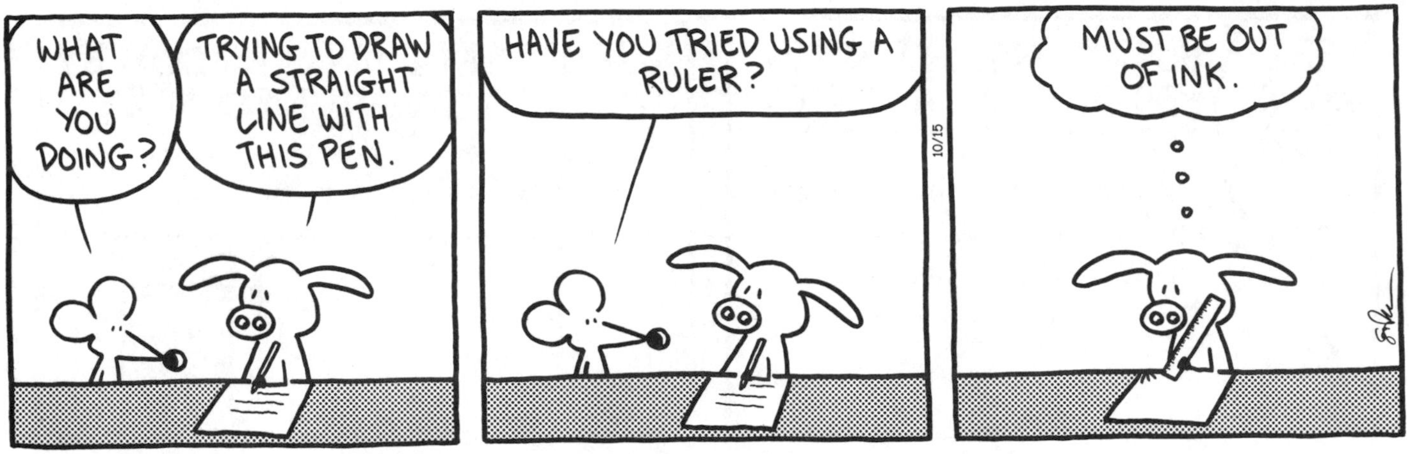
WHAT ARE YOU DOING?
TRYING TO DRAW A STRAIGHT LINE WITH THIS PEN.
HAVE YOU TRIED USING A RULER?
10/15
MUST BE OUT OF INK.

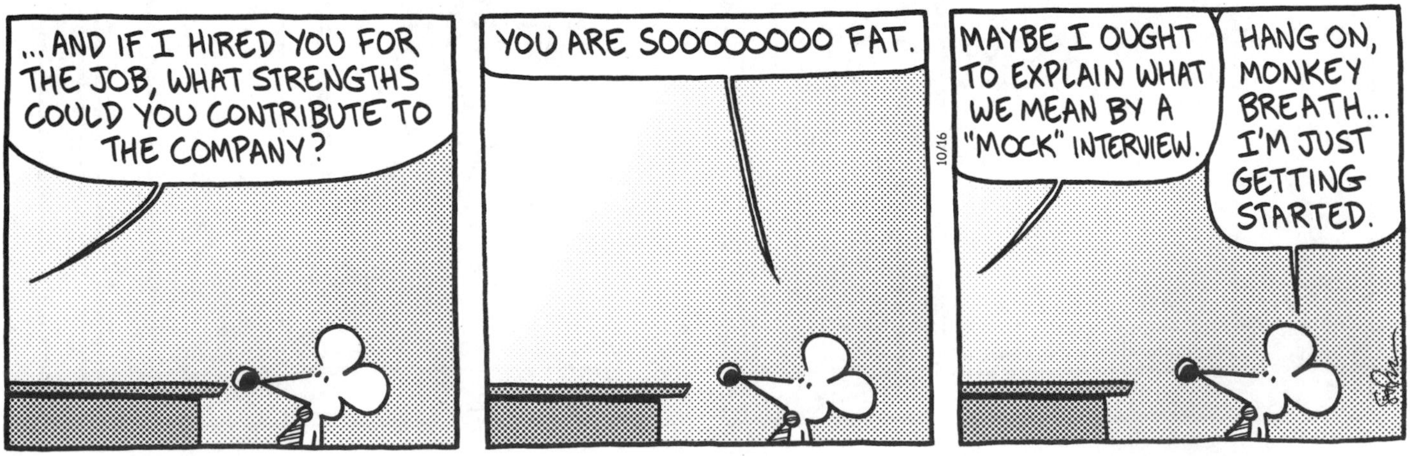
...AND IF I HIRED YOU FOR THE JOB, WHAT STRENGTHS COULD YOU CONTRIBUTE TO THE COMPANY?
YOU ARE SOOOOOOOO FAT.
10/16
MAYBE I OUGHT TO EXPLAIN WHAT WE MEAN BY A "MOCK" INTERVIEW.
HANG ON, MONKEY BREATH... I'M JUST GETTING STARTED.

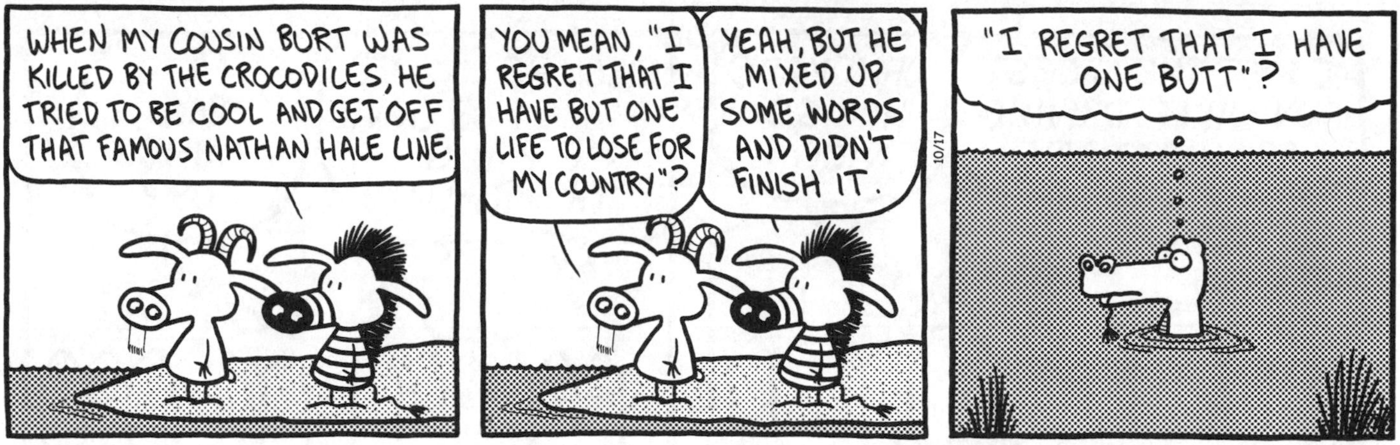
WHEN MY COUSIN BURT WAS KILLED BY THE CROCODILES, HE TRIED TO BE COOL AND GET OFF THAT FAMOUS NATHAN HALE LINE.
YOU MEAN, "I REGRET THAT I HAVE BUT ONE LIFE TO LOSE FOR MY COUNTRY"?
YEAH, BUT HE MIXED UP SOME WORDS AND DIDN'T FINISH IT.
10/17
"I REGRET THAT I HAVE ONE BUTT"?

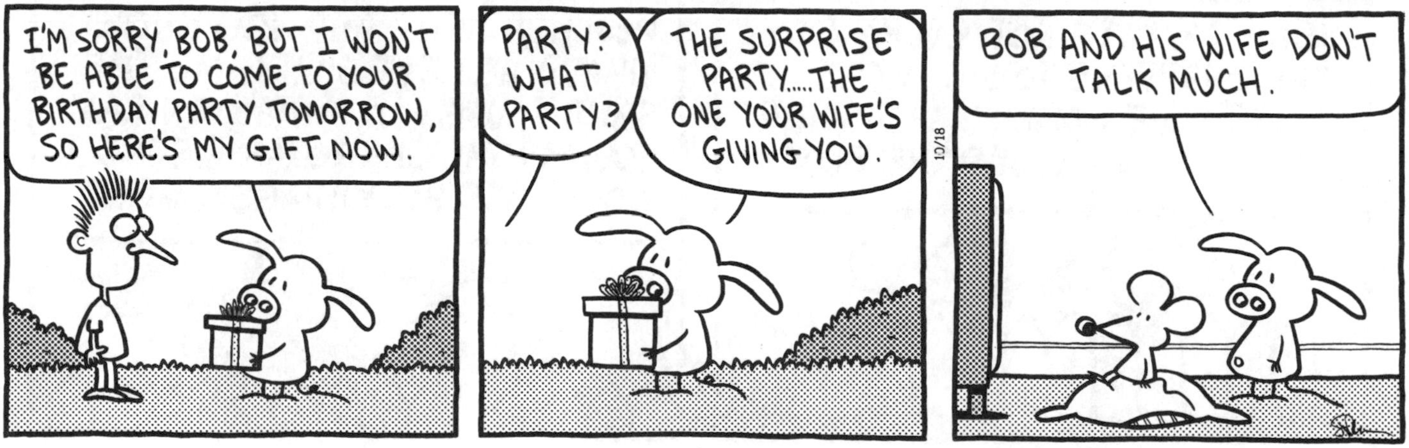
I'M SORRY, BOB, BUT I WON'T BE ABLE TO COME TO YOUR BIRTHDAY PARTY TOMORROW, SO HERE'S MY GIFT NOW.
PARTY? WHAT PARTY?
THE SURPRISE PARTY.....THE ONE YOUR WIFE'S GIVING YOU.
10/18
BOB AND HIS WIFE DON'T TALK MUCH.

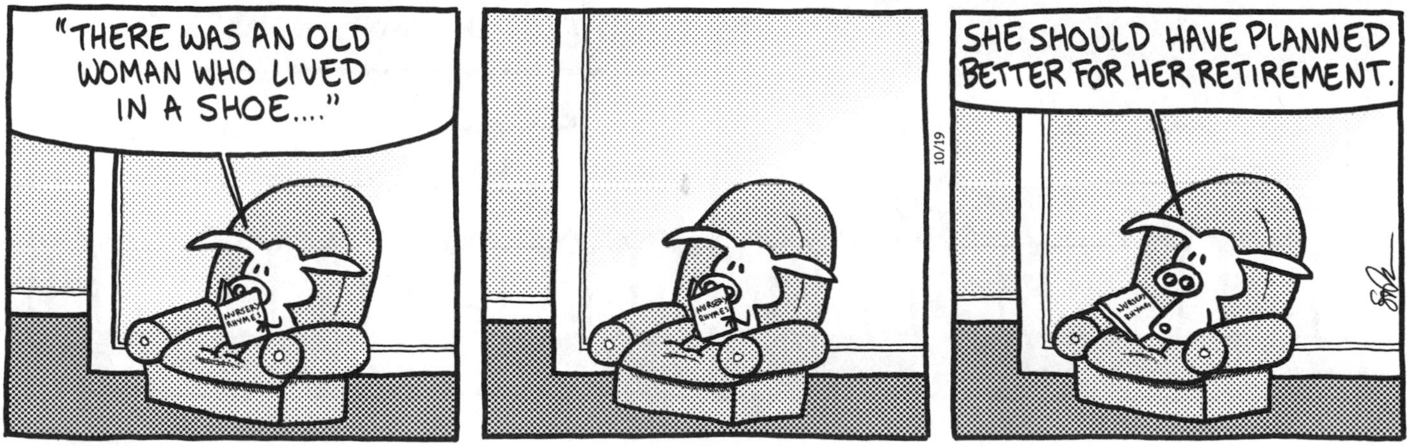
"THERE WAS AN OLD WOMAN WHO LIVED IN A SHOE...."
NURSERY RHYMES
10/19
SHE SHOULD HAVE PLANNED BETTER FOR HER RETIREMENT.

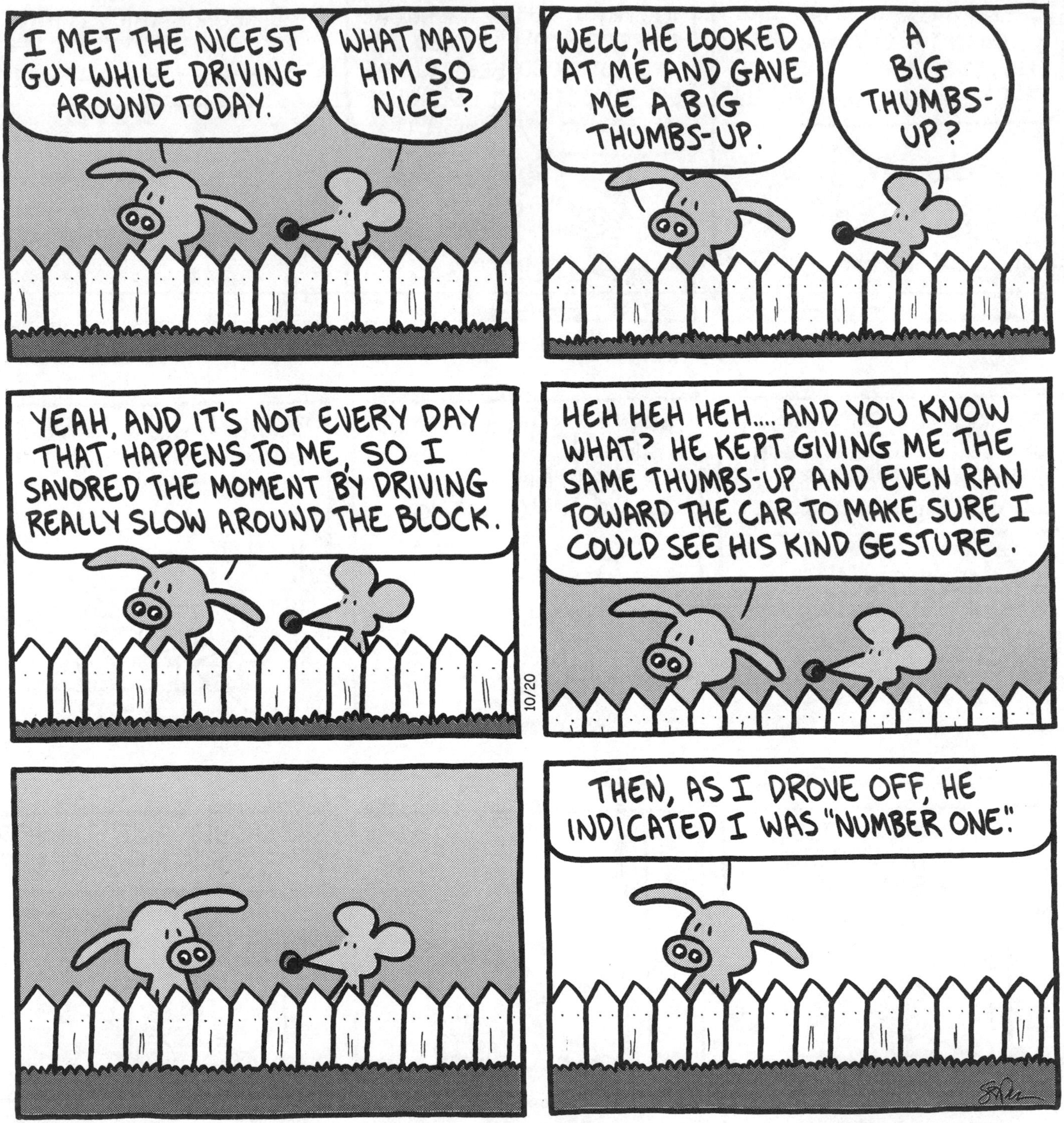
I MET THE NICEST GUY WHILE DRIVING AROUND TODAY.
WHAT MADE HIM SO NICE?
WELL, HE LOOKED AT ME AND GAVE ME A BIG THUMBS-UP.
A BIG THUMBS-UP?
YEAH, AND IT'S NOT EVERY DAY THAT HAPPENS TO ME, SO I SAVORED THE MOMENT BY DRIVING REALLY SLOW AROUND THE BLOCK.
10/20
HEH HEH HEH.... AND YOU KNOW WHAT? HE KEPT GIVING ME THE SAME THUMBS-UP AND EVEN RAN TOWARD THE CAR TO MAKE SURE I COULD SEE HIS KIND GESTURE.
THEN, AS I DROVE OFF, HE INDICATED I WAS "NUMBER ONE."

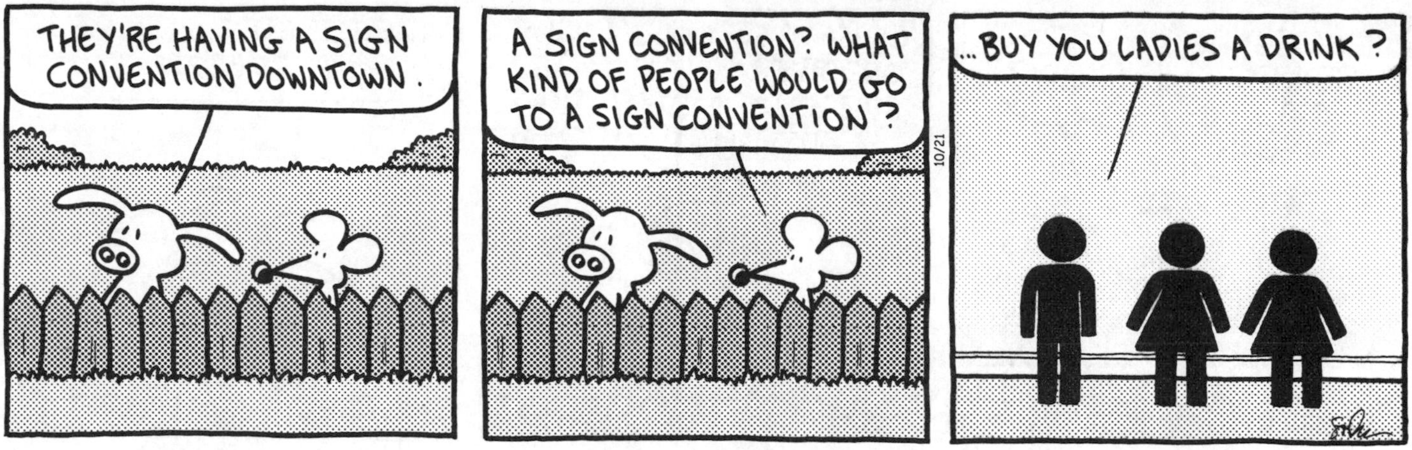
THEY'RE HAVING A SIGN CONVENTION DOWNTOWN.
A SIGN CONVENTION? WHAT KIND OF PEOPLE WOULD GO TO A SIGN CONVENTION?
10/21
...BUY YOU LADIES A DRINK?

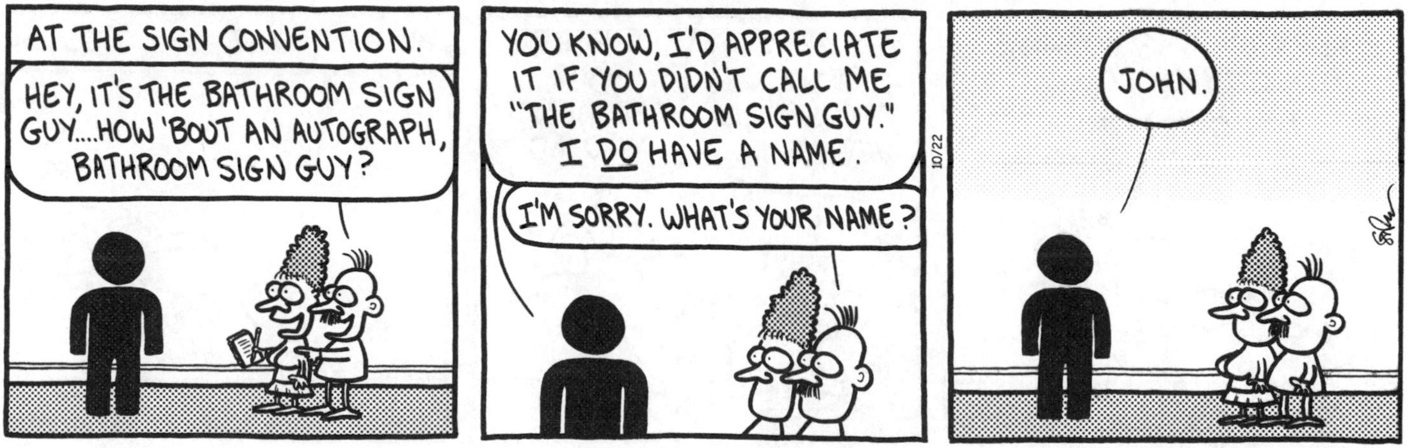
AT THE SIGN CONVENTION.
HEY, IT'S THE BATHROOM SIGN GUY....HOW 'BOUT AN AUTOGRAPH, BATHROOM SIGN GUY?
YOU KNOW, I'D APPRECIATE IT IF YOU DIDN'T CALL ME "THE BATHROOM SIGN GUY." I DO HAVE A NAME.
I'M SORRY. WHAT'S YOUR NAME?
10/22
JOHN.

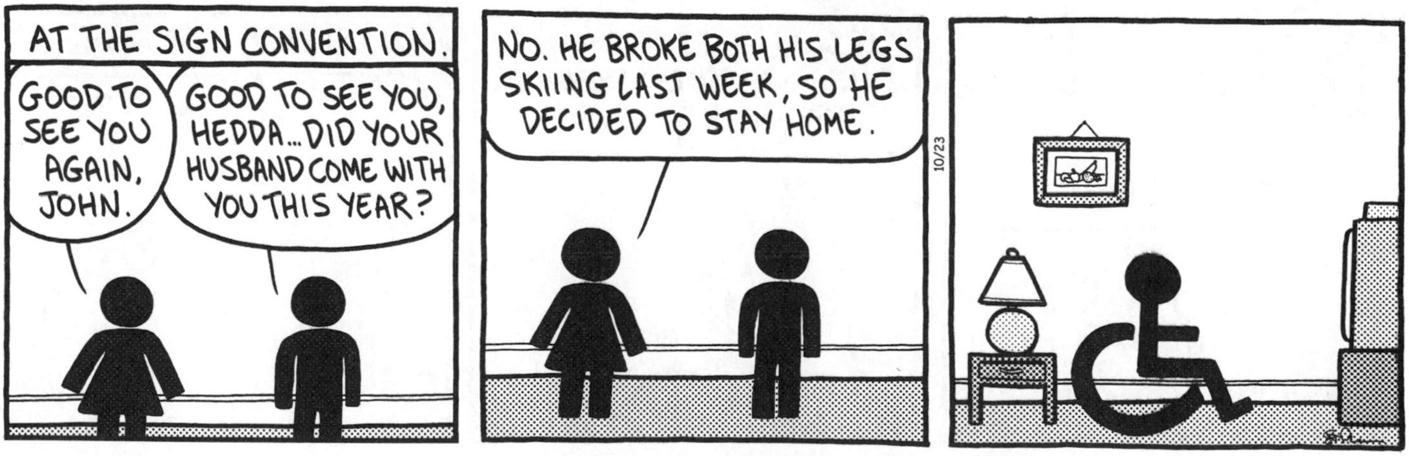
AT THE SIGN CONVENTION.
GOOD TO SEE YOU AGAIN, JOHN.
GOOD TO SEE YOU, HEDDA...DID YOUR HUSBAND COME WITH YOU THIS YEAR?
NO. HE BROKE BOTH HIS LEGS SKIING LAST WEEK, SO HE DECIDED TO STAY HOME.
10/23

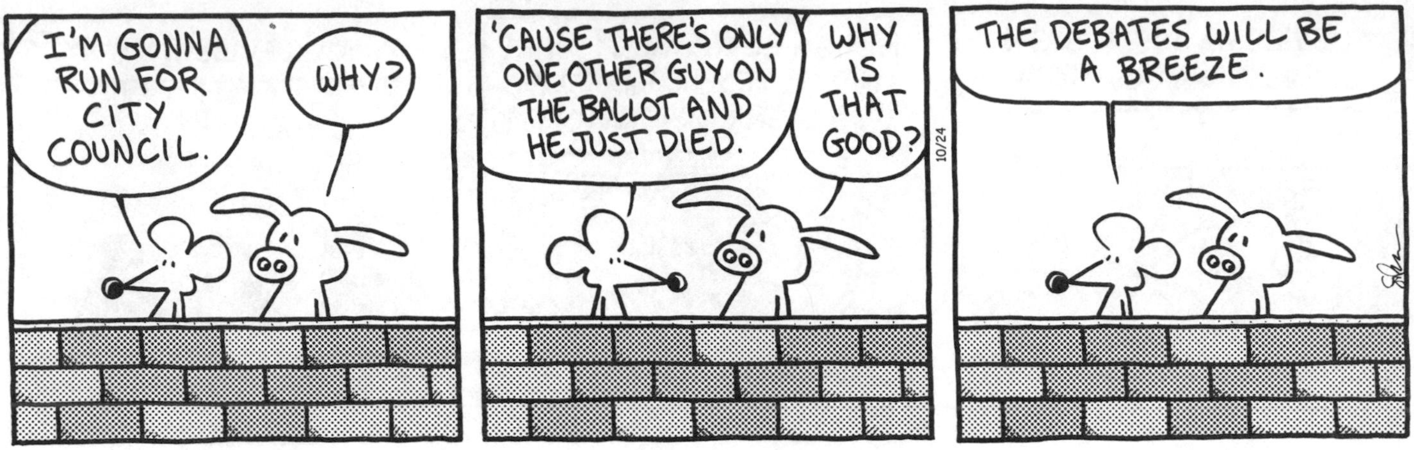
I'M GONNA RUN FOR CITY COUNCIL.
WHY?
'CAUSE THERE'S ONLY ONE OTHER GUY ON THE BALLOT AND HE JUST DIED.
WHY IS THAT GOOD?
10/24
THE DEBATES WILL BE A BREEZE.

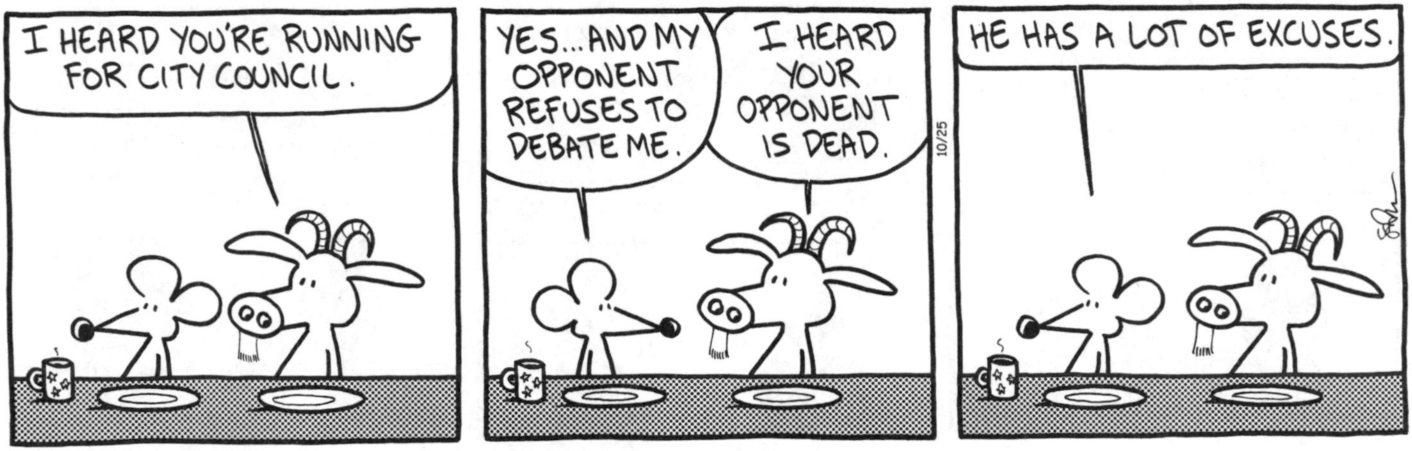
I HEARD YOU'RE RUNNING FOR CITY COUNCIL.
YES...AND MY OPPONENT REFUSES TO DEBATE ME.
I HEARD YOUR OPPONENT IS DEAD.
10/25
HE HAS A LOT OF EXCUSES.

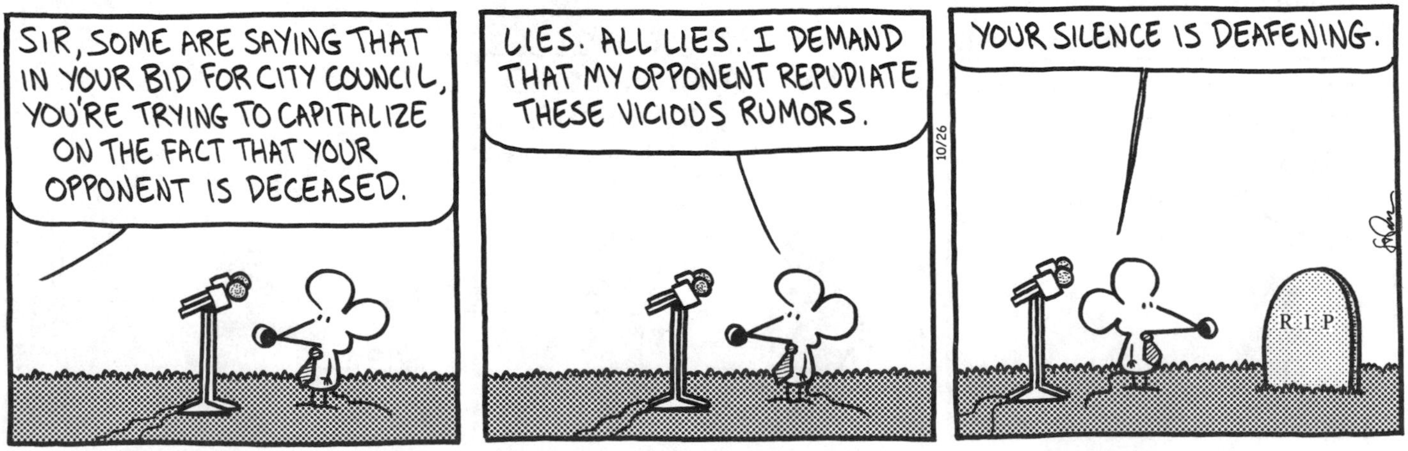
SIR, SOME ARE SAYING THAT IN YOUR BID FOR CITY COUNCIL, YOU'RE TRYING TO CAPITALIZE ON THE FACT THAT YOUR OPPONENT IS DECEASED.
LIES. ALL LIES. I DEMAND THAT MY OPPONENT REPUDIATE THESE VICIOUS RUMORS.
10/26
YOUR SILENCE IS DEAFENING.
R.I.P.

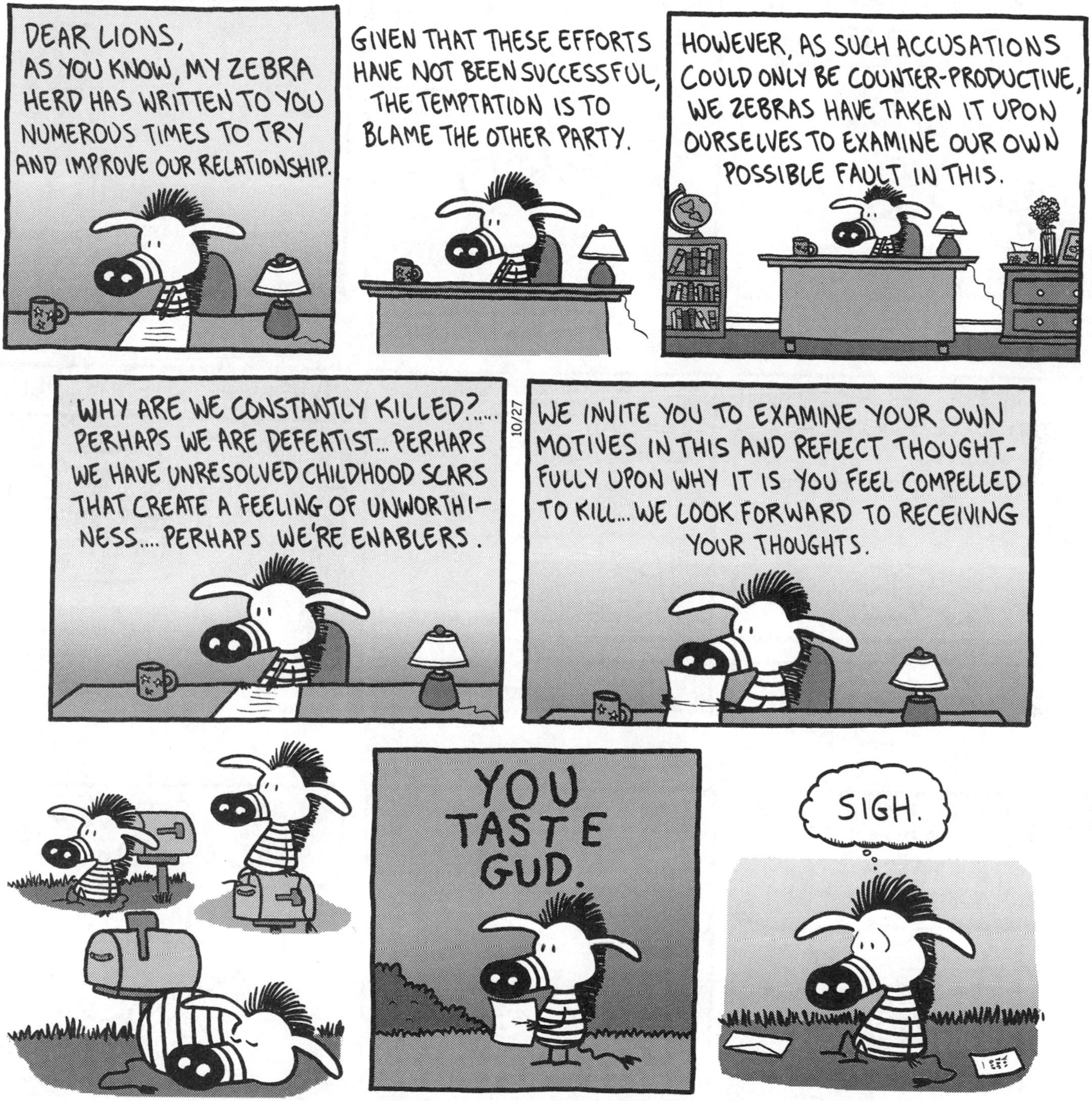
DEAR LIONS,
AS YOU KNOW, MY ZEBRA HERD HAS WRITTEN TO YOU NUMEROUS TIMES TO TRY AND IMPROVE OUR RELATIONSHIP.
GIVEN THAT THESE EFFORTS HAVE NOT BEEN SUCCESSFUL, THE TEMPTATION IS TO BLAME THE OTHER PARTY.
HOWEVER, AS SUCH ACCUSATIONS COULD ONLY BE COUNTER-PRODUCTIVE, WE ZEBRAS HAVE TAKEN IT UPON OURSELVES TO EXAMINE OUR OWN POSSIBLE FAULT IN THIS.
WHY ARE WE CONSTANTLY KILLED?..... PERHAPS WE ARE DEFEATIST... PERHAPS WE HAVE UNRESOLVED CHILDHOOD SCARS THAT CREATE A FEELING OF UNWORTHI-NESS.... PERHAPS WE'RE ENABLERS.
10/27
WE INVITE YOU TO EXAMINE YOUR OWN MOTIVES IN THIS AND REFLECT THOUGHT-FULLY UPON WHY IT IS YOU FEEL COMPELLED TO KILL... WE LOOK FORWARD TO RECEIVING YOUR THOUGHTS.
YOU TASTE GUD.
SIGH.

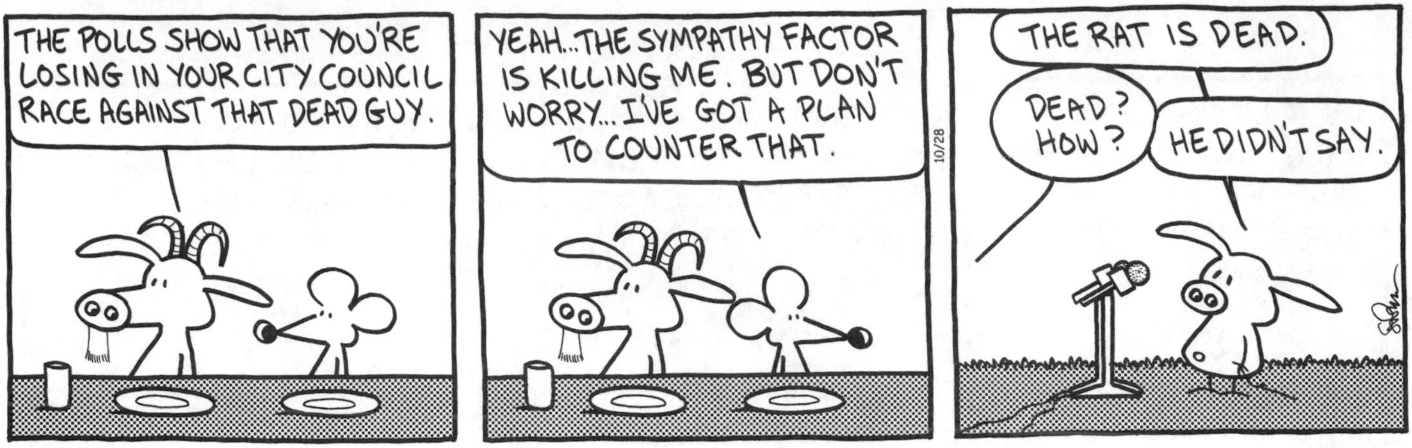
THE POLLS SHOW THAT YOU'RE LOSING IN YOUR CITY COUNCIL RACE AGAINST THAT DEAD GUY.
YEAH...THE SYMPATHY FACTOR IS KILLING ME. BUT DON'T WORRY... I'VE GOT A PLAN TO COUNTER THAT.
10/28
THE RAT IS DEAD.
DEAD? HOW?
HE DIDN'T SAY.

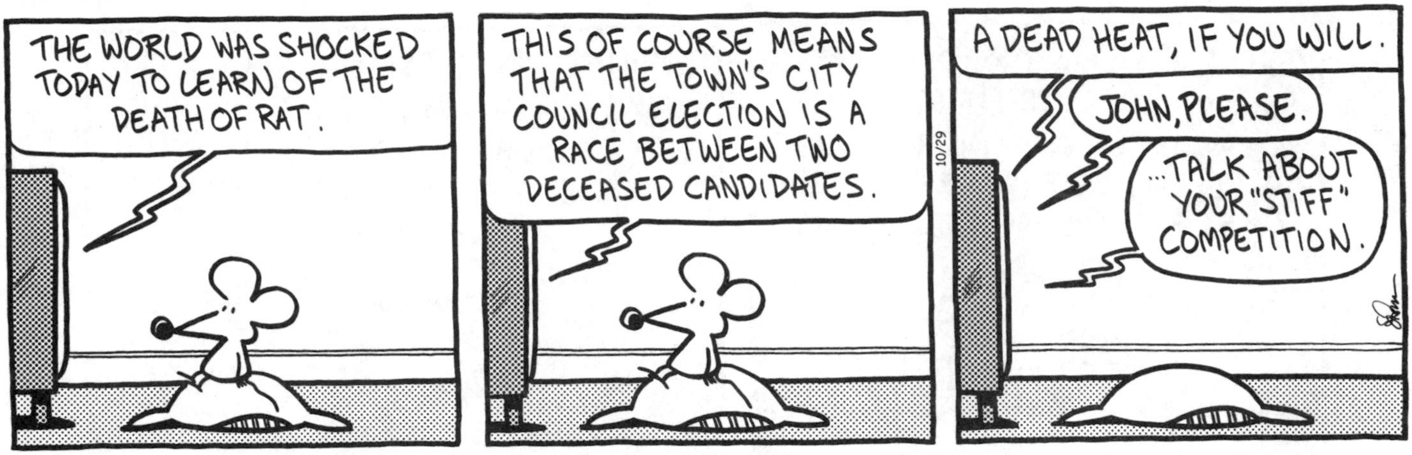
THE WORLD WAS SHOCKED TODAY TO LEARN OF THE DEATH OF RAT.
THIS OF COURSE MEANS THAT THE TOWN'S CITY COUNCIL ELECTION IS A RACE BETWEEN TWO DECEASED CANDIDATES.
10/29
A DEAD HEAT, IF YOU WILL.
JOHN, PLEASE.
...TALK ABOUT YOUR "STIFF" COMPETITION.

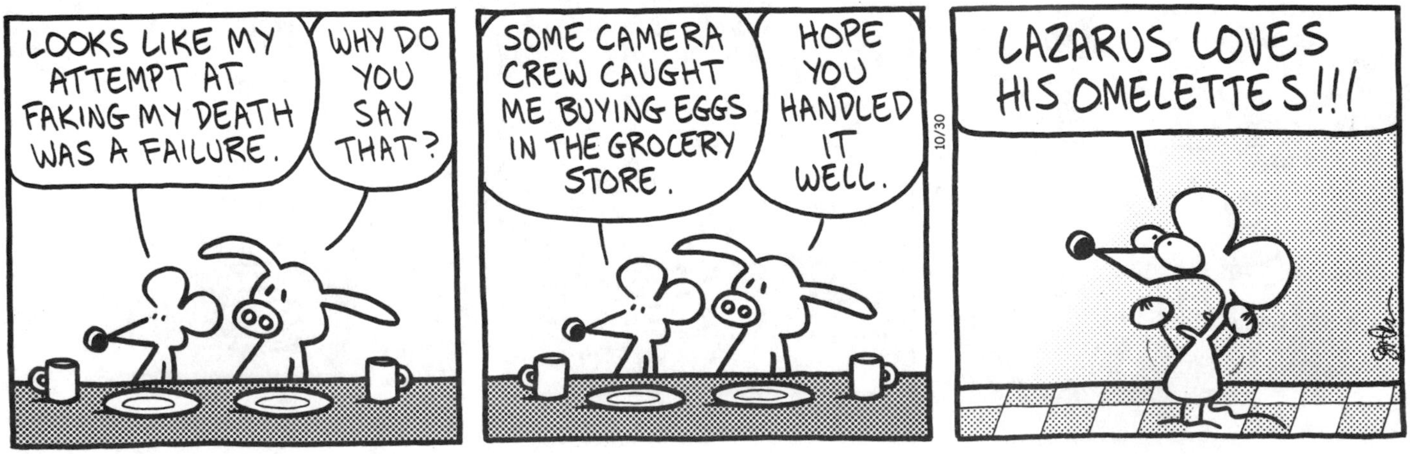
LOOKS LIKE MY ATTEMPT AT FAKING MY DEATH WAS A FAILURE.
WHY DO YOU SAY THAT?
SOME CAMERA CREW CAUGHT ME BUYING EGGS IN THE GROCERY STORE.
HOPE YOU HANDLED IT WELL.
10/30
LAZARUS LOVES HIS OMELETTES!!!

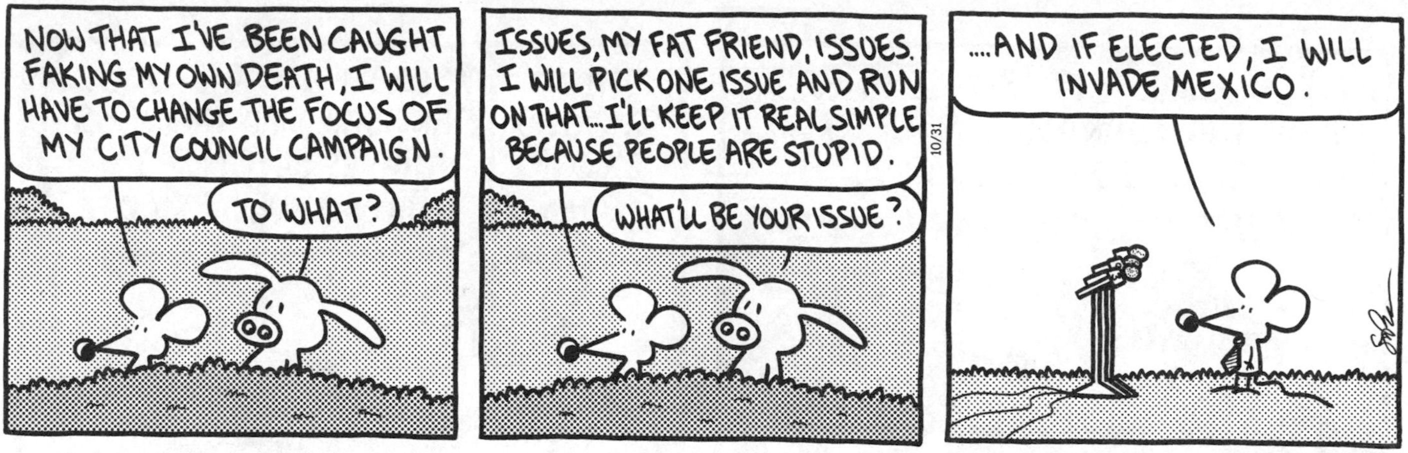
NOW THAT I'VE BEEN CAUGHT FAKING MY OWN DEATH, I WILL HAVE TO CHANGE THE FOCUS OF MY CITY COUNCIL CAMPAIGN.
TO WHAT?
ISSUES, MY FAT FRIEND, ISSUES. I WILL PICK ONE ISSUE AND RUN ON THAT... I'LL KEEP IT REAL SIMPLE BECAUSE PEOPLE ARE STUPID.
WHAT'LL BE YOUR ISSUE?
10/31
....AND IF ELECTED, I WILL INVADE MEXICO.

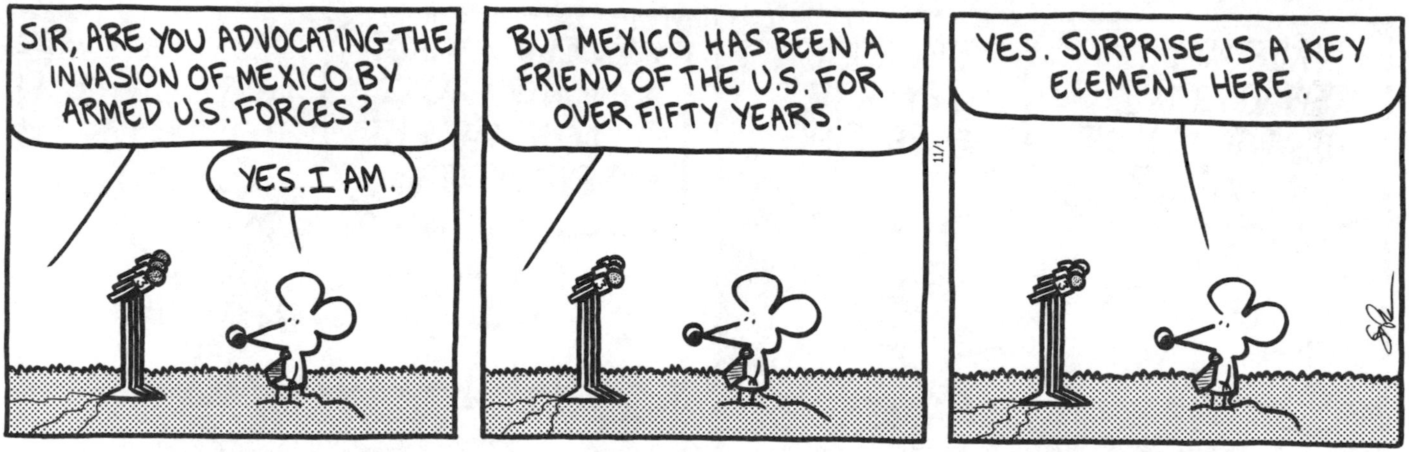
SIR, ARE YOU ADVOCATING THE INVASION OF MEXICO BY ARMED U.S. FORCES?
YES. I AM.
BUT MEXICO HAS BEEN A FRIEND OF THE U.S. FOR OVER FIFTY YEARS.
11/1
YES. SURPRISE IS A KEY ELEMENT HERE.

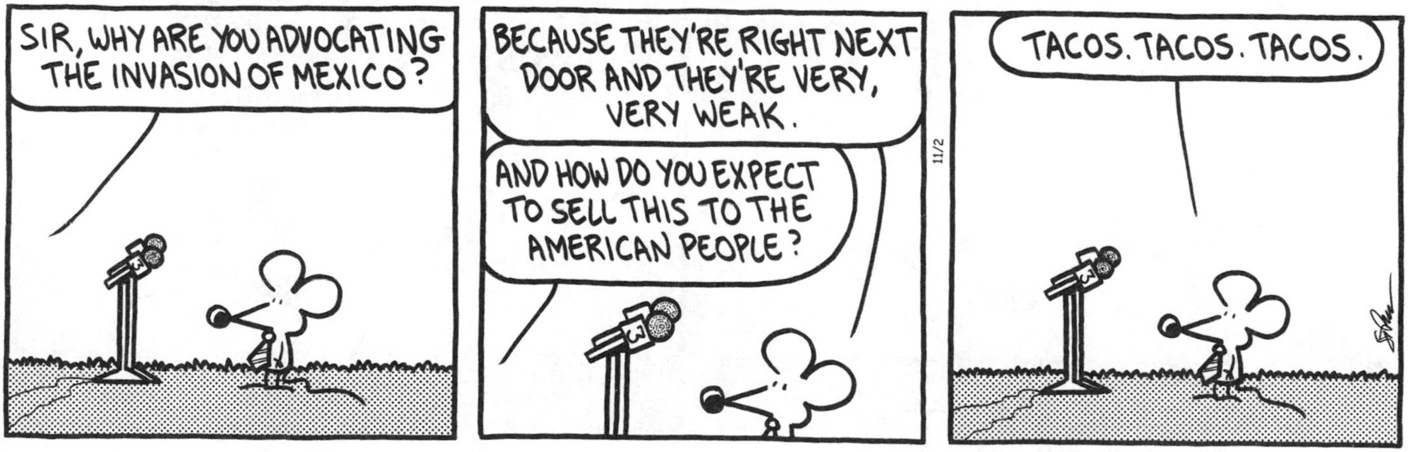
SIR, WHY ARE YOU ADVOCATING THE INVASION OF MEXICO?
BECAUSE THEY'RE RIGHT NEXT DOOR AND THEY'RE VERY, VERY WEAK.
AND HOW DO YOU EXPECT TO SELL THIS TO THE AMERICAN PEOPLE?
11/2
TACOS. TACOS. TACOS.

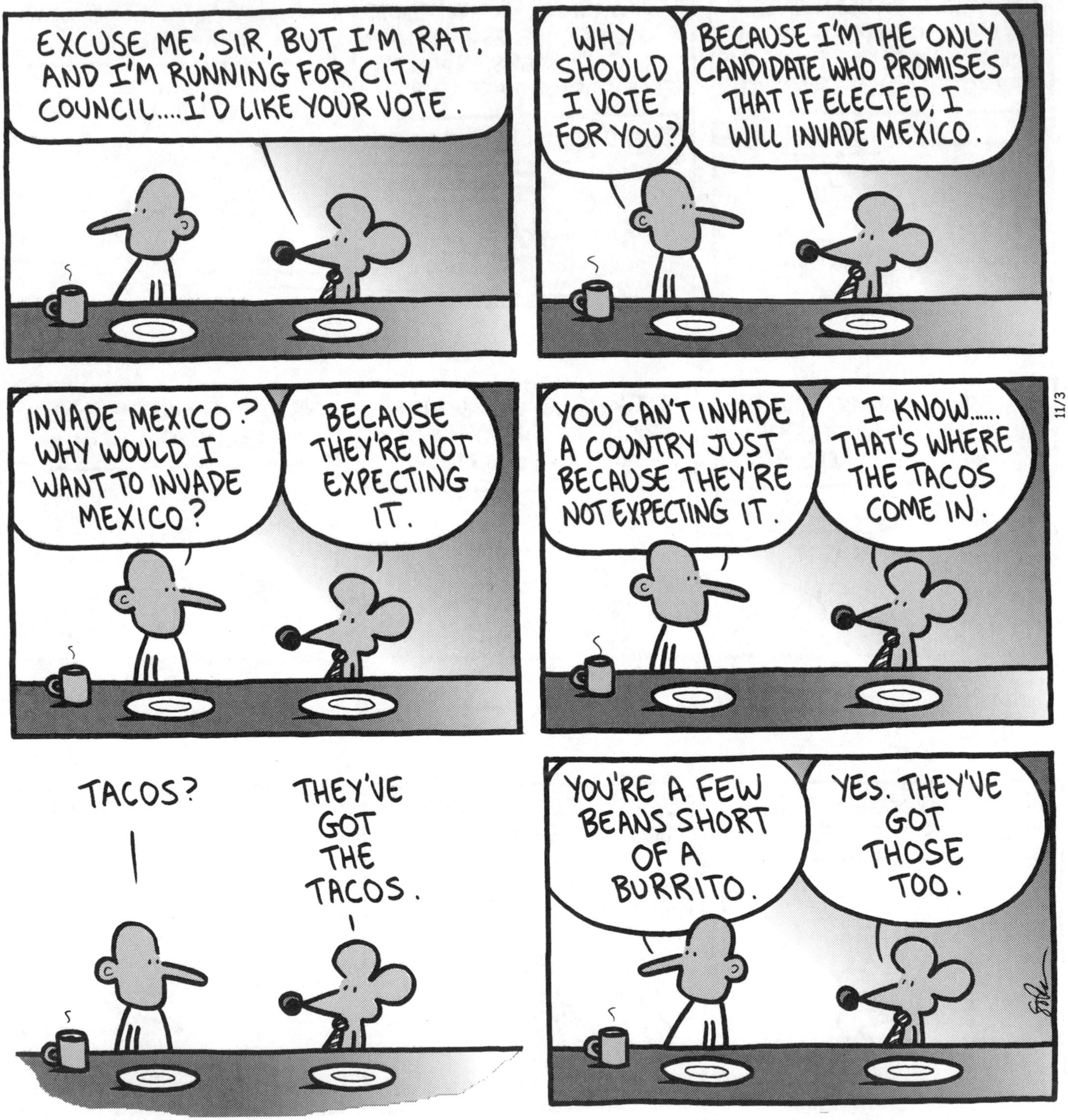
EXCUSE ME, SIR, BUT I'M RAT, AND I'M RUNNING FOR CITY COUNCIL.....I'D LIKE YOUR VOTE.
WHY SHOULD I VOTE FOR YOU?
BECAUSE I'M THE ONLY CANDIDATE WHO PROMISES THAT IF ELECTED, I WILL INVADE MEXICO.
INVADE MEXICO? WHY WOULD I WANT TO INVADE MEXICO?
BECAUSE THEY'RE NOT EXPECTING IT.
YOU CAN'T INVADE A COUNTRY JUST BECAUSE THEY'RE NOT EXPECTING IT.
I KNOW...... THAT'S WHERE THE TACOS COME IN.
11/3
TACOS?
THEY'VE GOT THE TACOS.
YOU'RE A FEW BEANS SHORT OF A BURRITO.
YES. THEY'VE GOT THOSE TOO.

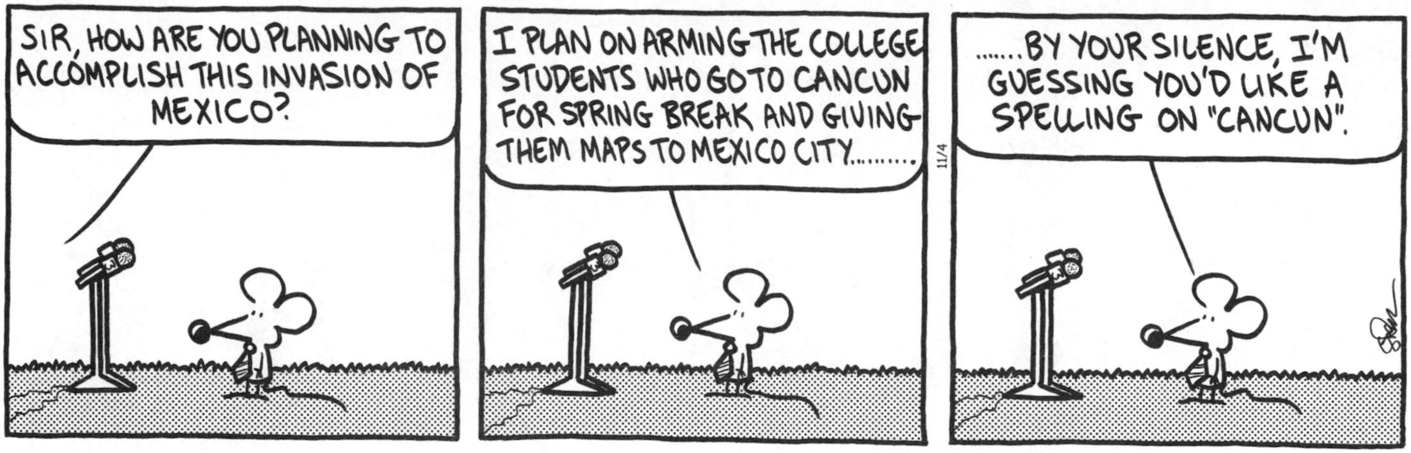
SIR, HOW ARE YOU PLANNING TO ACCOMPLISH THIS INVASION OF MEXICO?
I PLAN ON ARMING THE COLLEGE STUDENTS WHO GO TO CANCUN FOR SPRING BREAK AND GIVING THEM MAPS TO MEXICO CITY.........
11/4
.......BY YOUR SILENCE, I'M GUESSING YOU'D LIKE A SPELLING ON "CANCUN".

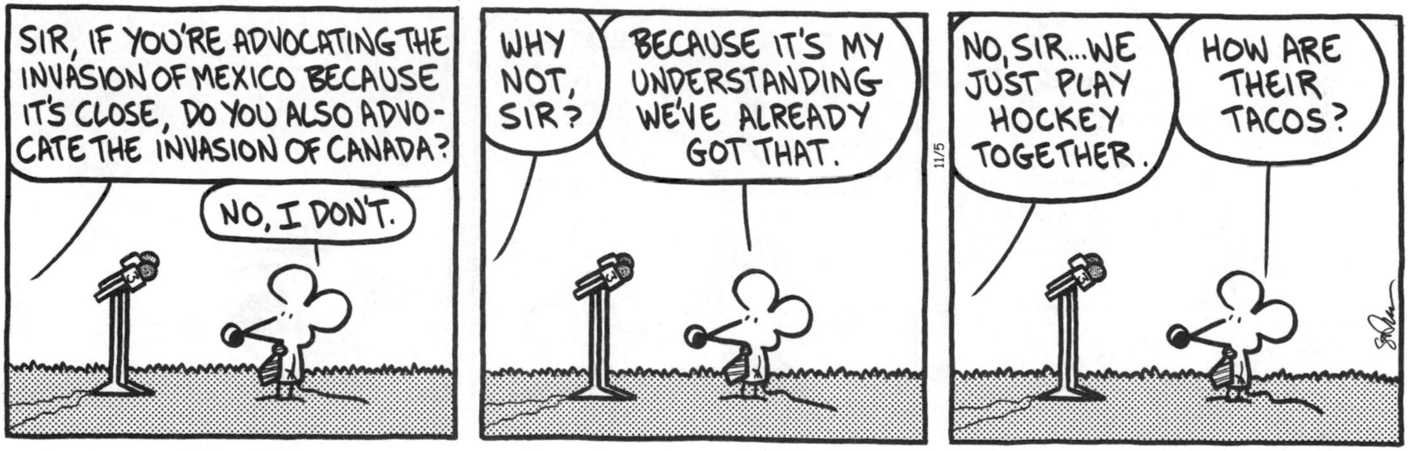
SIR, IF YOU'RE ADVOCATING THE INVASION OF MEXICO BECAUSE IT'S CLOSE, DO YOU ALSO ADVOCATE THE INVASION OF CANADA?
NO, I DON'T.
WHY NOT, SIR?
BECAUSE IT'S MY UNDERSTANDING WE'VE ALREADY GOT THAT.
11/5
NO, SIR...WE JUST PLAY HOCKEY TOGETHER.
HOW ARE THEIR TACOS?

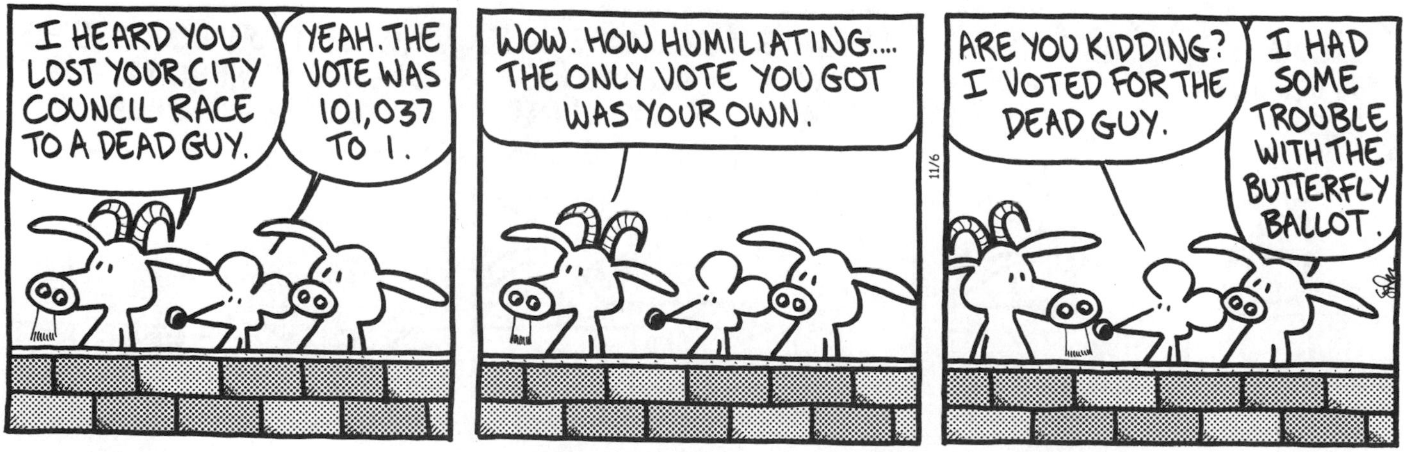
I HEARD YOU LOST YOUR CITY COUNCIL RACE TO A DEAD GUY.
YEAH. THE VOTE WAS 101,037 TO 1.
WOW. HOW HUMILIATING.... THE ONLY VOTE YOU GOT WAS YOUR OWN.
11/6
ARE YOU KIDDING? I VOTED FOR THE DEAD GUY.
I HAD SOME TROUBLE WITH THE BUTTERFLY BALLOT.

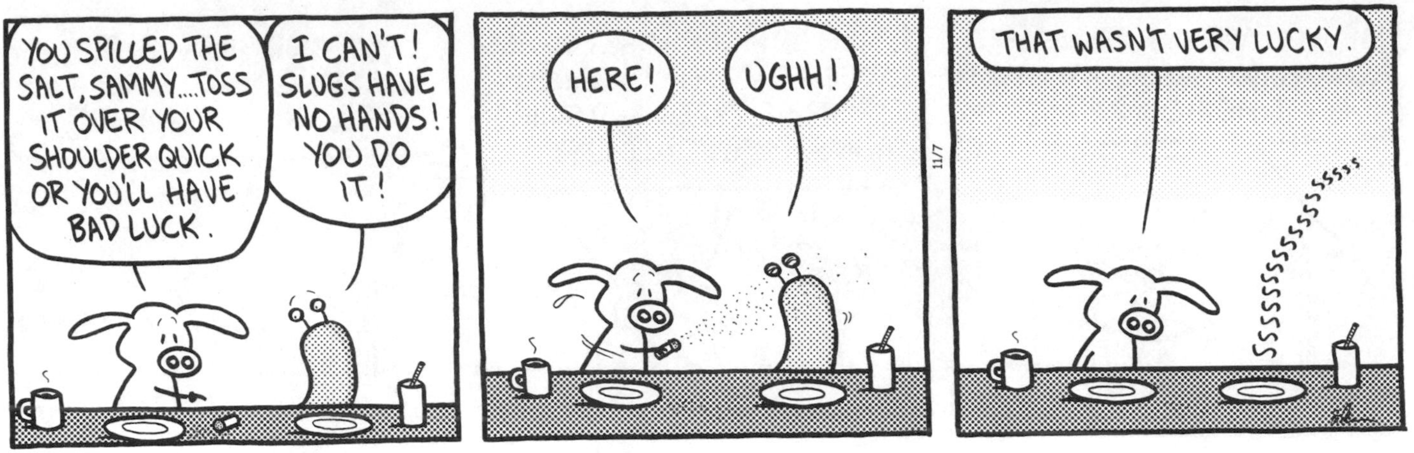
YOU SPILLED THE SALT, SAMMY....TOSS IT OVER YOUR SHOULDER QUICK OR YOU'LL HAVE BAD LUCK.
I CAN'T! SLUGS HAVE NO HANDS! YOU DO IT!
HERE!
UGHH!
11/7
THAT WASN'T VERY LUCKY.

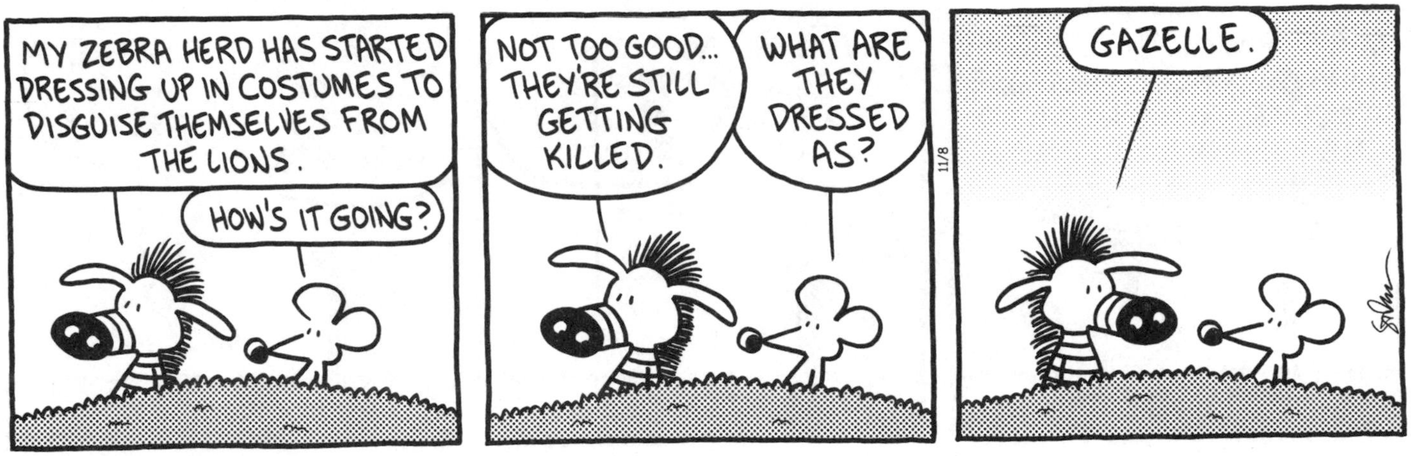
MY ZEBRA HERD HAS STARTED DRESSING UP IN COSTUMES TO DISGUISE THEMSELVES FROM THE LIONS.
HOW'S IT GOING?
NOT TOO GOOD... THEY'RE STILL GETTING KILLED.
WHAT ARE THEY DRESSED AS?
11/8
GAZELLE.

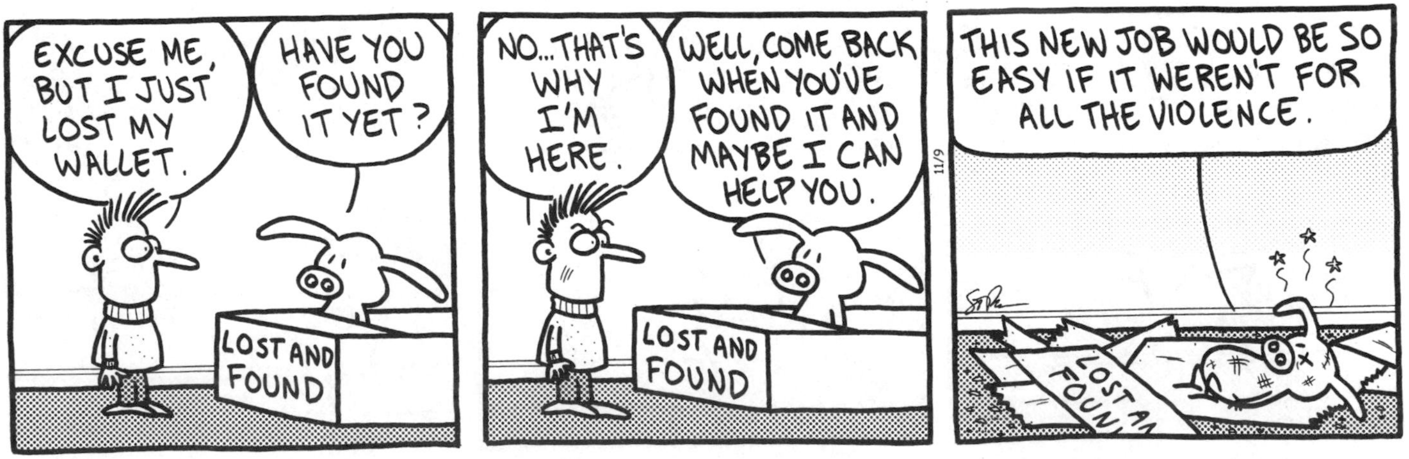
EXCUSE ME, BUT I JUST LOST MY WALLET.
HAVE YOU FOUND IT YET?
LOST AND FOUND
NO...THAT'S WHY I'M HERE.
WELL, COME BACK WHEN YOU'VE FOUND IT AND MAYBE I CAN HELP YOU.
LOST AND FOUND
11/9
THIS NEW JOB WOULD BE SO EASY IF IT WEREN'T FOR ALL THE VIOLENCE.

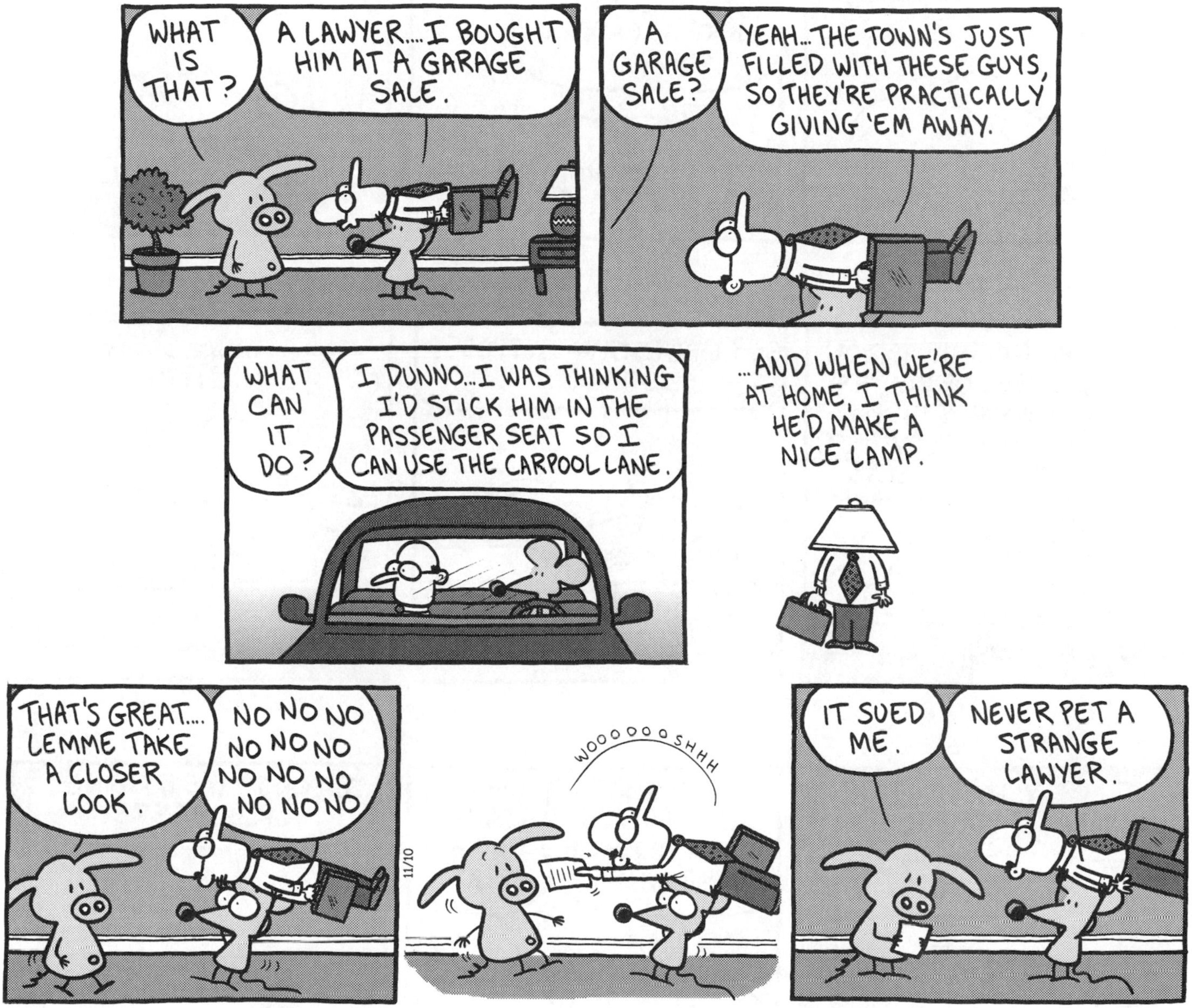
WHAT IS THAT?
A LAWYER.... I BOUGHT HIM AT A GARAGE SALE.
A GARAGE SALE?
YEAH... THE TOWN'S JUST FILLED WITH THESE GUYS, SO THEY'RE PRACTICALLY GIVING 'EM AWAY.
WHAT CAN IT DO?
I DUNNO... I WAS THINKING I'D STICK HIM IN THE PASSENGER SEAT SO I CAN USE THE CARPOOL LANE.
...AND WHEN WE'RE AT HOME, I THINK HE'D MAKE A NICE LAMP.
THAT'S GREAT.... LEMME TAKE A CLOSER LOOK.
NO NO NO NO NO NO NO NO NO NO NO NO
11/10
WOOOOOOSHHH
IT SUED ME.
NEVER PET A STRANGE LAWYER.

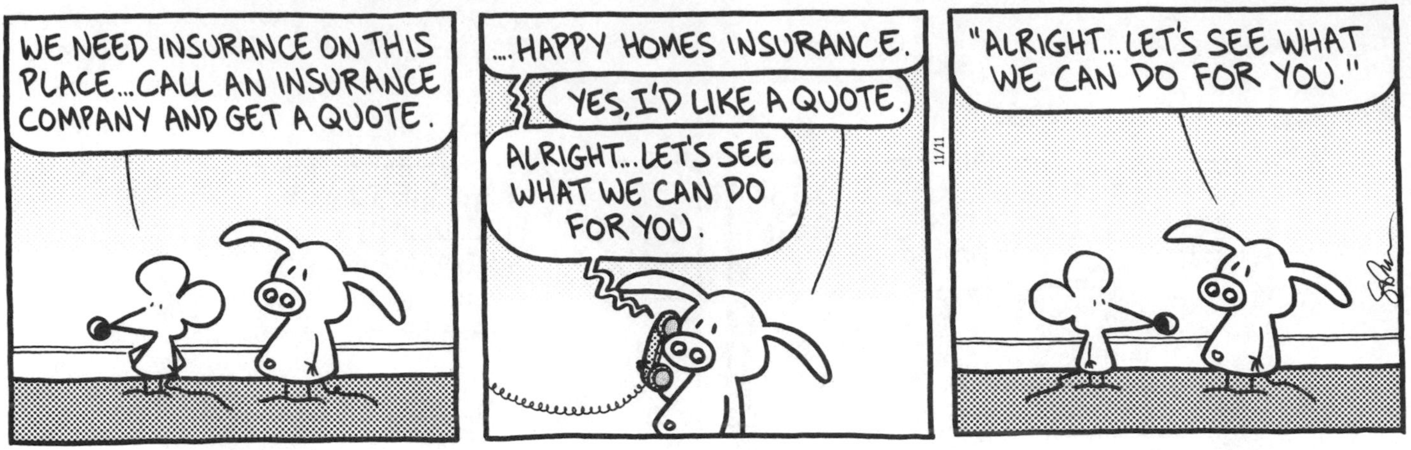
WE NEED INSURANCE ON THIS PLACE...CALL AN INSURANCE COMPANY AND GET A QUOTE.
....HAPPY HOMES INSURANCE.
YES, I'D LIKE A QUOTE.
ALRIGHT...LET'S SEE WHAT WE CAN DO FOR YOU.
11/11
"ALRIGHT...LET'S SEE WHAT WE CAN DO FOR YOU."

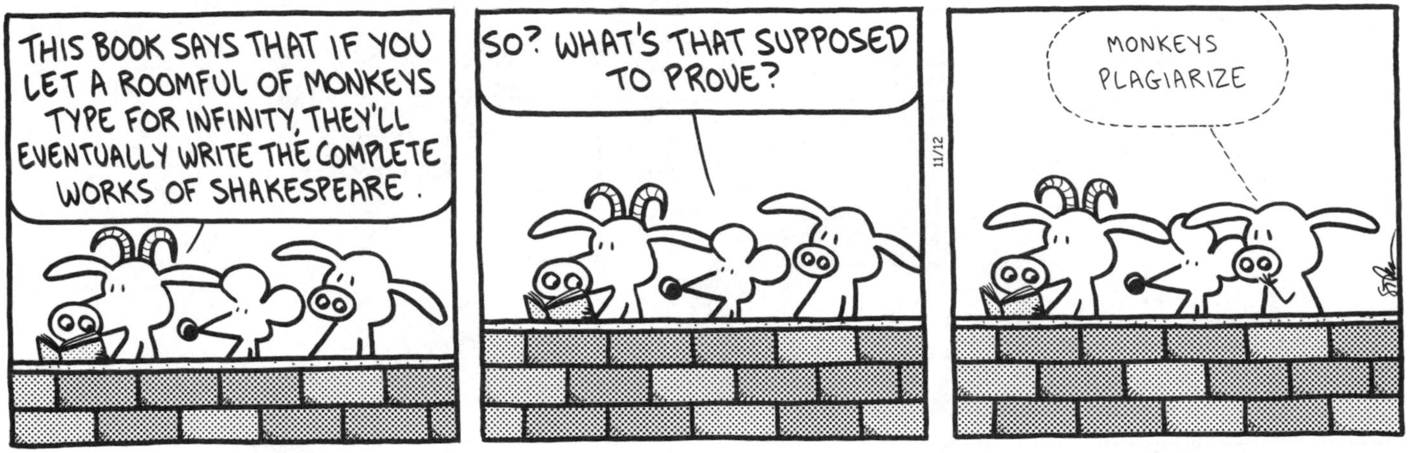
THIS BOOK SAYS THAT IF YOU LET A ROOMFUL OF MONKEYS TYPE FOR INFINITY, THEY'LL EVENTUALLY WRITE THE COMPLETE WORKS OF SHAKESPEARE.
SO? WHAT'S THAT SUPPOSED TO PROVE?
11/12
MONKEYS PLAGIARIZE

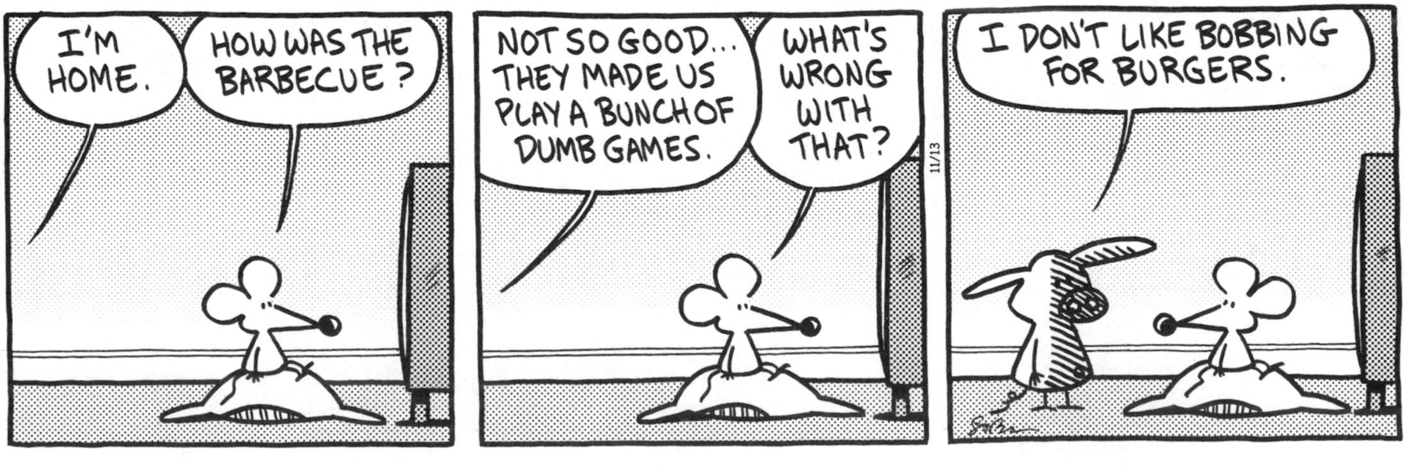
I'M HOME.
HOW WAS THE BARBECUE?
NOT SO GOOD... THEY MADE US PLAY A BUNCH OF DUMB GAMES.
WHAT'S WRONG WITH THAT?
11/13
I DON'T LIKE BOBBING FOR BURGERS.

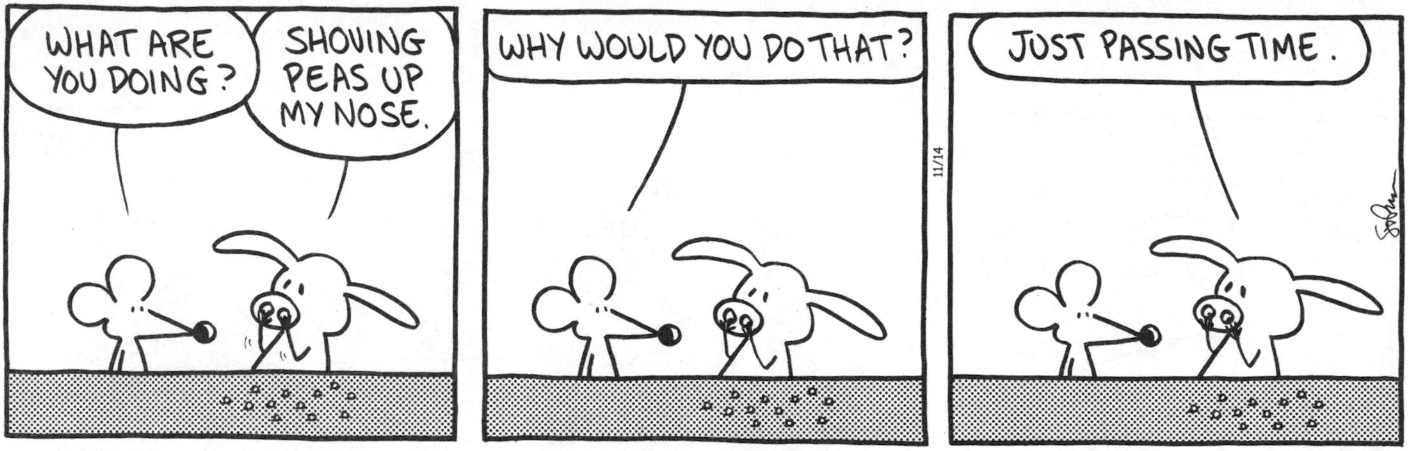
WHAT ARE YOU DOING?
SHOVING PEAS UP MY NOSE.
WHY WOULD YOU DO THAT?
11/14
JUST PASSING TIME.

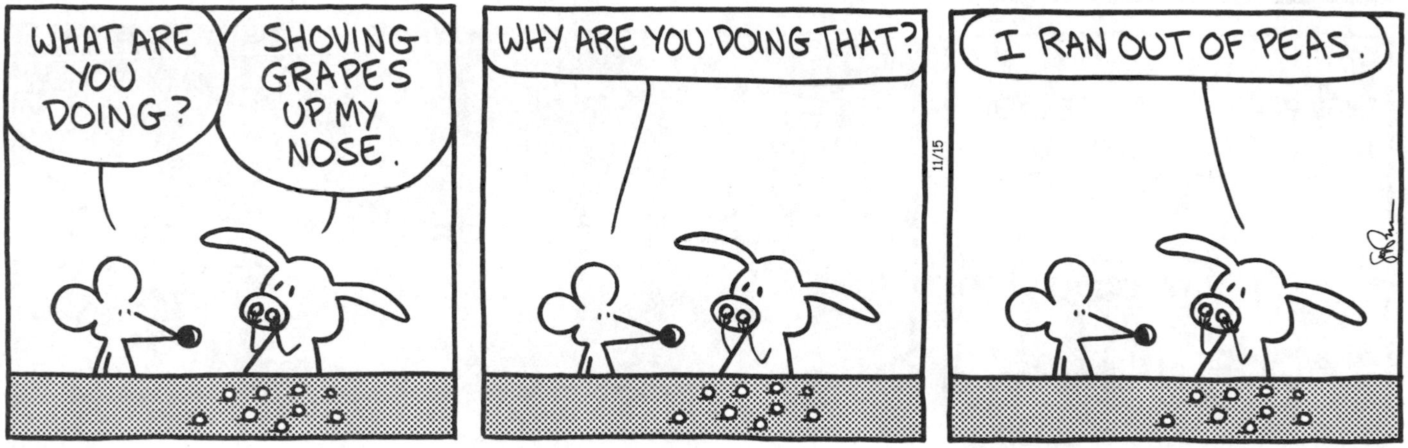
WHAT ARE YOU DOING?
SHOVING GRAPES UP MY NOSE.
WHY ARE YOU DOING THAT?
11/15
I RAN OUT OF PEAS.

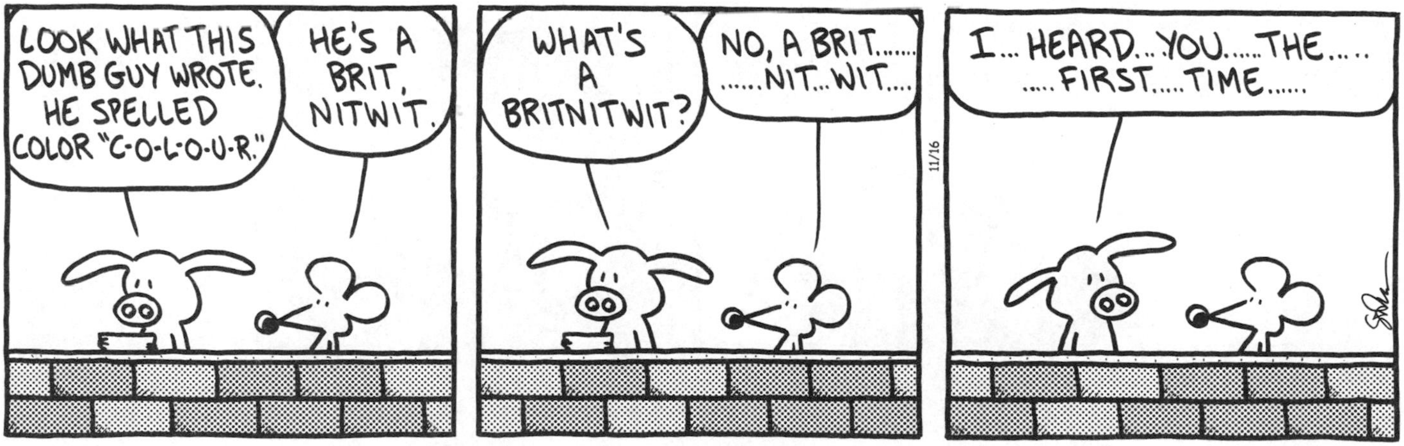
LOOK WHAT THIS DUMB GUY WROTE. HE SPELLED COLOR "C-O-L-O-U-R."
HE'S A BRIT, NITWIT.
WHAT'S A BRITNITWIT?
NO, A BRIT...... ......NIT...WIT....
11/16
I... HEARD... YOU...... THE..... ..... FIRST..... TIME......

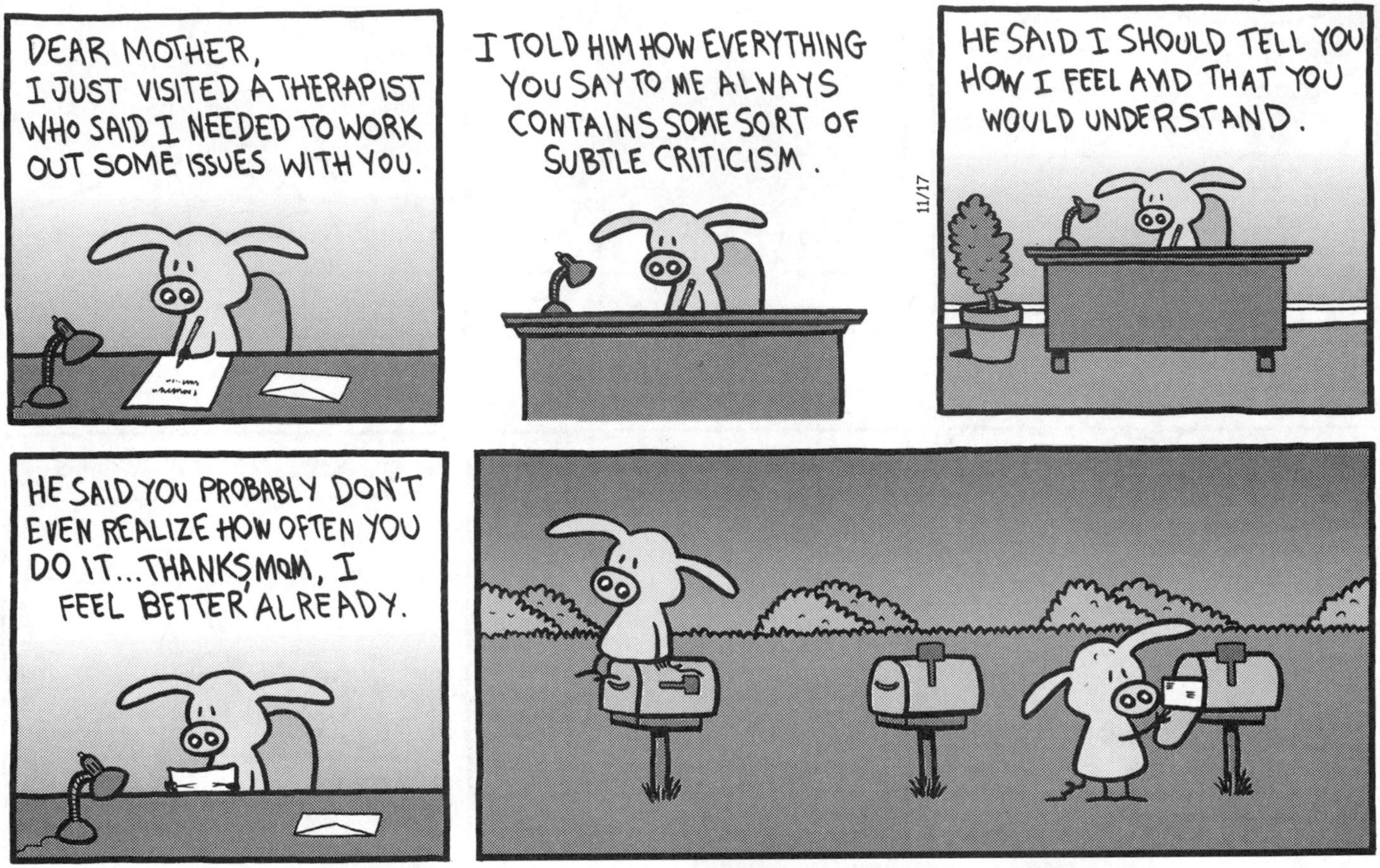
DEAR MOTHER,
I JUST VISITED A THERAPIST WHO SAID I NEEDED TO WORK OUT SOME ISSUES WITH YOU.
I TOLD HIM HOW EVERYTHING YOU SAY TO ME ALWAYS CONTAINS SOME SORT OF SUBTLE CRITICISM.
11/17
HE SAID I SHOULD TELL YOU HOW I FEEL AND THAT YOU WOULD UNDERSTAND.
HE SAID YOU PROBABLY DON'T EVEN REALIZE HOW OFTEN YOU DO IT... THANKS, MOM, I FEEL BETTER ALREADY.

Dear Monkeybrain,
Could you give me some examples?

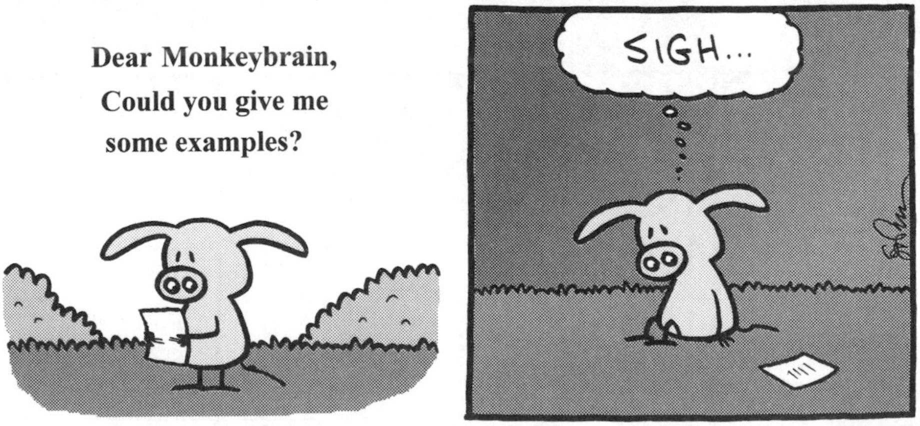
SIGH...

I'VE DECIDED TO EXPLOIT FAT PEOPLE BY CREATING A BOGUS WEIGHT-LOSS SCHEME THAT INVOLVES NO EXERCISE AND PROMISES GREAT RESULTS.
WHAT WILL IT BE?
IT'S CALLED "BOX ME IN." I WILL SELL THEM A CARDBOARD BOX AND TELL THEM TO SHOVE THEMSELVES INSIDE IT UNTIL THEY SEE RESULTS.
THAT'S RIDICULOUS.
11/18
A few days after sealing the box, you will become hungry. DO NOT BE AFRAID. The box is WORKING!
BOX ME IN!!

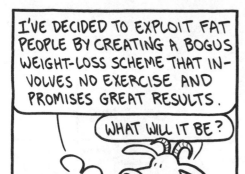

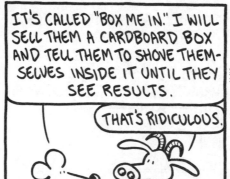

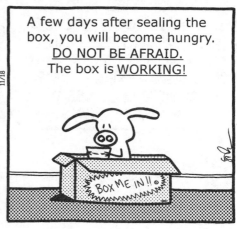

I CAN'T BELIEVE YOU'RE PROMOTING A DIET PLAN THAT INVOLVES SHOVING YOURSELF INTO A CARDBOARD BOX AND STAYING THERE FOR DAYS.
PLEASE..."BOX ME IN" IS A PROVEN WEIGHT-LOSS TECHNIQUE.
WHAT'S THE DIFFERENCE BETWEEN THAT AND STARVATION?
11/19
ABOUT THREE HUNDRED DOLLARS.

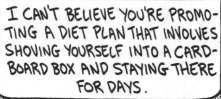

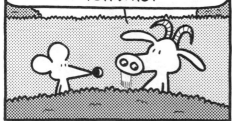

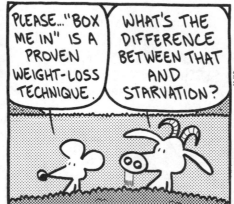

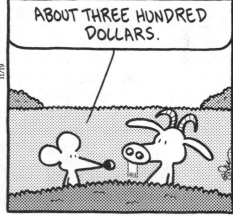

GOAT SAYS YOU'RE EXPLOITING FAT PEOPLE BY SELLING THEM A CARDBOARD BOX THEY HAVE TO SIT IN TO LOSE WEIGHT.
YES...."BOX ME IN" IS SWEEPING THE NATION.... SOME PEOPLE ARE BUYING THEM FOR THEIR ENTIRE FAMILY.
11/20
I CAN'T SEE THE TV, MOM.
ONLY A FEW MORE DAYS, TIMMY.
BOX ME IN!
BOX ME IN!
MEOW.
BOX ME IN!
BOX ME IN!

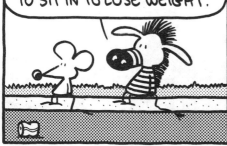

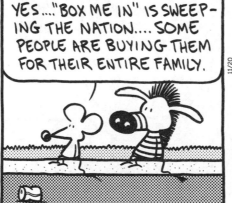

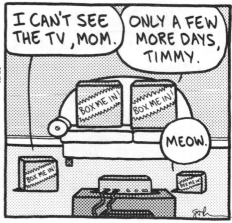

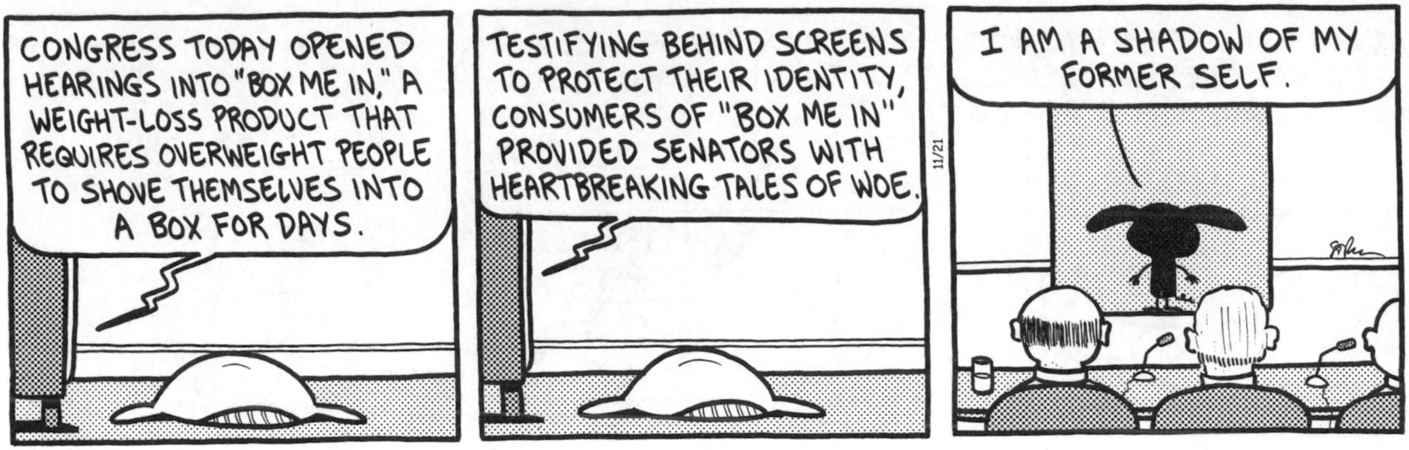
CONGRESS TODAY OPENED HEARINGS INTO "BOX ME IN," A WEIGHT-LOSS PRODUCT THAT REQUIRES OVERWEIGHT PEOPLE TO SHOVE THEMSELVES INTO A BOX FOR DAYS.
TESTIFYING BEHIND SCREENS TO PROTECT THEIR IDENTITY, CONSUMERS OF "BOX ME IN" PROVIDED SENATORS WITH HEARTBREAKING TALES OF WOE.
11/21
I AM A SHADOW OF MY FORMER SELF.

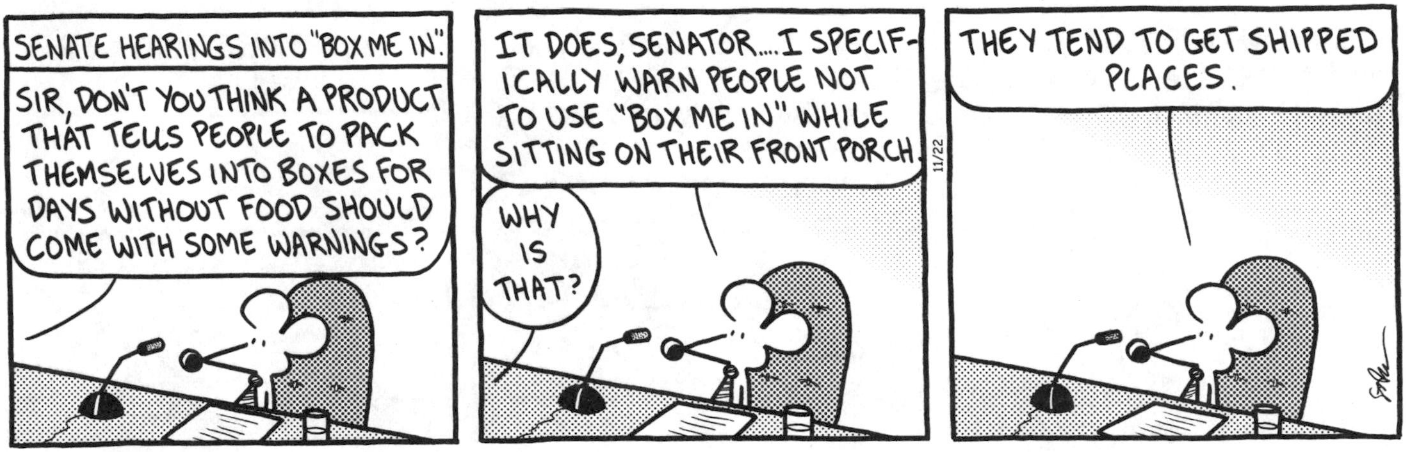
SENATE HEARINGS INTO "BOX ME IN".
SIR, DON'T YOU THINK A PRODUCT THAT TELLS PEOPLE TO PACK THEMSELVES INTO BOXES FOR DAYS WITHOUT FOOD SHOULD COME WITH SOME WARNINGS?
IT DOES, SENATOR....I SPECIFICALLY WARN PEOPLE NOT TO USE "BOX ME IN" WHILE SITTING ON THEIR FRONT PORCH.
WHY IS THAT?
11/22
THEY TEND TO GET SHIPPED PLACES.

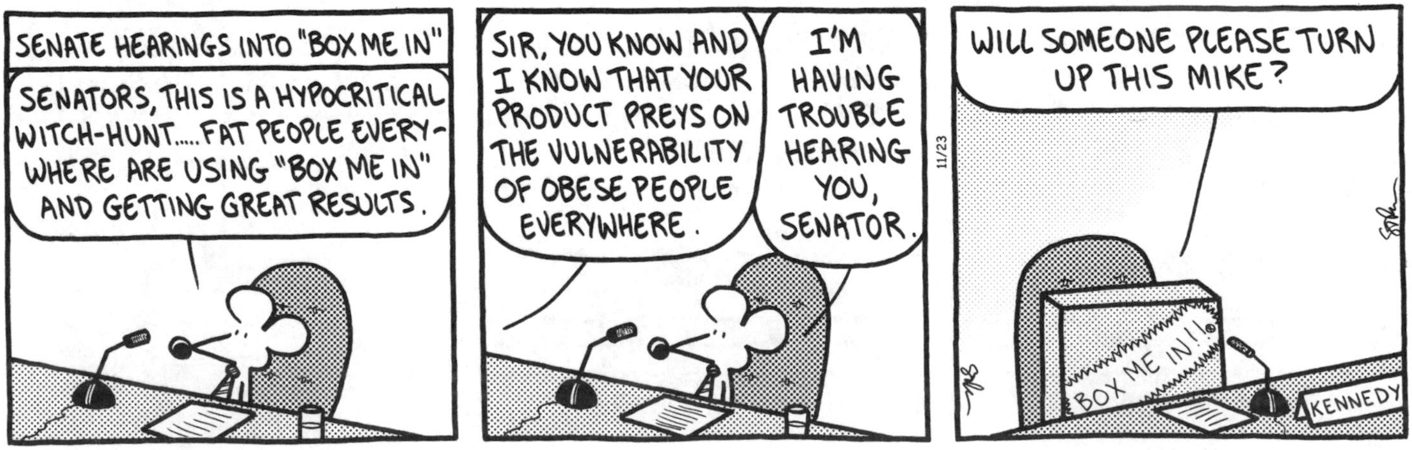
SENATE HEARINGS INTO "BOX ME IN"
SENATORS, THIS IS A HYPOCRITICAL WITCH-HUNT.....FAT PEOPLE EVERYWHERE ARE USING "BOX ME IN" AND GETTING GREAT RESULTS.
SIR, YOU KNOW AND I KNOW THAT YOUR PRODUCT PREYS ON THE VULNERABILITY OF OBESE PEOPLE EVERYWHERE.
I'M HAVING TROUBLE HEARING YOU, SENATOR.
11/23
WILL SOMEONE PLEASE TURN UP THIS MIKE?
BOX ME IN!!
KENNEDY

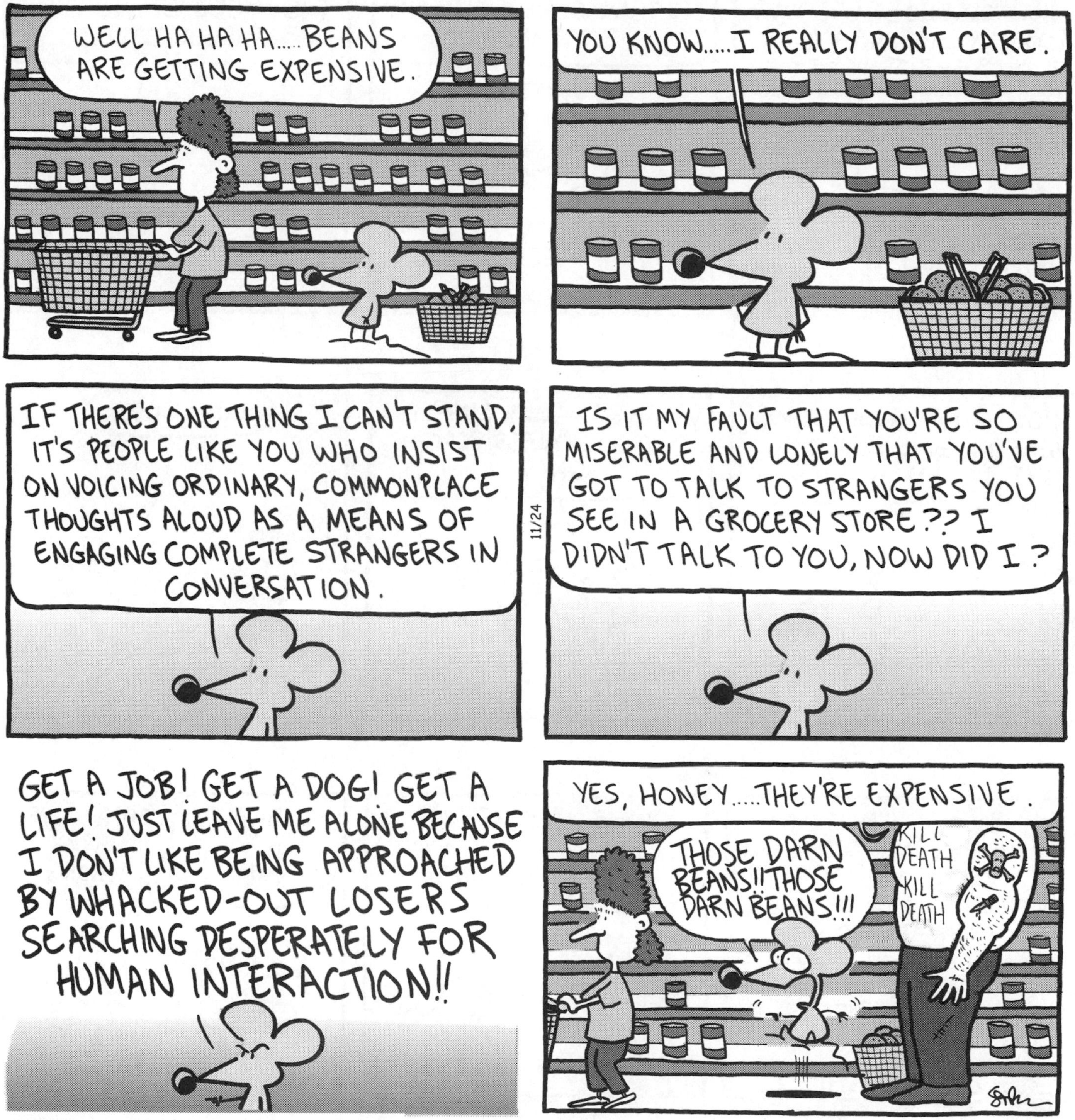
WELL HA HA HA..... BEANS ARE GETTING EXPENSIVE.
YOU KNOW..... I REALLY DON'T CARE.
IF THERE'S ONE THING I CAN'T STAND, IT'S PEOPLE LIKE YOU WHO INSIST ON VOICING ORDINARY, COMMONPLACE THOUGHTS ALOUD AS A MEANS OF ENGAGING COMPLETE STRANGERS IN CONVERSATION.
11/24
IS IT MY FAULT THAT YOU'RE SO MISERABLE AND LONELY THAT YOU'VE GOT TO TALK TO STRANGERS YOU SEE IN A GROCERY STORE?? I DIDN'T TALK TO YOU, NOW DID I?
GET A JOB! GET A DOG! GET A LIFE! JUST LEAVE ME ALONE BECAUSE I DON'T LIKE BEING APPROACHED BY WHACKED-OUT LOSERS SEARCHING DESPERATELY FOR HUMAN INTERACTION!!
YES, HONEY..... THEY'RE EXPENSIVE.
THOSE DARN BEANS!! THOSE DARN BEANS!!!
KILL DEATH KILL DEATH

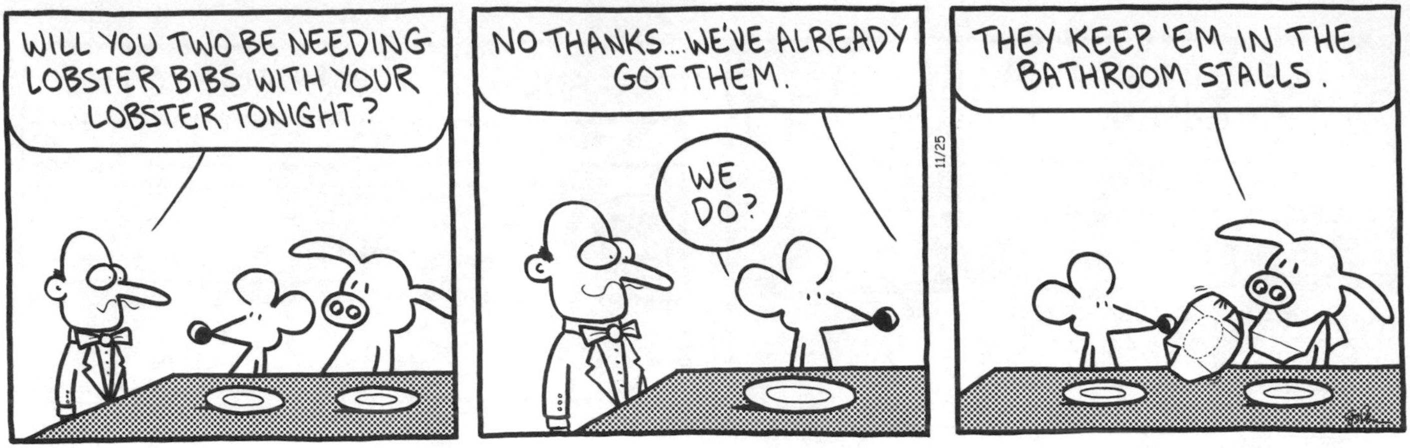
WILL YOU TWO BE NEEDING LOBSTER BIBS WITH YOUR LOBSTER TONIGHT?
NO THANKS....WE'VE ALREADY GOT THEM.
WE DO?
11/25
THEY KEEP 'EM IN THE BATHROOM STALLS.

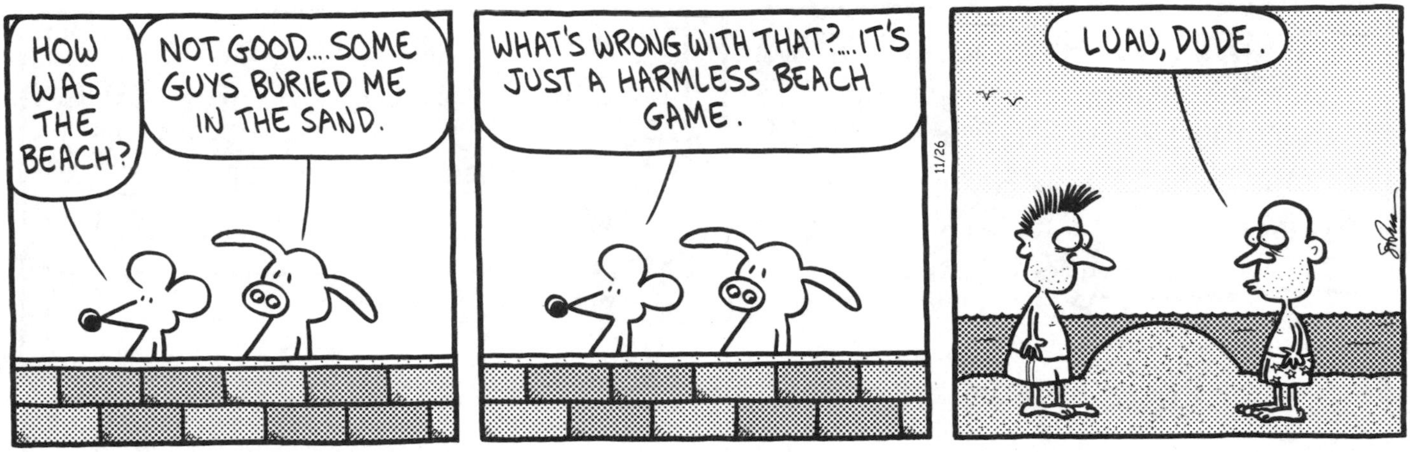
HOW WAS THE BEACH?
NOT GOOD....SOME GUYS BURIED ME IN THE SAND.
WHAT'S WRONG WITH THAT?....IT'S JUST A HARMLESS BEACH GAME.
11/26
LUAU, DUDE.

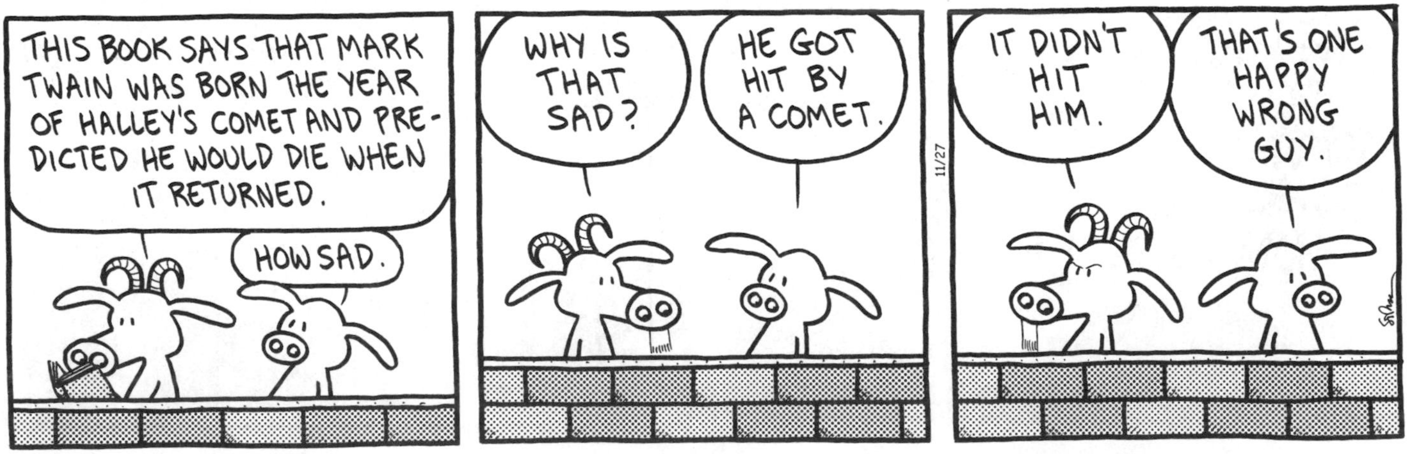
THIS BOOK SAYS THAT MARK TWAIN WAS BORN THE YEAR OF HALLEY'S COMET AND PREDICTED HE WOULD DIE WHEN IT RETURNED.
HOW SAD.
WHY IS THAT SAD?
HE GOT HIT BY A COMET.
11/27
IT DIDN'T HIT HIM.
THAT'S ONE HAPPY WRONG GUY.

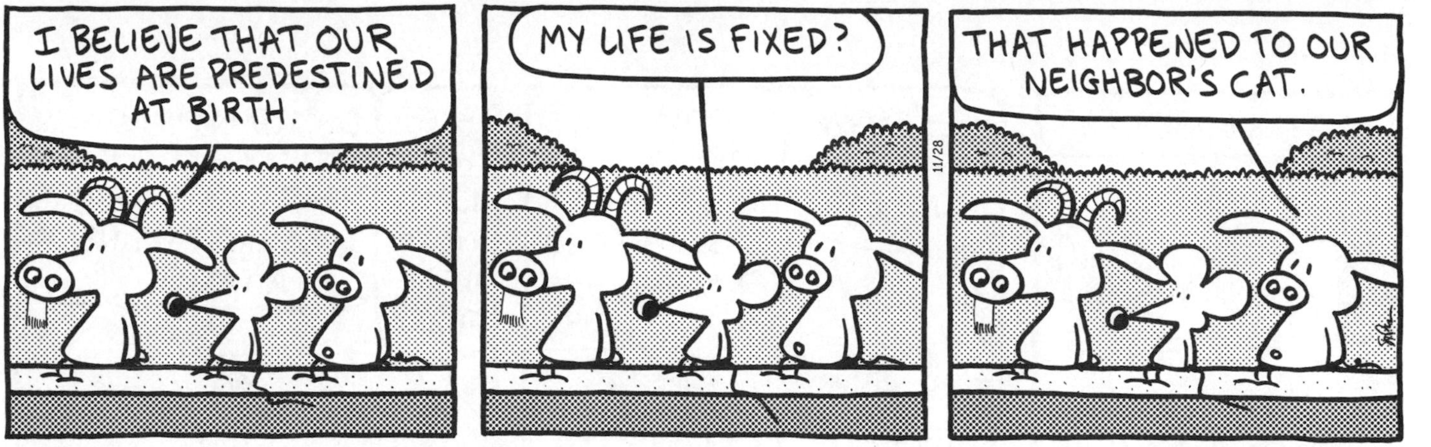
I BELIEVE THAT OUR LIVES ARE PREDESTINED AT BIRTH.
MY LIFE IS FIXED?
11/28
THAT HAPPENED TO OUR NEIGHBOR'S CAT.

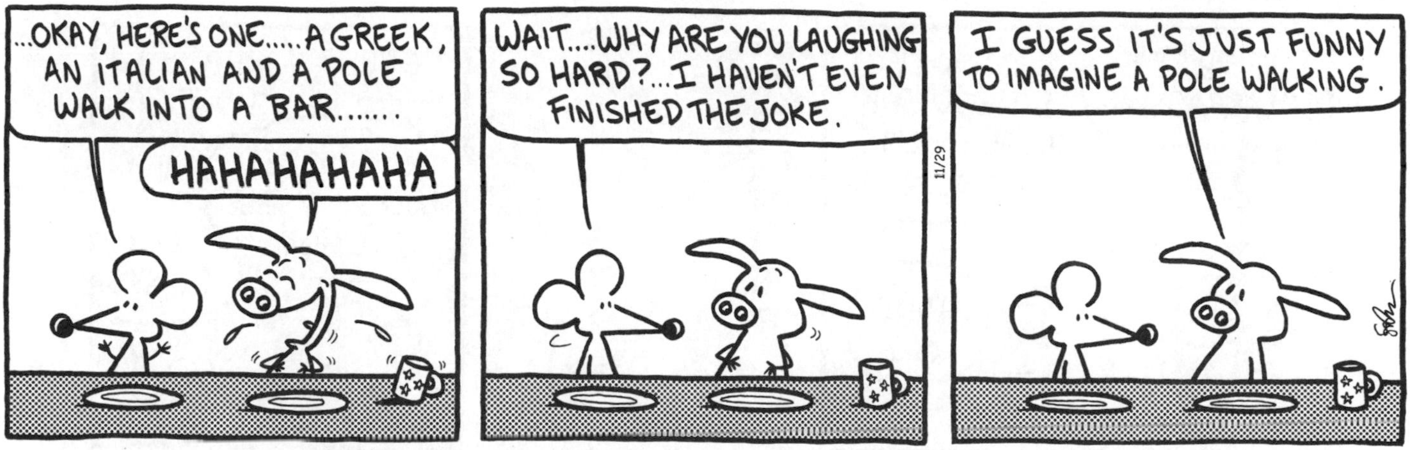
...OKAY, HERE'S ONE.....A GREEK, AN ITALIAN AND A POLE WALK INTO A BAR.......
HAHAHAHAHA
WAIT....WHY ARE YOU LAUGHING SO HARD?...I HAVEN'T EVEN FINISHED THE JOKE.
11/29
I GUESS IT'S JUST FUNNY TO IMAGINE A POLE WALKING.

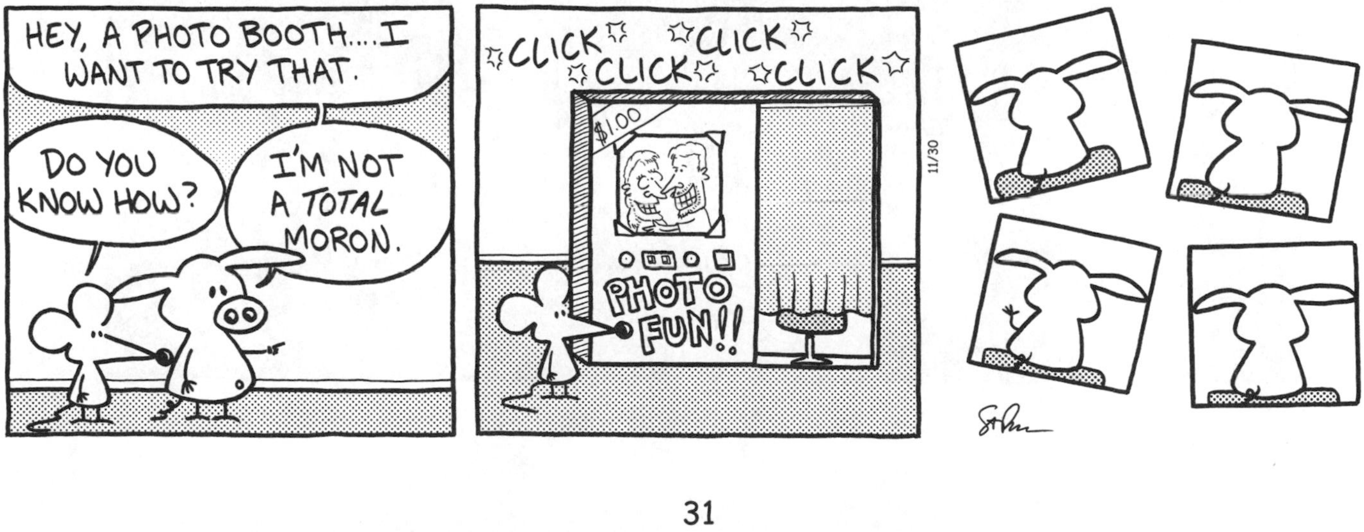
HEY, A PHOTO BOOTH....I WANT TO TRY THAT.
DO YOU KNOW HOW?
I'M NOT A TOTAL MORON.
CLICK CLICK CLICK CLICK
$1.00
PHOTO FUN!!
11/30

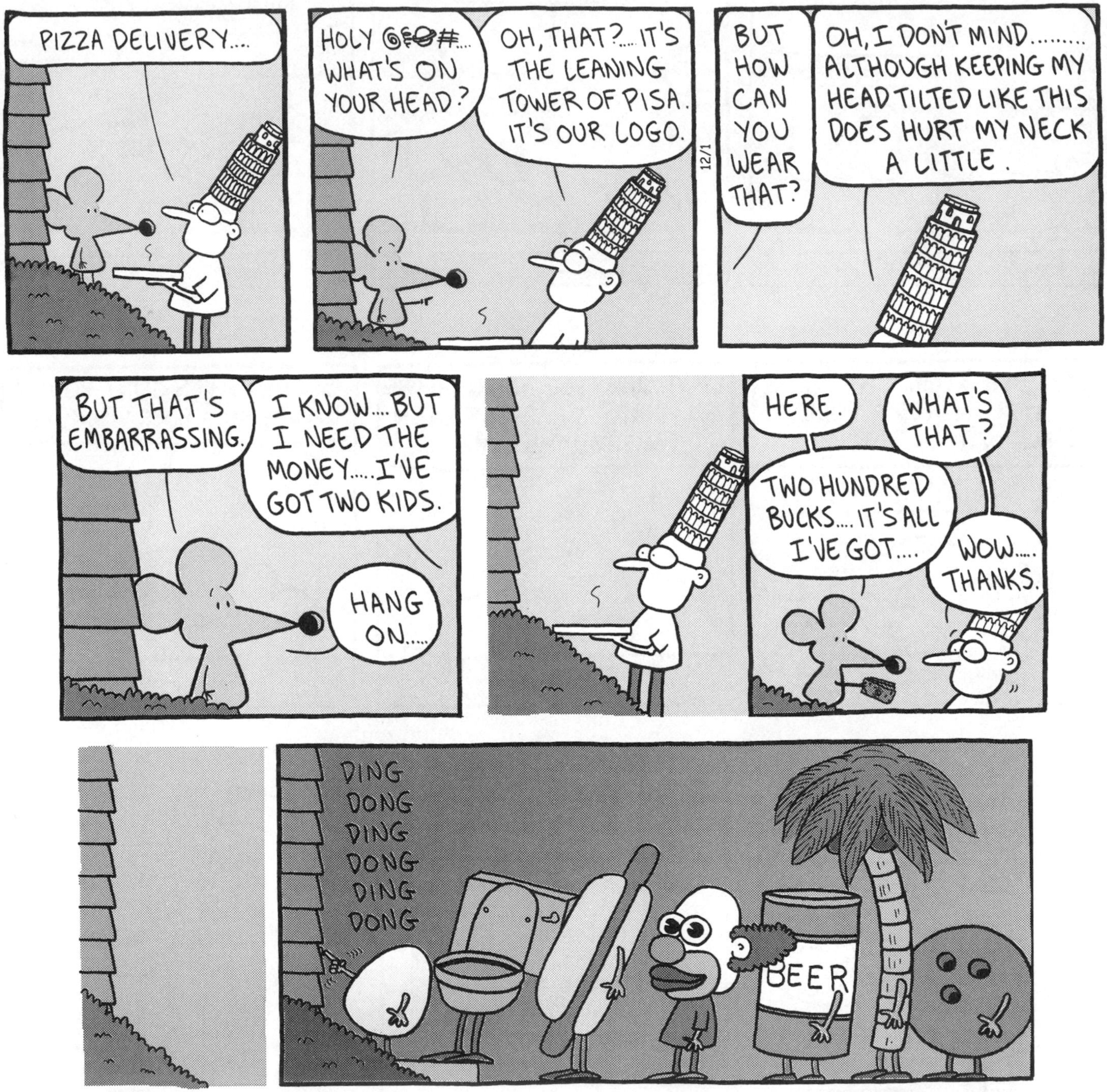
PIZZA DELIVERY....
HOLY @$@#.... WHAT'S ON YOUR HEAD?
OH, THAT?.... IT'S THE LEANING TOWER OF PISA. IT'S OUR LOGO.
12/1
BUT HOW CAN YOU WEAR THAT?
OH, I DON'T MIND......... ALTHOUGH KEEPING MY HEAD TILTED LIKE THIS DOES HURT MY NECK A LITTLE.
BUT THAT'S EMBARRASSING.
I KNOW.... BUT I NEED THE MONEY..... I'VE GOT TWO KIDS.
HANG ON.....
HERE.
TWO HUNDRED BUCKS.... IT'S ALL I'VE GOT....
WHAT'S THAT?
WOW..... THANKS.
DING DONG DING DONG DING DONG
BEER

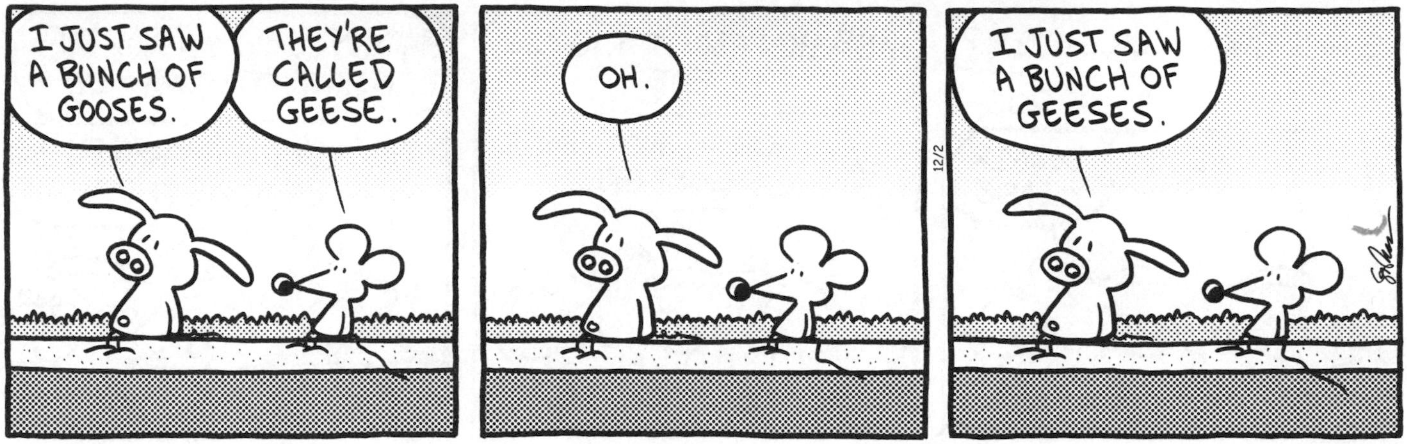
I JUST SAW A BUNCH OF GOOSES.
THEY'RE CALLED GEESE.
OH.
12/2
I JUST SAW A BUNCH OF GEESES.

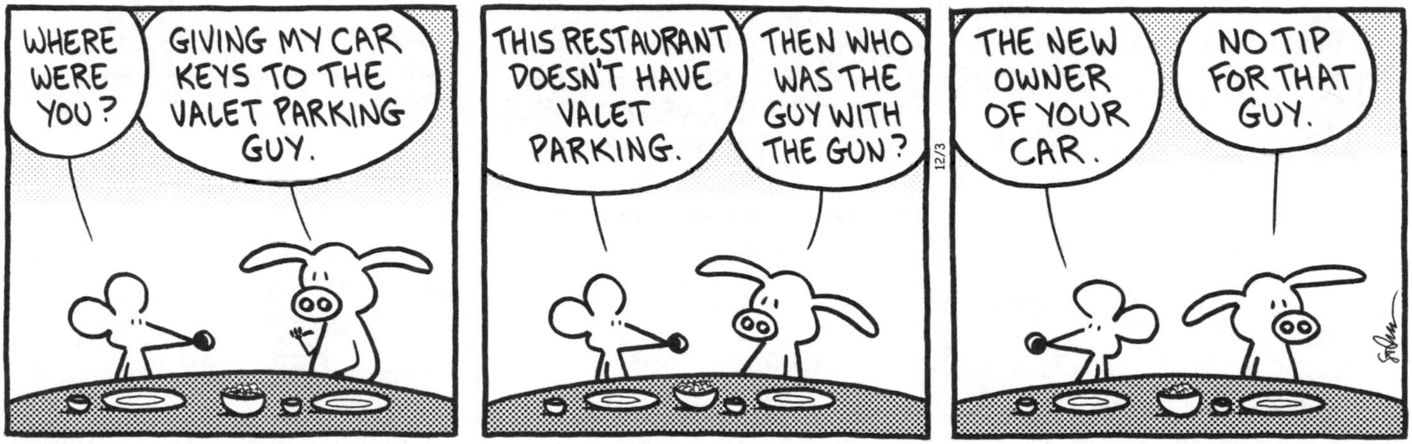
WHERE WERE YOU?
GIVING MY CAR KEYS TO THE VALET PARKING GUY.
THIS RESTAURANT DOESN'T HAVE VALET PARKING.
THEN WHO WAS THE GUY WITH THE GUN?
12/3
THE NEW OWNER OF YOUR CAR.
NO TIP FOR THAT GUY.

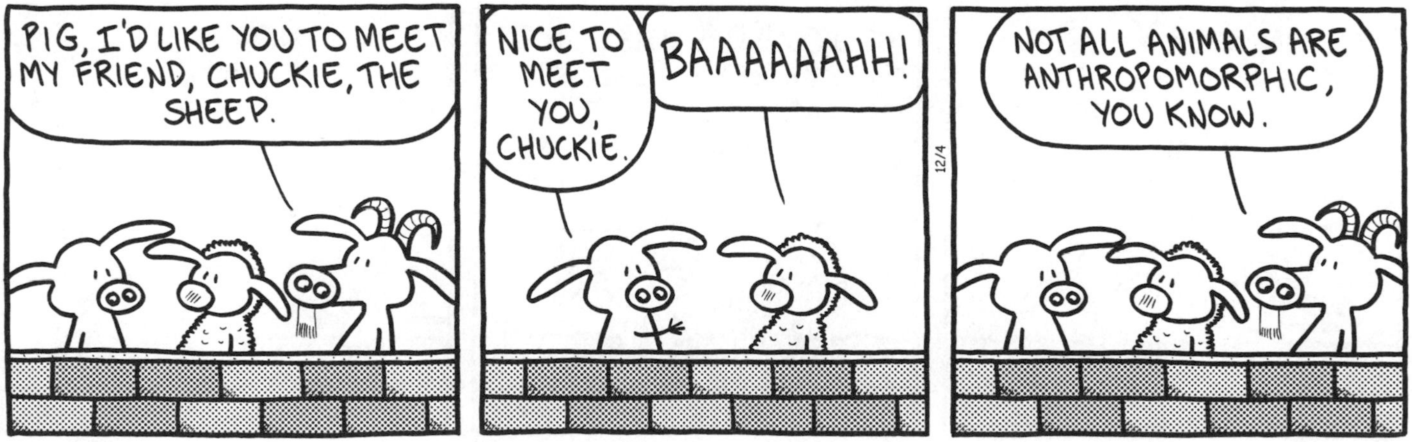
PIG, I'D LIKE YOU TO MEET MY FRIEND, CHUCKIE, THE SHEEP.
NICE TO MEET YOU, CHUCKIE.
BAAAAAAHH!
12/4
NOT ALL ANIMALS ARE ANTHROPOMORPHIC, YOU KNOW.

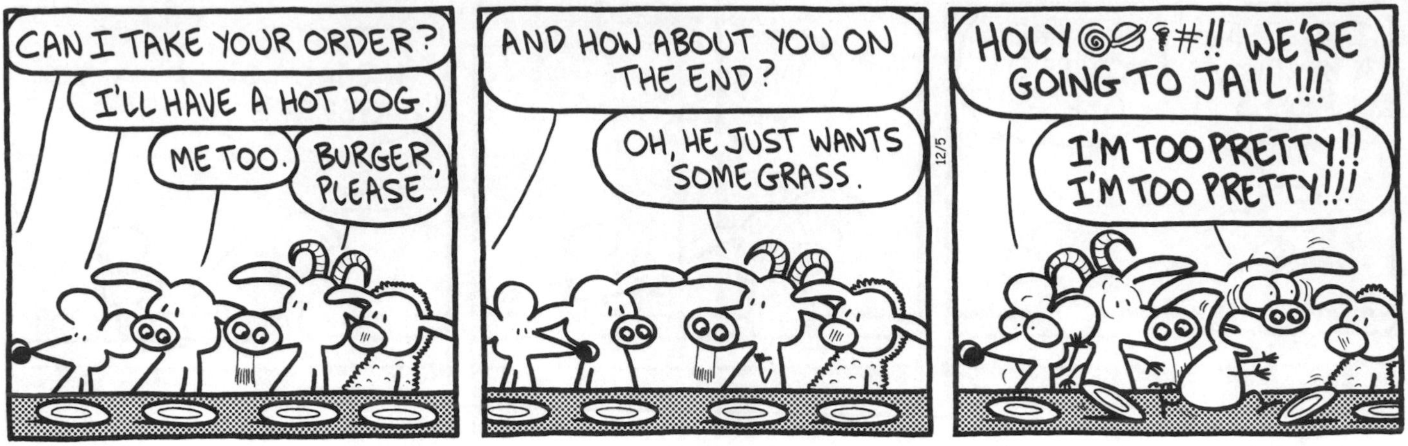
CAN I TAKE YOUR ORDER?
I'LL HAVE A HOT DOG.
ME TOO.
BURGER, PLEASE.
AND HOW ABOUT YOU ON THE END?
OH, HE JUST WANTS SOME GRASS.
12/5
HOLY #!! WE'RE GOING TO JAIL!!!
I'M TOO PRETTY!! I'M TOO PRETTY!!!

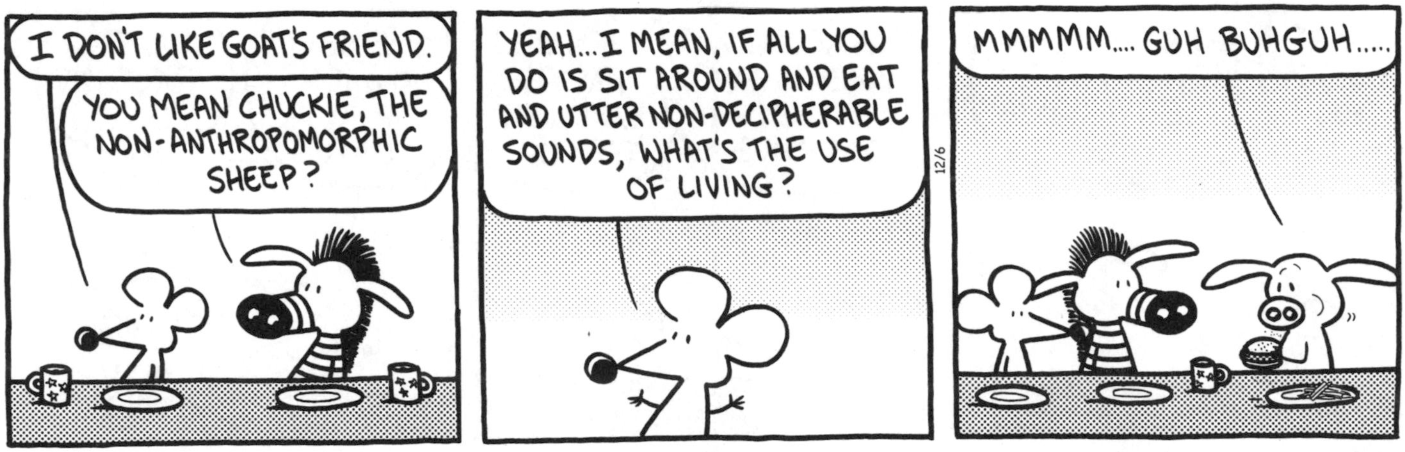
I DON'T LIKE GOAT'S FRIEND.
YOU MEAN CHUCKIE, THE NON-ANTHROPOMORPHIC SHEEP?
YEAH... I MEAN, IF ALL YOU DO IS SIT AROUND AND EAT AND UTTER NON-DECIPHERABLE SOUNDS, WHAT'S THE USE OF LIVING?
12/6
MMMMM.... GUH BUHGUH.....

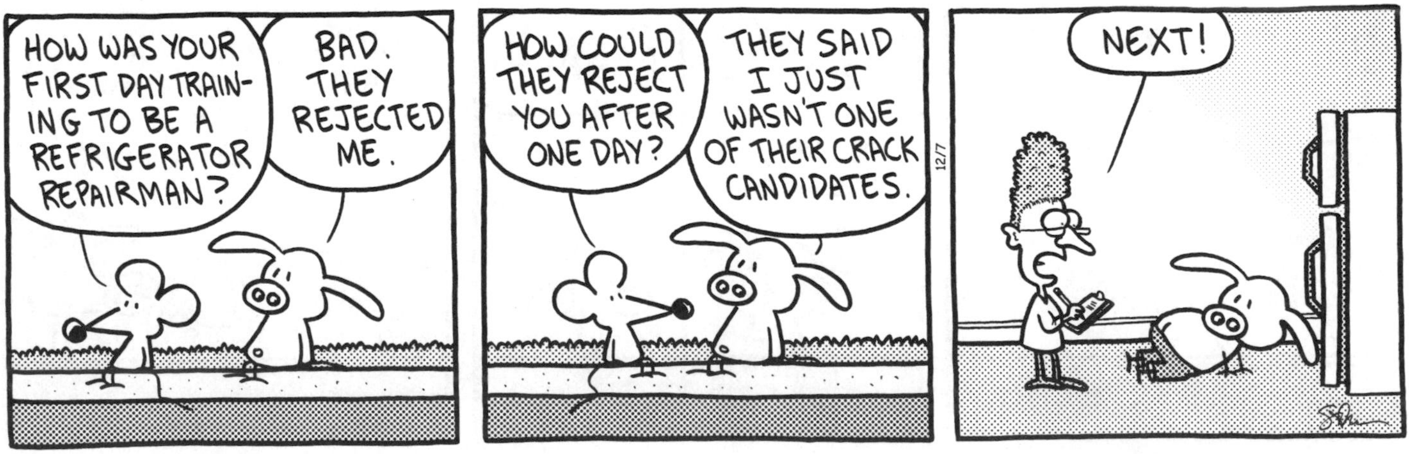
HOW WAS YOUR FIRST DAY TRAINING TO BE A REFRIGERATOR REPAIRMAN?
BAD. THEY REJECTED ME.
HOW COULD THEY REJECT YOU AFTER ONE DAY?
THEY SAID I JUST WASN'T ONE OF THEIR CRACK CANDIDATES.
12/7
NEXT!

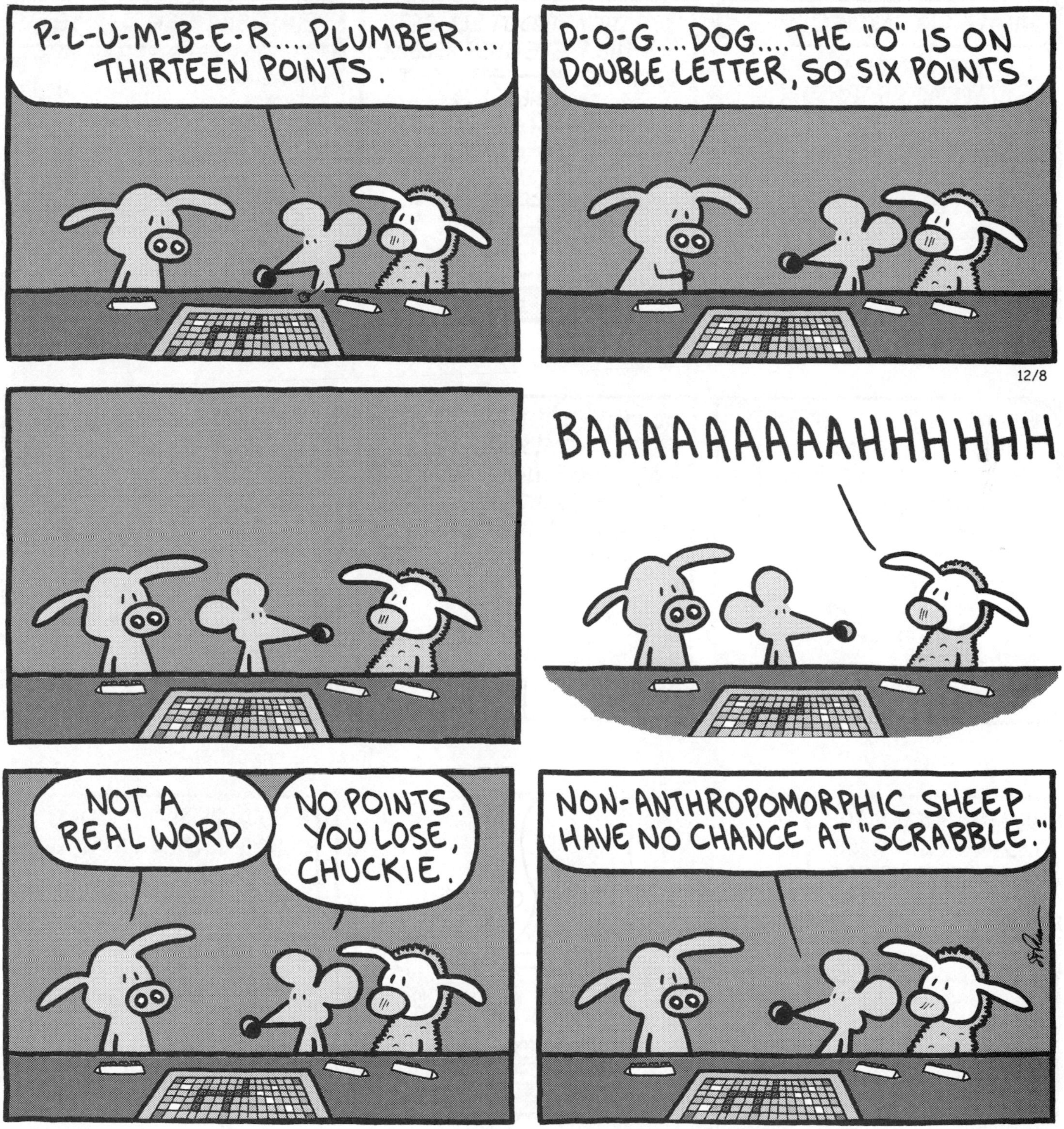
P-L-U-M-B-E-R.... PLUMBER.... THIRTEEN POINTS.
D-O-G.... DOG.... THE "O" IS ON DOUBLE LETTER, SO SIX POINTS.
12/8
BAAAAAAAAAHHHHHH
NOT A REAL WORD.
NO POINTS. YOU LOSE, CHUCKIE.
NON-ANTHROPOMORPHIC SHEEP HAVE NO CHANCE AT "SCRABBLE."

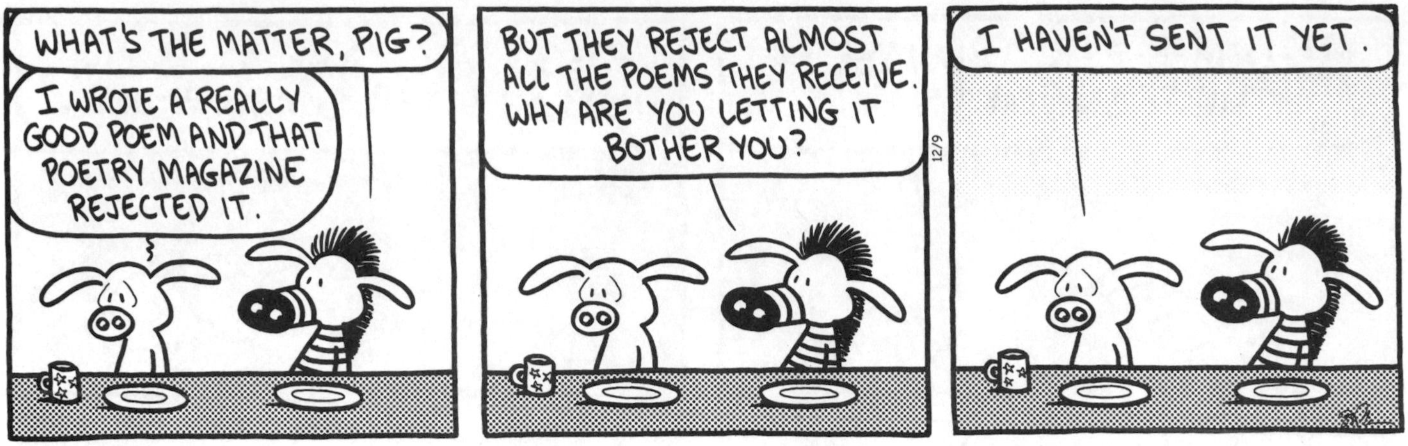
WHAT'S THE MATTER, PIG?
I WROTE A REALLY GOOD POEM AND THAT POETRY MAGAZINE REJECTED IT.
BUT THEY REJECT ALMOST ALL THE POEMS THEY RECEIVE. WHY ARE YOU LETTING IT BOTHER YOU?
12/9
I HAVEN'T SENT IT YET.

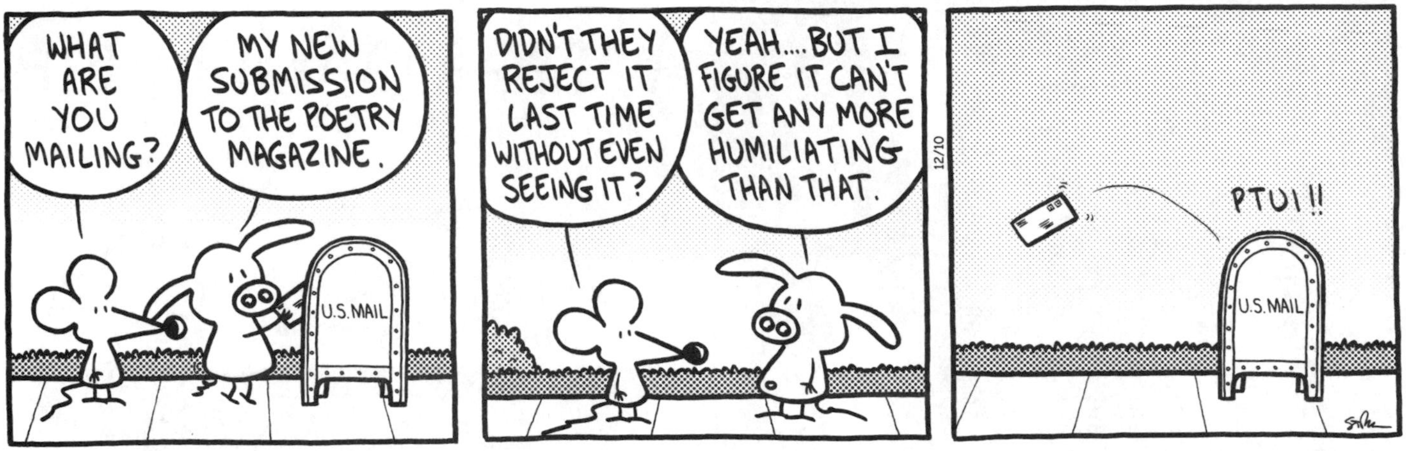
WHAT ARE YOU MAILING?
MY NEW SUBMISSION TO THE POETRY MAGAZINE.
U.S. MAIL
DIDN'T THEY REJECT IT LAST TIME WITHOUT EVEN SEEING IT?
YEAH.... BUT I FIGURE IT CAN'T GET ANY MORE HUMILIATING THAN THAT.
12/10
PTUI!!
U.S. MAIL

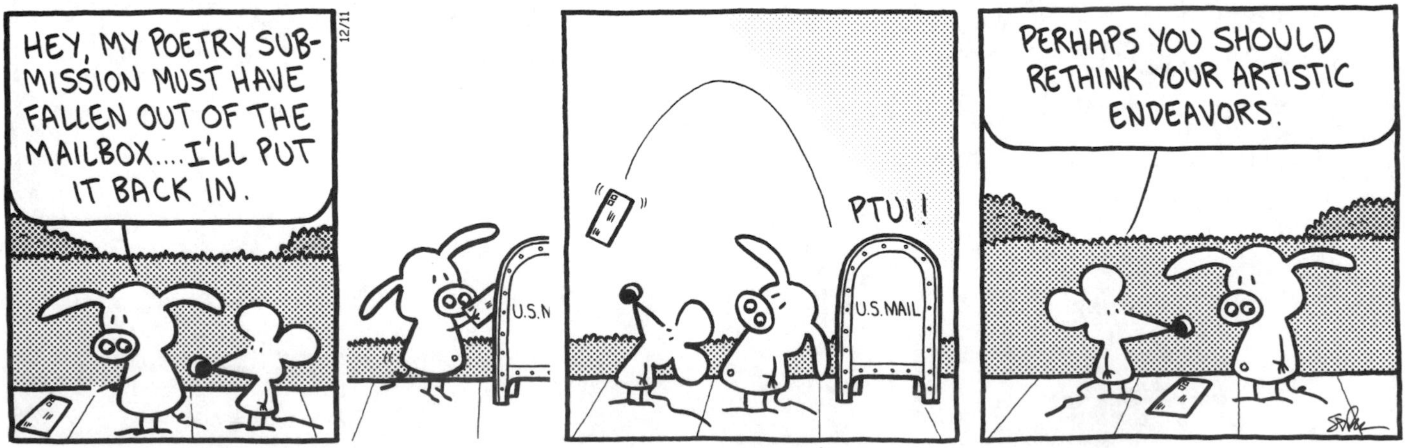
HEY, MY POETRY SUBMISSION MUST HAVE FALLEN OUT OF THE MAILBOX.... I'LL PUT IT BACK IN.
12/11
PTUI!
U.S. MAIL
PERHAPS YOU SHOULD RETHINK YOUR ARTISTIC ENDEAVORS.

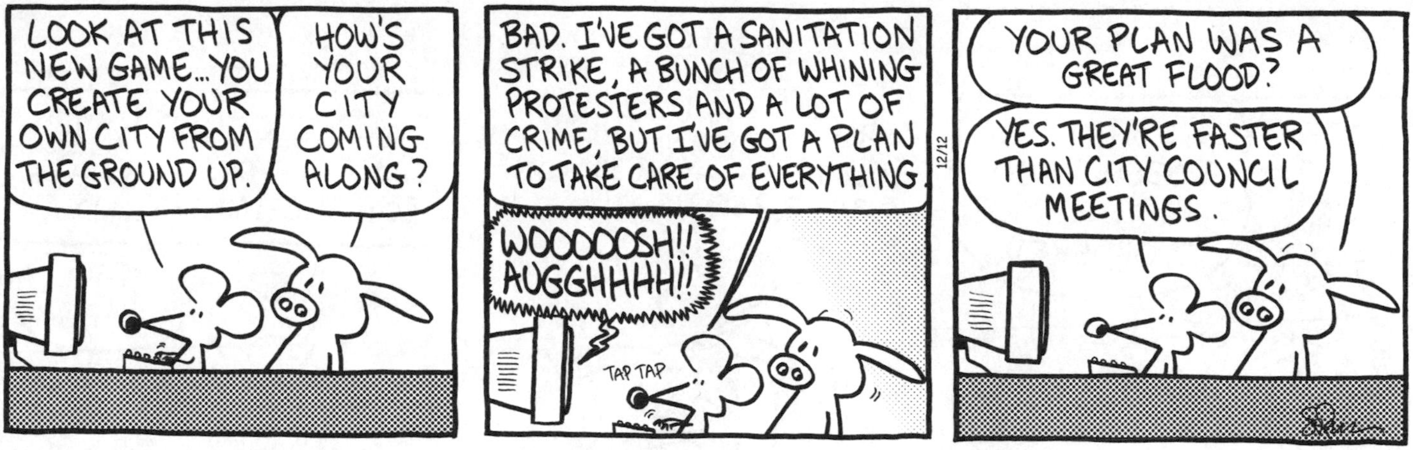
LOOK AT THIS NEW GAME... YOU CREATE YOUR OWN CITY FROM THE GROUND UP.
HOW'S YOUR CITY COMING ALONG?
BAD. I'VE GOT A SANITATION STRIKE, A BUNCH OF WHINING PROTESTERS AND A LOT OF CRIME, BUT I'VE GOT A PLAN TO TAKE CARE OF EVERYTHING.
WOOOOOSH!! AUGGHHHH!!
TAP TAP
12/12
YOUR PLAN WAS A GREAT FLOOD?
YES. THEY'RE FASTER THAN CITY COUNCIL MEETINGS.

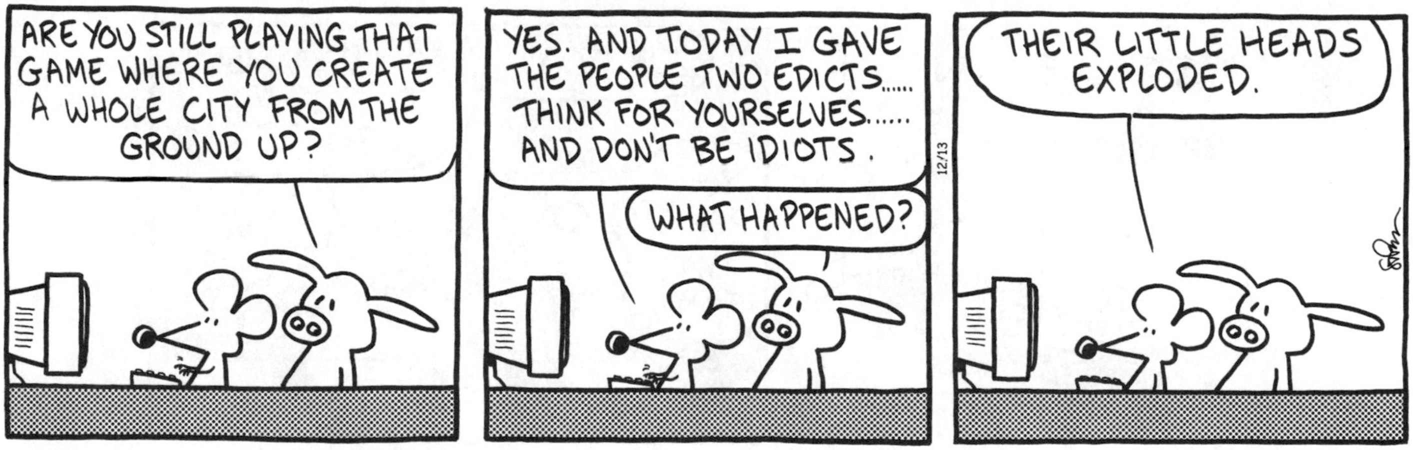
ARE YOU STILL PLAYING THAT GAME WHERE YOU CREATE A WHOLE CITY FROM THE GROUND UP?
YES. AND TODAY I GAVE THE PEOPLE TWO EDICTS...... THINK FOR YOURSELVES...... AND DON'T BE IDIOTS.
WHAT HAPPENED?
12/13
THEIR LITTLE HEADS EXPLODED.

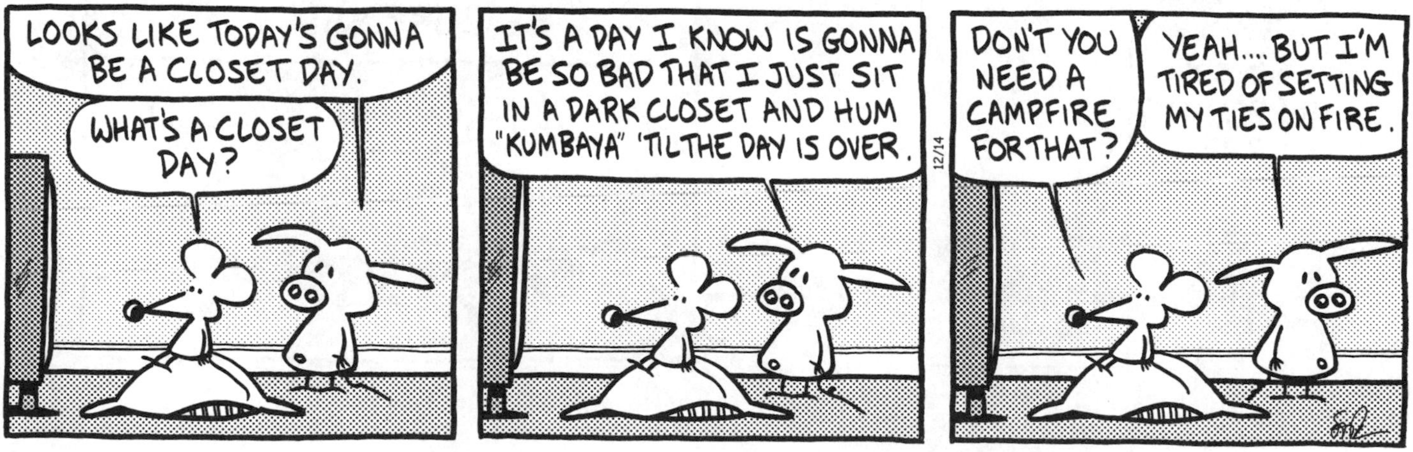
LOOKS LIKE TODAY'S GONNA BE A CLOSET DAY.
WHAT'S A CLOSET DAY?
IT'S A DAY I KNOW IS GONNA BE SO BAD THAT I JUST SIT IN A DARK CLOSET AND HUM "KUMBAYA" 'TIL THE DAY IS OVER.
12/14
DON'T YOU NEED A CAMPFIRE FOR THAT?
YEAH.... BUT I'M TIRED OF SETTING MY TIES ON FIRE.

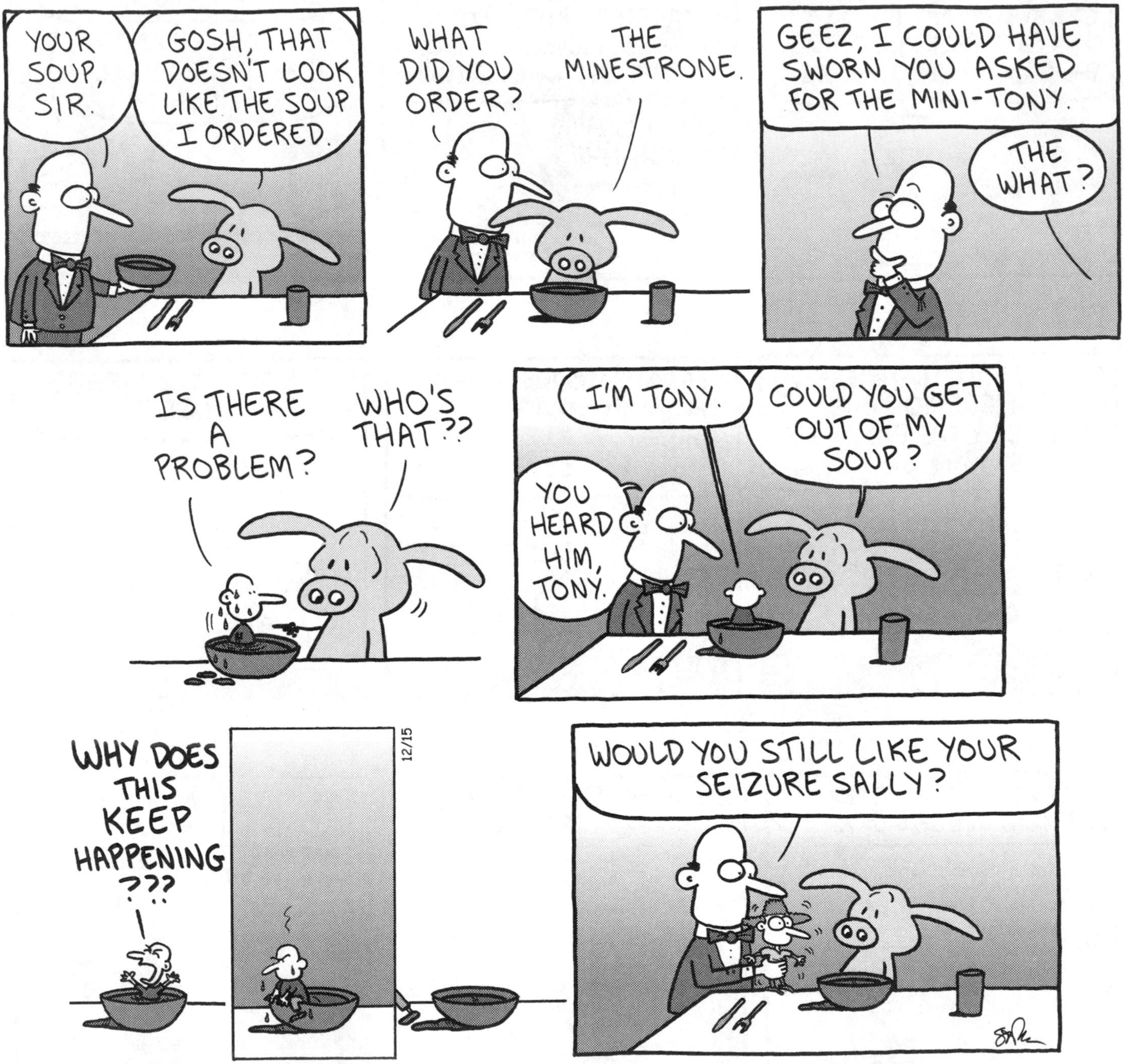
YOUR SOUP, SIR.
GOSH, THAT DOESN'T LOOK LIKE THE SOUP I ORDERED.
WHAT DID YOU ORDER?
THE MINESTRONE.
GEEZ, I COULD HAVE SWORN YOU ASKED FOR THE MINI-TONY.
THE WHAT?
IS THERE A PROBLEM?
WHO'S THAT??
I'M TONY.
COULD YOU GET OUT OF MY SOUP?
YOU HEARD HIM, TONY.
WHY DOES THIS KEEP HAPPENING???
12/15
WOULD YOU STILL LIKE YOUR SEIZURE SALLY?

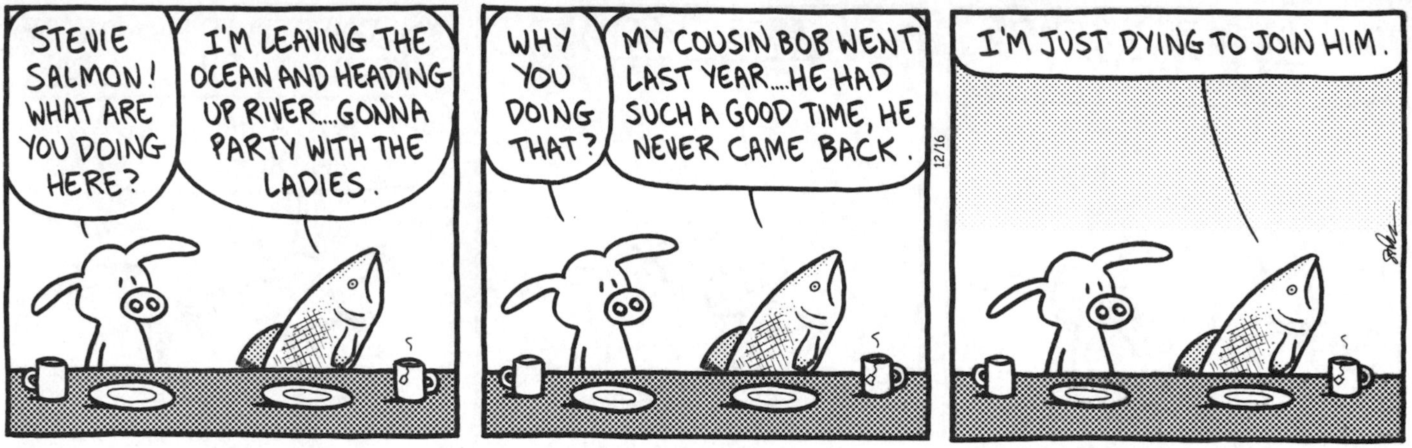
STEVIE SALMON! WHAT ARE YOU DOING HERE?
I'M LEAVING THE OCEAN AND HEADING UP RIVER....GONNA PARTY WITH THE LADIES.
WHY YOU DOING THAT?
MY COUSIN BOB WENT LAST YEAR....HE HAD SUCH A GOOD TIME, HE NEVER CAME BACK.
I'M JUST DYING TO JOIN HIM.
12/16

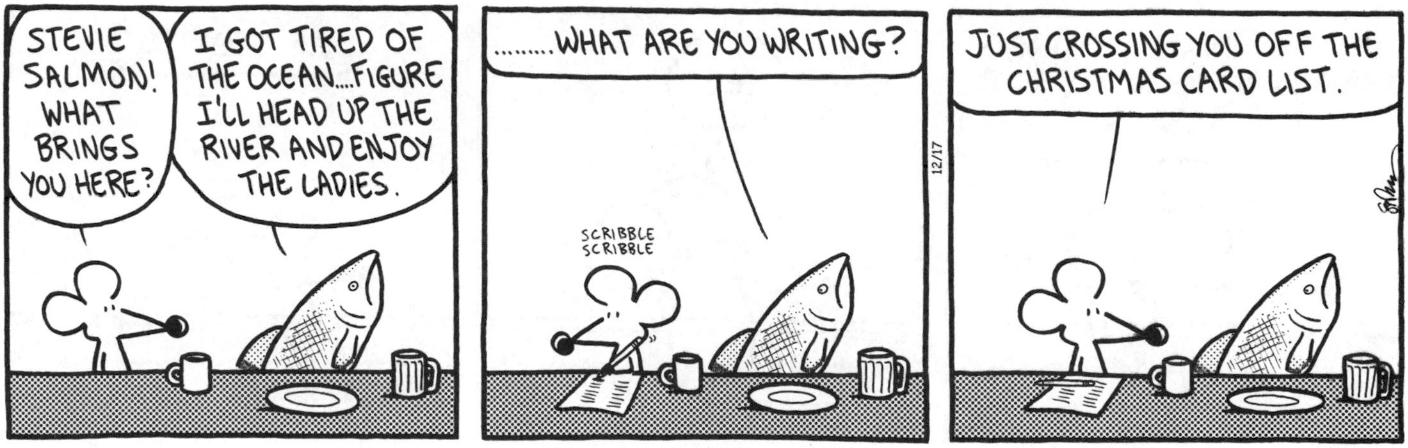
STEVIE SALMON! WHAT BRINGS YOU HERE?
I GOT TIRED OF THE OCEAN....FIGURE I'LL HEAD UP THE RIVER AND ENJOY THE LADIES.
.........WHAT ARE YOU WRITING?
SCRIBBLE SCRIBBLE
JUST CROSSING YOU OFF THE CHRISTMAS CARD LIST.
12/17

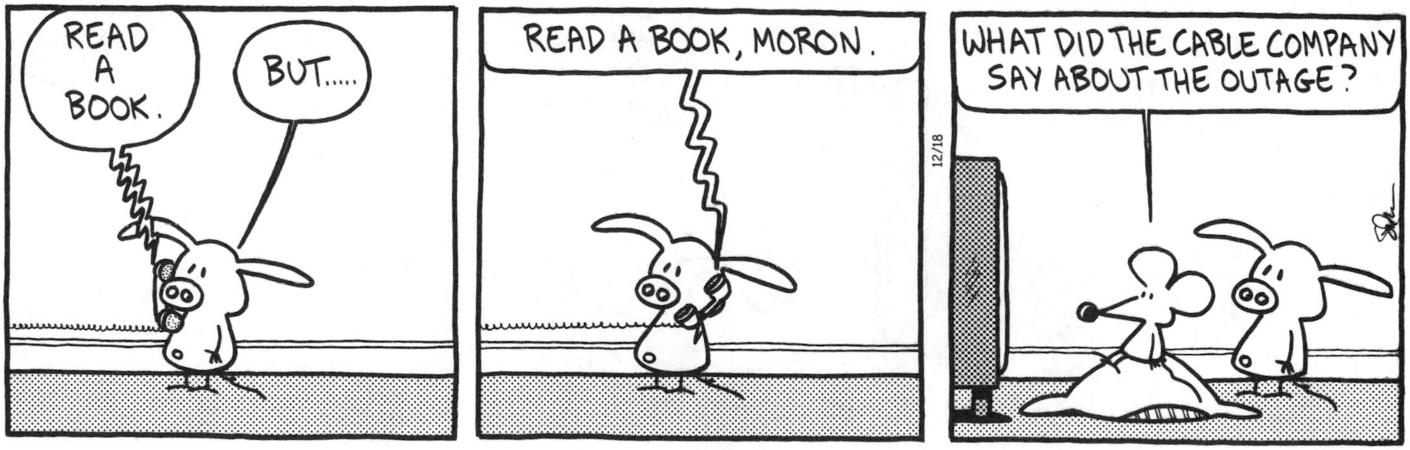
READ A BOOK.
BUT.....
READ A BOOK, MORON.
WHAT DID THE CABLE COMPANY SAY ABOUT THE OUTAGE?
12/18

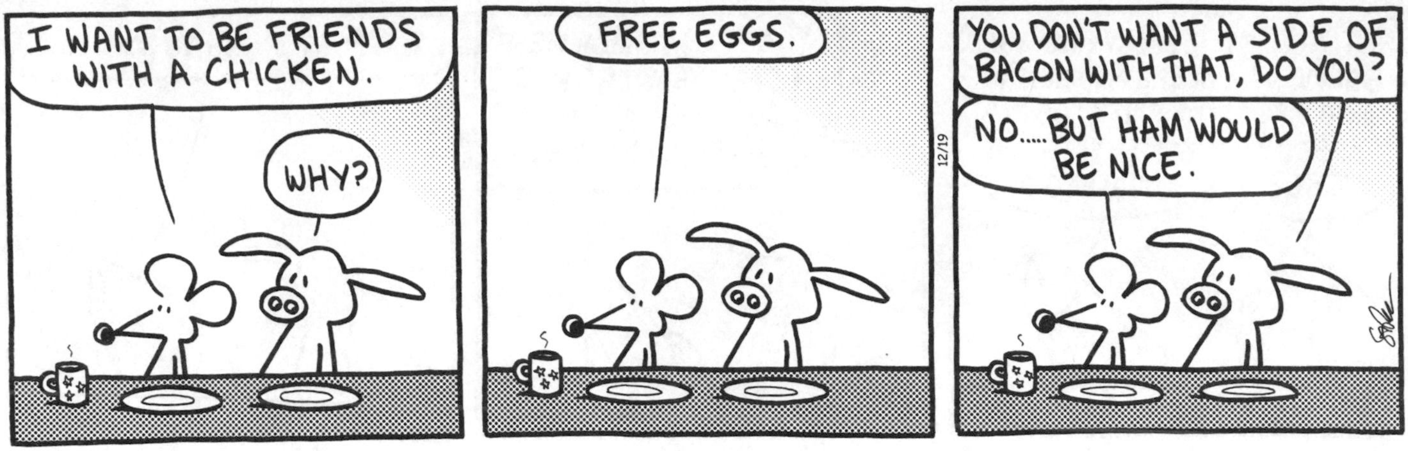
I WANT TO BE FRIENDS WITH A CHICKEN.
WHY?
FREE EGGS.
12/19
YOU DON'T WANT A SIDE OF BACON WITH THAT, DO YOU?
NO..... BUT HAM WOULD BE NICE.

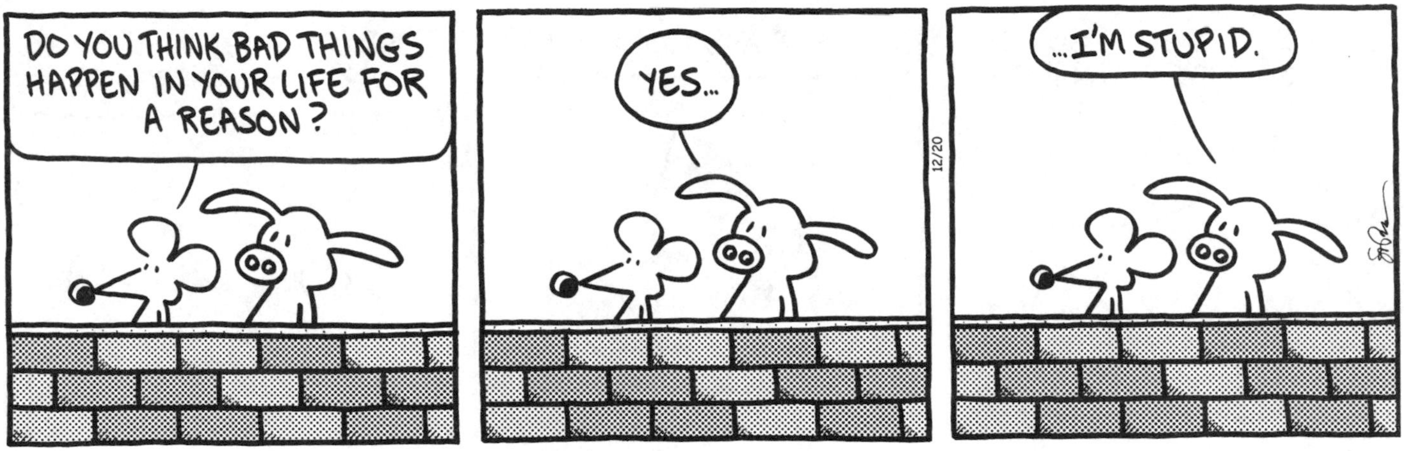
DO YOU THINK BAD THINGS HAPPEN IN YOUR LIFE FOR A REASON?
YES...
12/20
...I'M STUPID.

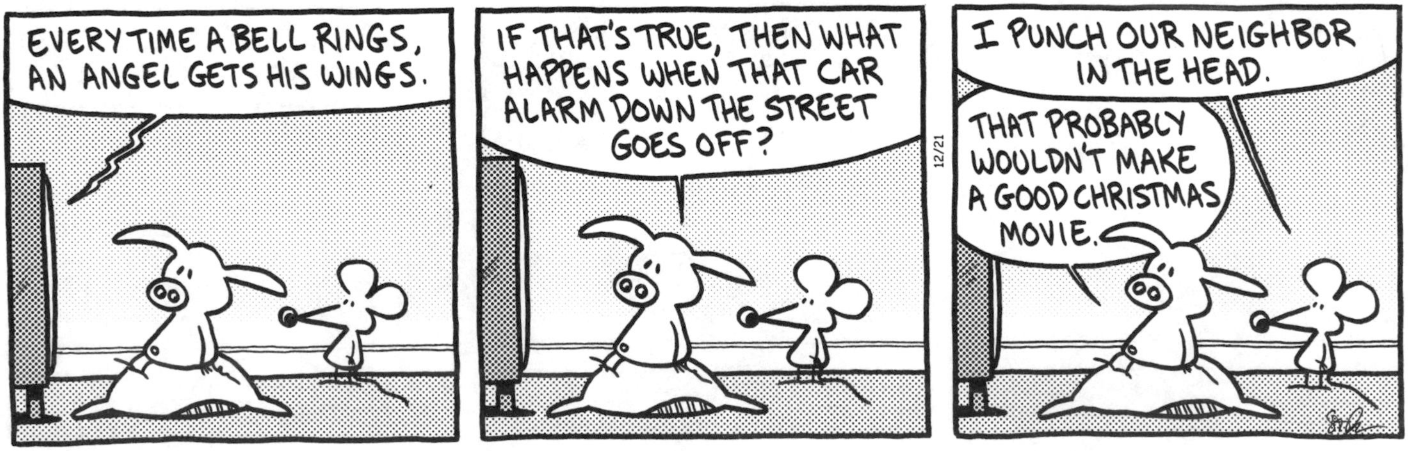
EVERY TIME A BELL RINGS, AN ANGEL GETS HIS WINGS.
IF THAT'S TRUE, THEN WHAT HAPPENS WHEN THAT CAR ALARM DOWN THE STREET GOES OFF?
12/21
I PUNCH OUR NEIGHBOR IN THE HEAD.
THAT PROBABLY WOULDN'T MAKE A GOOD CHRISTMAS MOVIE.

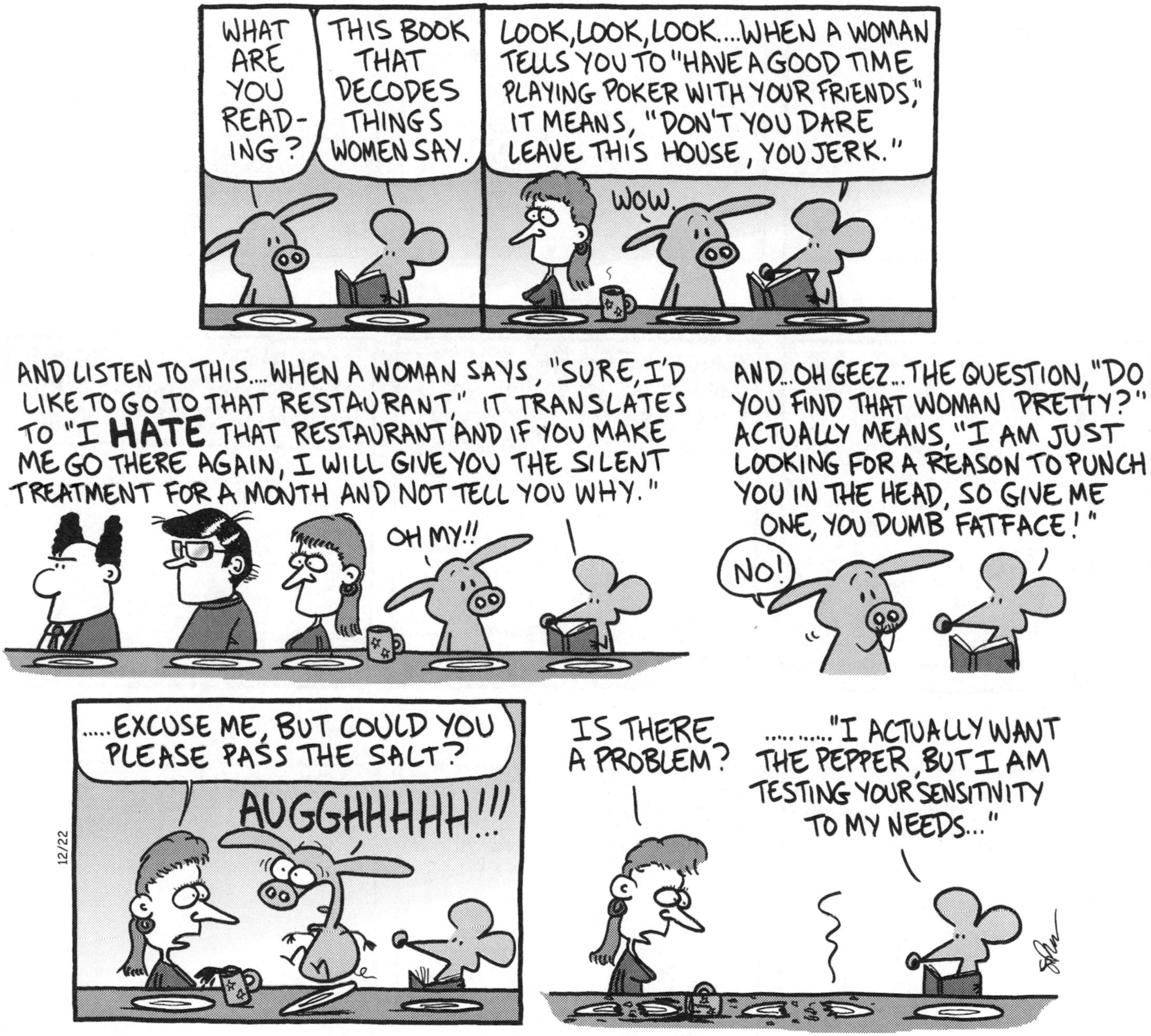
WHAT ARE YOU READING?
THIS BOOK THAT DECODES THINGS WOMEN SAY.
LOOK, LOOK, LOOK.... WHEN A WOMAN TELLS YOU TO "HAVE A GOOD TIME PLAYING POKER WITH YOUR FRIENDS," IT MEANS, "DON'T YOU DARE LEAVE THIS HOUSE, YOU JERK."
WOW.
AND LISTEN TO THIS.... WHEN A WOMAN SAYS, "SURE, I'D LIKE TO GO TO THAT RESTAURANT," IT TRANSLATES TO "I HATE THAT RESTAURANT AND IF YOU MAKE ME GO THERE AGAIN, I WILL GIVE YOU THE SILENT TREATMENT FOR A MONTH AND NOT TELL YOU WHY."
OH MY!!
AND...OH GEEZ...THE QUESTION, "DO YOU FIND THAT WOMAN PRETTY?" ACTUALLY MEANS, "I AM JUST LOOKING FOR A REASON TO PUNCH YOU IN THE HEAD, SO GIVE ME ONE, YOU DUMB FATFACE!"
NO!
.....EXCUSE ME, BUT COULD YOU PLEASE PASS THE SALT?
AUGGHHHHH!!!...
12/22
IS THERE A PROBLEM?
.........."I ACTUALLY WANT THE PEPPER, BUT I AM TESTING YOUR SENSITIVITY TO MY NEEDS..."

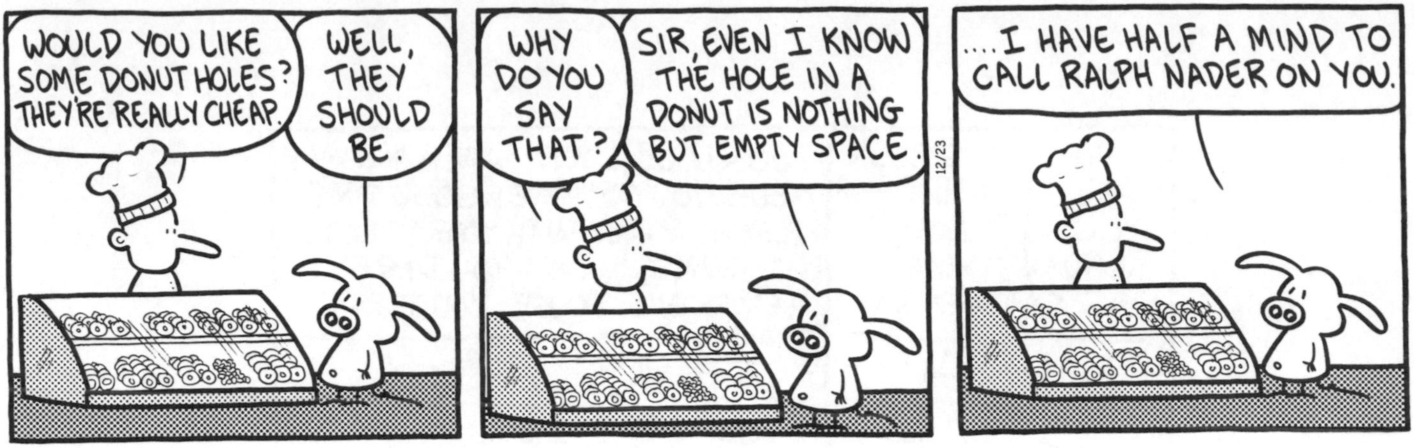
WOULD YOU LIKE SOME DONUT HOLES? THEY'RE REALLY CHEAP.
WELL, THEY SHOULD BE.
WHY DO YOU SAY THAT?
SIR, EVEN I KNOW THE HOLE IN A DONUT IS NOTHING BUT EMPTY SPACE.
12/23
....I HAVE HALF A MIND TO CALL RALPH NADER ON YOU.

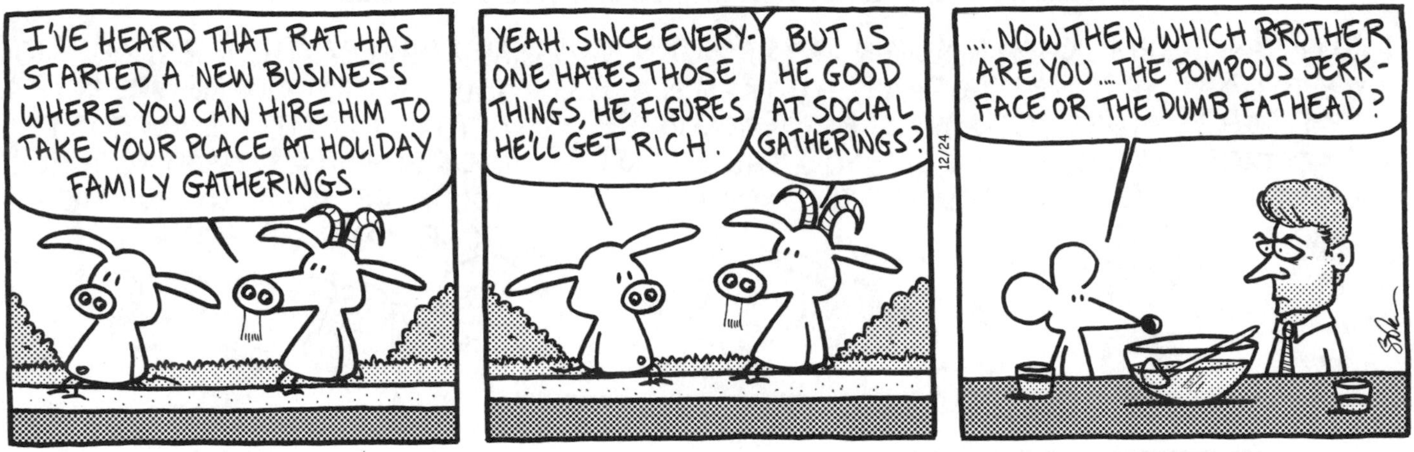
I'VE HEARD THAT RAT HAS STARTED A NEW BUSINESS WHERE YOU CAN HIRE HIM TO TAKE YOUR PLACE AT HOLIDAY FAMILY GATHERINGS.
YEAH. SINCE EVERYONE HATES THOSE THINGS, HE FIGURES HE'LL GET RICH.
BUT IS HE GOOD AT SOCIAL GATHERINGS?
12/24
....NOW THEN, WHICH BROTHER ARE YOU....THE POMPOUS JERK-FACE OR THE DUMB FATHEAD?

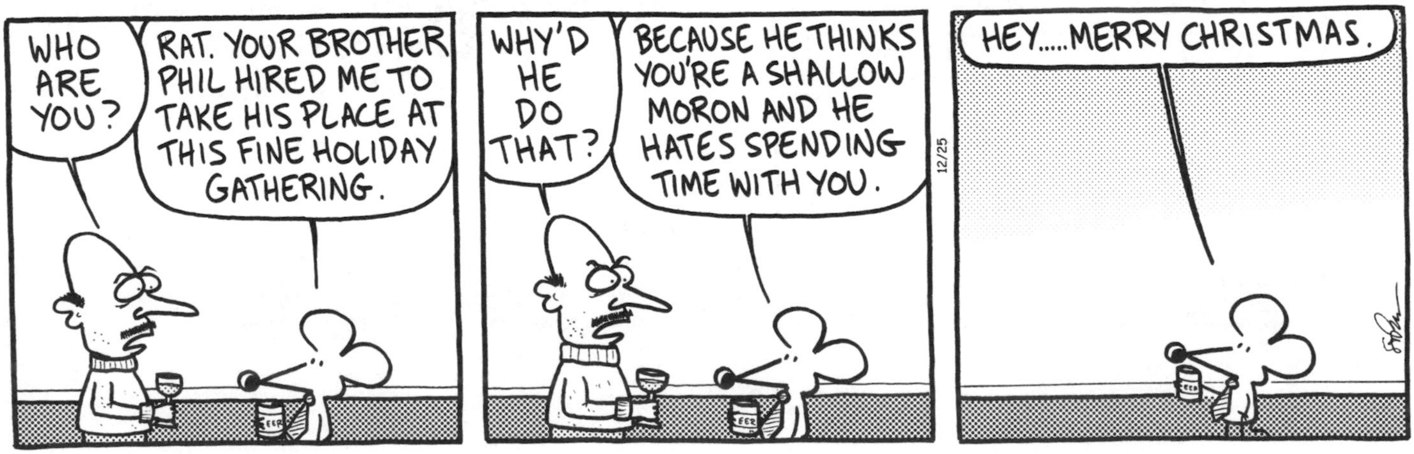
WHO ARE YOU?
RAT. YOUR BROTHER PHIL HIRED ME TO TAKE HIS PLACE AT THIS FINE HOLIDAY GATHERING.
WHY'D HE DO THAT?
BECAUSE HE THINKS YOU'RE A SHALLOW MORON AND HE HATES SPENDING TIME WITH YOU.
12/25
HEY.....MERRY CHRISTMAS.

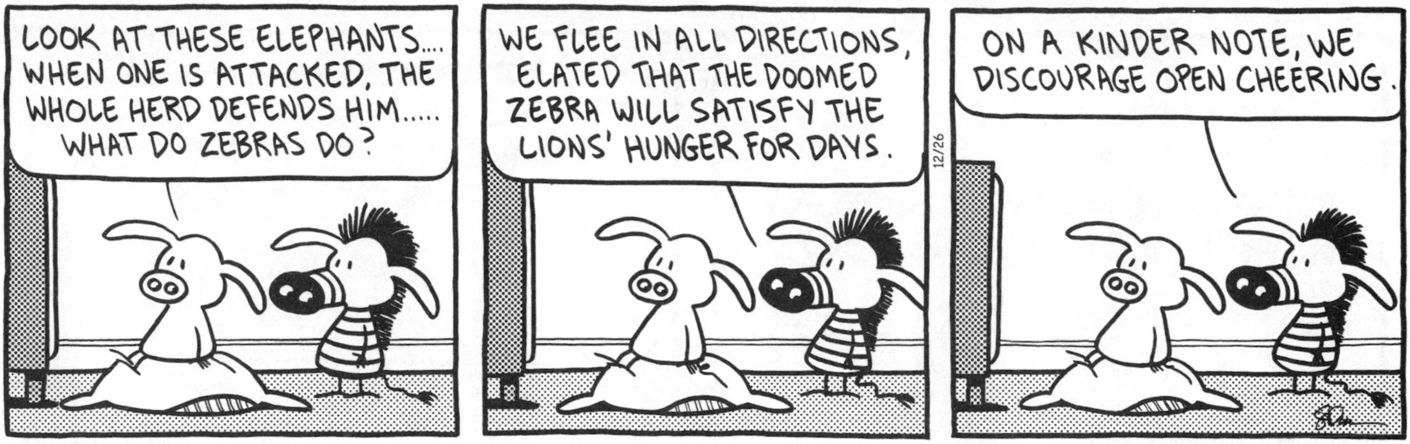
LOOK AT THESE ELEPHANTS.... WHEN ONE IS ATTACKED, THE WHOLE HERD DEFENDS HIM..... WHAT DO ZEBRAS DO?
WE FLEE IN ALL DIRECTIONS, ELATED THAT THE DOOMED ZEBRA WILL SATISFY THE LIONS' HUNGER FOR DAYS.
12/26
ON A KINDER NOTE, WE DISCOURAGE OPEN CHEERING.

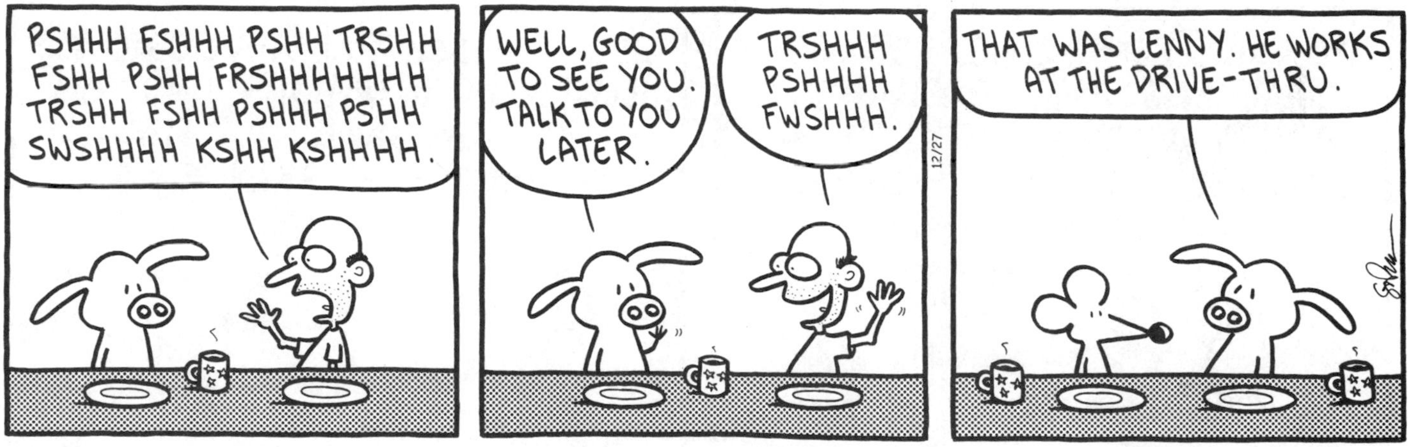
PSHHH FSHHH PSHH TRSHH FSHH PSHH FRSHHHHHHH TRSHH FSHH PSHHH PSHH SWSHHHH KSHH KSHHHH.
WELL, GOOD TO SEE YOU. TALK TO YOU LATER.
TRSHHH PSHHHH FWSHHH.
12/27
THAT WAS LENNY. HE WORKS AT THE DRIVE-THRU.

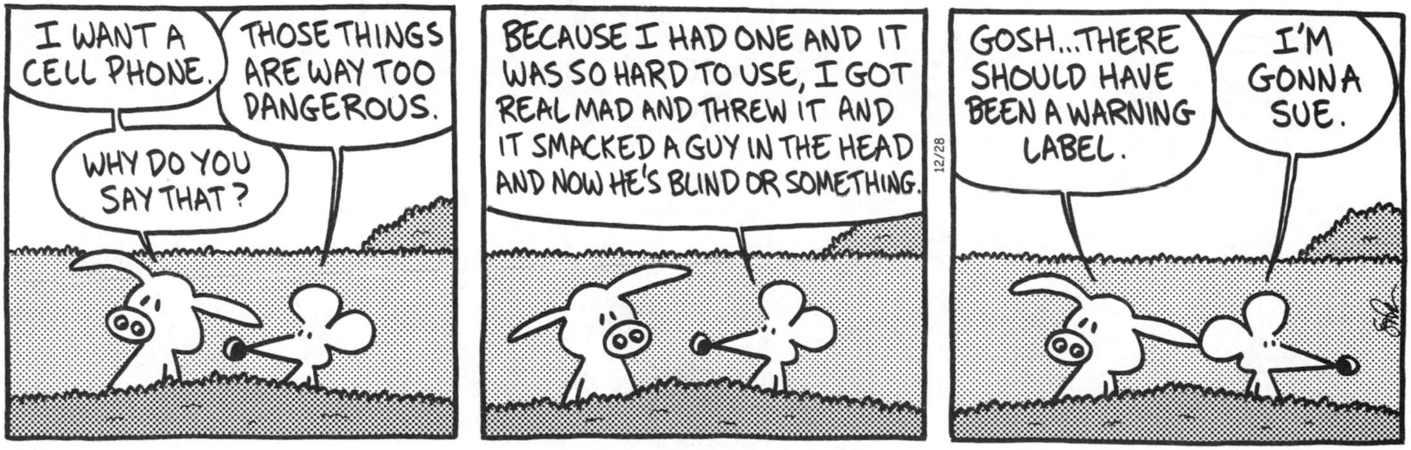
I WANT A CELL PHONE.
WHY DO YOU SAY THAT?
THOSE THINGS ARE WAY TOO DANGEROUS.
BECAUSE I HAD ONE AND IT WAS SO HARD TO USE, I GOT REAL MAD AND THREW IT AND IT SMACKED A GUY IN THE HEAD AND NOW HE'S BLIND OR SOMETHING.
12/28
GOSH...THERE SHOULD HAVE BEEN A WARNING LABEL.
I'M GONNA SUE.

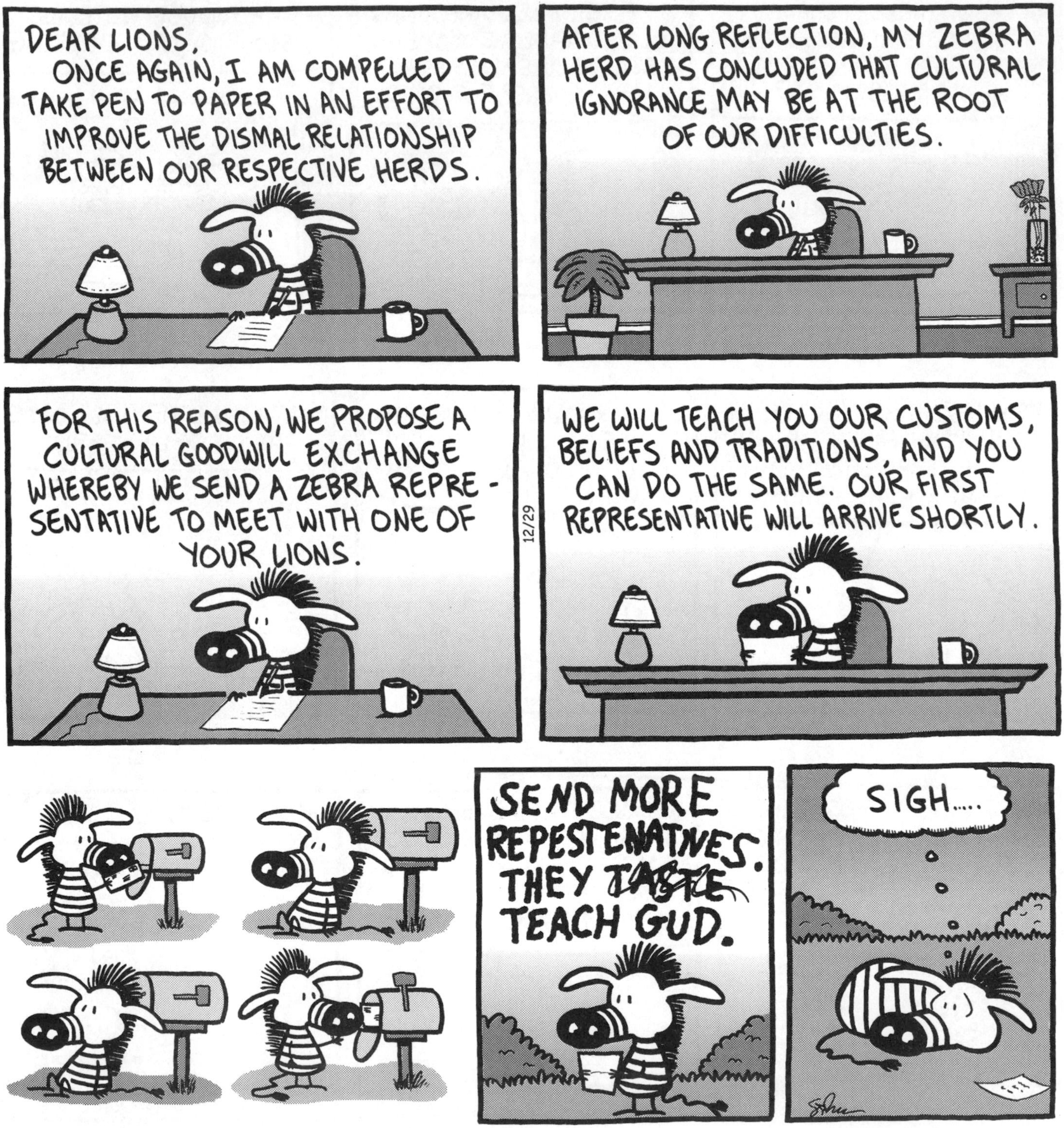
DEAR LIONS,
ONCE AGAIN, I AM COMPELLED TO TAKE PEN TO PAPER IN AN EFFORT TO IMPROVE THE DISMAL RELATIONSHIP BETWEEN OUR RESPECTIVE HERDS.
AFTER LONG REFLECTION, MY ZEBRA HERD HAS CONCLUDED THAT CULTURAL IGNORANCE MAY BE AT THE ROOT OF OUR DIFFICULTIES.
FOR THIS REASON, WE PROPOSE A CULTURAL GOODWILL EXCHANGE WHEREBY WE SEND A ZEBRA REPRE-SENTATIVE TO MEET WITH ONE OF YOUR LIONS.
12/29
WE WILL TEACH YOU OUR CUSTOMS, BELIEFS AND TRADITIONS, AND YOU CAN DO THE SAME. OUR FIRST REPRESENTATIVE WILL ARRIVE SHORTLY.
SEND MORE REPESTENATIVES. THEY ~~TASTE~~ TEACH GUD.
SIGH.....

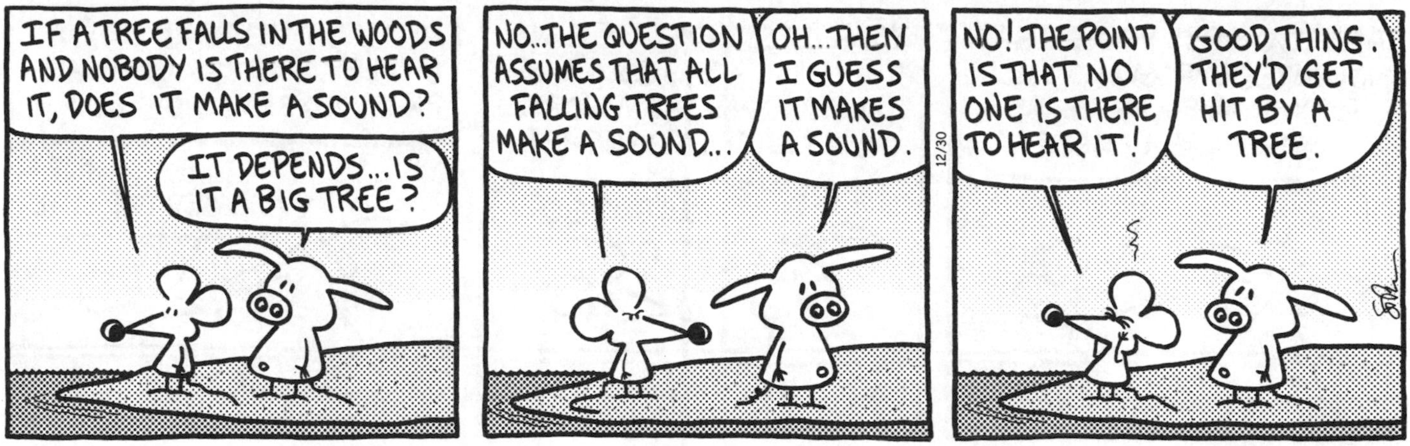
IF A TREE FALLS IN THE WOODS AND NOBODY IS THERE TO HEAR IT, DOES IT MAKE A SOUND?
IT DEPENDS...IS IT A BIG TREE?
NO...THE QUESTION ASSUMES THAT ALL FALLING TREES MAKE A SOUND...
OH...THEN I GUESS IT MAKES A SOUND.
12/30
NO! THE POINT IS THAT NO ONE IS THERE TO HEAR IT!
GOOD THING. THEY'D GET HIT BY A TREE.

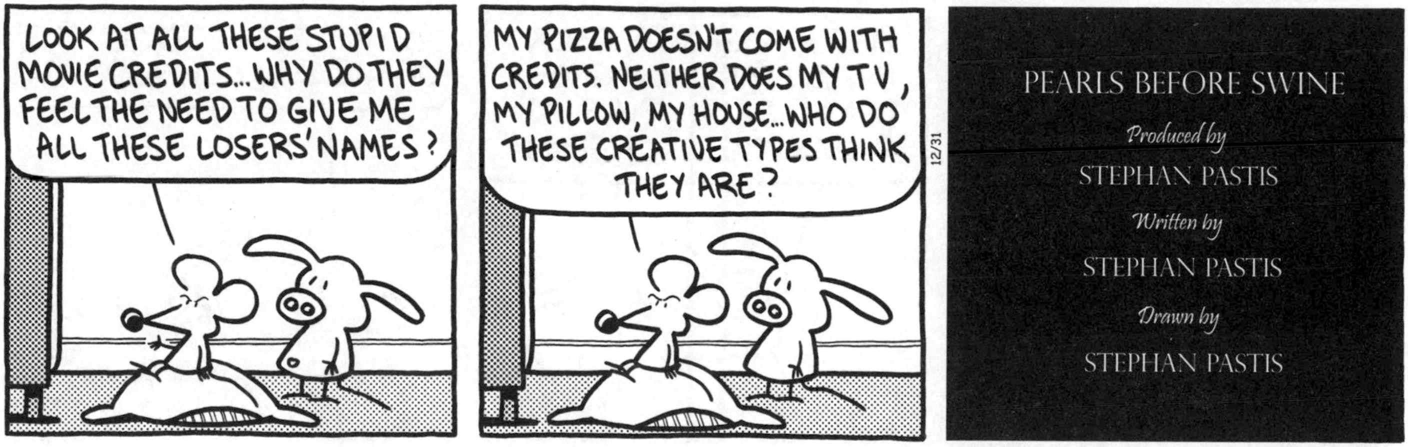
LOOK AT ALL THESE STUPID MOVIE CREDITS...WHY DO THEY FEEL THE NEED TO GIVE ME ALL THESE LOSERS' NAMES?
MY PIZZA DOESN'T COME WITH CREDITS. NEITHER DOES MY TV, MY PILLOW, MY HOUSE...WHO DO THESE CREATIVE TYPES THINK THEY ARE?
12/31
PEARLS BEFORE SWINE
Produced by
STEPHAN PASTIS
Written by
STEPHAN PASTIS
Drawn by
STEPHAN PASTIS

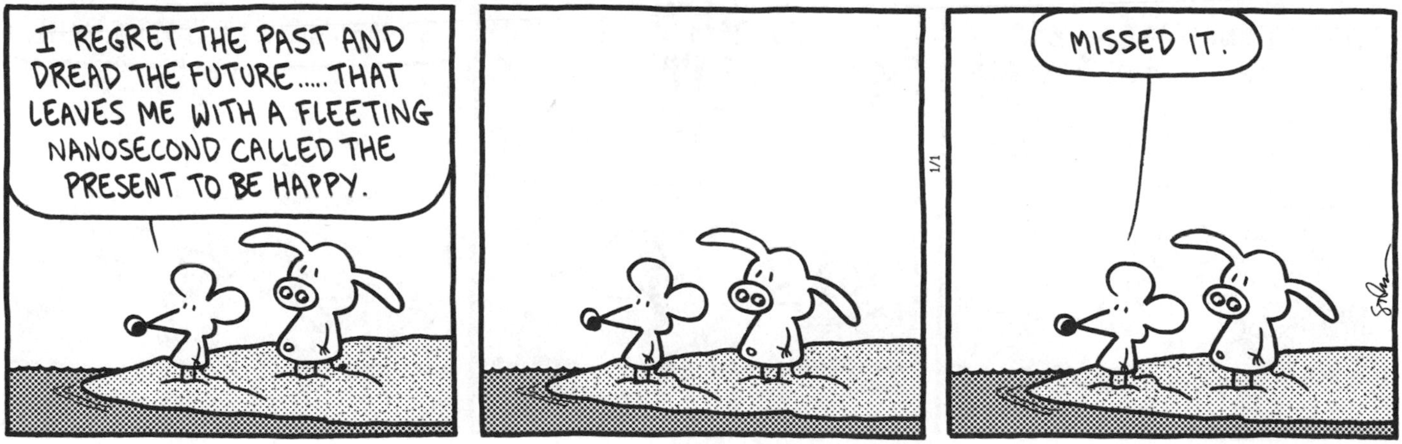
I REGRET THE PAST AND DREAD THE FUTURE.....THAT LEAVES ME WITH A FLEETING NANOSECOND CALLED THE PRESENT TO BE HAPPY.
1/1
MISSED IT.

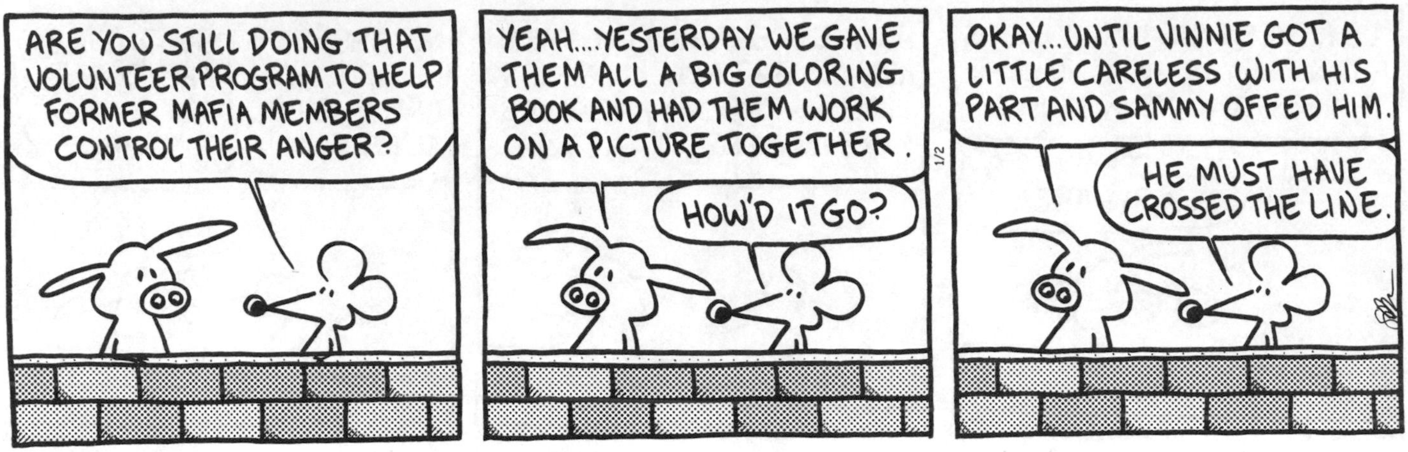
ARE YOU STILL DOING THAT VOLUNTEER PROGRAM TO HELP FORMER MAFIA MEMBERS CONTROL THEIR ANGER?
YEAH....YESTERDAY WE GAVE THEM ALL A BIG COLORING BOOK AND HAD THEM WORK ON A PICTURE TOGETHER.
HOW'D IT GO?
1/2
OKAY...UNTIL VINNIE GOT A LITTLE CARELESS WITH HIS PART AND SAMMY OFFED HIM.
HE MUST HAVE CROSSED THE LINE.

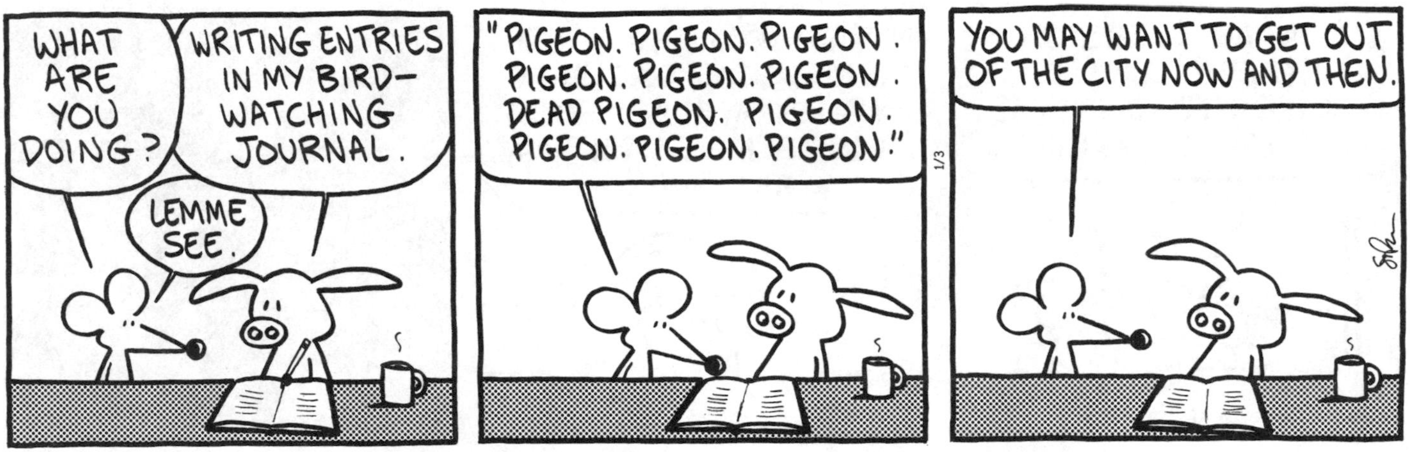
WHAT ARE YOU DOING?
WRITING ENTRIES IN MY BIRD-WATCHING JOURNAL.
LEMME SEE.
"PIGEON. PIGEON. PIGEON. PIGEON. PIGEON. PIGEON. DEAD PIGEON. PIGEON. PIGEON. PIGEON. PIGEON."
1/3
YOU MAY WANT TO GET OUT OF THE CITY NOW AND THEN.

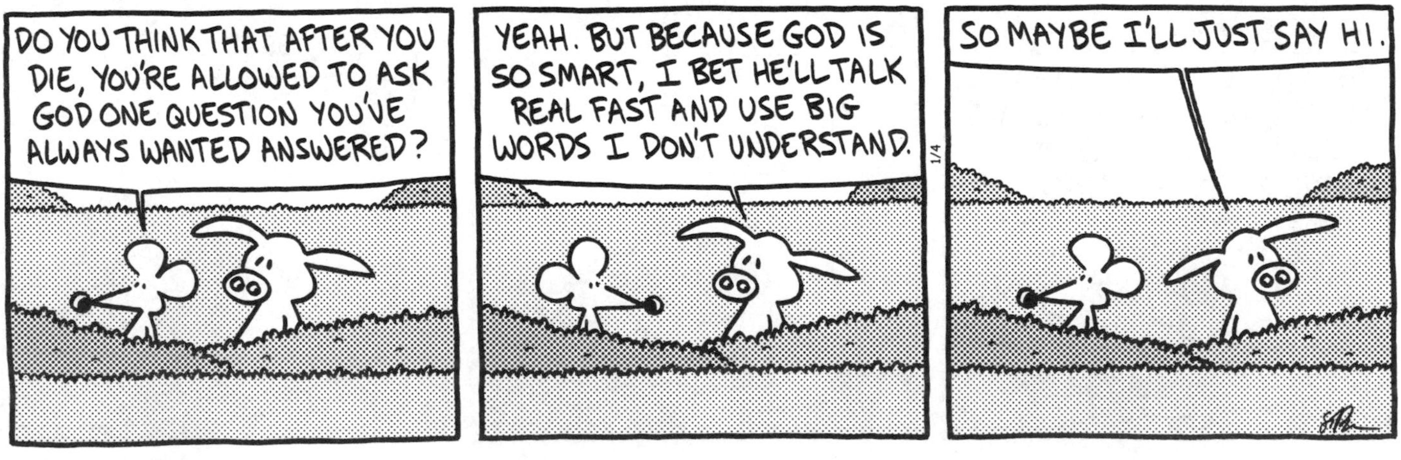
DO YOU THINK THAT AFTER YOU DIE, YOU'RE ALLOWED TO ASK GOD ONE QUESTION YOU'VE ALWAYS WANTED ANSWERED?
YEAH. BUT BECAUSE GOD IS SO SMART, I BET HE'LL TALK REAL FAST AND USE BIG WORDS I DON'T UNDERSTAND.
1/4
SO MAYBE I'LL JUST SAY HI.

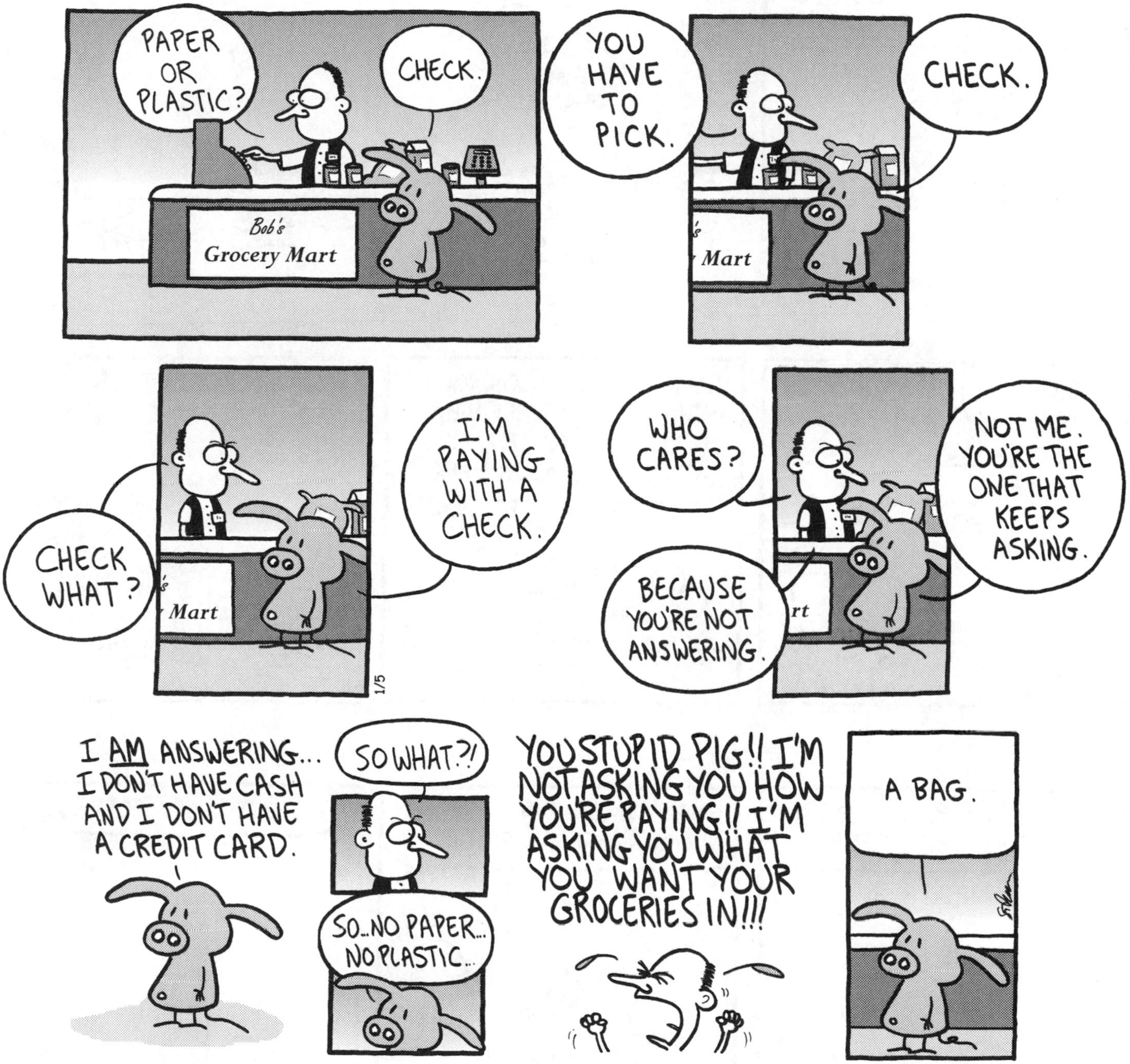

PAPER OR PLASTIC?
CHECK.
Bob's Grocery Mart
YOU HAVE TO PICK.
CHECK.
CHECK WHAT?
I'M PAYING WITH A CHECK.
1/5
WHO CARES?
NOT ME. YOU'RE THE ONE THAT KEEPS ASKING.
BECAUSE YOU'RE NOT ANSWERING.
I AM ANSWERING... I DON'T HAVE CASH AND I DON'T HAVE A CREDIT CARD.
SO WHAT?!
SO...NO PAPER... NO PLASTIC...
YOU STUPID PIG!! I'M NOT ASKING YOU HOW YOU'RE PAYING!! I'M ASKING YOU WHAT YOU WANT YOUR GROCERIES IN!!!
A BAG.

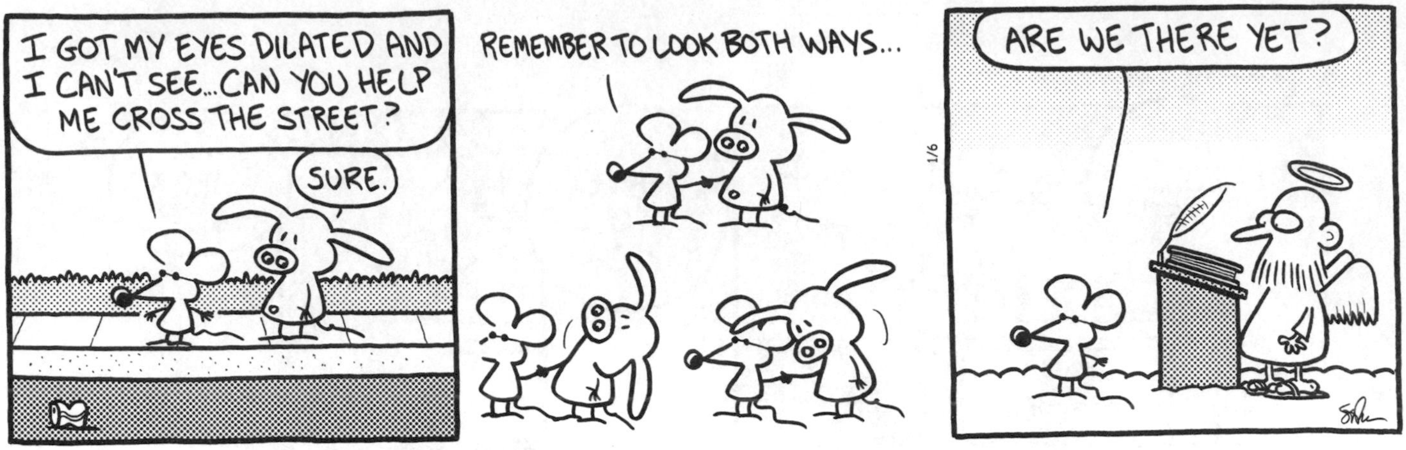
I GOT MY EYES DILATED AND I CAN'T SEE...CAN YOU HELP ME CROSS THE STREET?
SURE.
REMEMBER TO LOOK BOTH WAYS...
1/6
ARE WE THERE YET?

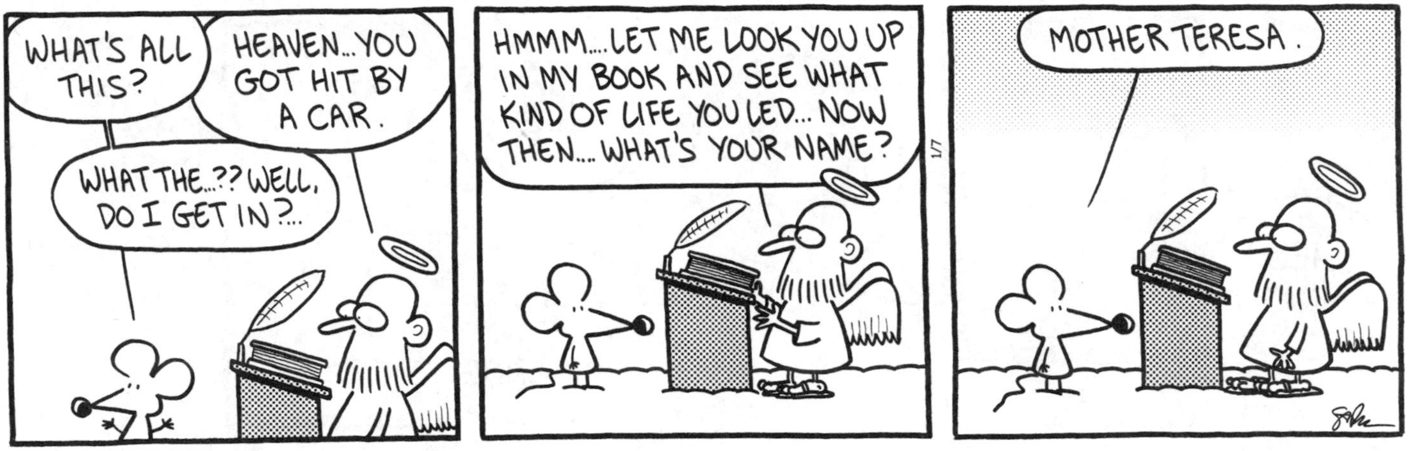
WHAT'S ALL THIS?
HEAVEN...YOU GOT HIT BY A CAR.
WHAT THE...?? WELL, DO I GET IN?...
HMMM....LET ME LOOK YOU UP IN MY BOOK AND SEE WHAT KIND OF LIFE YOU LED... NOW THEN.... WHAT'S YOUR NAME?
1/7
MOTHER TERESA.

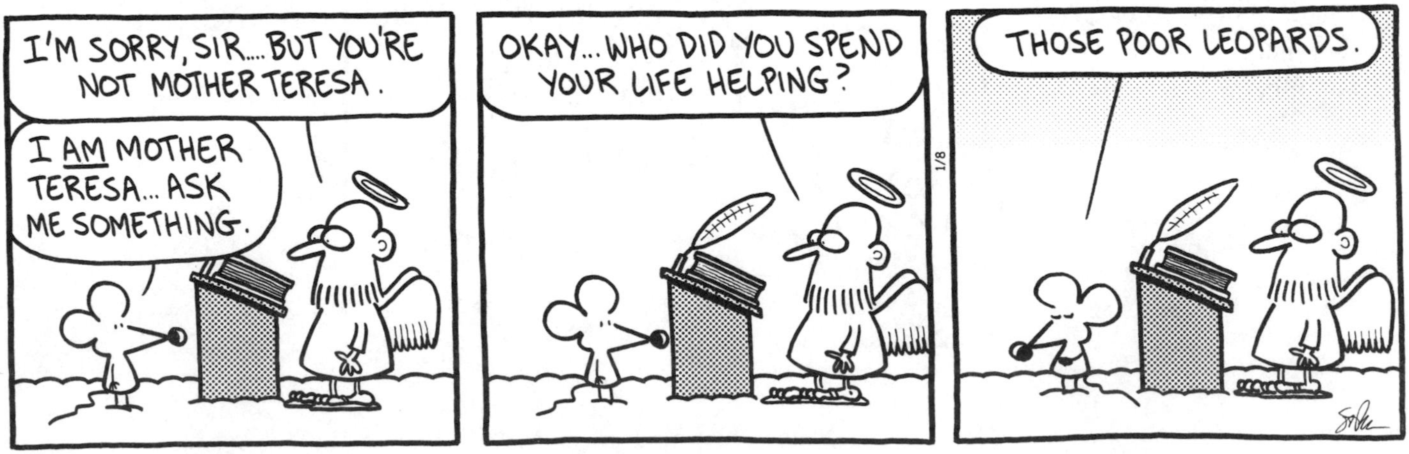
I'M SORRY, SIR....BUT YOU'RE NOT MOTHER TERESA.
I AM MOTHER TERESA... ASK ME SOMETHING.
OKAY... WHO DID YOU SPEND YOUR LIFE HELPING?
1/8
THOSE POOR LEOPARDS.

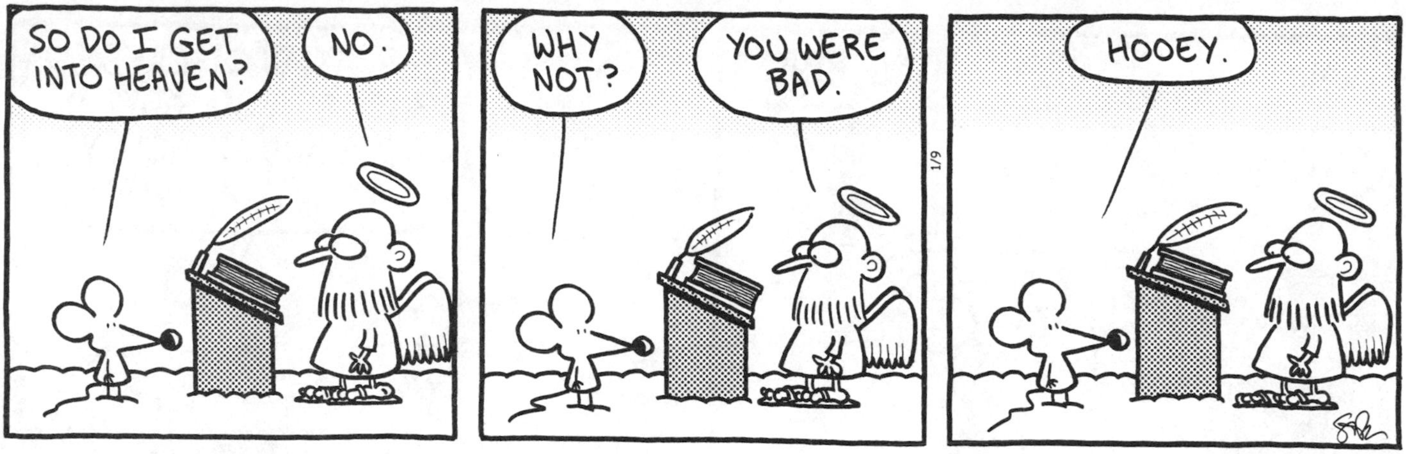
SO DO I GET INTO HEAVEN?
NO.
WHY NOT?
YOU WERE BAD.
1/9
HOOEY.

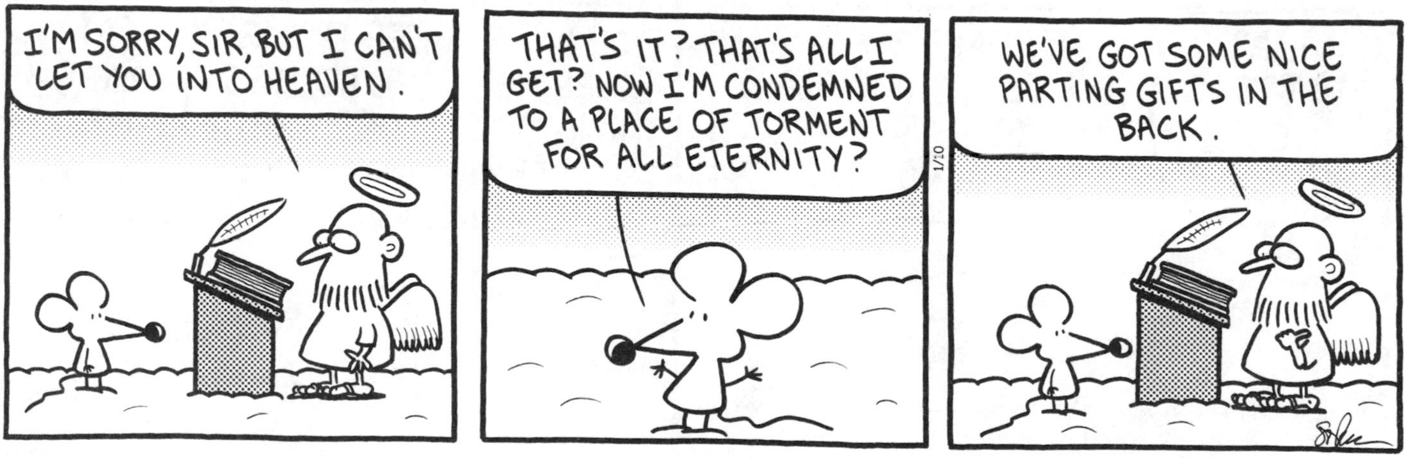
I'M SORRY, SIR, BUT I CAN'T LET YOU INTO HEAVEN.
THAT'S IT? THAT'S ALL I GET? NOW I'M CONDEMNED TO A PLACE OF TORMENT FOR ALL ETERNITY?
1/10
WE'VE GOT SOME NICE PARTING GIFTS IN THE BACK.

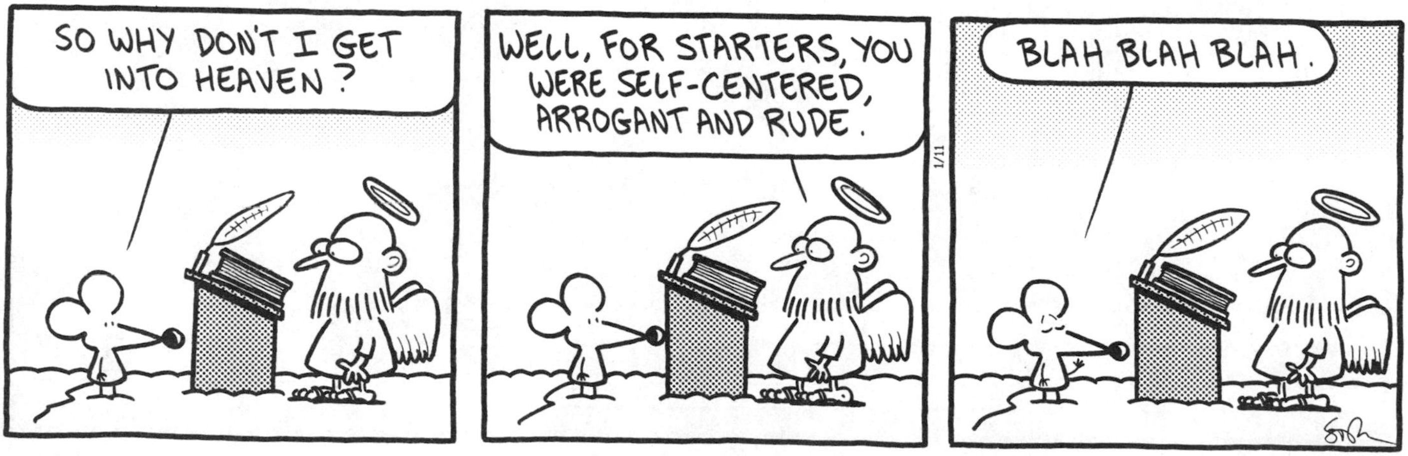
SO WHY DON'T I GET INTO HEAVEN?
WELL, FOR STARTERS, YOU WERE SELF-CENTERED, ARROGANT AND RUDE.
1/11
BLAH BLAH BLAH.

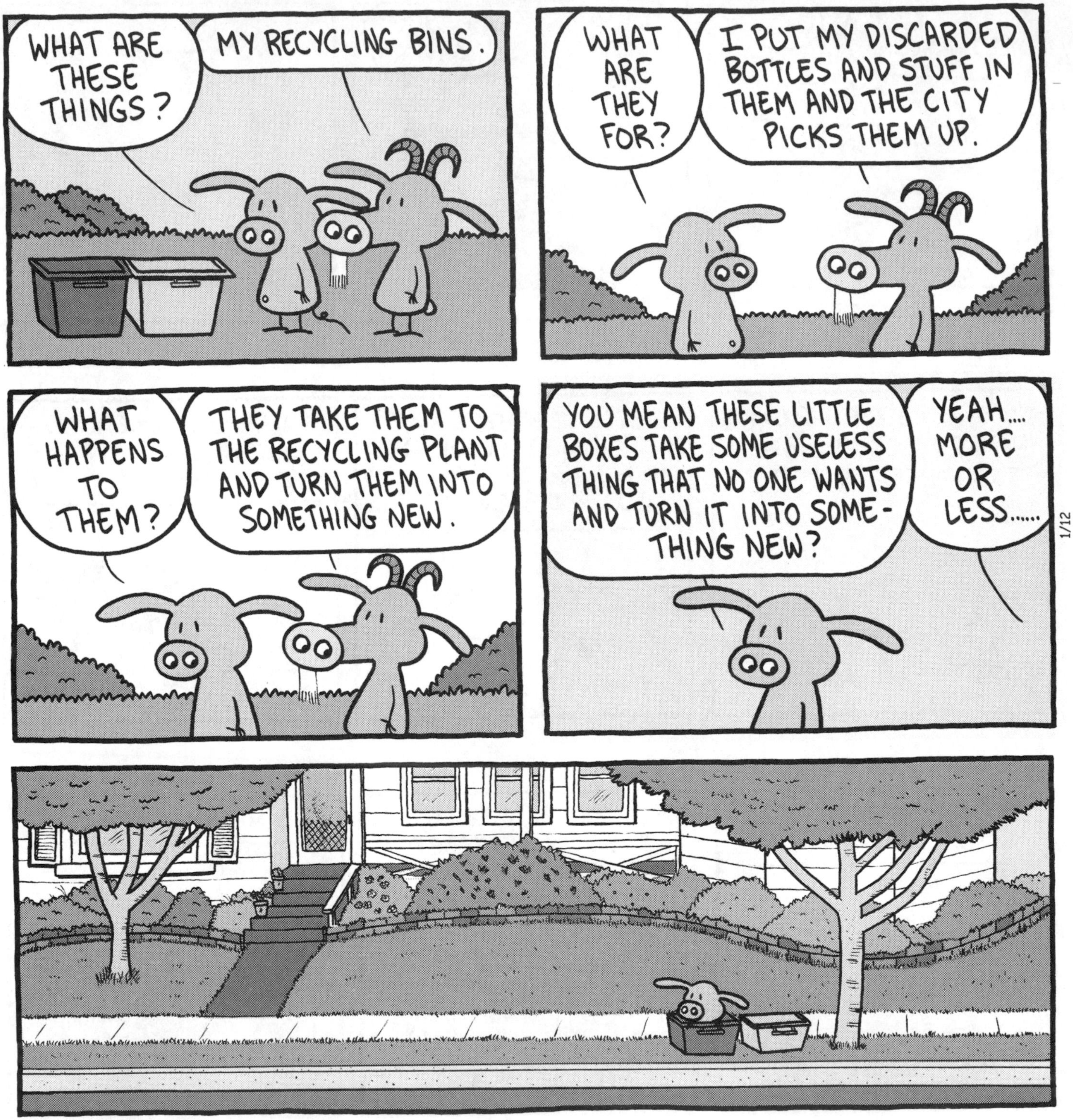
WHAT ARE THESE THINGS?
MY RECYCLING BINS.
WHAT ARE THEY FOR?
I PUT MY DISCARDED BOTTLES AND STUFF IN THEM AND THE CITY PICKS THEM UP.
WHAT HAPPENS TO THEM?
THEY TAKE THEM TO THE RECYCLING PLANT AND TURN THEM INTO SOMETHING NEW.
YOU MEAN THESE LITTLE BOXES TAKE SOME USELESS THING THAT NO ONE WANTS AND TURN IT INTO SOMETHING NEW?
YEAH.... MORE OR LESS......
1/12

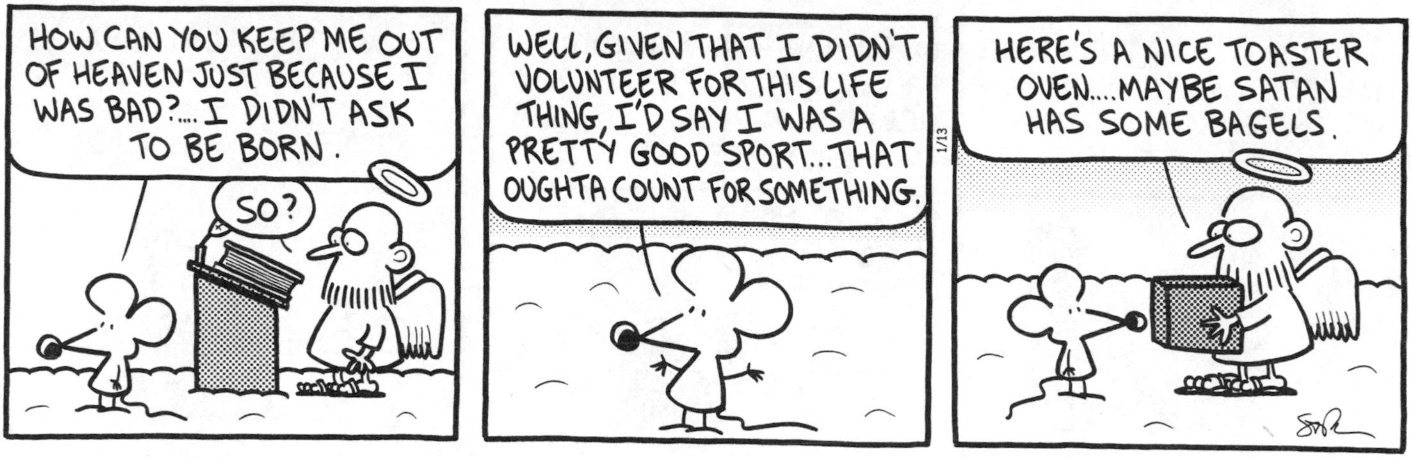
HOW CAN YOU KEEP ME OUT OF HEAVEN JUST BECAUSE I WAS BAD?.... I DIDN'T ASK TO BE BORN.
SO?
WELL, GIVEN THAT I DIDN'T VOLUNTEER FOR THIS LIFE THING, I'D SAY I WAS A PRETTY GOOD SPORT...THAT OUGHTA COUNT FOR SOMETHING.
HERE'S A NICE TOASTER OVEN....MAYBE SATAN HAS SOME BAGELS.

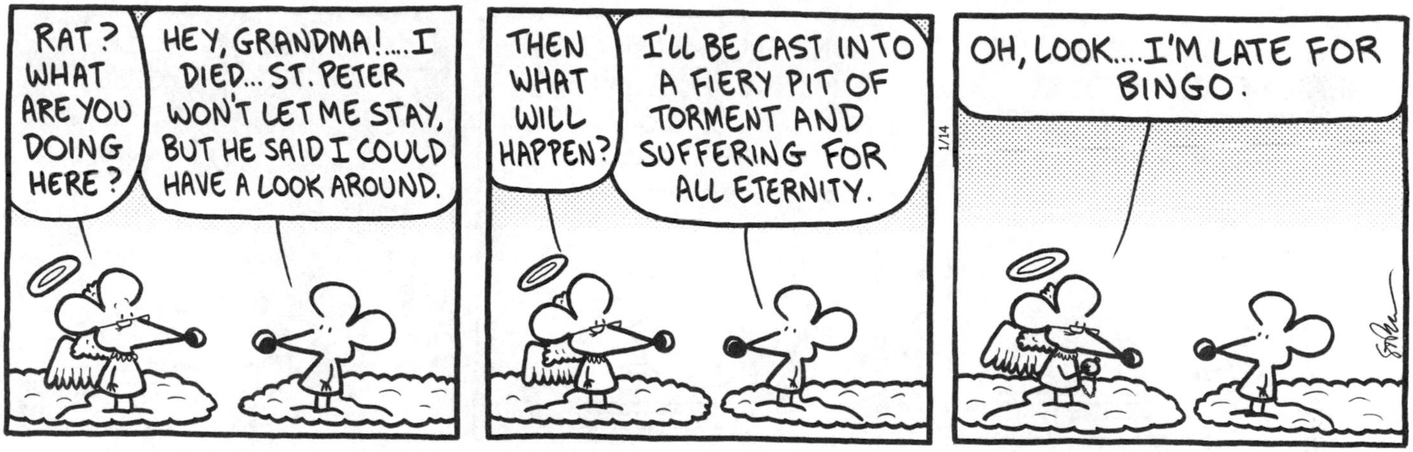
RAT? WHAT ARE YOU DOING HERE?
HEY, GRANDMA!.....I DIED... ST. PETER WON'T LET ME STAY, BUT HE SAID I COULD HAVE A LOOK AROUND.
THEN WHAT WILL HAPPEN?
I'LL BE CAST INTO A FIERY PIT OF TORMENT AND SUFFERING FOR ALL ETERNITY.
OH, LOOK.... I'M LATE FOR BINGO.

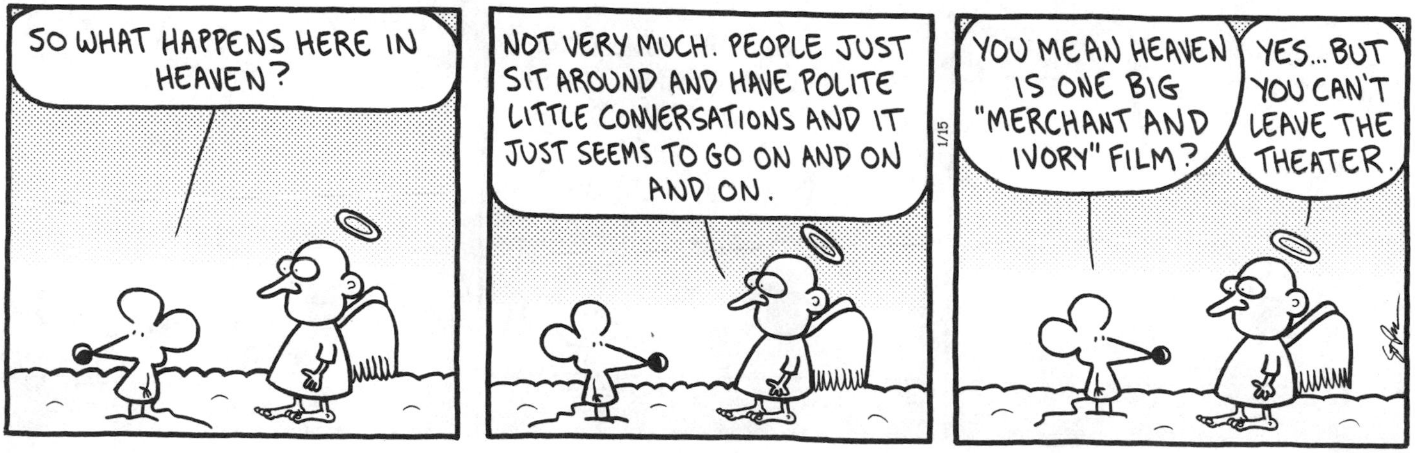
SO WHAT HAPPENS HERE IN HEAVEN?
NOT VERY MUCH. PEOPLE JUST SIT AROUND AND HAVE POLITE LITTLE CONVERSATIONS AND IT JUST SEEMS TO GO ON AND ON AND ON.
YOU MEAN HEAVEN IS ONE BIG "MERCHANT AND IVORY" FILM?
YES... BUT YOU CAN'T LEAVE THE THEATER.

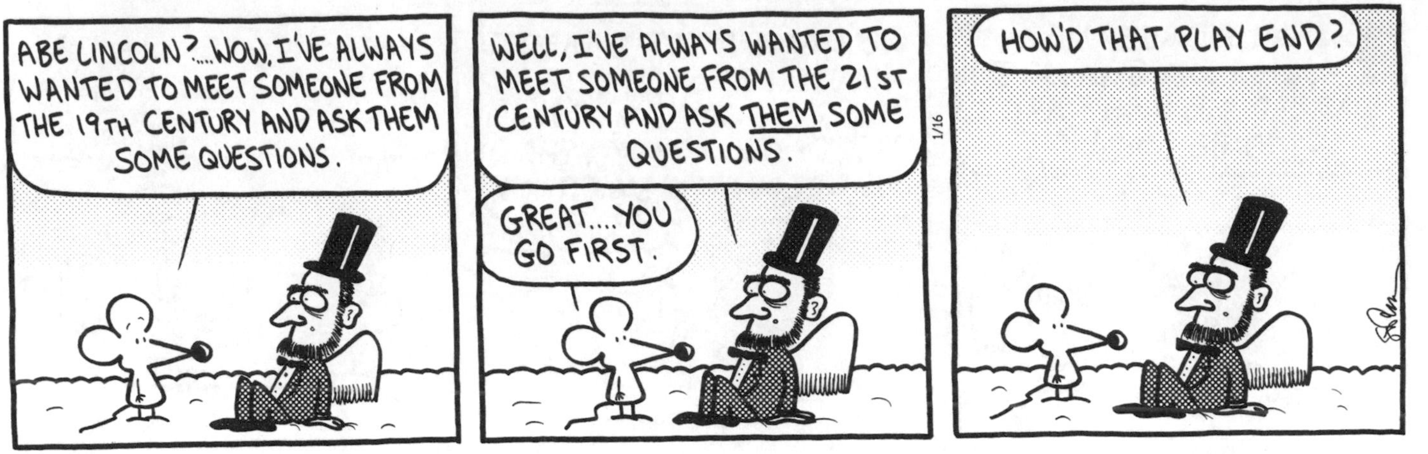
ABE LINCOLN?....WOW, I'VE ALWAYS WANTED TO MEET SOMEONE FROM THE 19TH CENTURY AND ASK THEM SOME QUESTIONS.
WELL, I'VE ALWAYS WANTED TO MEET SOMEONE FROM THE 21ST CENTURY AND ASK THEM SOME QUESTIONS.
GREAT....YOU GO FIRST.
1/16
HOW'D THAT PLAY END?

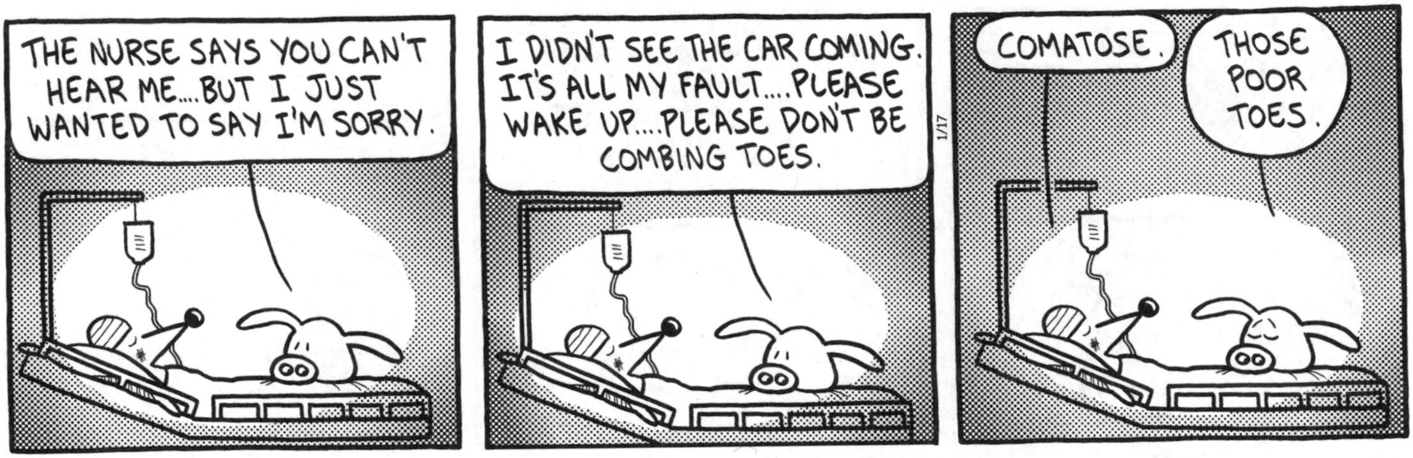
THE NURSE SAYS YOU CAN'T HEAR ME....BUT I JUST WANTED TO SAY I'M SORRY.
I DIDN'T SEE THE CAR COMING. IT'S ALL MY FAULT....PLEASE WAKE UP....PLEASE DON'T BE COMBING TOES.
1/17
COMATOSE.
THOSE POOR TOES.

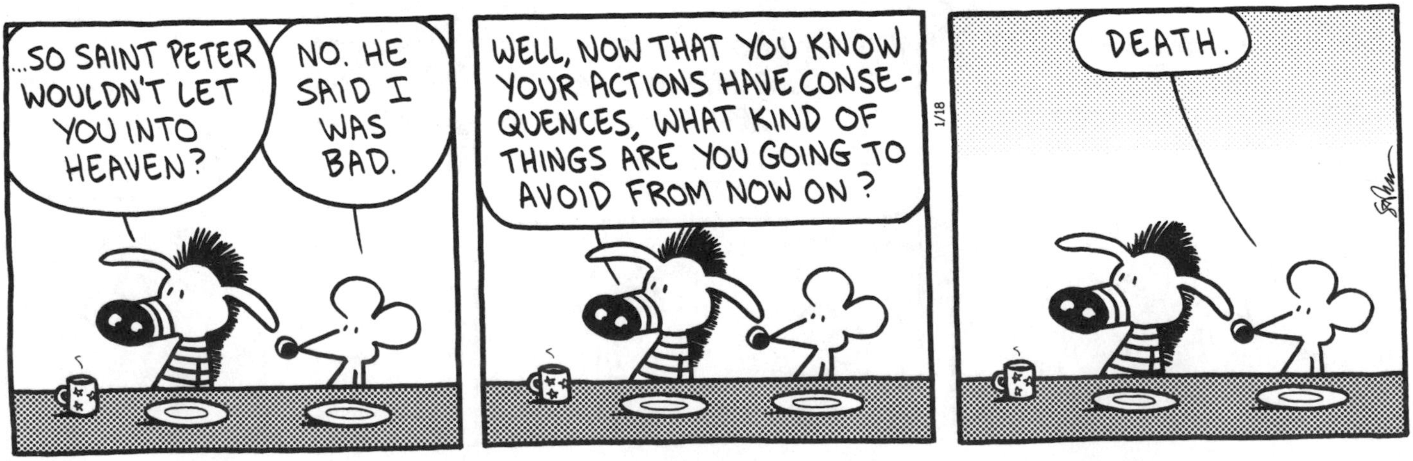
...SO SAINT PETER WOULDN'T LET YOU INTO HEAVEN?
NO. HE SAID I WAS BAD.
WELL, NOW THAT YOU KNOW YOUR ACTIONS HAVE CONSE-QUENCES, WHAT KIND OF THINGS ARE YOU GOING TO AVOID FROM NOW ON?
1/18
DEATH.

HEY THERE, DAN. HOW ARE THINGS?
GOOD... I JUST GOT MARRIED... THIS IS MY WIFE, STEPHANIE.
HOW YOU STAYING BUSY THESE DAYS?
I OPENED MY OWN FLORIST SHOP... MATTER OF FACT, I JUST GOT MY SIGN MADE.... WHADDYA THINK?
DAN'S FLOWERS
THAT ONE LEAF LOOKS A LITTLE BIG.
YEAH... IT DOES... I BETTER TAKE IT BACK.... I'LL SEE YOU GUYS LATER.
1/19
THAT'S ONE SMALL STEPH FOR DAN, ONE GIANT LEAF FOR DAN'S SIGN.

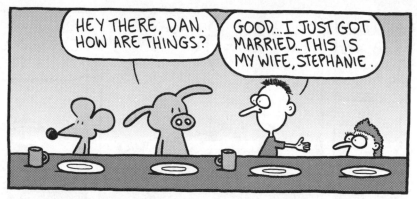

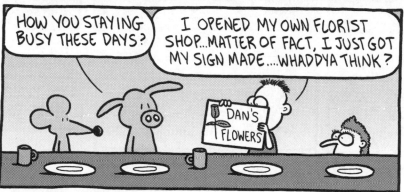

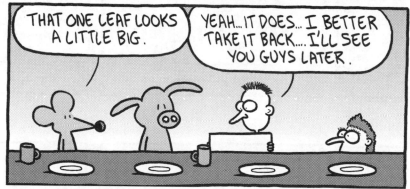

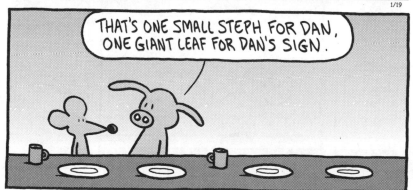

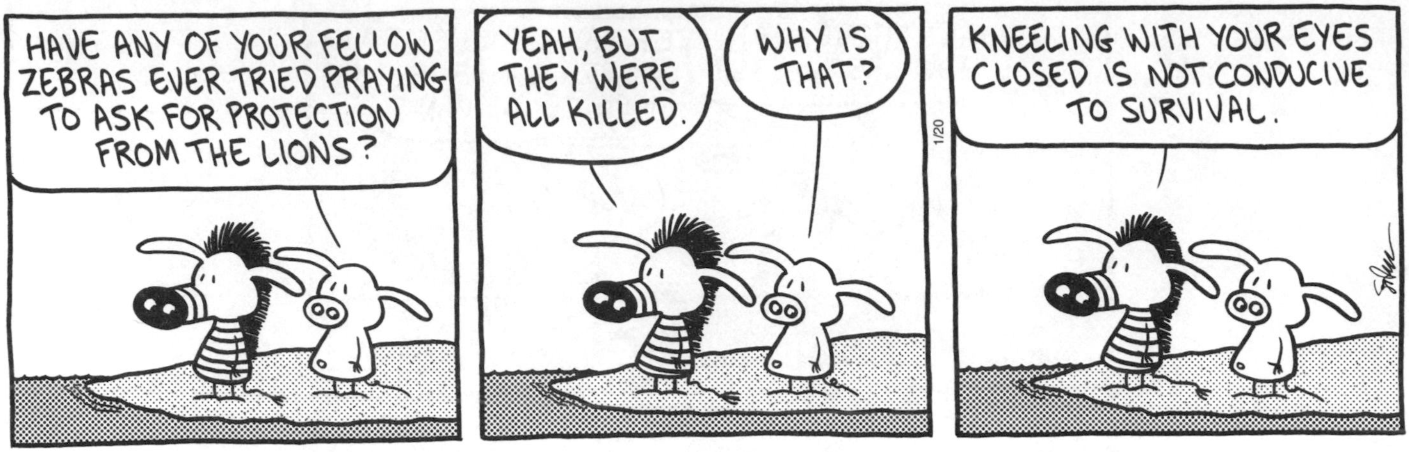
HAVE ANY OF YOUR FELLOW ZEBRAS EVER TRIED PRAYING TO ASK FOR PROTECTION FROM THE LIONS?
YEAH, BUT THEY WERE ALL KILLED.
WHY IS THAT?
1/20
KNEELING WITH YOUR EYES CLOSED IS NOT CONDUCIVE TO SURVIVAL.

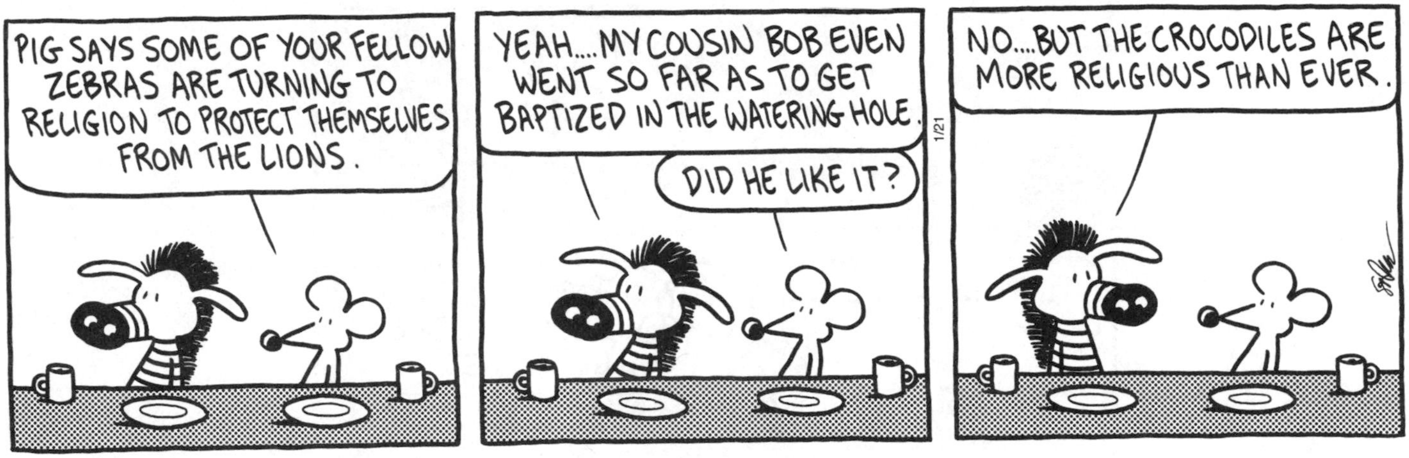
PIG SAYS SOME OF YOUR FELLOW ZEBRAS ARE TURNING TO RELIGION TO PROTECT THEMSELVES FROM THE LIONS.
YEAH....MY COUSIN BOB EVEN WENT SO FAR AS TO GET BAPTIZED IN THE WATERING HOLE.
DID HE LIKE IT?
1/21
NO....BUT THE CROCODILES ARE MORE RELIGIOUS THAN EVER.

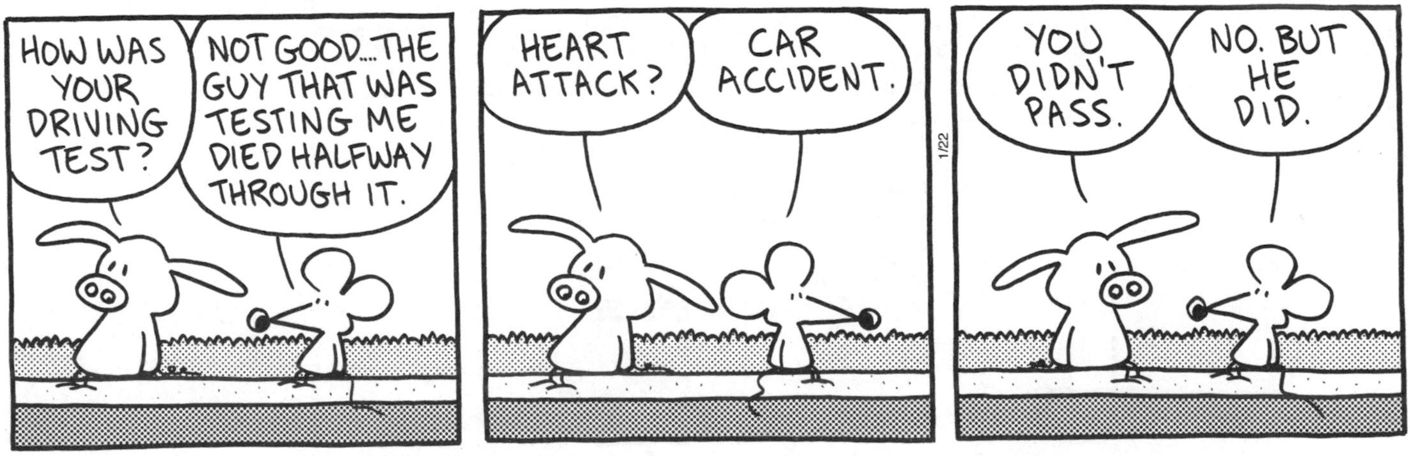
HOW WAS YOUR DRIVING TEST?
NOT GOOD...THE GUY THAT WAS TESTING ME DIED HALFWAY THROUGH IT.
HEART ATTACK?
CAR ACCIDENT.
1/22
YOU DIDN'T PASS.
NO. BUT HE DID.

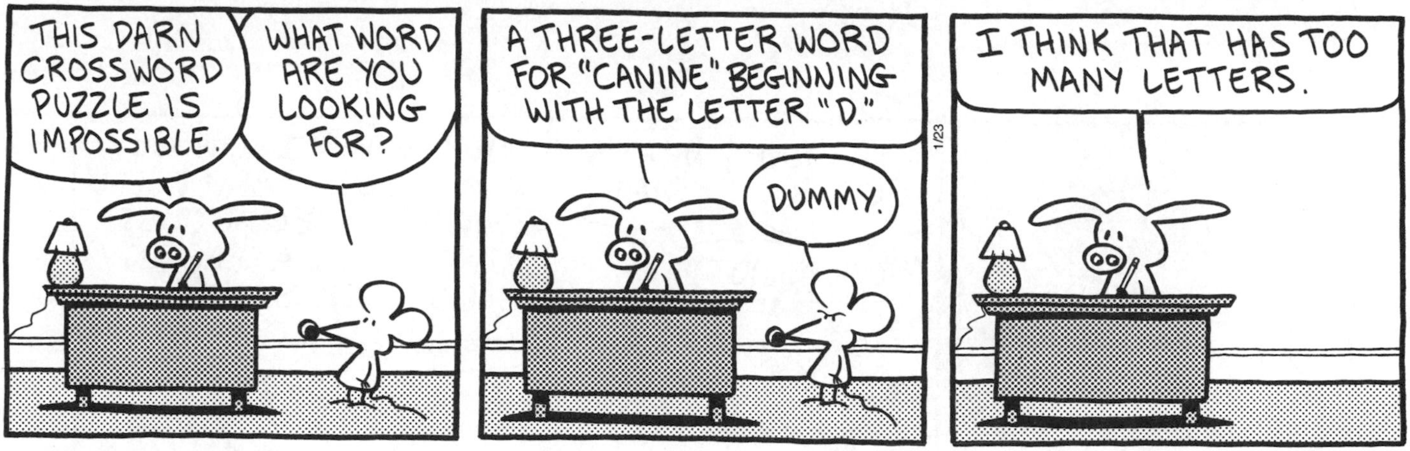
THIS DARN CROSSWORD PUZZLE IS IMPOSSIBLE.
WHAT WORD ARE YOU LOOKING FOR?
A THREE-LETTER WORD FOR "CANINE" BEGINNING WITH THE LETTER "D."
DUMMY.
1/23
I THINK THAT HAS TOO MANY LETTERS.

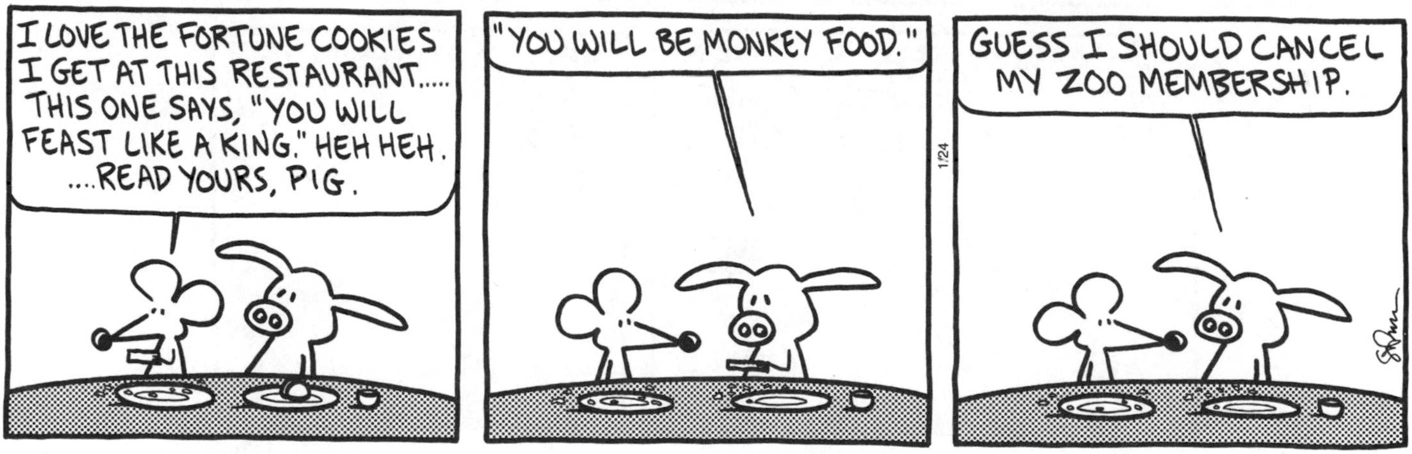
I LOVE THE FORTUNE COOKIES I GET AT THIS RESTAURANT..... THIS ONE SAYS, "YOU WILL FEAST LIKE A KING." HEH HEH. ....READ YOURS, PIG.
"YOU WILL BE MONKEY FOOD."
1/24
GUESS I SHOULD CANCEL MY ZOO MEMBERSHIP.

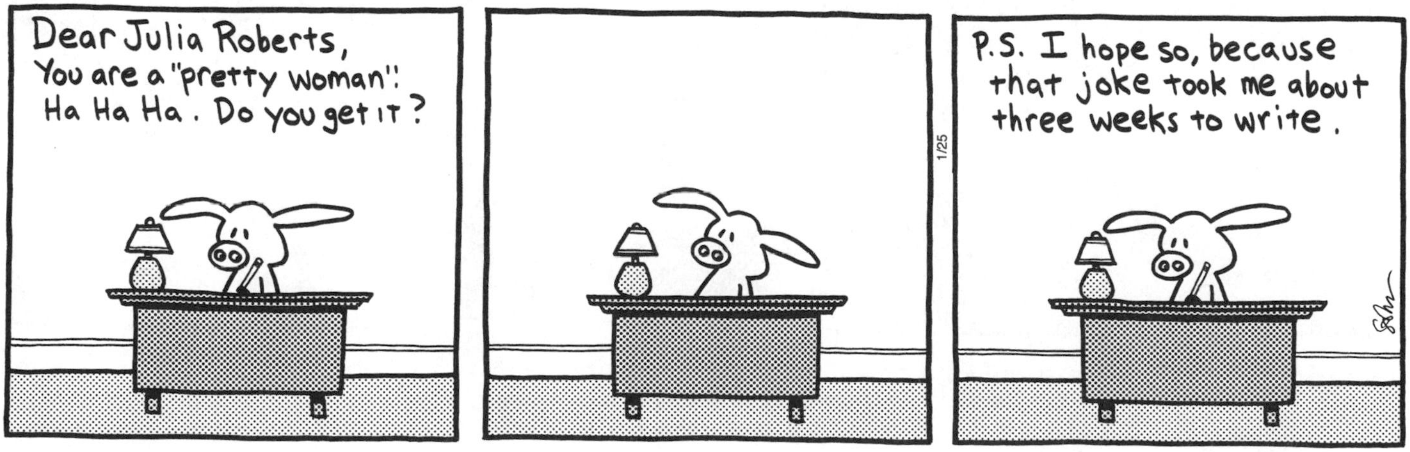
Dear Julia Roberts, You are a "pretty woman". Ha Ha Ha. Do you get it?
1/25
P.S. I hope so, because that joke took me about three weeks to write.

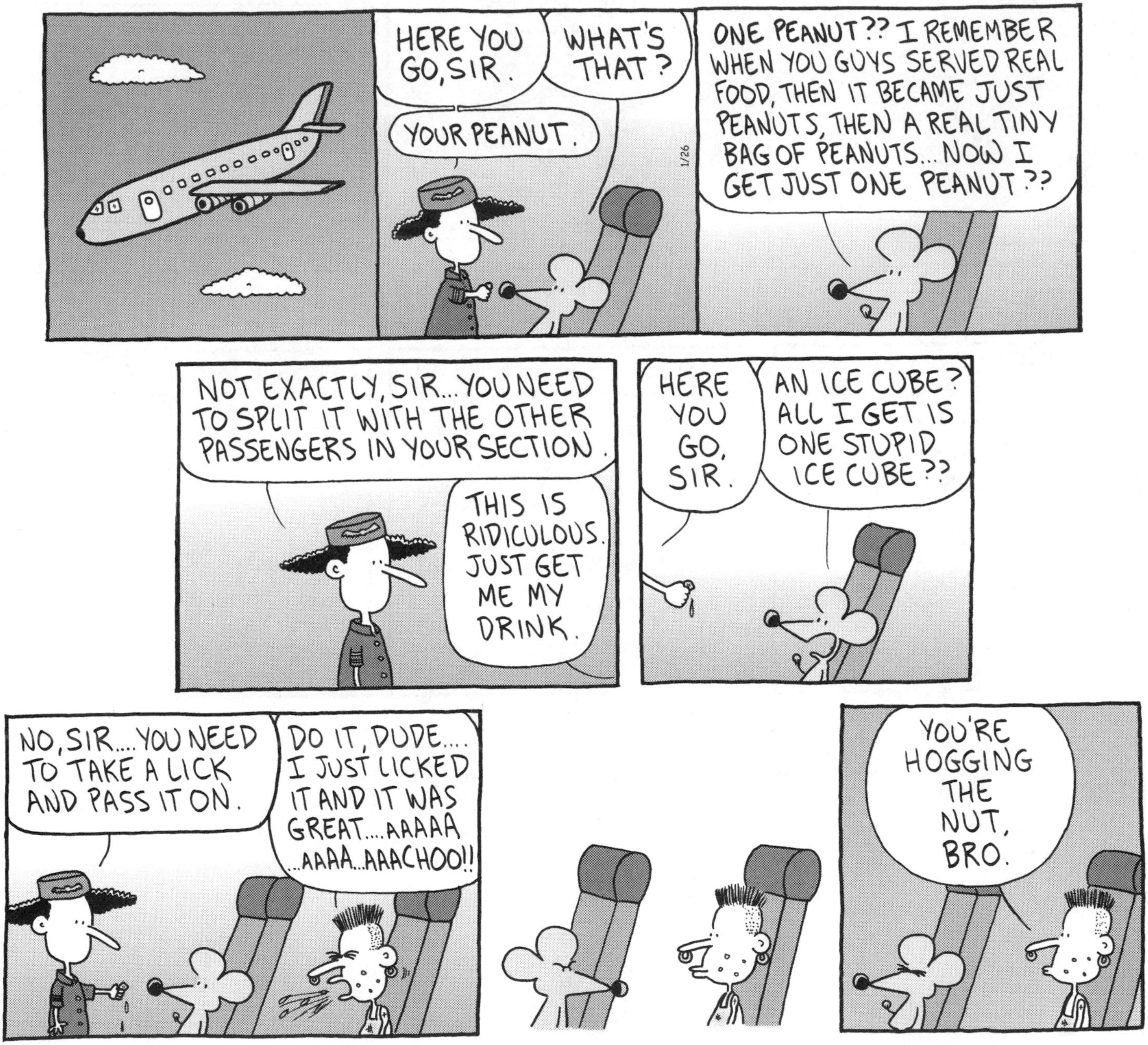
HERE YOU GO, SIR.
YOUR PEANUT.
WHAT'S THAT?
1/26
ONE PEANUT?? I REMEMBER WHEN YOU GUYS SERVED REAL FOOD, THEN IT BECAME JUST PEANUTS, THEN A REAL TINY BAG OF PEANUTS... NOW I GET JUST ONE PEANUT??
NOT EXACTLY, SIR... YOU NEED TO SPLIT IT WITH THE OTHER PASSENGERS IN YOUR SECTION.
THIS IS RIDICULOUS. JUST GET ME MY DRINK.
HERE YOU GO, SIR.
AN ICE CUBE? ALL I GET IS ONE STUPID ICE CUBE??
NO, SIR.... YOU NEED TO TAKE A LICK AND PASS IT ON.
DO IT, DUDE.... I JUST LICKED IT AND IT WAS GREAT....AAAAA ...AAAA...AAACHOO!!
YOU'RE HOGGING THE NUT, BRO.

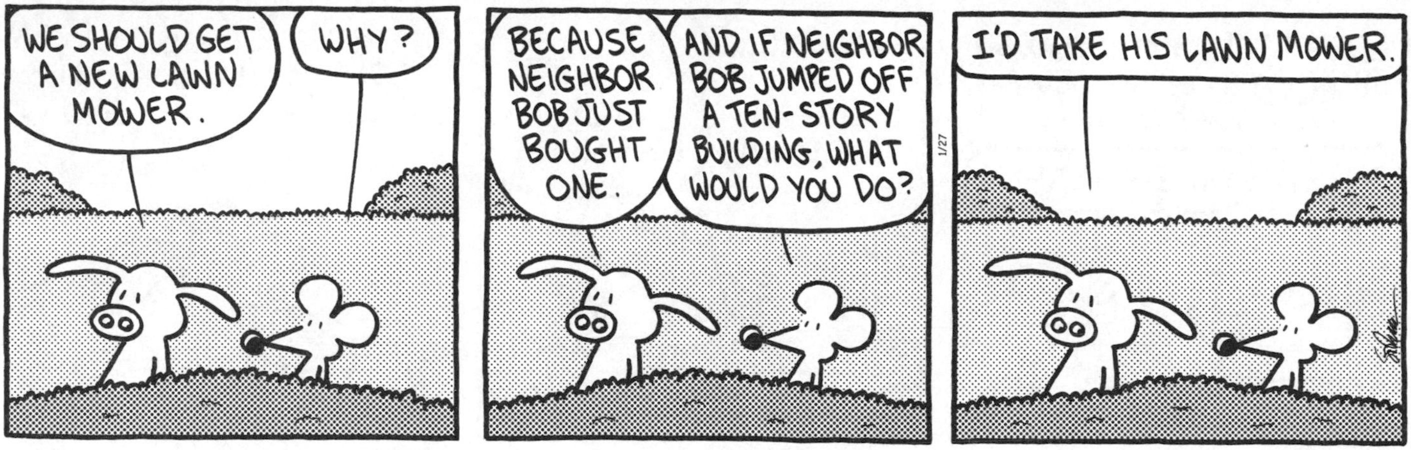
WE SHOULD GET A NEW LAWN MOWER.
WHY?
BECAUSE NEIGHBOR BOB JUST BOUGHT ONE.
AND IF NEIGHBOR BOB JUMPED OFF A TEN-STORY BUILDING, WHAT WOULD YOU DO?
1/27
I'D TAKE HIS LAWN MOWER.

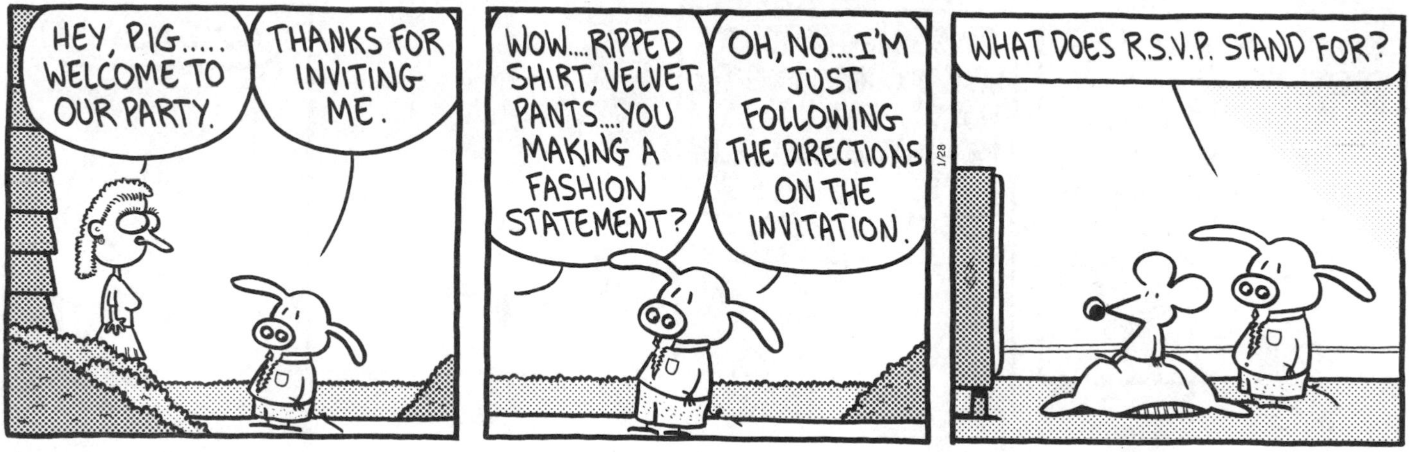
HEY, PIG..... WELCOME TO OUR PARTY.
THANKS FOR INVITING ME.
WOW....RIPPED SHIRT, VELVET PANTS....YOU MAKING A FASHION STATEMENT?
OH, NO....I'M JUST FOLLOWING THE DIRECTIONS ON THE INVITATION.
1/28
WHAT DOES R.S.V.P. STAND FOR?

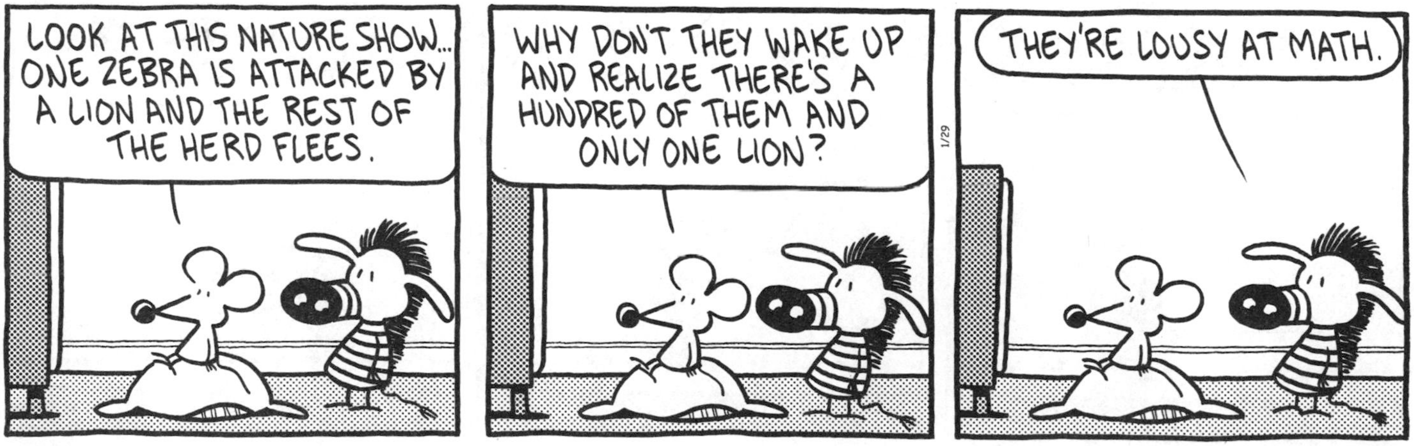
LOOK AT THIS NATURE SHOW... ONE ZEBRA IS ATTACKED BY A LION AND THE REST OF THE HERD FLEES.
WHY DON'T THEY WAKE UP AND REALIZE THERE'S A HUNDRED OF THEM AND ONLY ONE LION?
1/29
THEY'RE LOUSY AT MATH.

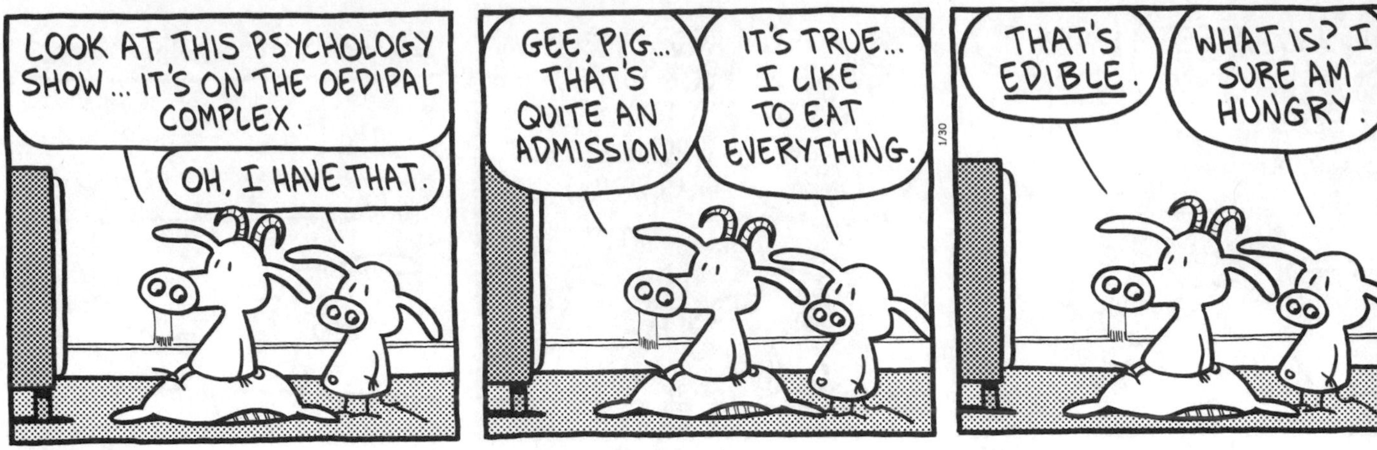
LOOK AT THIS PSYCHOLOGY SHOW ... IT'S ON THE OEDIPAL COMPLEX.
OH, I HAVE THAT.
GEE, PIG... THAT'S QUITE AN ADMISSION.
IT'S TRUE... I LIKE TO EAT EVERYTHING.
1/30
THAT'S EDIBLE.
WHAT IS? I SURE AM HUNGRY.

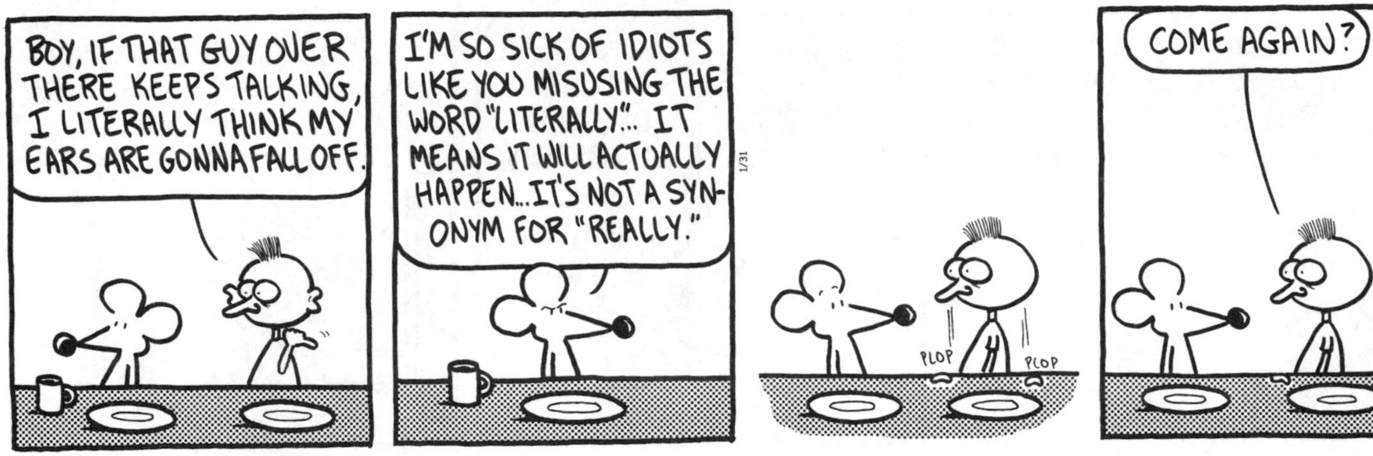
BOY, IF THAT GUY OVER THERE KEEPS TALKING, I LITERALLY THINK MY EARS ARE GONNA FALL OFF.
I'M SO SICK OF IDIOTS LIKE YOU MISUSING THE WORD "LITERALLY"... IT MEANS IT WILL ACTUALLY HAPPEN...IT'S NOT A SYN-ONYM FOR "REALLY."
1/31
PLOP
PLOP
COME AGAIN?

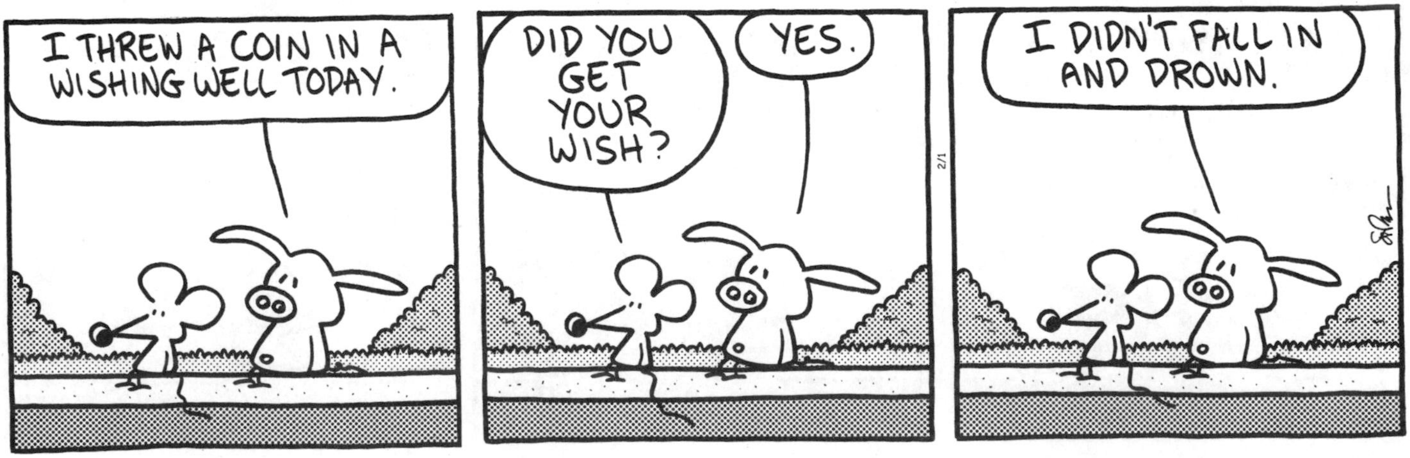
I THREW A COIN IN A WISHING WELL TODAY.
DID YOU GET YOUR WISH?
YES.
2/1
I DIDN'T FALL IN AND DROWN.

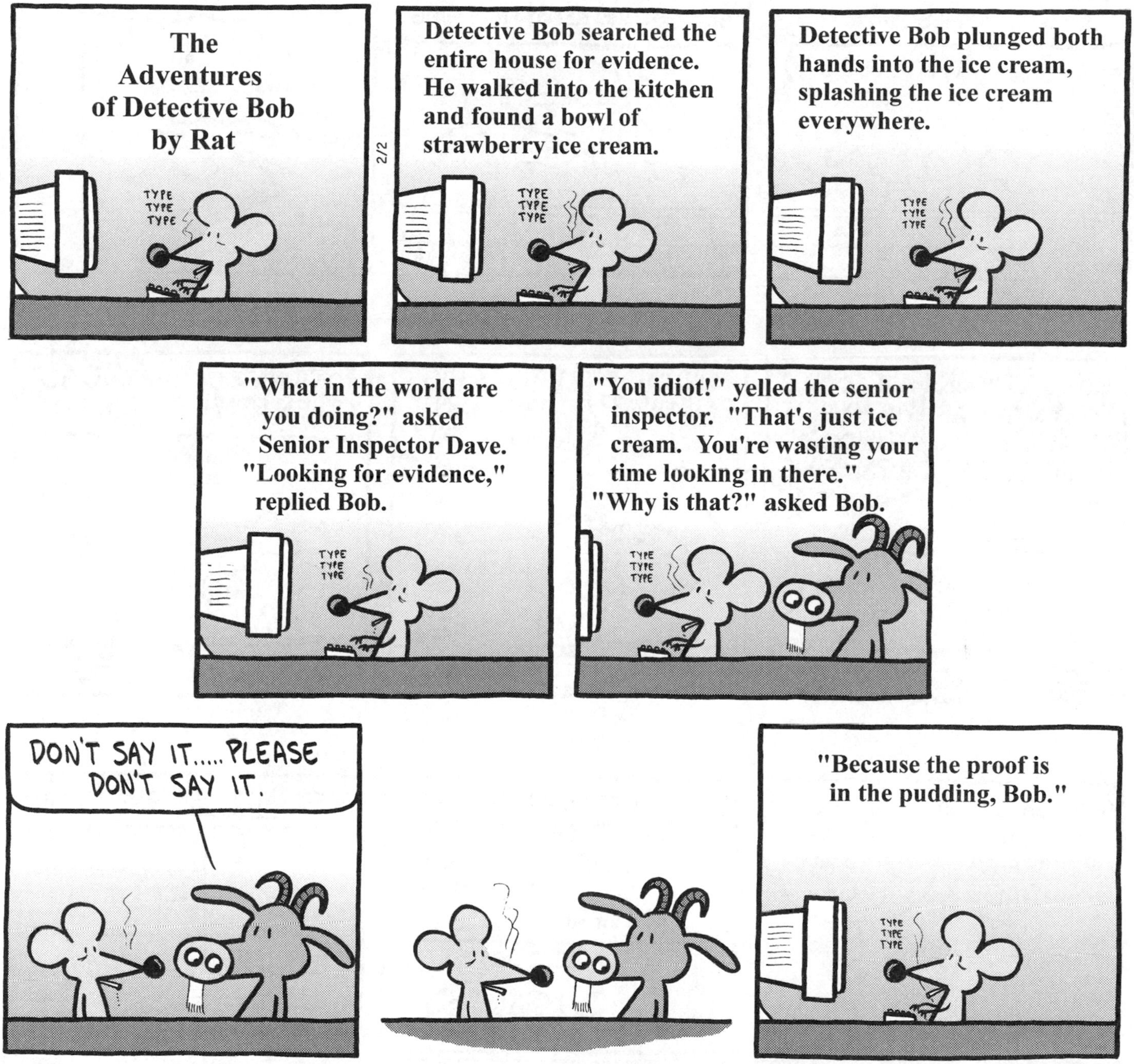
The Adventures of Detective Bob by Rat
TYPE TYPE TYPE
2/2
Detective Bob searched the entire house for evidence. He walked into the kitchen and found a bowl of strawberry ice cream.
TYPE TYPE TYPE
Detective Bob plunged both hands into the ice cream, splashing the ice cream everywhere.
TYPE TYPE TYPE
"What in the world are you doing?" asked Senior Inspector Dave. "Looking for evidence," replied Bob.
TYPE TYPE TYPE
"You idiot!" yelled the senior inspector. "That's just ice cream. You're wasting your time looking in there." "Why is that?" asked Bob.
TYPE TYPE TYPE
DON'T SAY IT..... PLEASE DON'T SAY IT.
"Because the proof is in the pudding, Bob."
TYPE TYPE TYPE

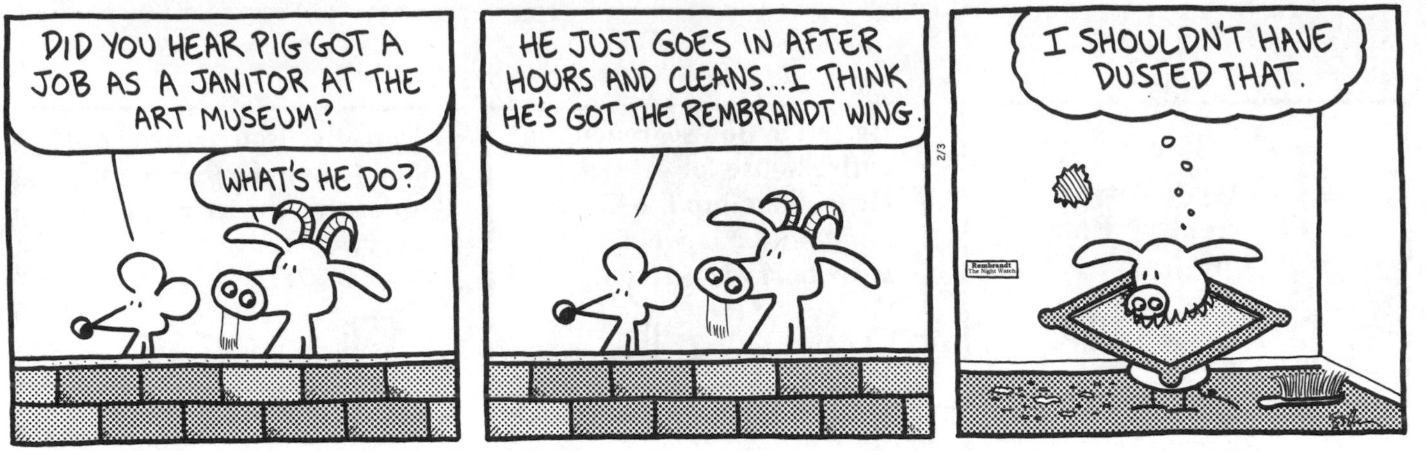
DID YOU HEAR PIG GOT A JOB AS A JANITOR AT THE ART MUSEUM?
WHAT'S HE DO?
HE JUST GOES IN AFTER HOURS AND CLEANS...I THINK HE'S GOT THE REMBRANDT WING.
2/3
I SHOULDN'T HAVE DUSTED THAT.
Rembrandt
The Night Watch

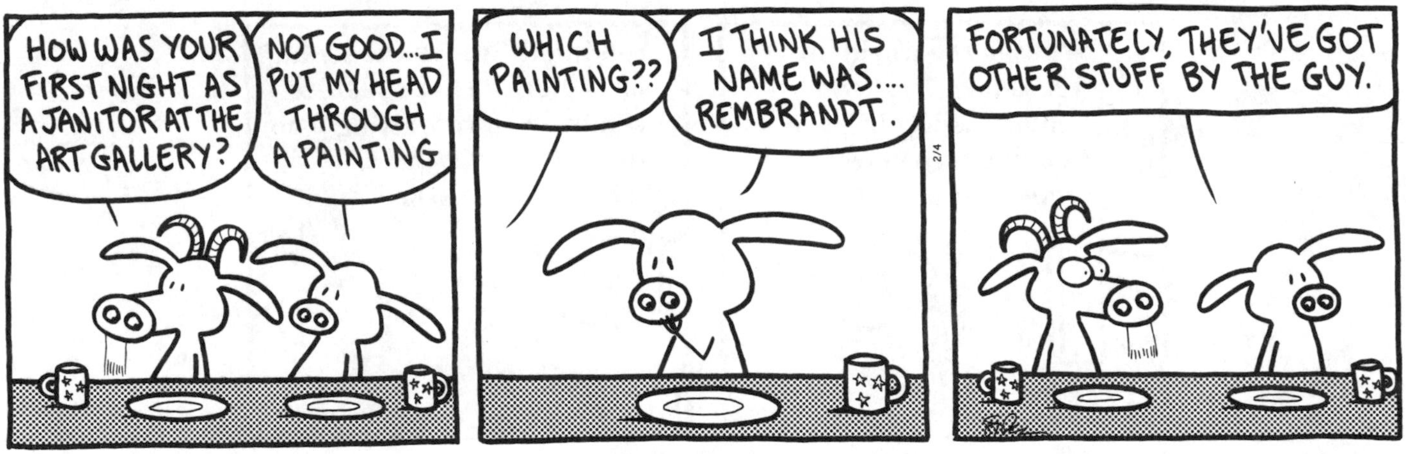
HOW WAS YOUR FIRST NIGHT AS A JANITOR AT THE ART GALLERY?
NOT GOOD...I PUT MY HEAD THROUGH A PAINTING
WHICH PAINTING??
I THINK HIS NAME WAS.... REMBRANDT.
2/4
FORTUNATELY, THEY'VE GOT OTHER STUFF BY THE GUY.

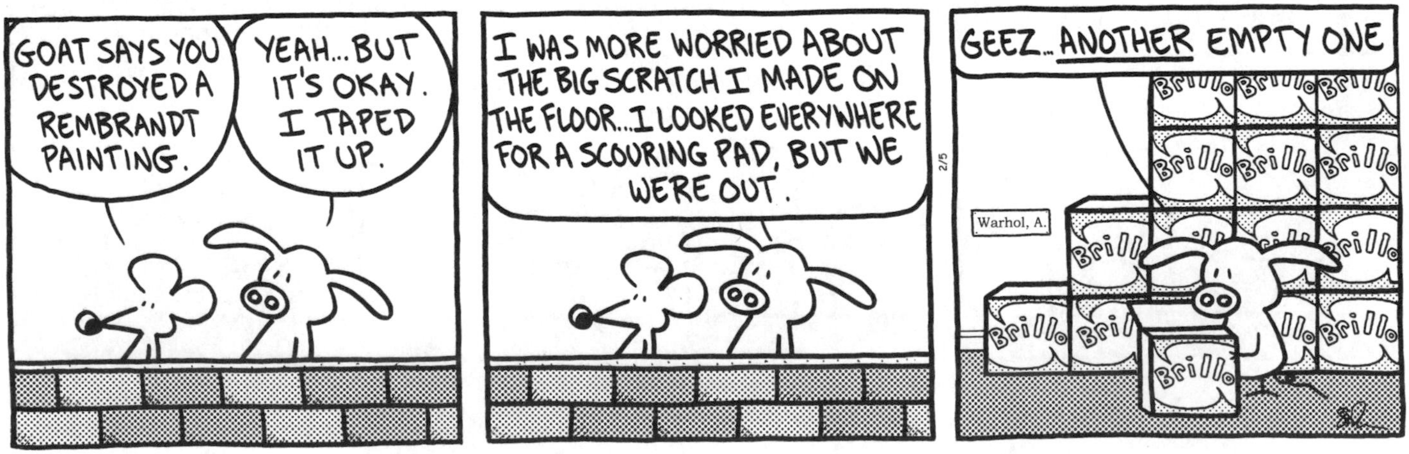
GOAT SAYS YOU DESTROYED A REMBRANDT PAINTING.
YEAH...BUT IT'S OKAY. I TAPED IT UP.
I WAS MORE WORRIED ABOUT THE BIG SCRATCH I MADE ON THE FLOOR...I LOOKED EVERYWHERE FOR A SCOURING PAD, BUT WE WERE OUT.
2/5
GEEZ... ANOTHER EMPTY ONE
Warhol, A.
Brillo

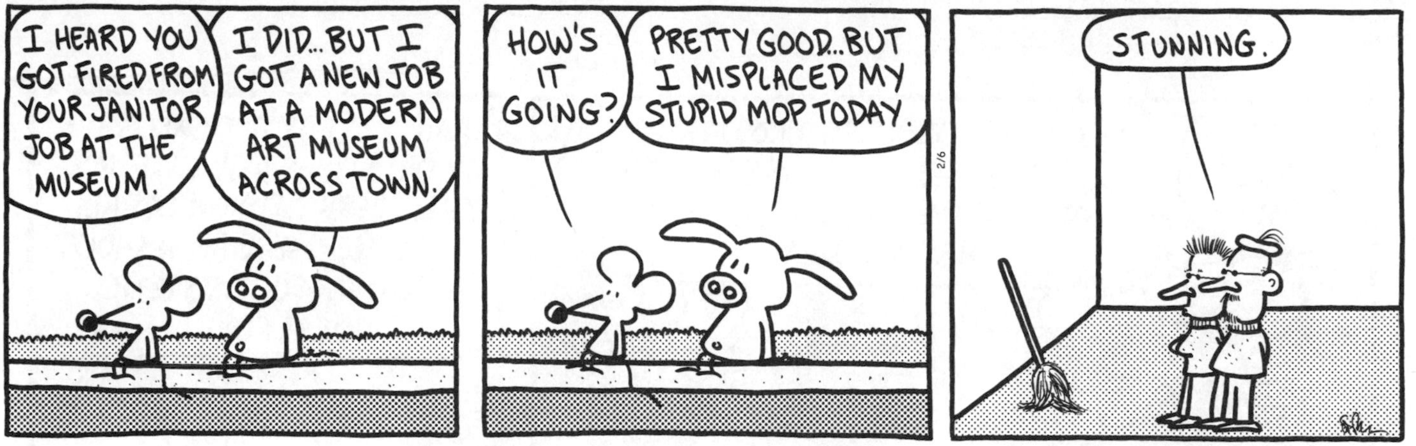
I HEARD YOU GOT FIRED FROM YOUR JANITOR JOB AT THE MUSEUM.
I DID...BUT I GOT A NEW JOB AT A MODERN ART MUSEUM ACROSS TOWN.
HOW'S IT GOING?
PRETTY GOOD...BUT I MISPLACED MY STUPID MOP TODAY.
STUNNING.

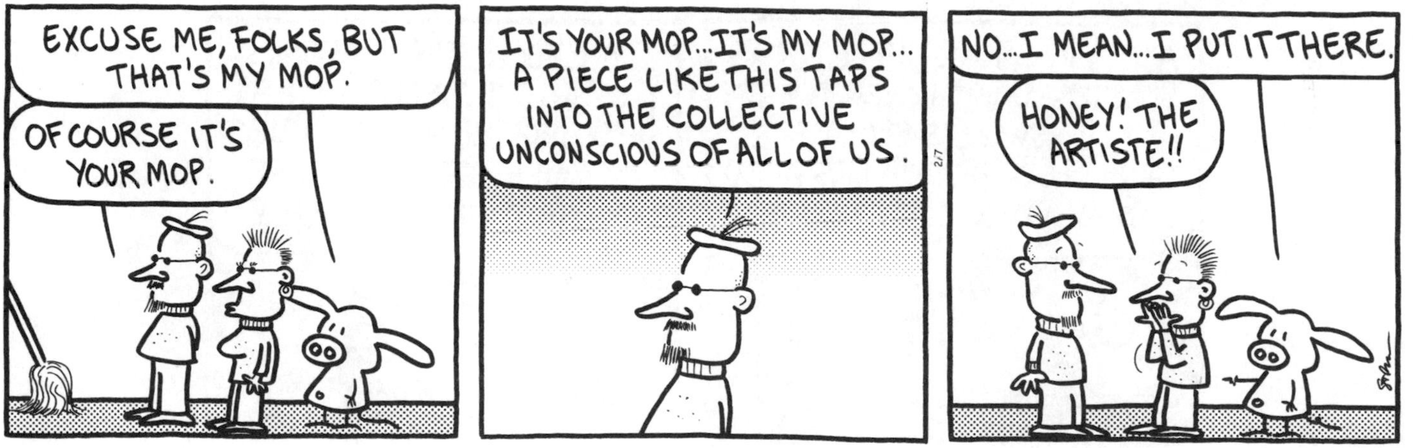
EXCUSE ME, FOLKS, BUT THAT'S MY MOP.
OF COURSE IT'S YOUR MOP.
IT'S YOUR MOP...IT'S MY MOP... A PIECE LIKE THIS TAPS INTO THE COLLECTIVE UNCONSCIOUS OF ALL OF US.
NO...I MEAN...I PUT IT THERE.
HONEY! THE ARTISTE!!

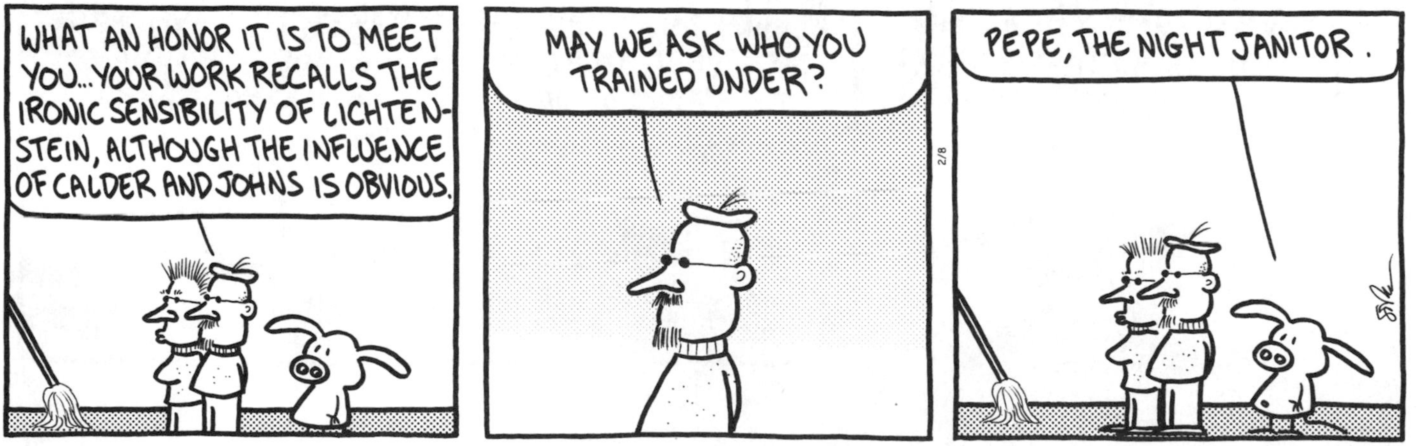
WHAT AN HONOR IT IS TO MEET YOU...YOUR WORK RECALLS THE IRONIC SENSIBILITY OF LICHTEN-STEIN, ALTHOUGH THE INFLUENCE OF CALDER AND JOHNS IS OBVIOUS.
MAY WE ASK WHO YOU TRAINED UNDER?
PEPE, THE NIGHT JANITOR.

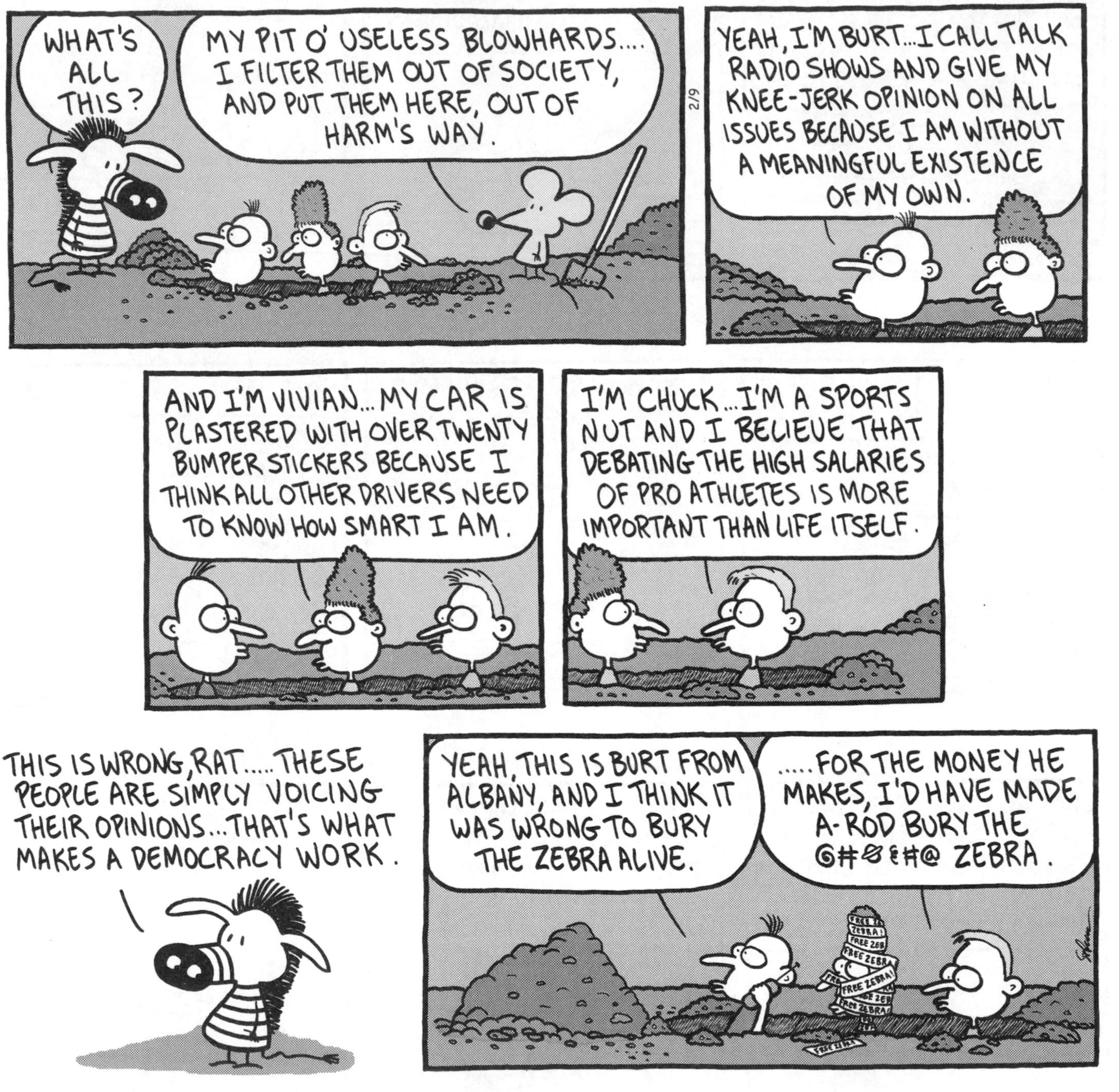
WHAT'S ALL THIS?
MY PIT O' USELESS BLOWHARDS.... I FILTER THEM OUT OF SOCIETY, AND PUT THEM HERE, OUT OF HARM'S WAY.
2/9
YEAH, I'M BURT...I CALL TALK RADIO SHOWS AND GIVE MY KNEE-JERK OPINION ON ALL ISSUES BECAUSE I AM WITHOUT A MEANINGFUL EXISTENCE OF MY OWN.
AND I'M VIVIAN... MY CAR IS PLASTERED WITH OVER TWENTY BUMPER STICKERS BECAUSE I THINK ALL OTHER DRIVERS NEED TO KNOW HOW SMART I AM.
I'M CHUCK...I'M A SPORTS NUT AND I BELIEVE THAT DEBATING THE HIGH SALARIES OF PRO ATHLETES IS MORE IMPORTANT THAN LIFE ITSELF.
THIS IS WRONG, RAT..... THESE PEOPLE ARE SIMPLY VOICING THEIR OPINIONS...THAT'S WHAT MAKES A DEMOCRACY WORK.
YEAH, THIS IS BURT FROM ALBANY, AND I THINK IT WAS WRONG TO BURY THE ZEBRA ALIVE.
.....FOR THE MONEY HE MAKES, I'D HAVE MADE A-ROD BURY THE @#$&#@ ZEBRA.

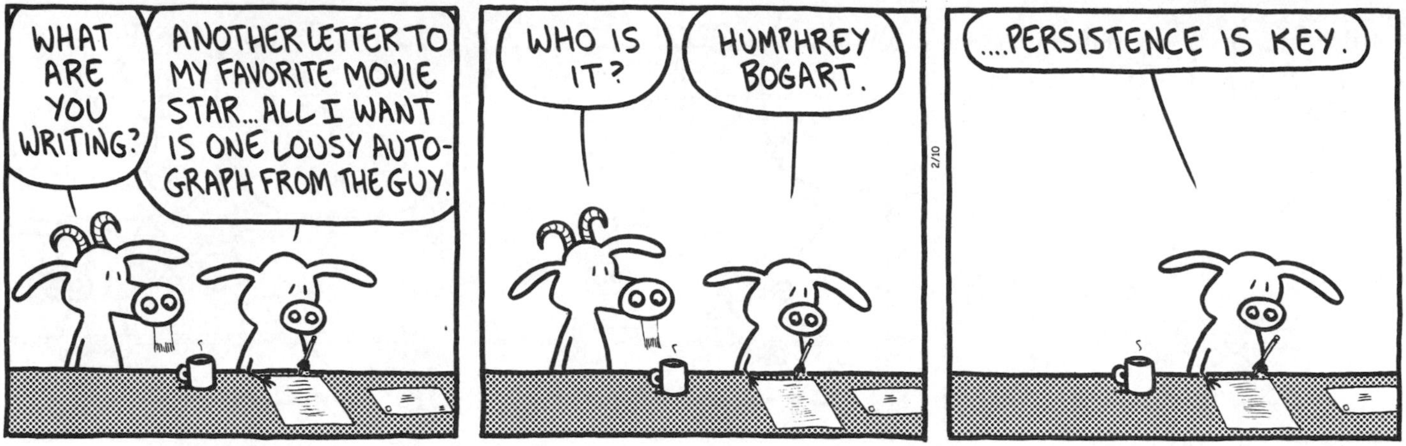
WHAT ARE YOU WRITING?
ANOTHER LETTER TO MY FAVORITE MOVIE STAR... ALL I WANT IS ONE LOUSY AUTOGRAPH FROM THE GUY.
WHO IS IT?
HUMPHREY BOGART.
2/10
....PERSISTENCE IS KEY.

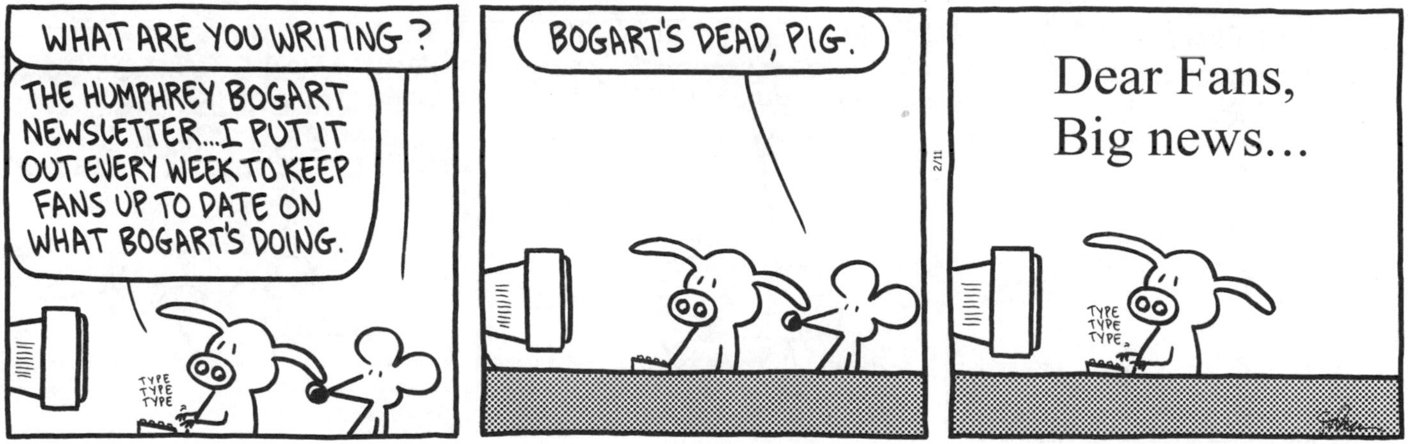
WHAT ARE YOU WRITING?
THE HUMPHREY BOGART NEWSLETTER... I PUT IT OUT EVERY WEEK TO KEEP FANS UP TO DATE ON WHAT BOGART'S DOING.
TYPE TYPE TYPE
BOGART'S DEAD, PIG.
2/11
Dear Fans,
Big news...
TYPE TYPE TYPE

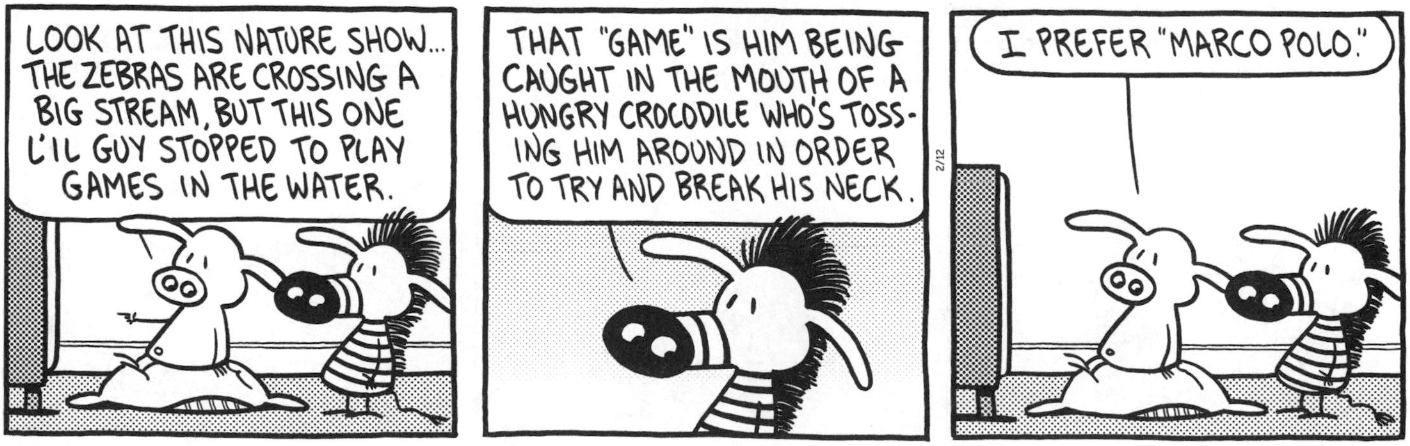
LOOK AT THIS NATURE SHOW... THE ZEBRAS ARE CROSSING A BIG STREAM, BUT THIS ONE L'IL GUY STOPPED TO PLAY GAMES IN THE WATER.
THAT "GAME" IS HIM BEING CAUGHT IN THE MOUTH OF A HUNGRY CROCODILE WHO'S TOSSING HIM AROUND IN ORDER TO TRY AND BREAK HIS NECK.
2/12
I PREFER "MARCO POLO."

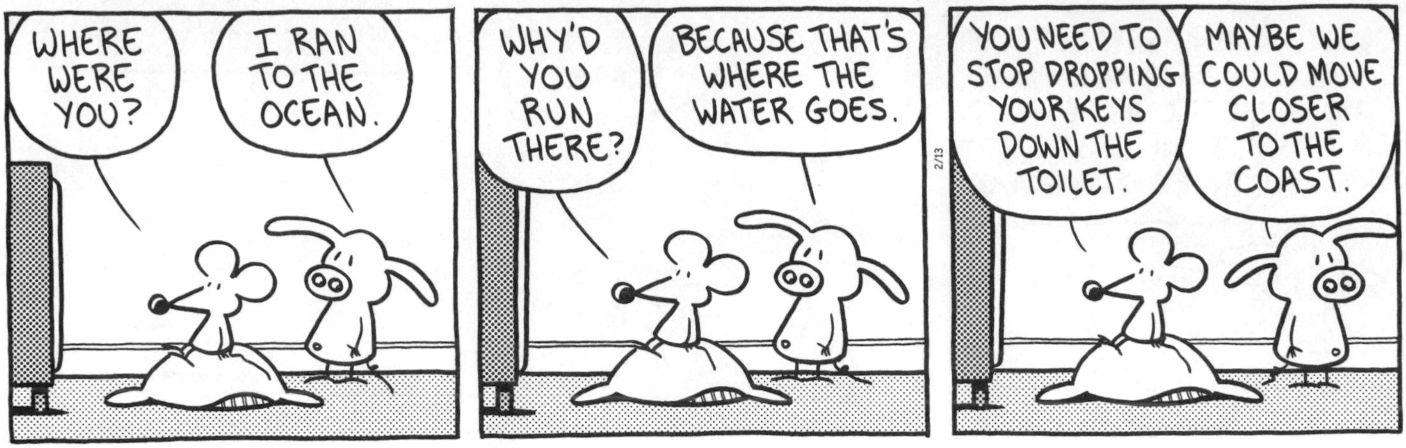
WHERE WERE YOU?
I RAN TO THE OCEAN.
WHY'D YOU RUN THERE?
BECAUSE THAT'S WHERE THE WATER GOES.
2/13
YOU NEED TO STOP DROPPING YOUR KEYS DOWN THE TOILET.
MAYBE WE COULD MOVE CLOSER TO THE COAST.

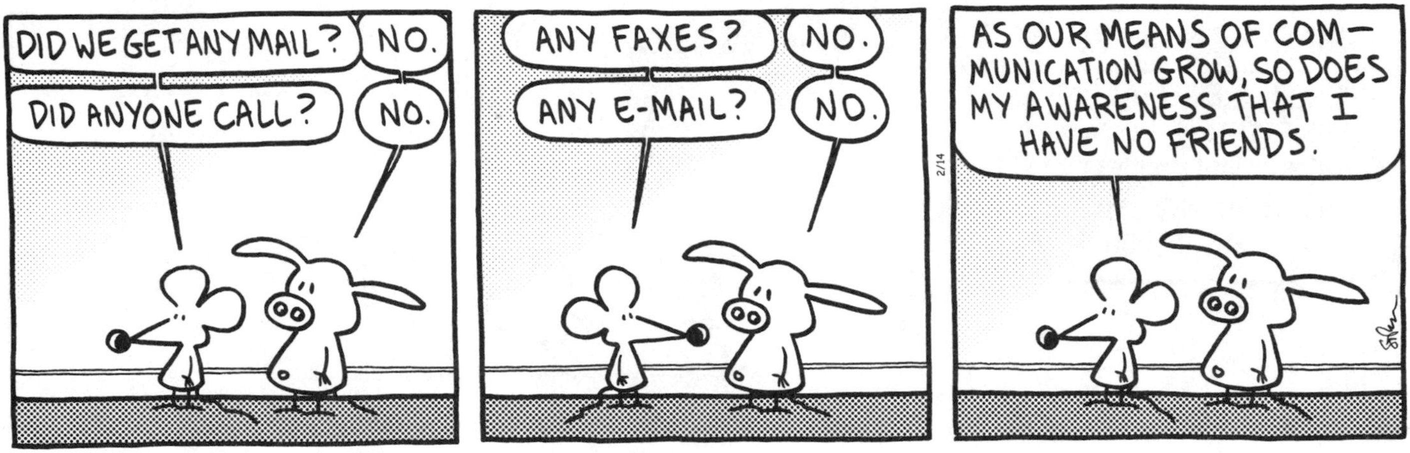
DID WE GET ANY MAIL?
NO.
DID ANYONE CALL?
NO.
ANY FAXES?
NO.
ANY E-MAIL?
NO.
2/14
AS OUR MEANS OF COM-MUNICATION GROW, SO DOES MY AWARENESS THAT I HAVE NO FRIENDS.

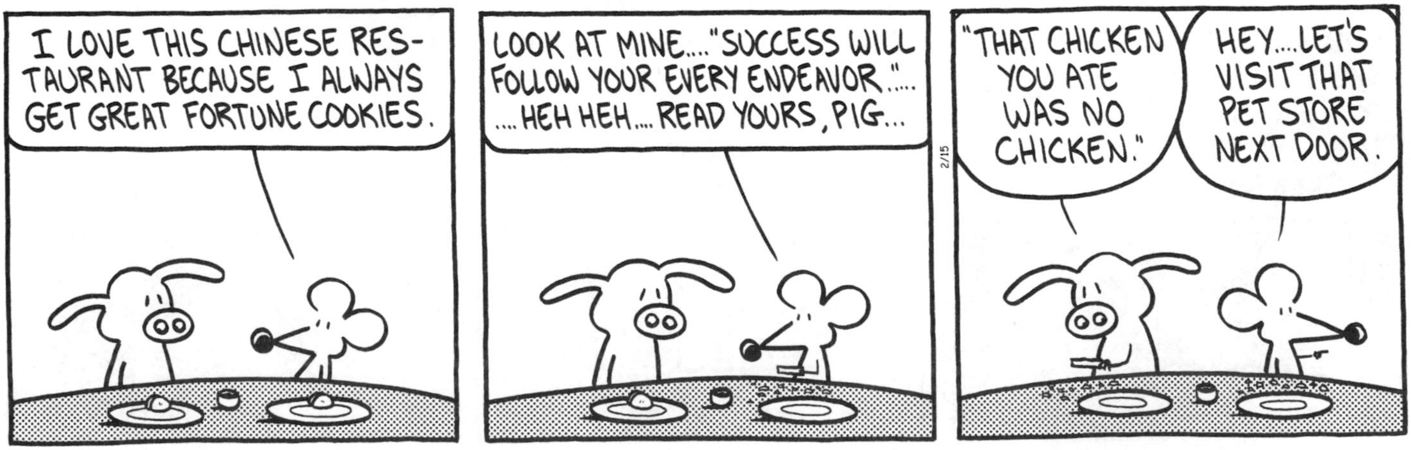
I LOVE THIS CHINESE RES-TAURANT BECAUSE I ALWAYS GET GREAT FORTUNE COOKIES.
LOOK AT MINE...."SUCCESS WILL FOLLOW YOUR EVERY ENDEAVOR."..... ....HEH HEH.... READ YOURS, PIG...
2/15
"THAT CHICKEN YOU ATE WAS NO CHICKEN."
HEY....LET'S VISIT THAT PET STORE NEXT DOOR.

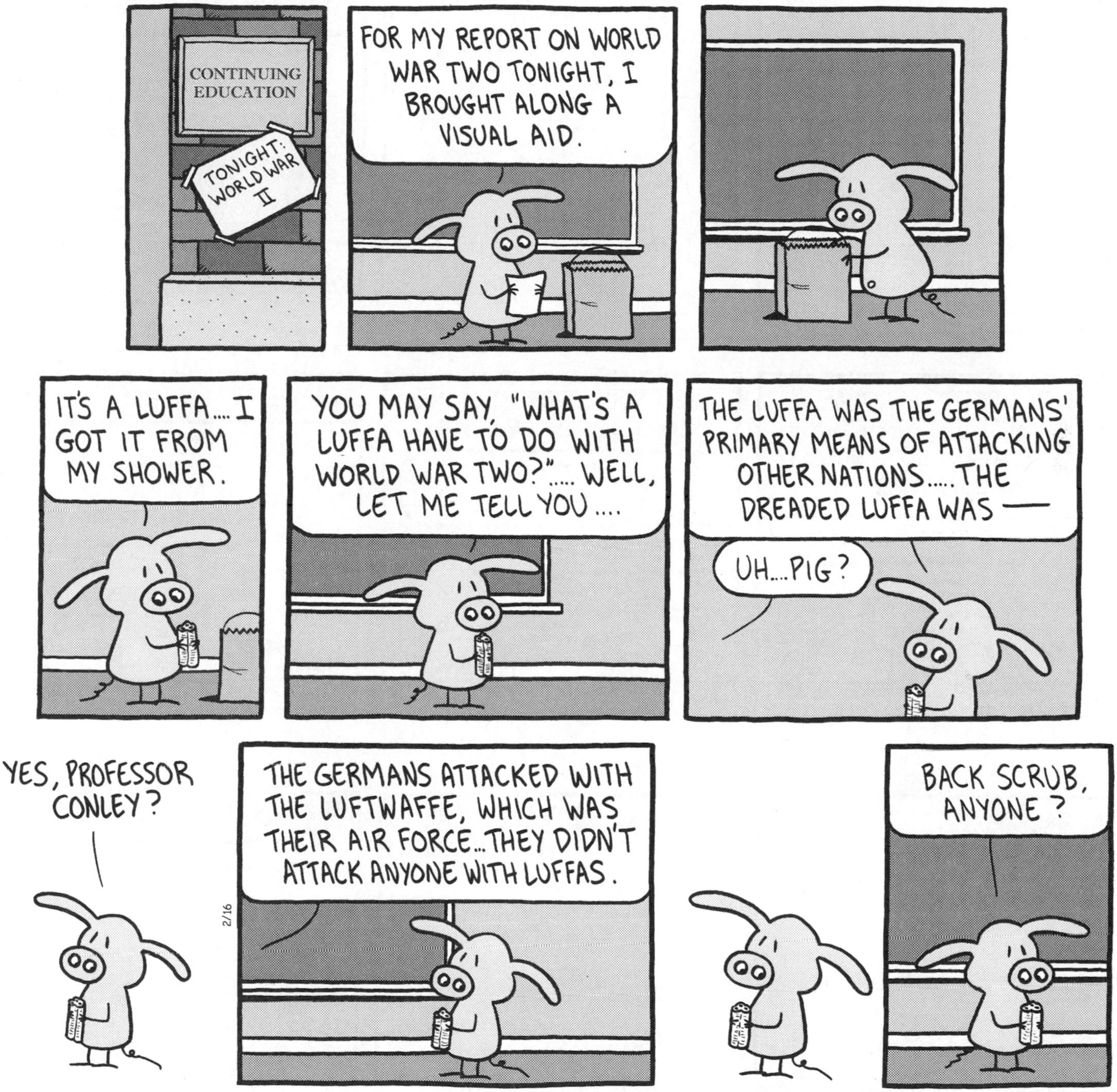
CONTINUING EDUCATION
TONIGHT: WORLD WAR II
FOR MY REPORT ON WORLD WAR TWO TONIGHT, I BROUGHT ALONG A VISUAL AID.
IT'S A LUFFA.... I GOT IT FROM MY SHOWER.
YOU MAY SAY, "WHAT'S A LUFFA HAVE TO DO WITH WORLD WAR TWO?"..... WELL, LET ME TELL YOU ....
THE LUFFA WAS THE GERMANS' PRIMARY MEANS OF ATTACKING OTHER NATIONS..... THE DREADED LUFFA WAS —
UH....PIG?
YES, PROFESSOR CONLEY?
THE GERMANS ATTACKED WITH THE LUFTWAFFE, WHICH WAS THEIR AIR FORCE...THEY DIDN'T ATTACK ANYONE WITH LUFFAS.
BACK SCRUB, ANYONE?
2/16

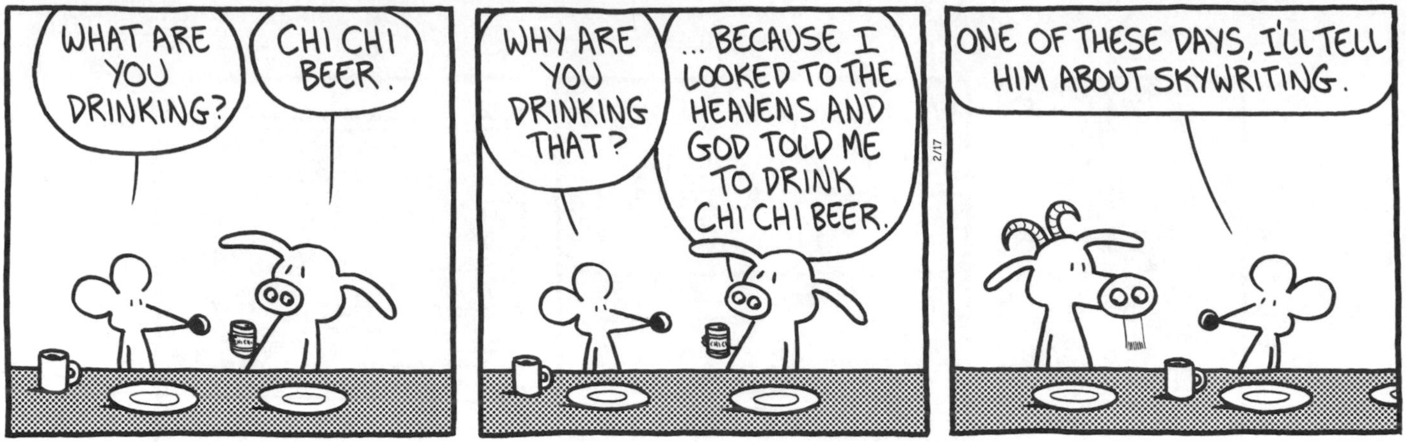
WHAT ARE YOU DRINKING?
CHI CHI BEER.
WHY ARE YOU DRINKING THAT?
... BECAUSE I LOOKED TO THE HEAVENS AND GOD TOLD ME TO DRINK CHI CHI BEER.
2/17
ONE OF THESE DAYS, I'LL TELL HIM ABOUT SKYWRITING.

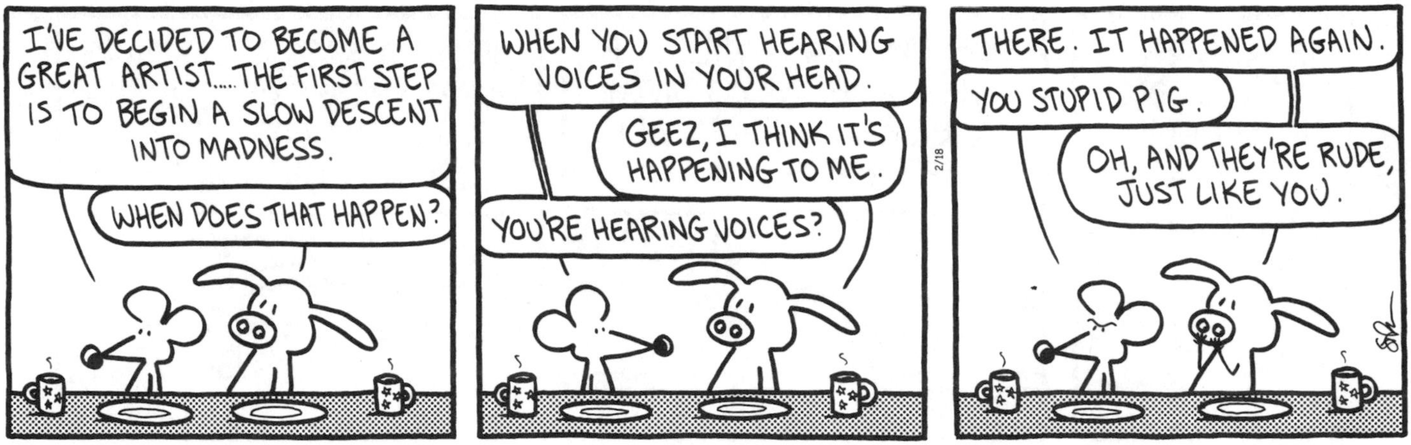
I'VE DECIDED TO BECOME A GREAT ARTIST.....THE FIRST STEP IS TO BEGIN A SLOW DESCENT INTO MADNESS.
WHEN DOES THAT HAPPEN?
WHEN YOU START HEARING VOICES IN YOUR HEAD.
GEEZ, I THINK IT'S HAPPENING TO ME.
YOU'RE HEARING VOICES?
2/18
THERE. IT HAPPENED AGAIN.
YOU STUPID PIG.
OH, AND THEY'RE RUDE, JUST LIKE YOU.

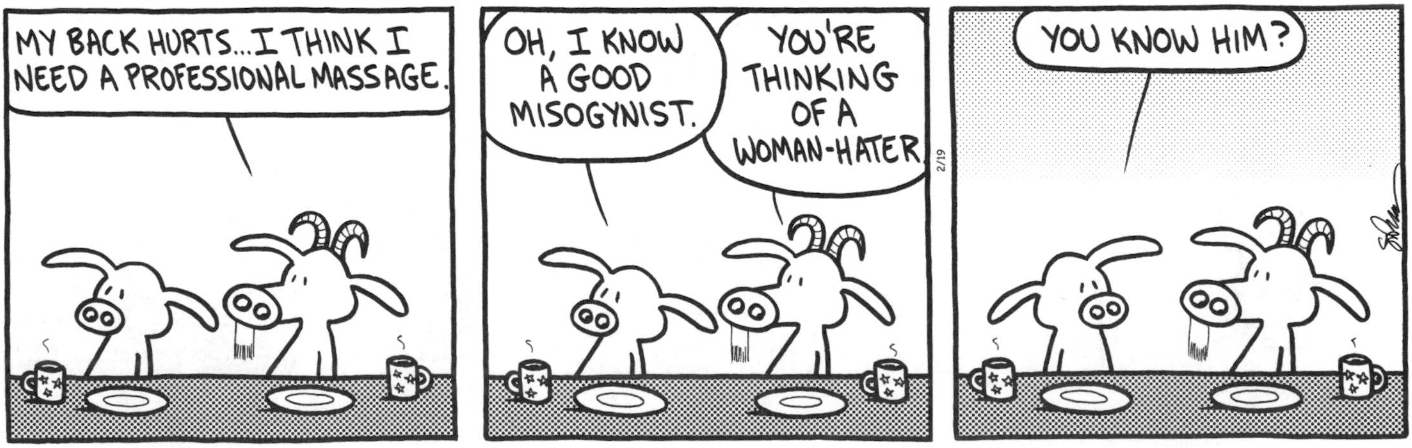
MY BACK HURTS...I THINK I NEED A PROFESSIONAL MASSAGE.
OH, I KNOW A GOOD MISOGYNIST.
YOU'RE THINKING OF A WOMAN-HATER.
2/19
YOU KNOW HIM?

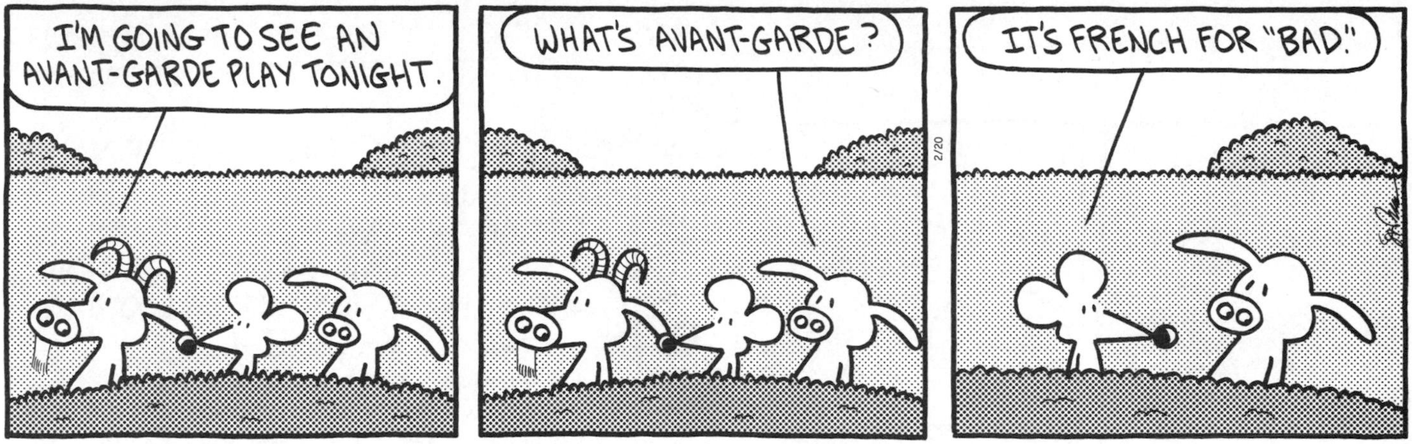
I'M GOING TO SEE AN AVANT-GARDE PLAY TONIGHT.
WHAT'S AVANT-GARDE?
IT'S FRENCH FOR "BAD."
2/20

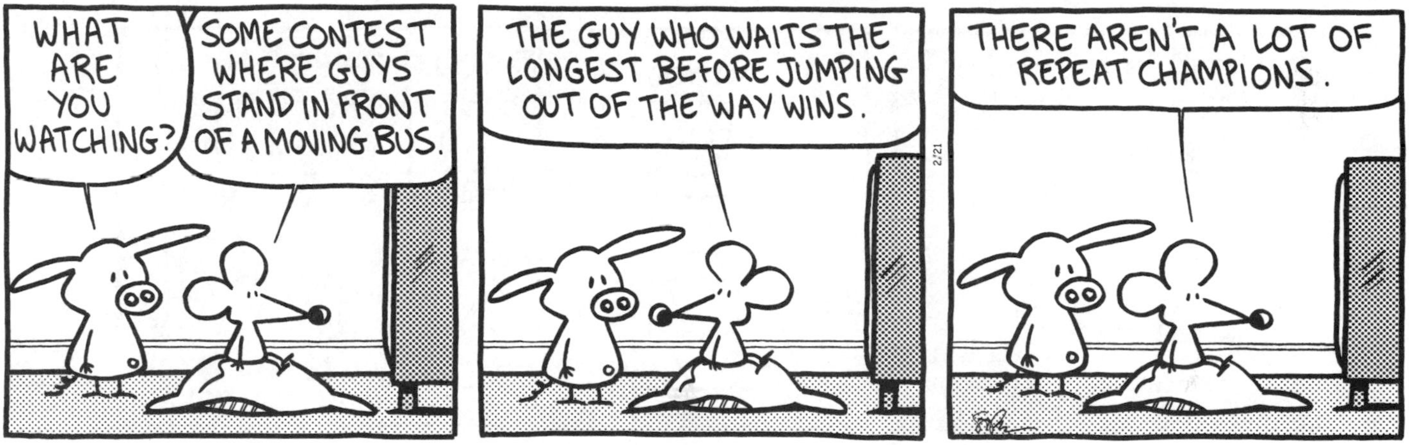
WHAT ARE YOU WATCHING?
SOME CONTEST WHERE GUYS STAND IN FRONT OF A MOVING BUS.
THE GUY WHO WAITS THE LONGEST BEFORE JUMPING OUT OF THE WAY WINS.
THERE AREN'T A LOT OF REPEAT CHAMPIONS.
2/21

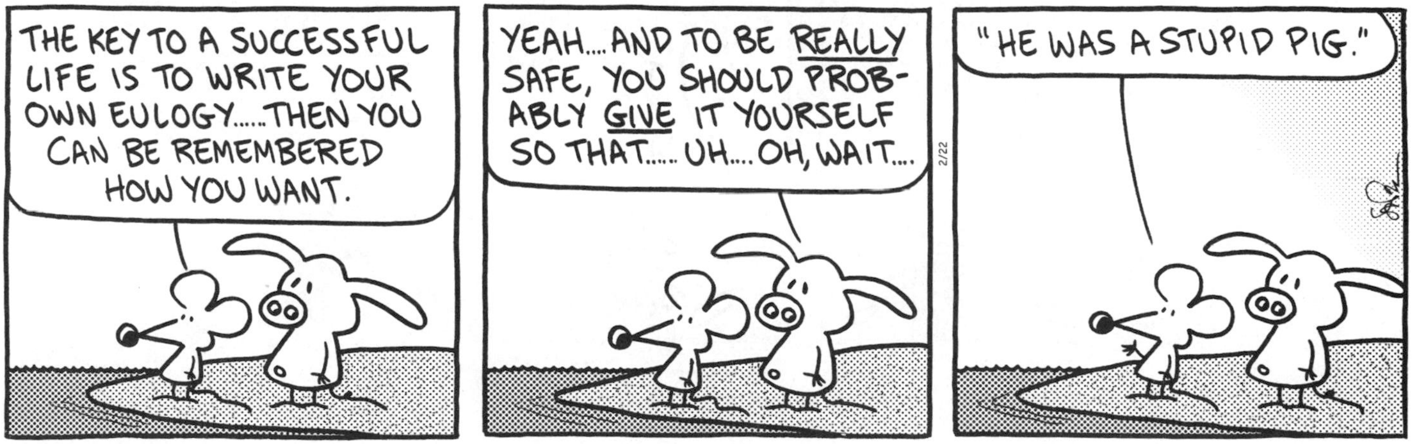
THE KEY TO A SUCCESSFUL LIFE IS TO WRITE YOUR OWN EULOGY...... THEN YOU CAN BE REMEMBERED HOW YOU WANT.
YEAH.... AND TO BE REALLY SAFE, YOU SHOULD PROBABLY GIVE IT YOURSELF SO THAT...... UH.... OH, WAIT....
"HE WAS A STUPID PIG."
2/22

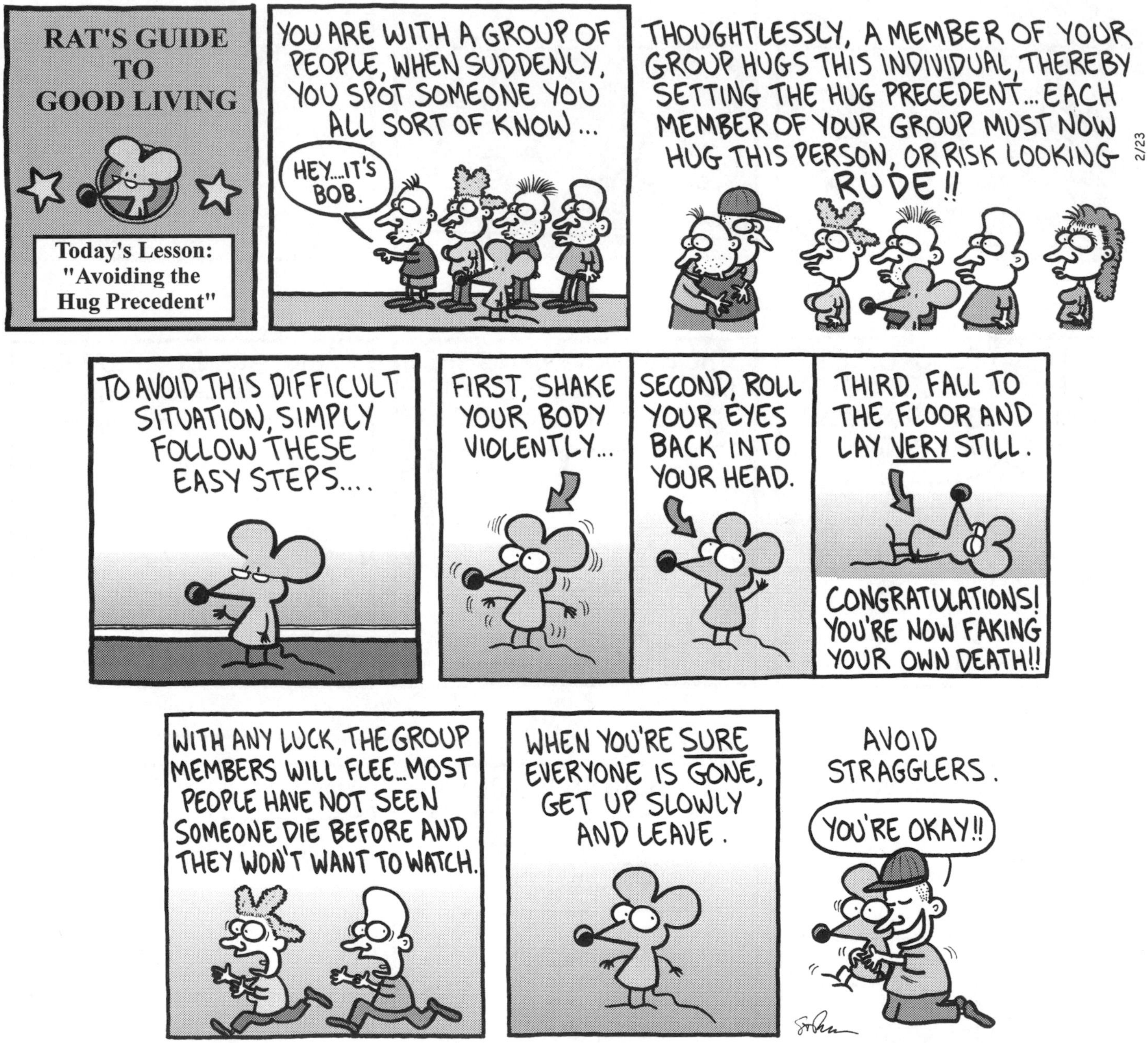
RAT'S GUIDE TO GOOD LIVING
Today's Lesson: "Avoiding the Hug Precedent"
YOU ARE WITH A GROUP OF PEOPLE, WHEN SUDDENLY, YOU SPOT SOMEONE YOU ALL SORT OF KNOW...
HEY...IT'S BOB.
THOUGHTLESSLY, A MEMBER OF YOUR GROUP HUGS THIS INDIVIDUAL, THEREBY SETTING THE HUG PRECEDENT... EACH MEMBER OF YOUR GROUP MUST NOW HUG THIS PERSON, OR RISK LOOKING RUDE!!
2/23
TO AVOID THIS DIFFICULT SITUATION, SIMPLY FOLLOW THESE EASY STEPS....
FIRST, SHAKE YOUR BODY VIOLENTLY...
SECOND, ROLL YOUR EYES BACK INTO YOUR HEAD.
THIRD, FALL TO THE FLOOR AND LAY VERY STILL.
CONGRATULATIONS! YOU'RE NOW FAKING YOUR OWN DEATH!!
WITH ANY LUCK, THE GROUP MEMBERS WILL FLEE...MOST PEOPLE HAVE NOT SEEN SOMEONE DIE BEFORE AND THEY WON'T WANT TO WATCH.
WHEN YOU'RE SURE EVERYONE IS GONE, GET UP SLOWLY AND LEAVE.
AVOID STRAGGLERS.
YOU'RE OKAY!!

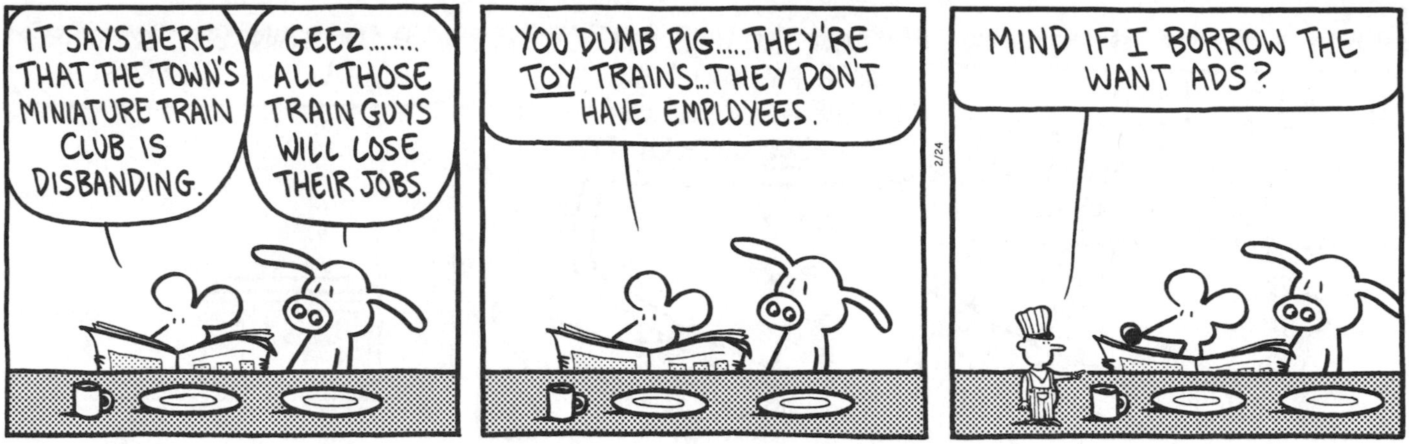
IT SAYS HERE THAT THE TOWN'S MINIATURE TRAIN CLUB IS DISBANDING.
GEEZ........ ALL THOSE TRAIN GUYS WILL LOSE THEIR JOBS.
YOU DUMB PIG.....THEY'RE TOY TRAINS...THEY DON'T HAVE EMPLOYEES.
MIND IF I BORROW THE WANT ADS?
2/24

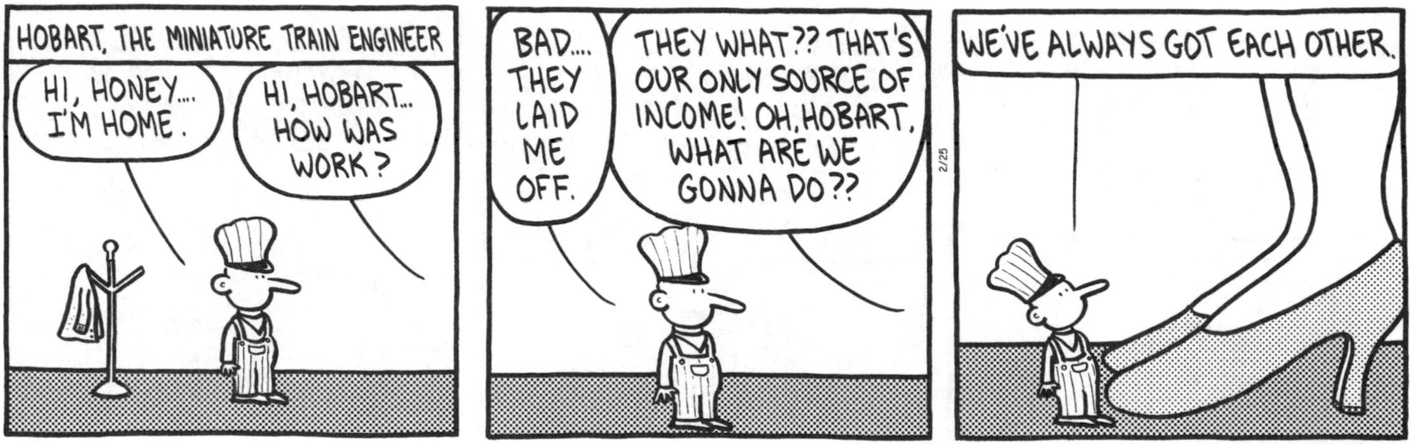
HOBART, THE MINIATURE TRAIN ENGINEER
HI, HONEY.... I'M HOME.
HI, HOBART... HOW WAS WORK?
BAD.... THEY LAID ME OFF.
THEY WHAT?? THAT'S OUR ONLY SOURCE OF INCOME! OH, HOBART, WHAT ARE WE GONNA DO??
WE'VE ALWAYS GOT EACH OTHER.
2/25

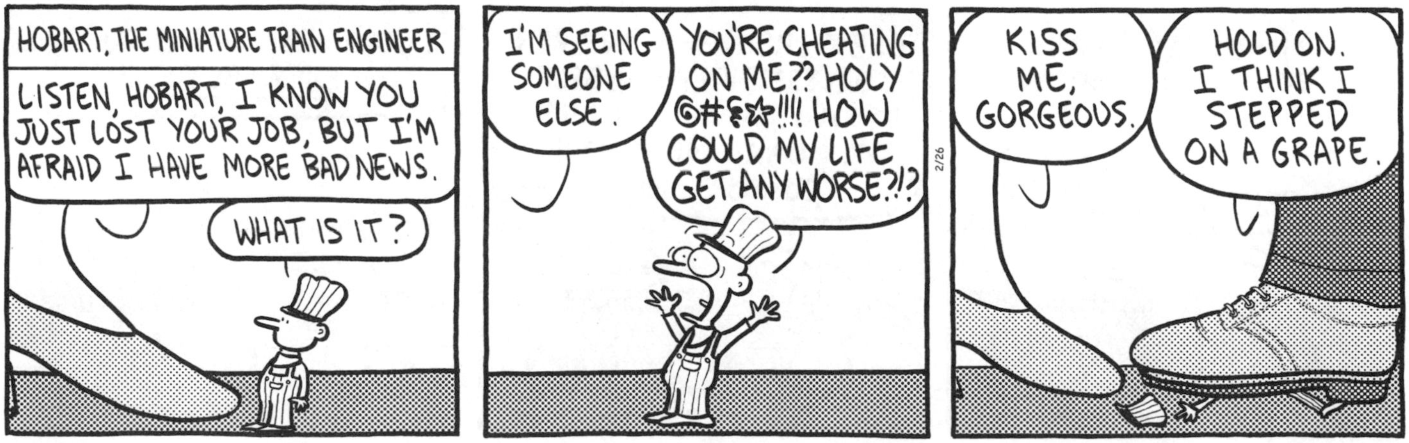
HOBART, THE MINIATURE TRAIN ENGINEER
LISTEN, HOBART, I KNOW YOU JUST LOST YOUR JOB, BUT I'M AFRAID I HAVE MORE BAD NEWS.
WHAT IS IT?
I'M SEEING SOMEONE ELSE.
YOU'RE CHEATING ON ME?? HOLY @#$☆!!!! HOW COULD MY LIFE GET ANY WORSE?!?
KISS ME, GORGEOUS.
HOLD ON. I THINK I STEPPED ON A GRAPE.
2/26

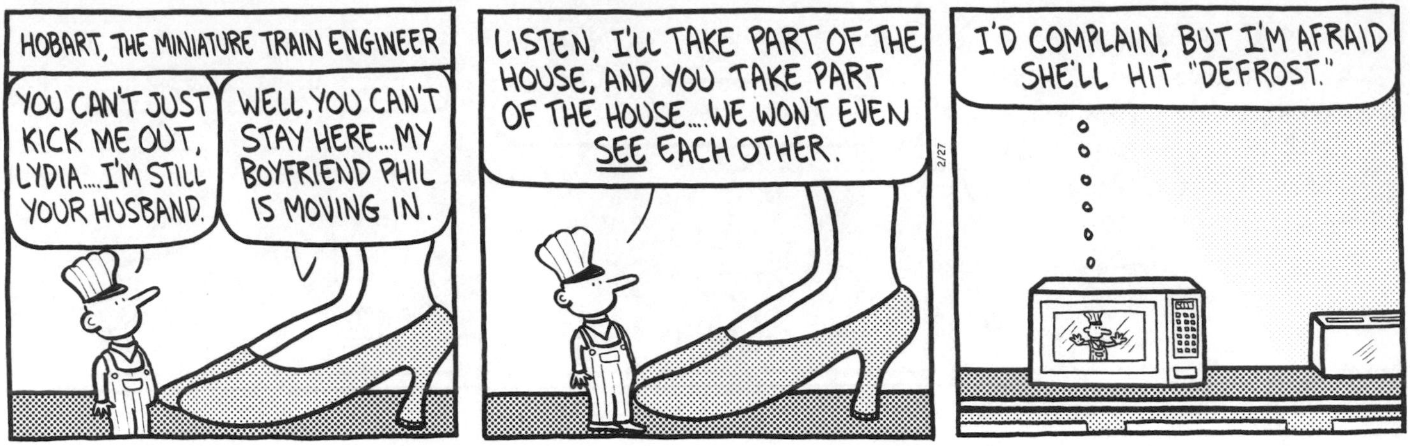
HOBART, THE MINIATURE TRAIN ENGINEER
YOU CAN'T JUST KICK ME OUT, LYDIA....I'M STILL YOUR HUSBAND.
WELL, YOU CAN'T STAY HERE...MY BOYFRIEND PHIL IS MOVING IN.
LISTEN, I'LL TAKE PART OF THE HOUSE, AND YOU TAKE PART OF THE HOUSE....WE WON'T EVEN SEE EACH OTHER.
2/27
I'D COMPLAIN, BUT I'M AFRAID SHE'LL HIT "DEFROST."

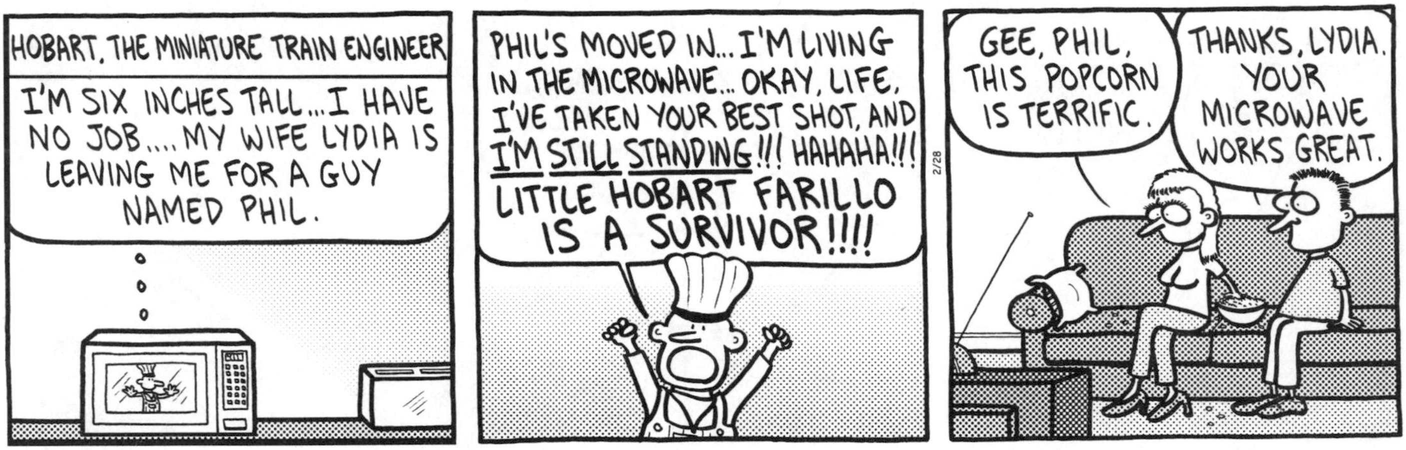
HOBART, THE MINIATURE TRAIN ENGINEER
I'M SIX INCHES TALL...I HAVE NO JOB.... MY WIFE LYDIA IS LEAVING ME FOR A GUY NAMED PHIL.
PHIL'S MOVED IN... I'M LIVING IN THE MICROWAVE... OKAY, LIFE, I'VE TAKEN YOUR BEST SHOT, AND I'M STILL STANDING!!! HAHAHA!!! LITTLE HOBART FARILLO IS A SURVIVOR!!!!
2/28
GEE, PHIL, THIS POPCORN IS TERRIFIC.
THANKS, LYDIA. YOUR MICROWAVE WORKS GREAT.

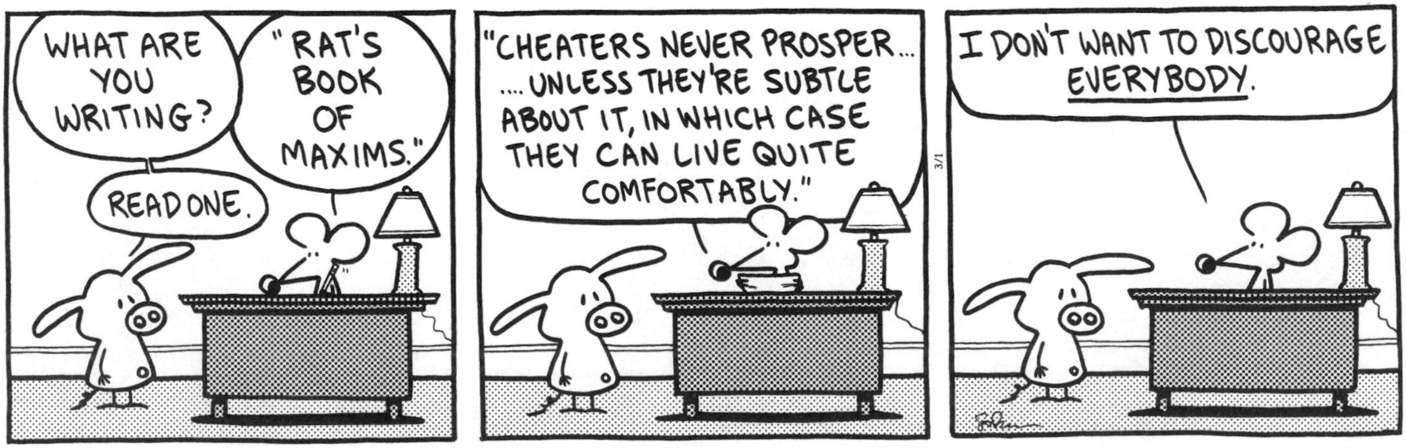
WHAT ARE YOU WRITING?
"RAT'S BOOK OF MAXIMS."
READ ONE.
"CHEATERS NEVER PROSPER... ....UNLESS THEY'RE SUBTLE ABOUT IT, IN WHICH CASE THEY CAN LIVE QUITE COMFORTABLY."
3/1
I DON'T WANT TO DISCOURAGE EVERYBODY.

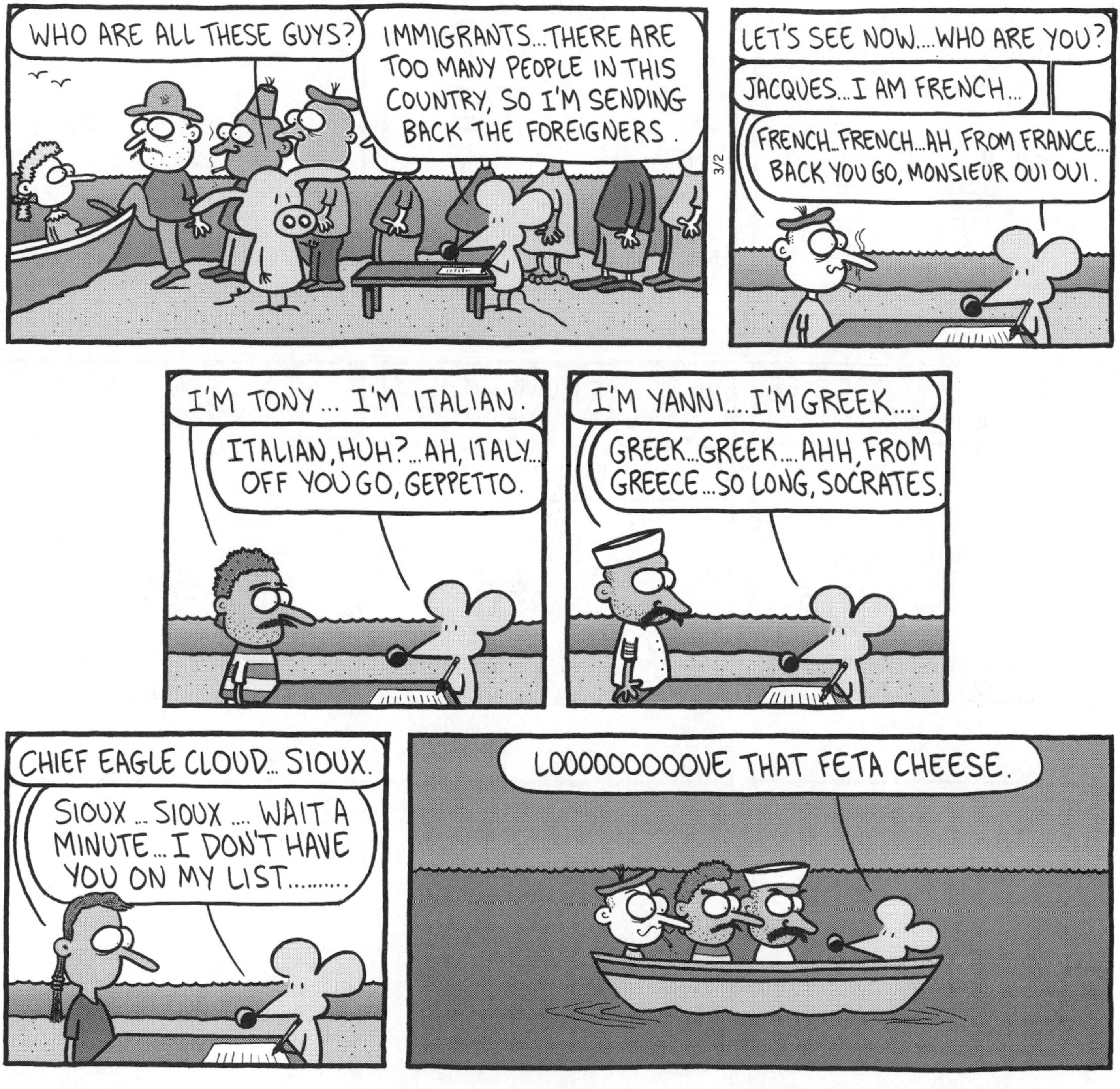
WHO ARE ALL THESE GUYS?
IMMIGRANTS...THERE ARE TOO MANY PEOPLE IN THIS COUNTRY, SO I'M SENDING BACK THE FOREIGNERS.
3/2
LET'S SEE NOW....WHO ARE YOU?
JACQUES...I AM FRENCH...
FRENCH...FRENCH...AH, FROM FRANCE... BACK YOU GO, MONSIEUR OUI OUI.
I'M TONY... I'M ITALIAN.
ITALIAN, HUH?...AH, ITALY... OFF YOU GO, GEPPETTO.
I'M YANNI....I'M GREEK....
GREEK...GREEK.... AHH, FROM GREECE...SO LONG, SOCRATES.
CHIEF EAGLE CLOUD... SIOUX.
SIOUX ... SIOUX .... WAIT A MINUTE... I DON'T HAVE YOU ON MY LIST.........
LOOOOOOOOOVE THAT FETA CHEESE.

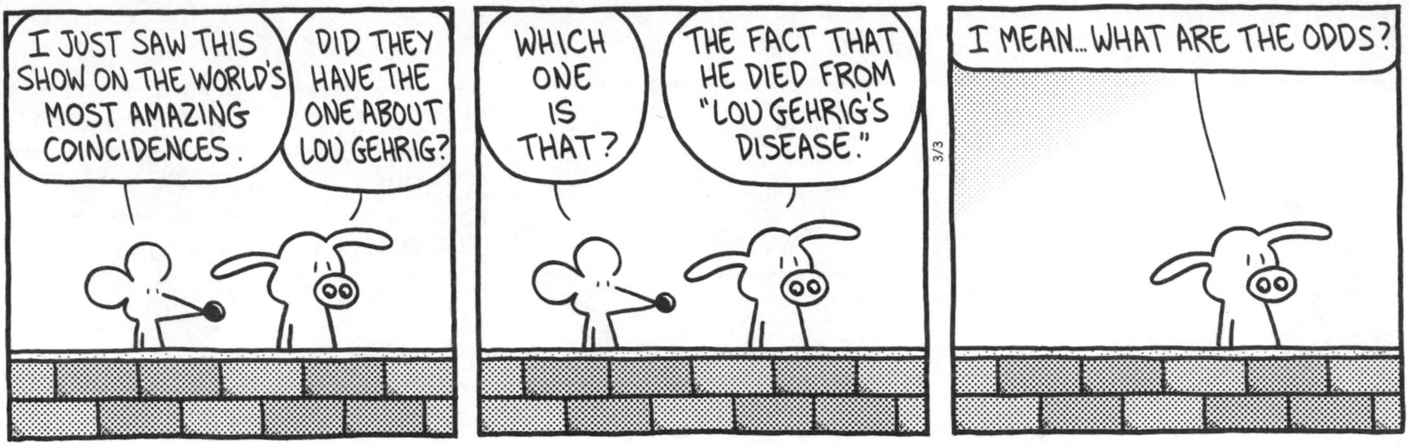
I JUST SAW THIS SHOW ON THE WORLD'S MOST AMAZING COINCIDENCES.
DID THEY HAVE THE ONE ABOUT LOU GEHRIG?
WHICH ONE IS THAT?
THE FACT THAT HE DIED FROM "LOU GEHRIG'S DISEASE."
3/3
I MEAN... WHAT ARE THE ODDS?

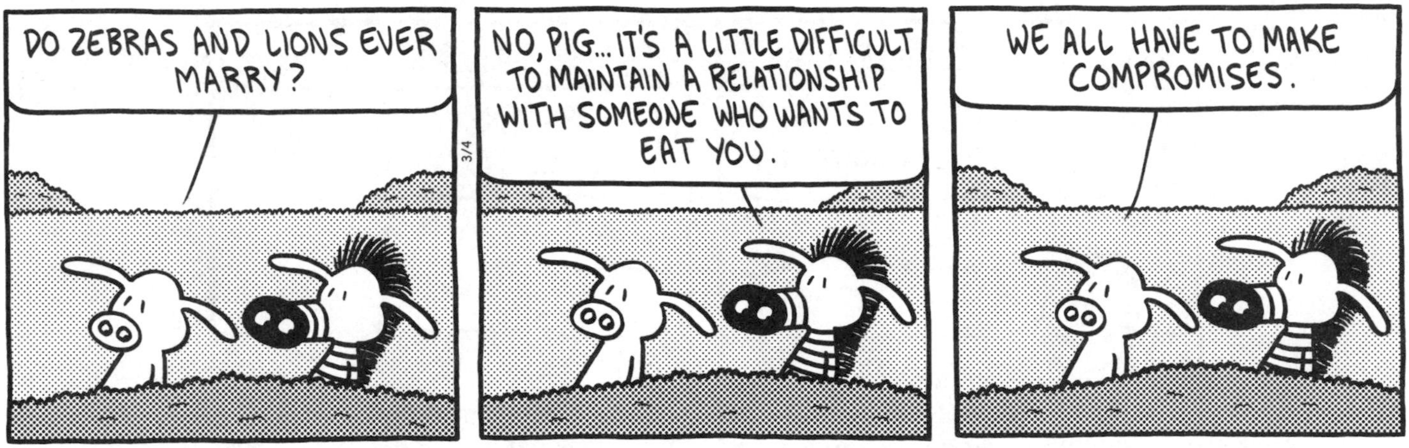
DO ZEBRAS AND LIONS EVER MARRY?
3/4
NO, PIG... IT'S A LITTLE DIFFICULT TO MAINTAIN A RELATIONSHIP WITH SOMEONE WHO WANTS TO EAT YOU.
WE ALL HAVE TO MAKE COMPROMISES.

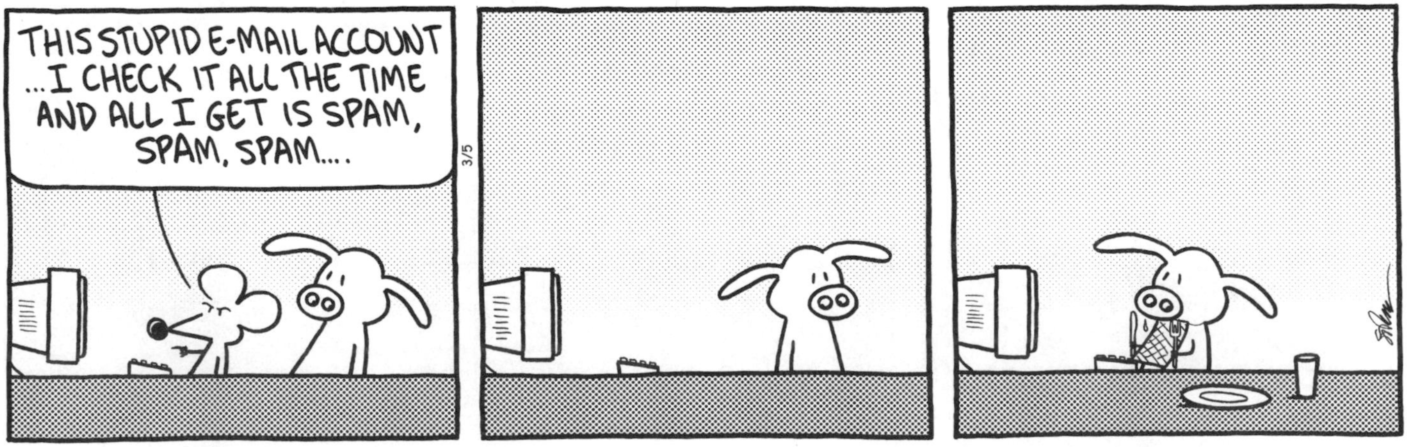
THIS STUPID E-MAIL ACCOUNT ...I CHECK IT ALL THE TIME AND ALL I GET IS SPAM, SPAM, SPAM....
3/5

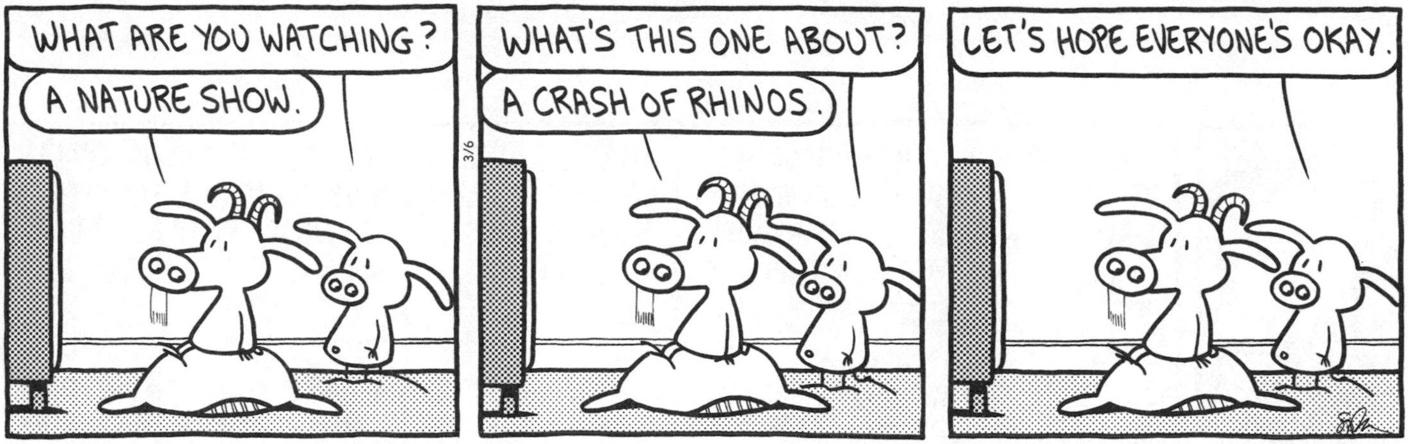
WHAT ARE YOU WATCHING?
A NATURE SHOW.
3/6
WHAT'S THIS ONE ABOUT?
A CRASH OF RHINOS.
LET'S HOPE EVERYONE'S OKAY.

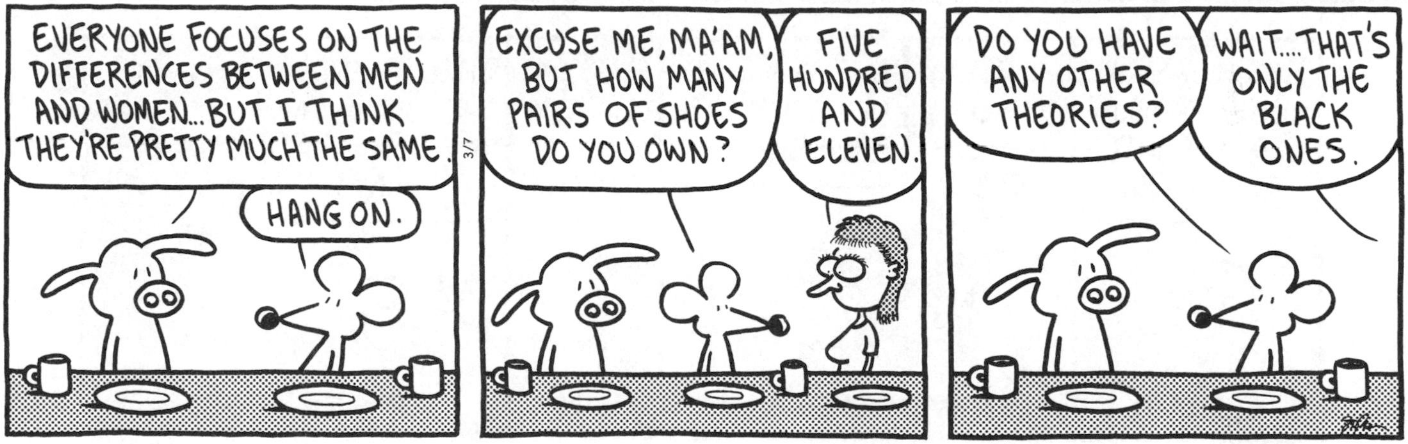
EVERYONE FOCUSES ON THE DIFFERENCES BETWEEN MEN AND WOMEN...BUT I THINK THEY'RE PRETTY MUCH THE SAME.
HANG ON.
3/7
EXCUSE ME, MA'AM, BUT HOW MANY PAIRS OF SHOES DO YOU OWN?
FIVE HUNDRED AND ELEVEN.
DO YOU HAVE ANY OTHER THEORIES?
WAIT....THAT'S ONLY THE BLACK ONES.

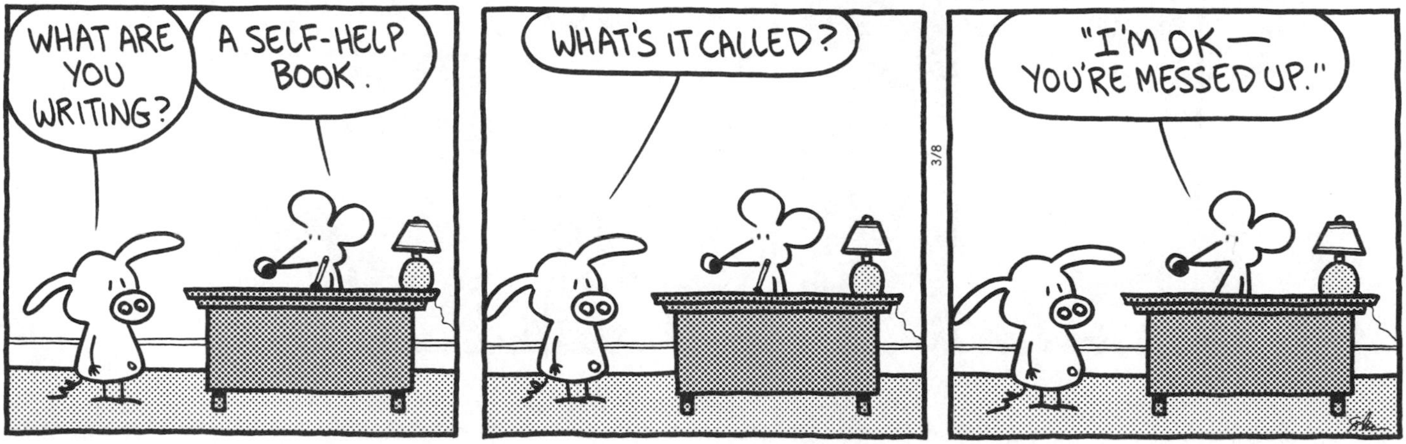
WHAT ARE YOU WRITING?
A SELF-HELP BOOK.
WHAT'S IT CALLED?
3/8
"I'M OK — YOU'RE MESSED UP."

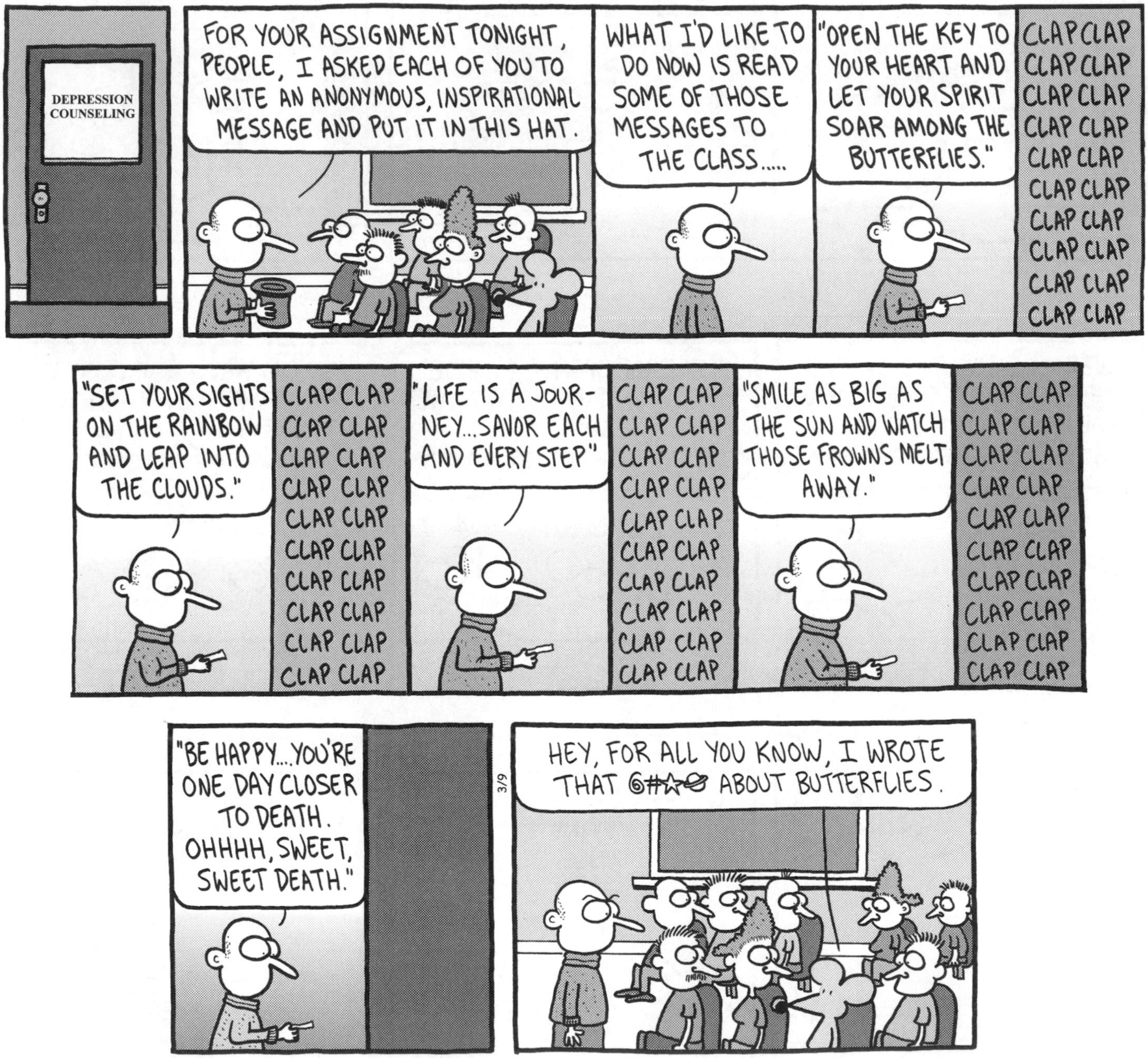
DEPRESSION COUNSELING
FOR YOUR ASSIGNMENT TONIGHT, PEOPLE, I ASKED EACH OF YOU TO WRITE AN ANONYMOUS, INSPIRATIONAL MESSAGE AND PUT IT IN THIS HAT.
WHAT I'D LIKE TO DO NOW IS READ SOME OF THOSE MESSAGES TO THE CLASS.....
"OPEN THE KEY TO YOUR HEART AND LET YOUR SPIRIT SOAR AMONG THE BUTTERFLIES."
CLAP CLAP CLAP CLAP CLAP CLAP CLAP CLAP CLAP CLAP CLAP CLAP CLAP CLAP CLAP CLAP CLAP CLAP CLAP CLAP
"SET YOUR SIGHTS ON THE RAINBOW AND LEAP INTO THE CLOUDS."
CLAP CLAP CLAP CLAP CLAP CLAP CLAP CLAP CLAP CLAP CLAP CLAP CLAP CLAP CLAP CLAP CLAP CLAP CLAP CLAP
"LIFE IS A JOURNEY...SAVOR EACH AND EVERY STEP"
CLAP CLAP CLAP CLAP CLAP CLAP CLAP CLAP CLAP CLAP CLAP CLAP CLAP CLAP CLAP CLAP CLAP CLAP CLAP CLAP
"SMILE AS BIG AS THE SUN AND WATCH THOSE FROWNS MELT AWAY."
CLAP CLAP CLAP CLAP CLAP CLAP CLAP CLAP CLAP CLAP CLAP CLAP CLAP CLAP CLAP CLAP CLAP CLAP CLAP CLAP
"BE HAPPY....YOU'RE ONE DAY CLOSER TO DEATH. OHHHH, SWEET, SWEET DEATH."
3/9
HEY, FOR ALL YOU KNOW, I WROTE THAT @#☆ ABOUT BUTTERFLIES.

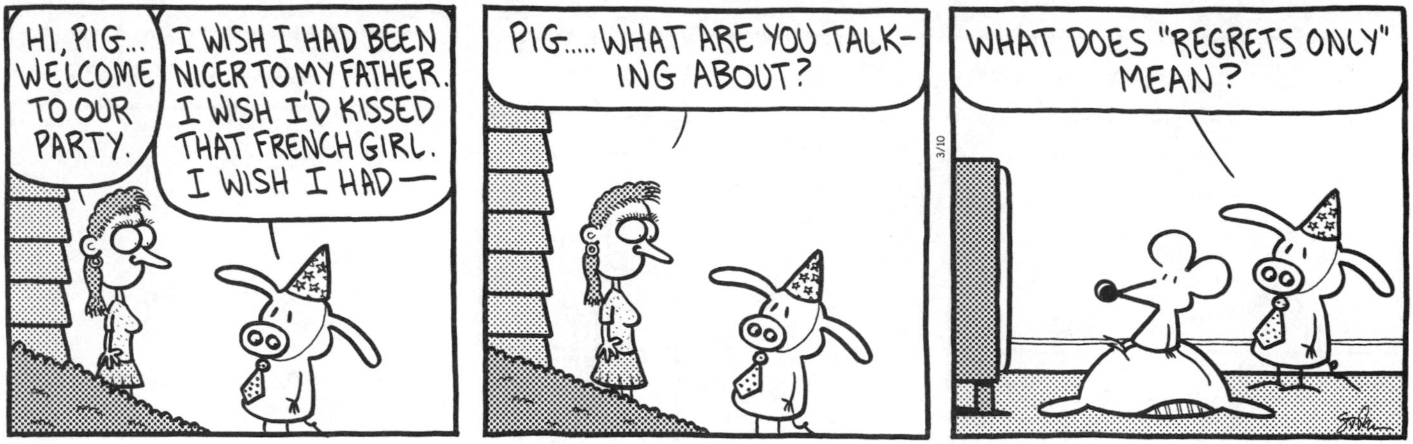
HI, PIG... WELCOME TO OUR PARTY.
I WISH I HAD BEEN NICER TO MY FATHER. I WISH I'D KISSED THAT FRENCH GIRL. I WISH I HAD—
PIG..... WHAT ARE YOU TALKING ABOUT?
3/10
WHAT DOES "REGRETS ONLY" MEAN?

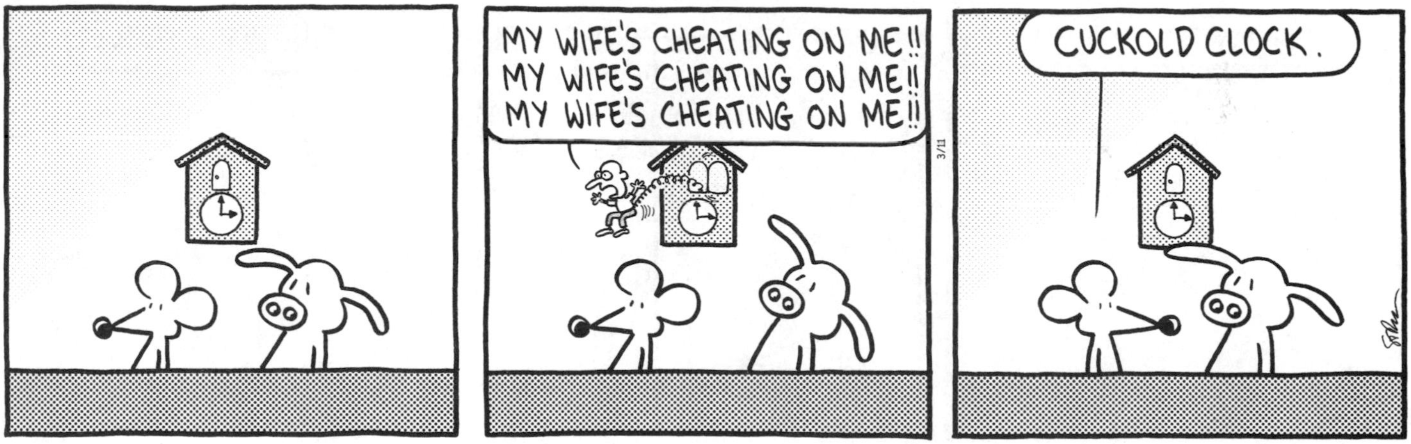
MY WIFE'S CHEATING ON ME!! MY WIFE'S CHEATING ON ME!! MY WIFE'S CHEATING ON ME!!
3/11
CUCKOLD CLOCK.

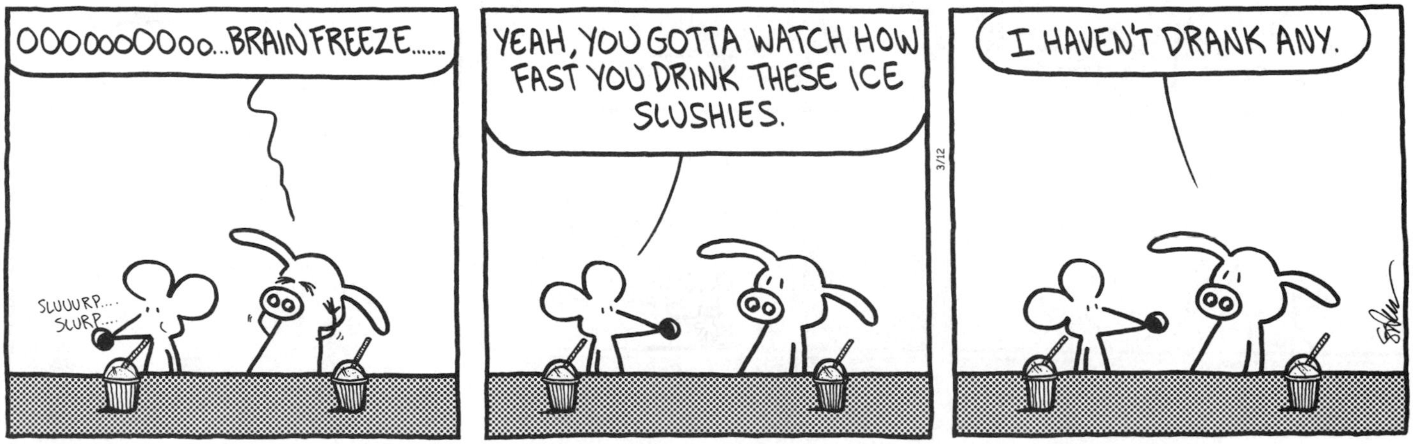
OOOOOOOOOo... BRAIN FREEZE......
SLUUURP.... SLURP....
YEAH, YOU GOTTA WATCH HOW FAST YOU DRINK THESE ICE SLUSHIES.
3/12
I HAVEN'T DRANK ANY.

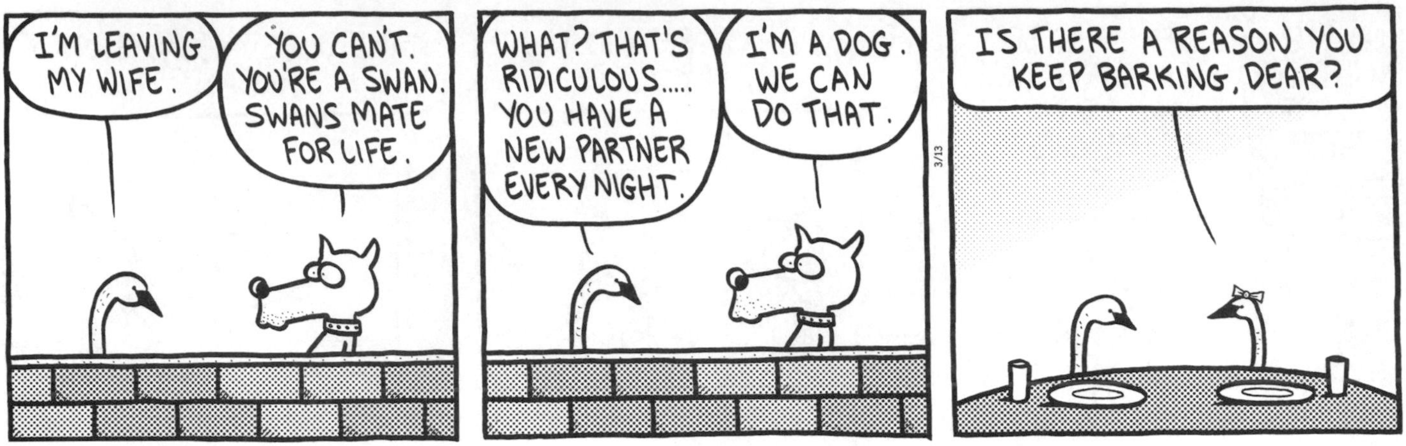
I'M LEAVING MY WIFE.
YOU CAN'T. YOU'RE A SWAN. SWANS MATE FOR LIFE.
WHAT? THAT'S RIDICULOUS..... YOU HAVE A NEW PARTNER EVERY NIGHT.
I'M A DOG. WE CAN DO THAT.
3/13
IS THERE A REASON YOU KEEP BARKING, DEAR?

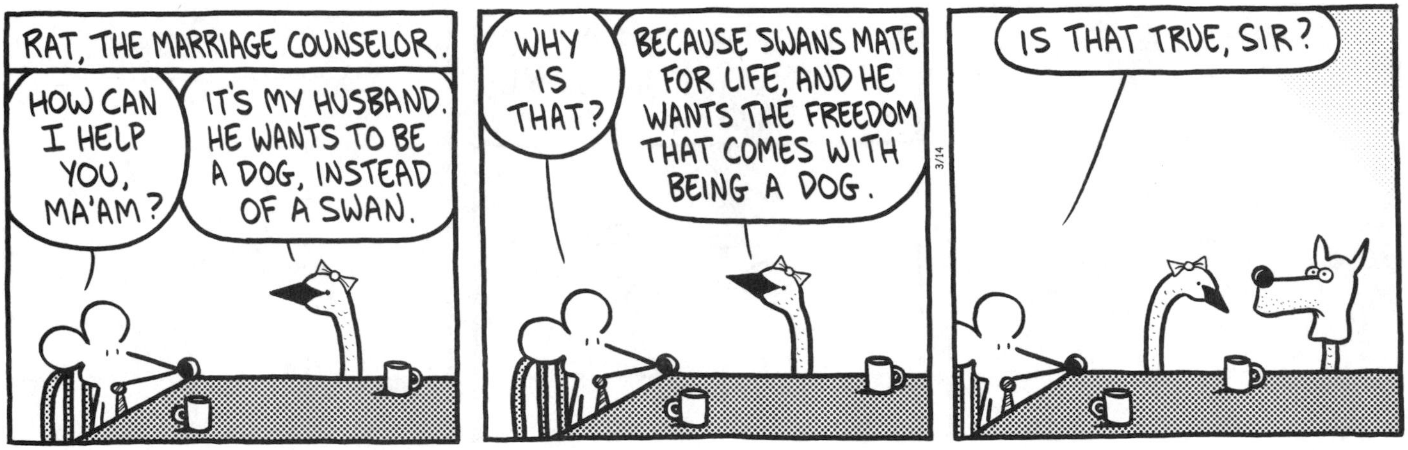
RAT, THE MARRIAGE COUNSELOR.
HOW CAN I HELP YOU, MA'AM?
IT'S MY HUSBAND. HE WANTS TO BE A DOG, INSTEAD OF A SWAN.
WHY IS THAT?
BECAUSE SWANS MATE FOR LIFE, AND HE WANTS THE FREEDOM THAT COMES WITH BEING A DOG.
3/14
IS THAT TRUE, SIR?

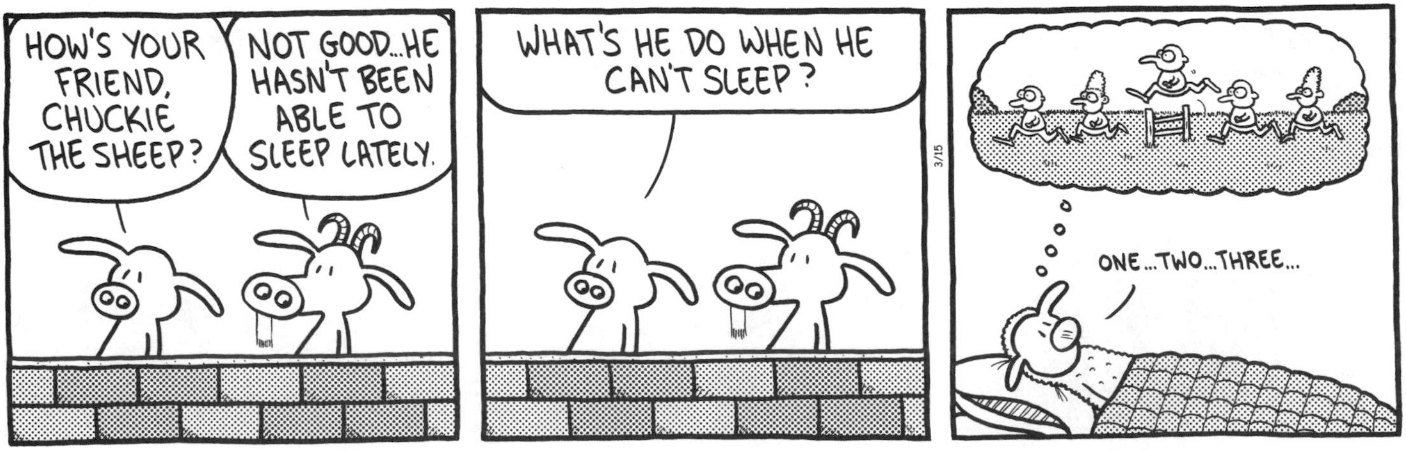
HOW'S YOUR FRIEND, CHUCKIE THE SHEEP?
NOT GOOD...HE HASN'T BEEN ABLE TO SLEEP LATELY.
WHAT'S HE DO WHEN HE CAN'T SLEEP?
3/15
ONE...TWO...THREE...

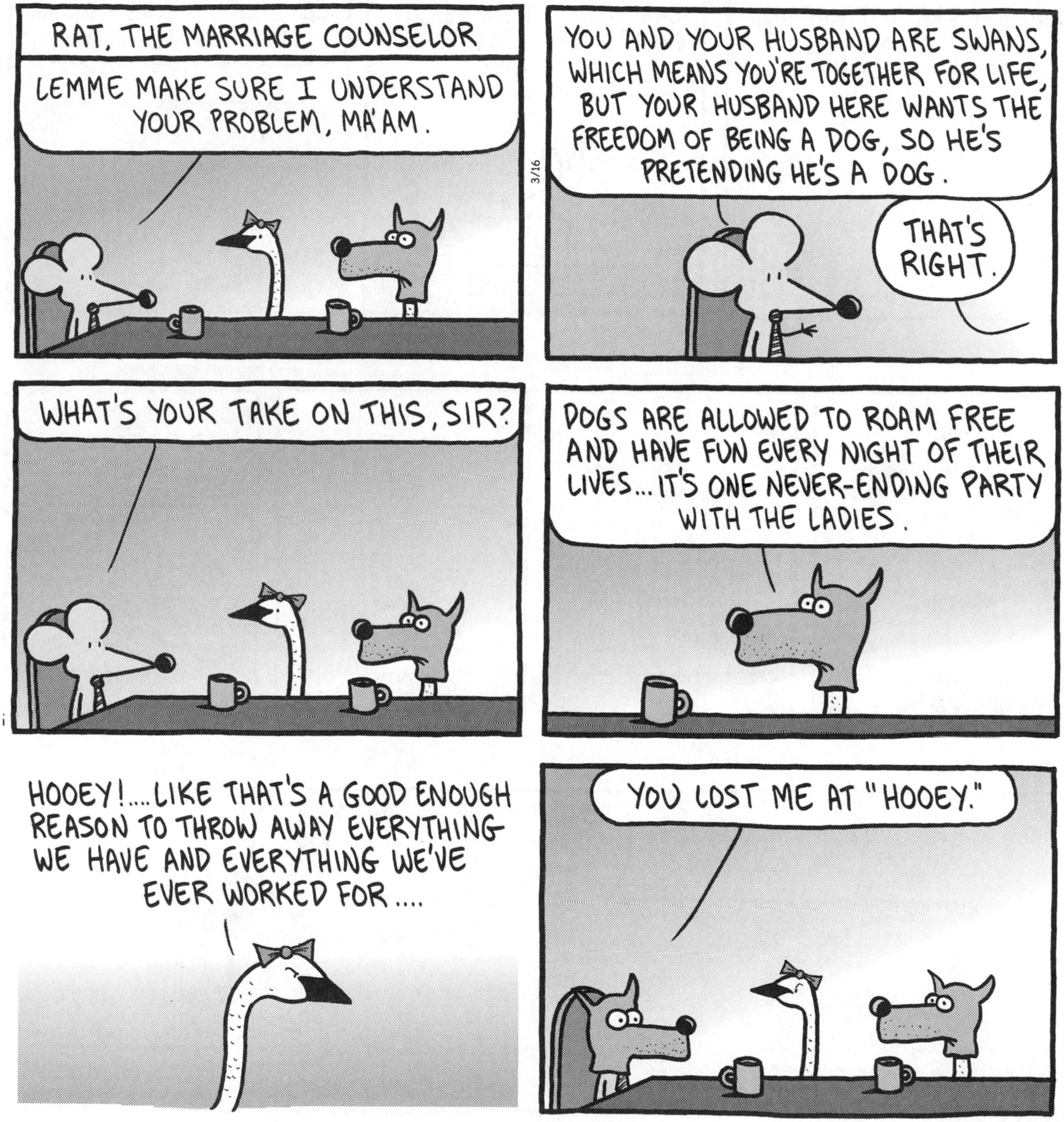
RAT, THE MARRIAGE COUNSELOR
LEMME MAKE SURE I UNDERSTAND YOUR PROBLEM, MA'AM.
3/16
YOU AND YOUR HUSBAND ARE SWANS, WHICH MEANS YOU'RE TOGETHER FOR LIFE, BUT YOUR HUSBAND HERE WANTS THE FREEDOM OF BEING A DOG, SO HE'S PRETENDING HE'S A DOG.
THAT'S RIGHT.
WHAT'S YOUR TAKE ON THIS, SIR?
DOGS ARE ALLOWED TO ROAM FREE AND HAVE FUN EVERY NIGHT OF THEIR LIVES... IT'S ONE NEVER-ENDING PARTY WITH THE LADIES.
HOOEY!.... LIKE THAT'S A GOOD ENOUGH REASON TO THROW AWAY EVERYTHING WE HAVE AND EVERYTHING WE'VE EVER WORKED FOR....
YOU LOST ME AT "HOOEY."

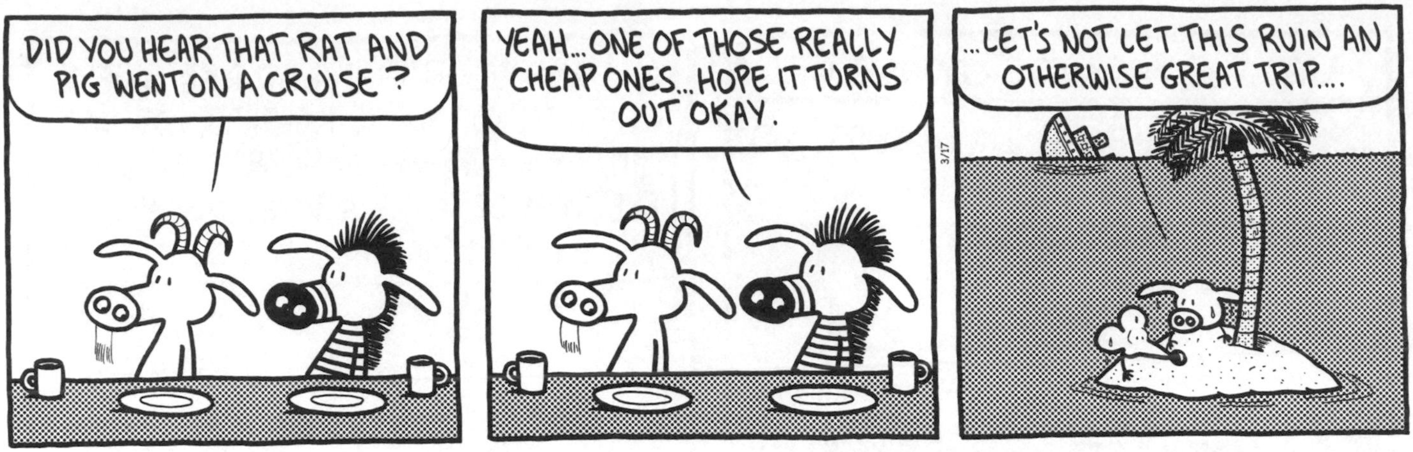
DID YOU HEAR THAT RAT AND PIG WENT ON A CRUISE?
YEAH... ONE OF THOSE REALLY CHEAP ONES... HOPE IT TURNS OUT OKAY.
3/17
...LET'S NOT LET THIS RUIN AN OTHERWISE GREAT TRIP....

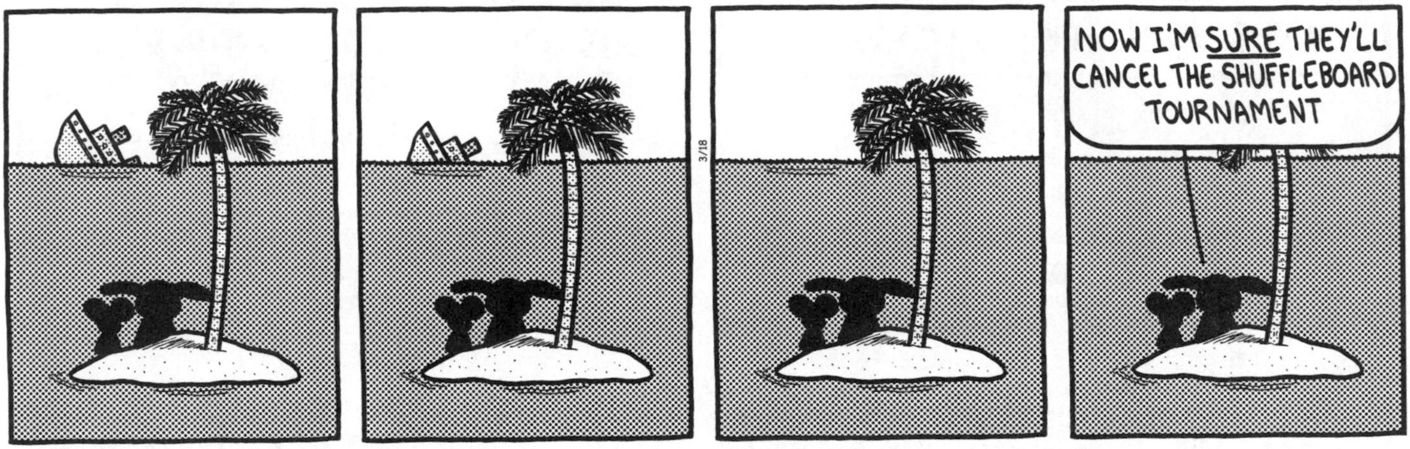
3/18
NOW I'M SURE THEY'LL CANCEL THE SHUFFLEBOARD TOURNAMENT

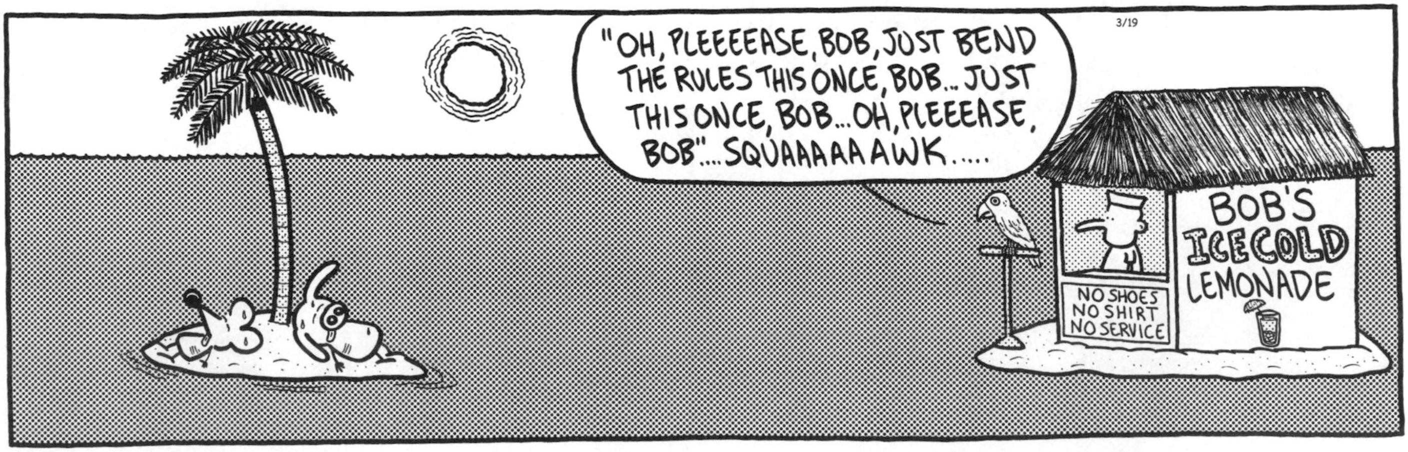
"OH, PLEEEEASE, BOB, JUST BEND THE RULES THIS ONCE, BOB... JUST THIS ONCE, BOB... OH, PLEEEASE, BOB"... SQUAAAAAAWK.....
3/19
BOB'S ICE COLD LEMONADE
NO SHOES NO SHIRT NO SERVICE

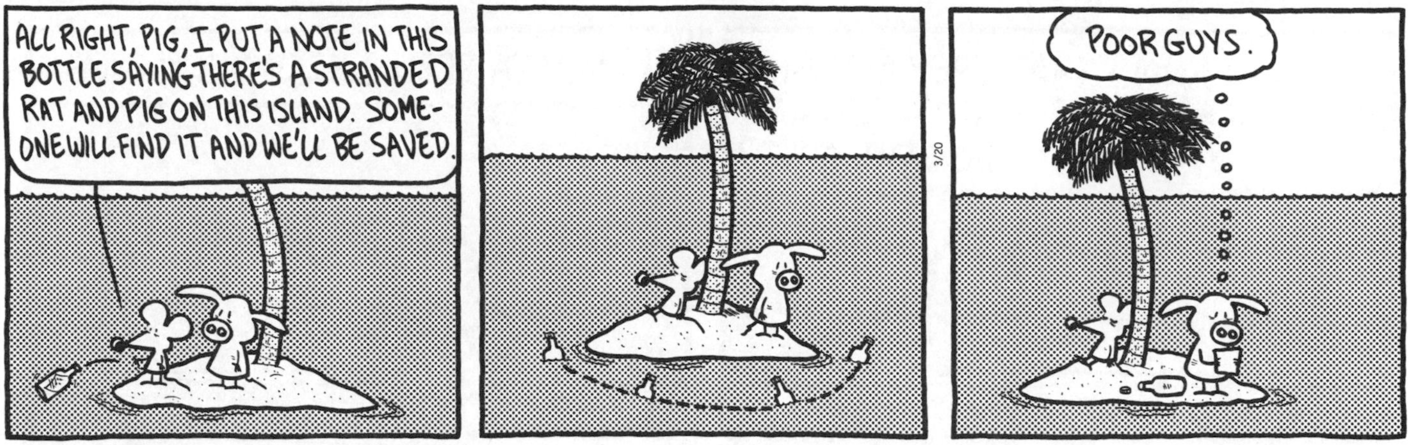
ALL RIGHT, PIG, I PUT A NOTE IN THIS BOTTLE SAYING THERE'S A STRANDED RAT AND PIG ON THIS ISLAND. SOMEONE WILL FIND IT AND WE'LL BE SAVED.
3/20
POOR GUYS.

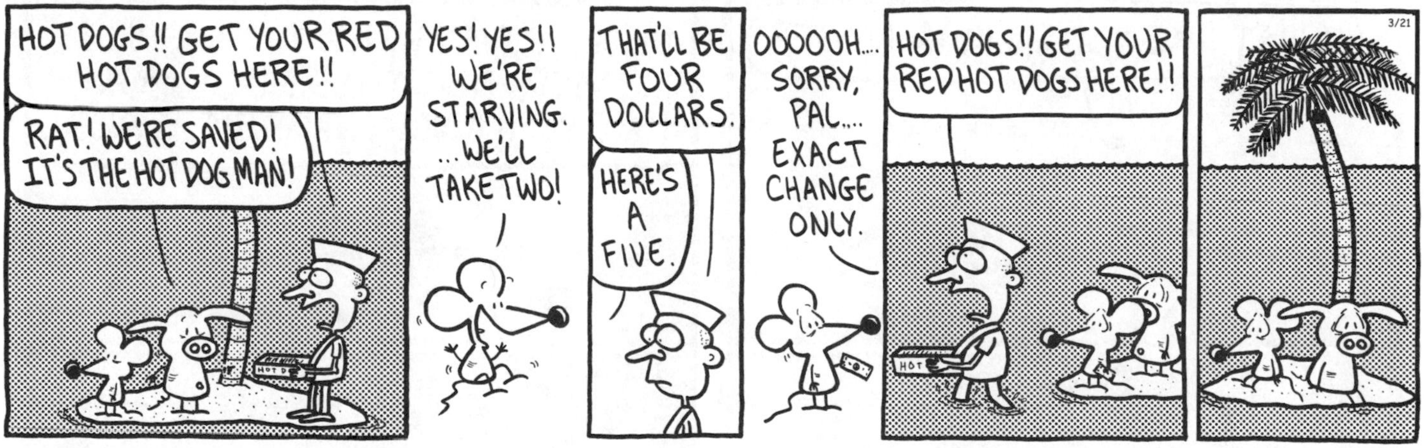
HOT DOGS!! GET YOUR RED HOT DOGS HERE!!
RAT! WE'RE SAVED! IT'S THE HOT DOG MAN!
HOT D
YES! YES!! WE'RE STARVING. ...WE'LL TAKE TWO!
THAT'LL BE FOUR DOLLARS.
HERE'S A FIVE.
OOOOOH.... SORRY, PAL.... EXACT CHANGE ONLY.
HOT DOGS!! GET YOUR RED HOT DOGS HERE!!
HOT
3/21

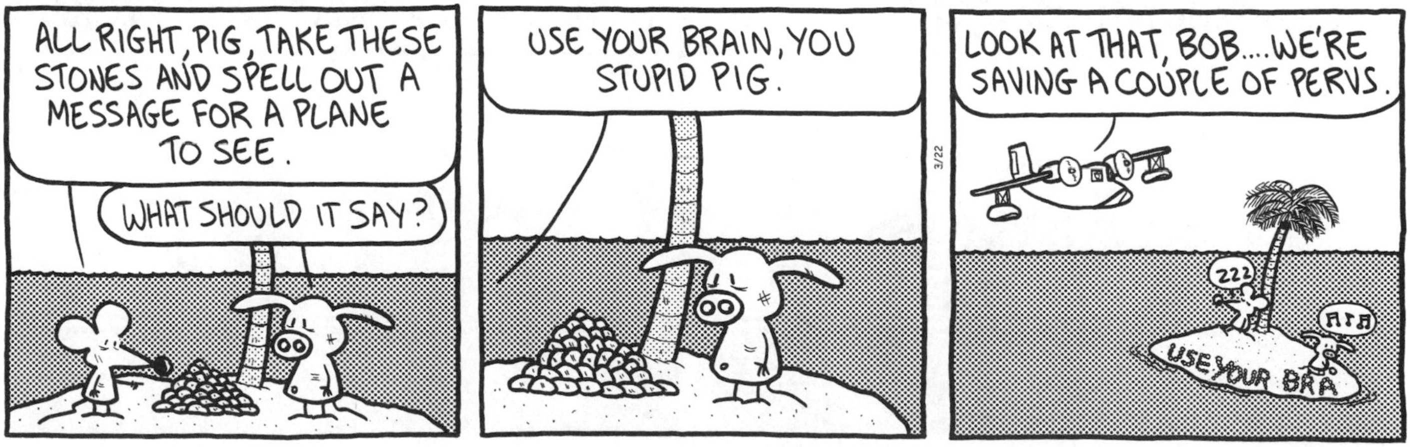
ALL RIGHT, PIG, TAKE THESE STONES AND SPELL OUT A MESSAGE FOR A PLANE TO SEE.
WHAT SHOULD IT SAY?
USE YOUR BRAIN, YOU STUPID PIG.
3/22
LOOK AT THAT, BOB....WE'RE SAVING A COUPLE OF PERVS.
ZZZ
USE YOUR BRA

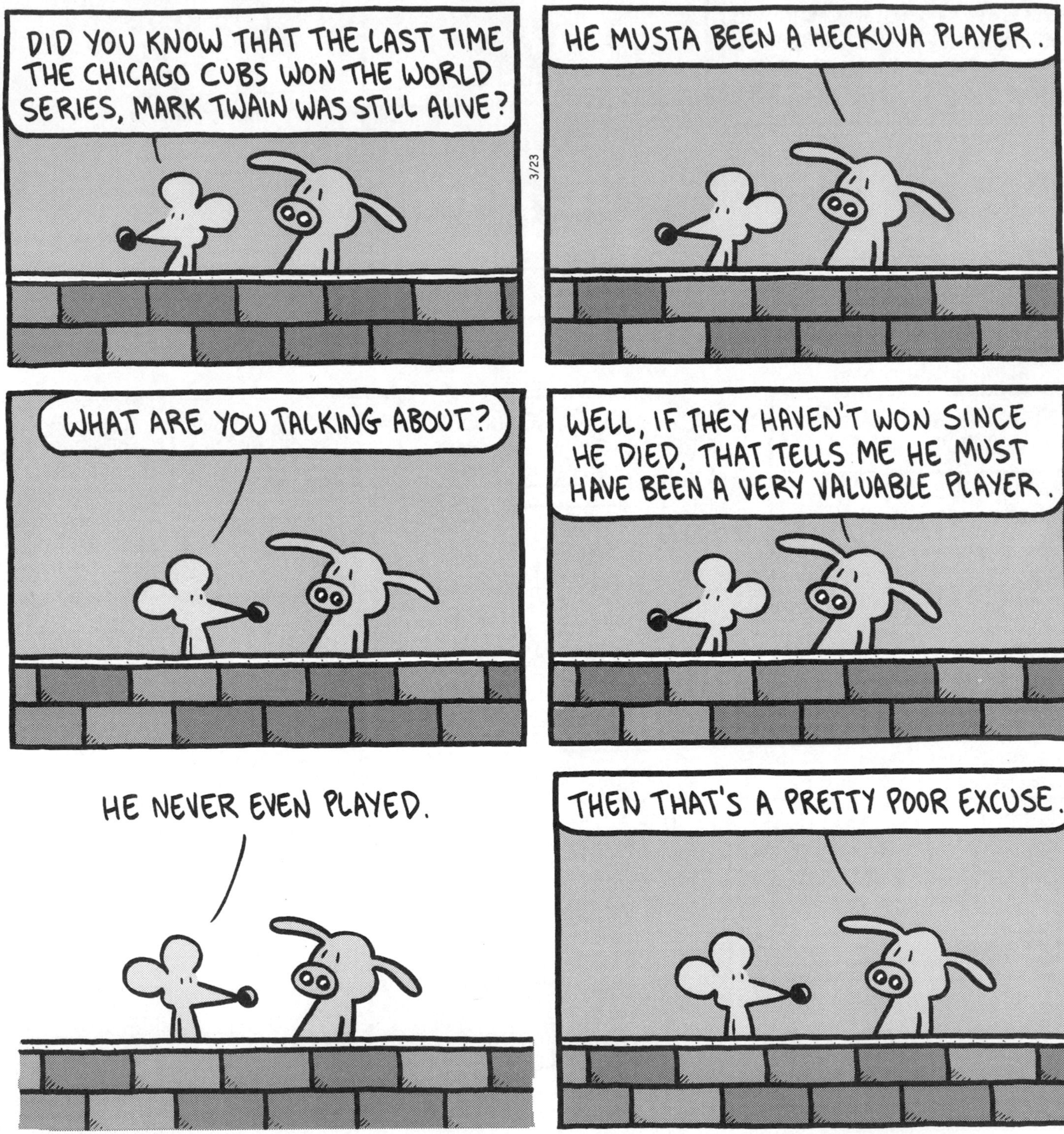
DID YOU KNOW THAT THE LAST TIME THE CHICAGO CUBS WON THE WORLD SERIES, MARK TWAIN WAS STILL ALIVE?
3/23
HE MUSTA BEEN A HECKUVA PLAYER.
WHAT ARE YOU TALKING ABOUT?
WELL, IF THEY HAVEN'T WON SINCE HE DIED, THAT TELLS ME HE MUST HAVE BEEN A VERY VALUABLE PLAYER.
HE NEVER EVEN PLAYED.
THEN THAT'S A PRETTY POOR EXCUSE.

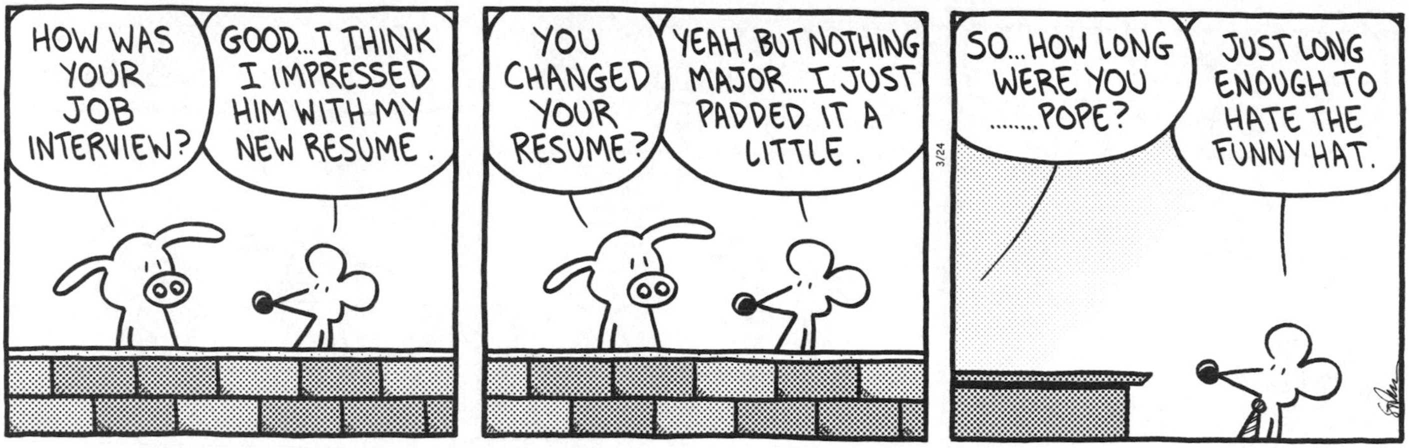
HOW WAS YOUR JOB INTERVIEW?
GOOD...I THINK I IMPRESSED HIM WITH MY NEW RESUME.
YOU CHANGED YOUR RESUME?
YEAH, BUT NOTHING MAJOR....I JUST PADDED IT A LITTLE.
3/24
SO...HOW LONG WERE YOU ....POPE?
JUST LONG ENOUGH TO HATE THE FUNNY HAT.

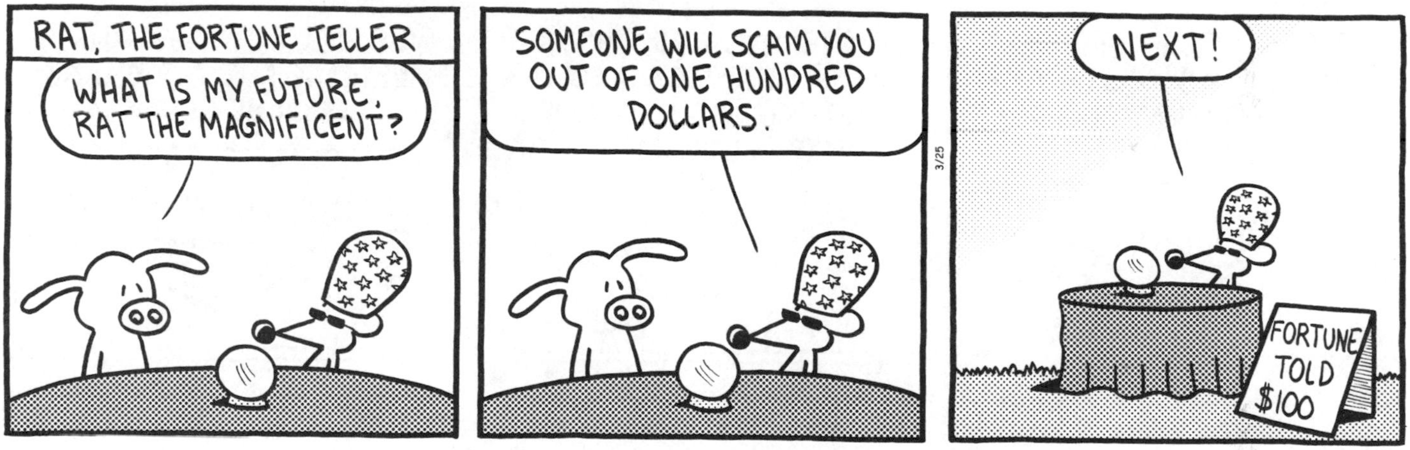
RAT, THE FORTUNE TELLER
WHAT IS MY FUTURE, RAT THE MAGNIFICENT?
SOMEONE WILL SCAM YOU OUT OF ONE HUNDRED DOLLARS.
3/25
NEXT!
FORTUNE TOLD $100

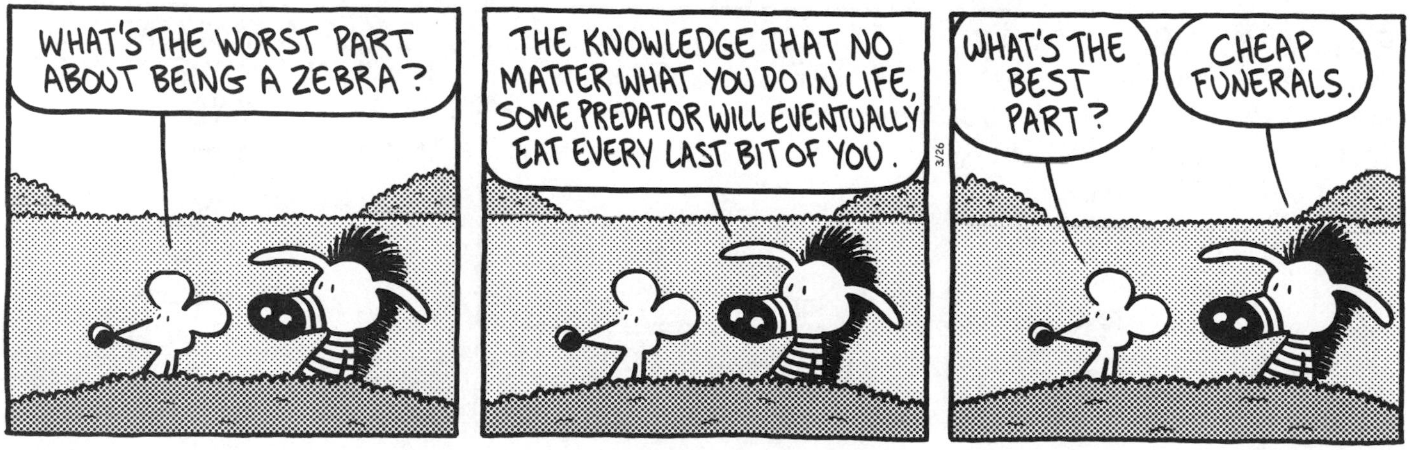
WHAT'S THE WORST PART ABOUT BEING A ZEBRA?
THE KNOWLEDGE THAT NO MATTER WHAT YOU DO IN LIFE, SOME PREDATOR WILL EVENTUALLY EAT EVERY LAST BIT OF YOU.
3/26
WHAT'S THE BEST PART?
CHEAP FUNERALS.

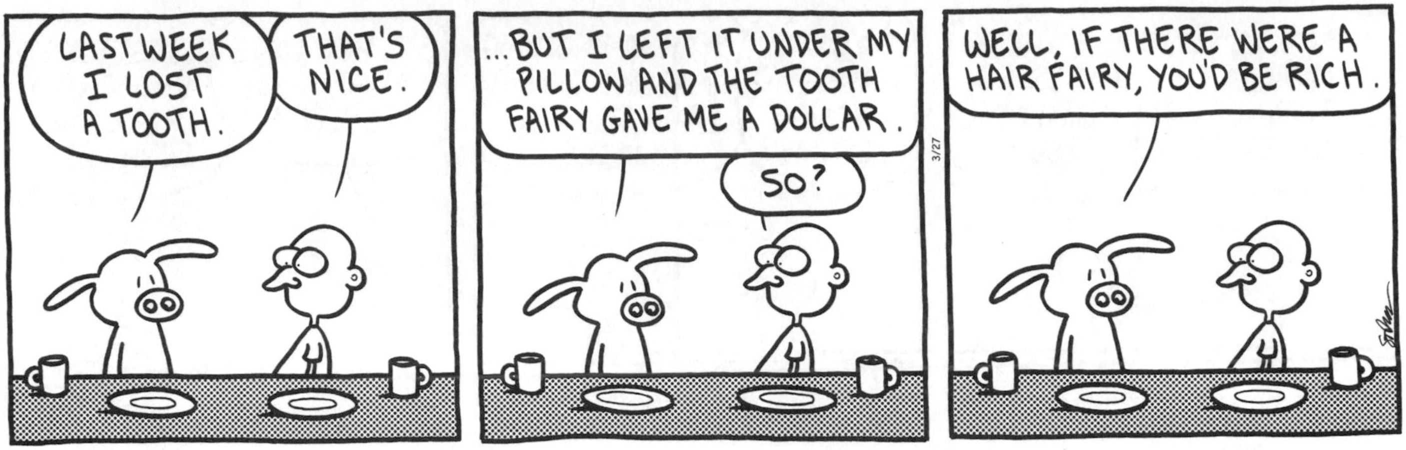
LAST WEEK I LOST A TOOTH.
THAT'S NICE.
...BUT I LEFT IT UNDER MY PILLOW AND THE TOOTH FAIRY GAVE ME A DOLLAR.
SO?
3/27
WELL, IF THERE WERE A HAIR FAIRY, YOU'D BE RICH.

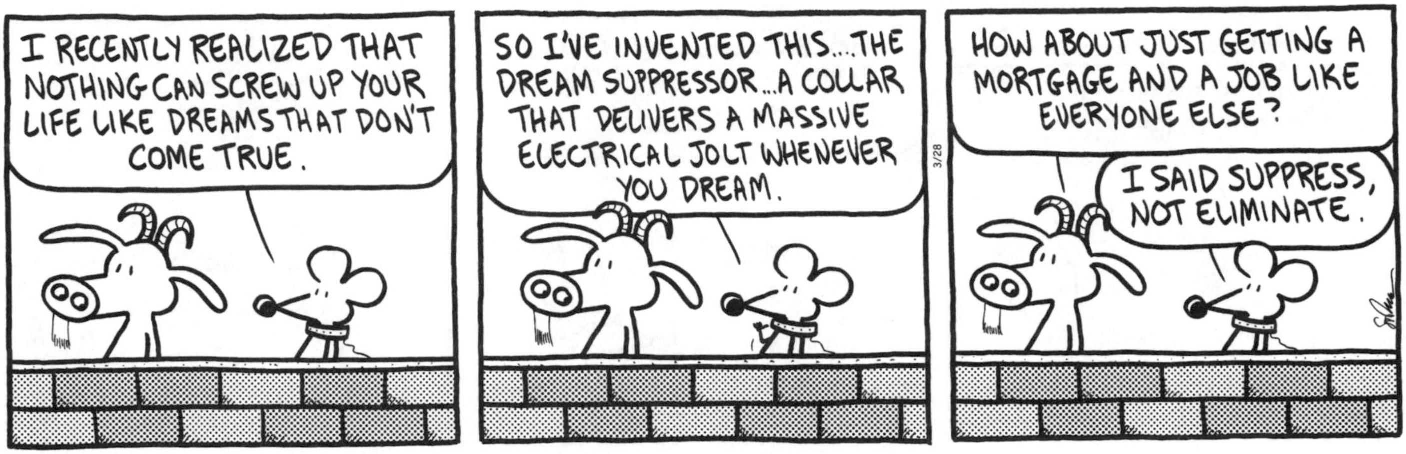
I RECENTLY REALIZED THAT NOTHING CAN SCREW UP YOUR LIFE LIKE DREAMS THAT DON'T COME TRUE.
SO I'VE INVENTED THIS....THE DREAM SUPPRESSOR...A COLLAR THAT DELIVERS A MASSIVE ELECTRICAL JOLT WHENEVER YOU DREAM.
3/28
HOW ABOUT JUST GETTING A MORTGAGE AND A JOB LIKE EVERYONE ELSE?
I SAID SUPPRESS, NOT ELIMINATE.

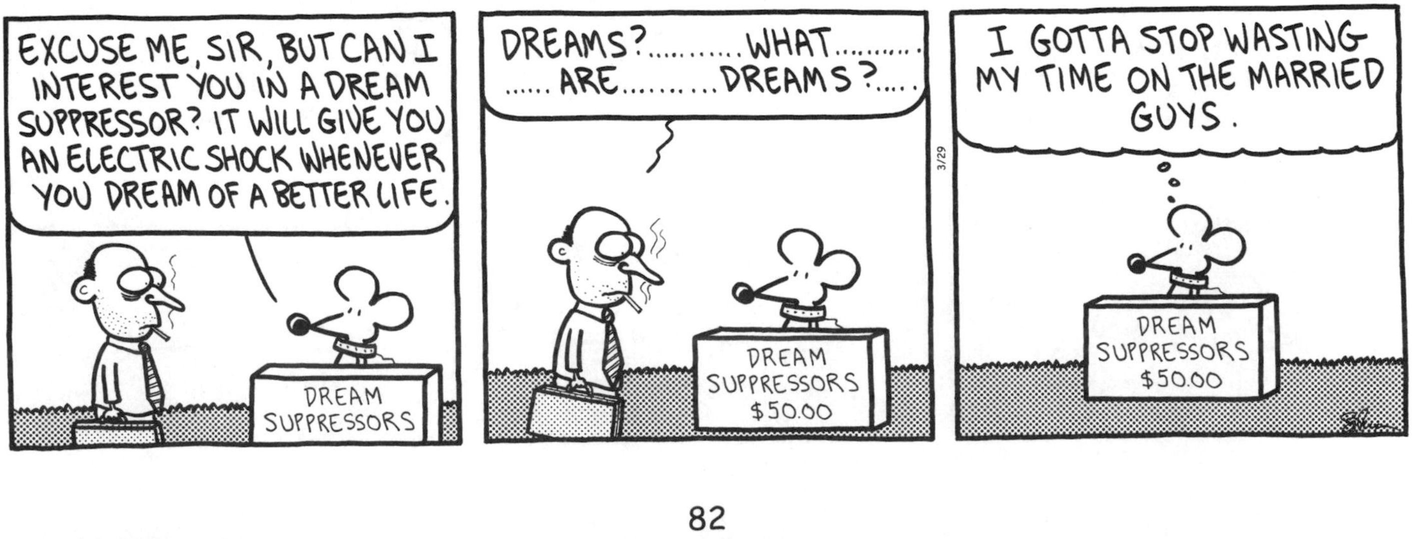
EXCUSE ME, SIR, BUT CAN I INTEREST YOU IN A DREAM SUPPRESSOR? IT WILL GIVE YOU AN ELECTRIC SHOCK WHENEVER YOU DREAM OF A BETTER LIFE.
DREAM SUPPRESSORS
DREAMS?..........WHAT.......... ......ARE..........DREAMS?.....
DREAM SUPPRESSORS $50.00
3/29
I GOTTA STOP WASTING MY TIME ON THE MARRIED GUYS.
DREAM SUPPRESSORS $50.00

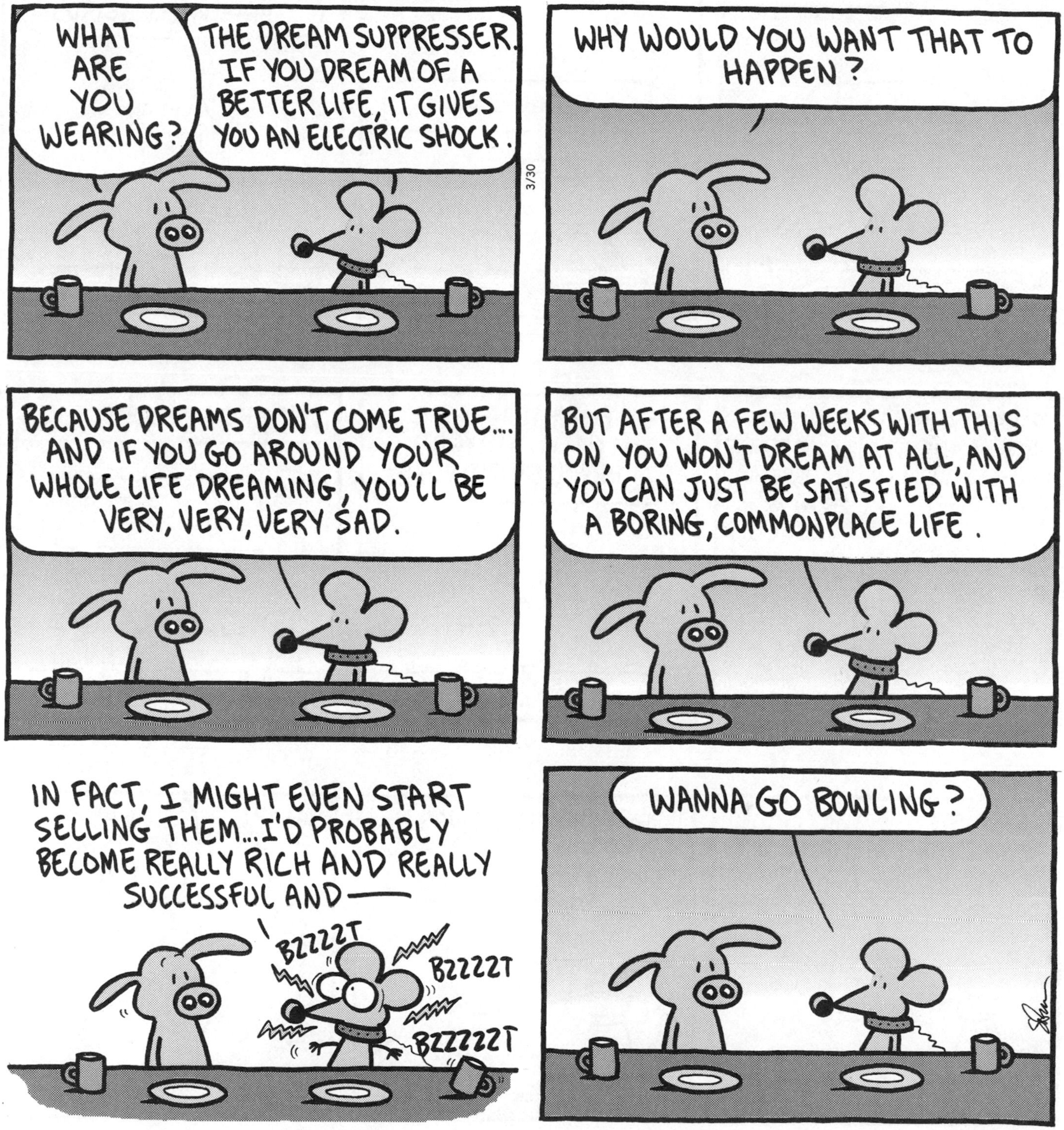
WHAT ARE YOU WEARING?
THE DREAM SUPPRESSER. IF YOU DREAM OF A BETTER LIFE, IT GIVES YOU AN ELECTRIC SHOCK.
3/30
WHY WOULD YOU WANT THAT TO HAPPEN?
BECAUSE DREAMS DON'T COME TRUE.... AND IF YOU GO AROUND YOUR WHOLE LIFE DREAMING, YOU'LL BE VERY, VERY, VERY SAD.
BUT AFTER A FEW WEEKS WITH THIS ON, YOU WON'T DREAM AT ALL, AND YOU CAN JUST BE SATISFIED WITH A BORING, COMMONPLACE LIFE.
IN FACT, I MIGHT EVEN START SELLING THEM...I'D PROBABLY BECOME REALLY RICH AND REALLY SUCCESSFUL AND—
BZZZZT
BZZZZT
BZZZZZT
WANNA GO BOWLING?

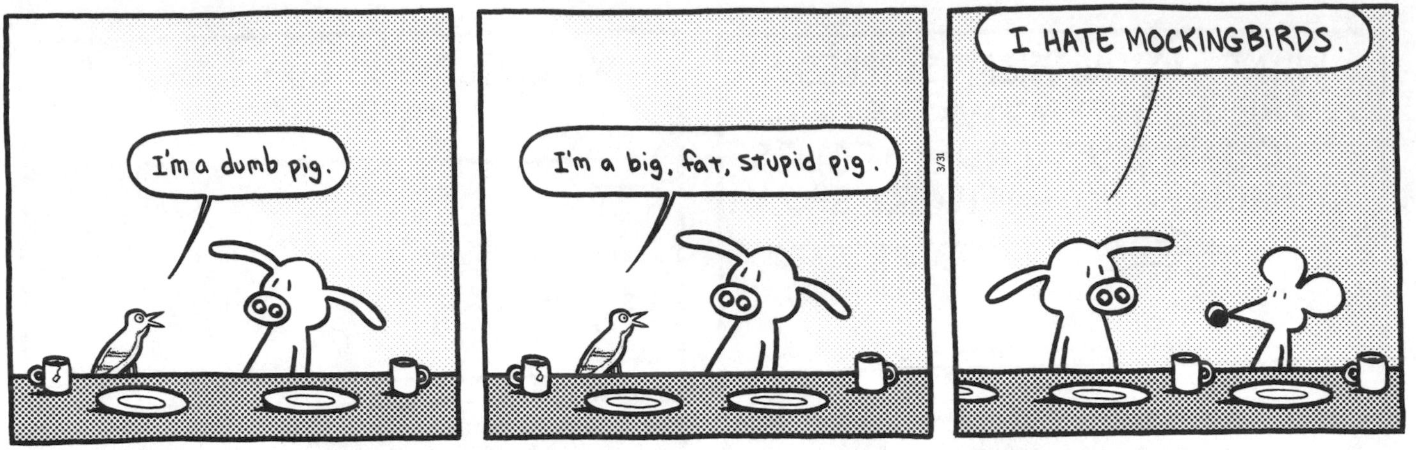
I'm a dumb pig.
I'm a big, fat, stupid pig.
3/31
I HATE MOCKINGBIRDS.

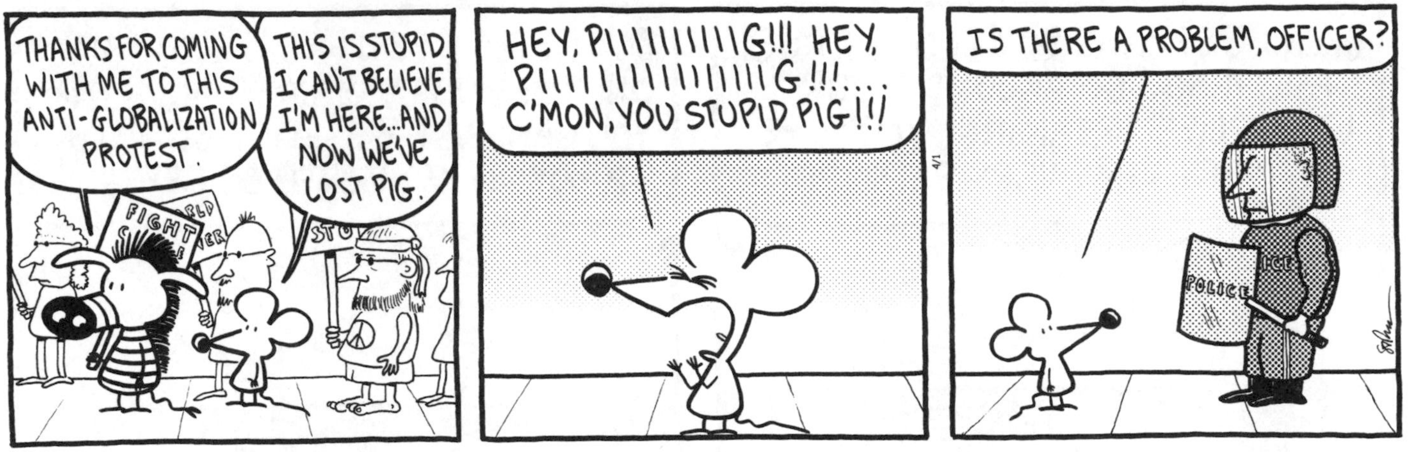
THANKS FOR COMING WITH ME TO THIS ANTI-GLOBALIZATION PROTEST.
THIS IS STUPID. I CAN'T BELIEVE I'M HERE...AND NOW WE'VE LOST PIG.
FIGHT
4/1
HEY, PIIIIIIIIIIG!!! HEY, PIIIIIIIIIIIIIIIIG!!!.... C'MON, YOU STUPID PIG!!!
IS THERE A PROBLEM, OFFICER?
POLICE

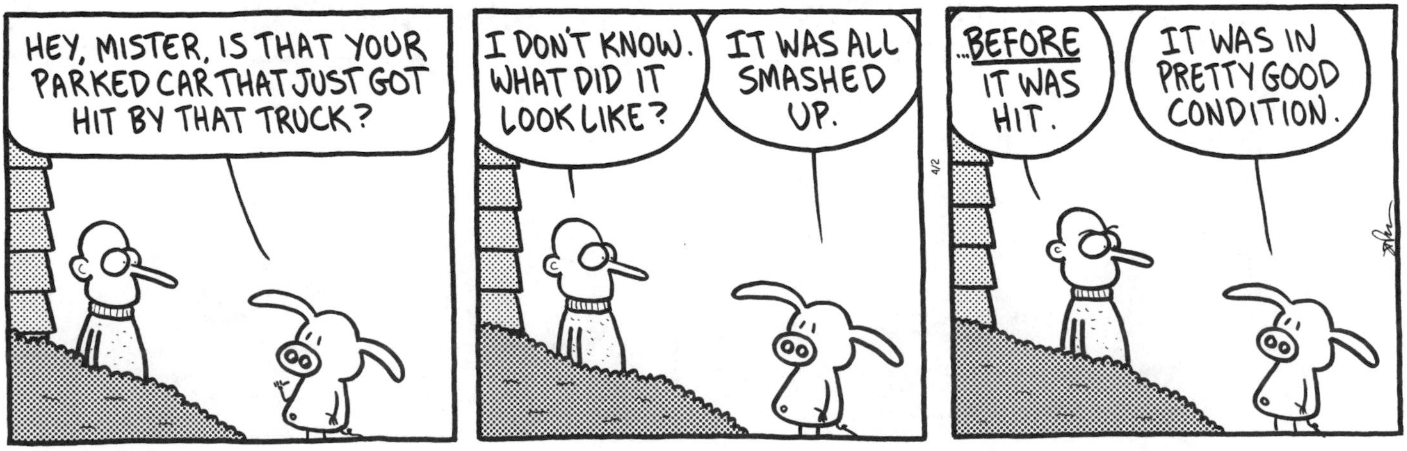
HEY, MISTER, IS THAT YOUR PARKED CAR THAT JUST GOT HIT BY THAT TRUCK?
I DON'T KNOW. WHAT DID IT LOOK LIKE?
IT WAS ALL SMASHED UP.
4/2
...BEFORE IT WAS HIT.
IT WAS IN PRETTY GOOD CONDITION.

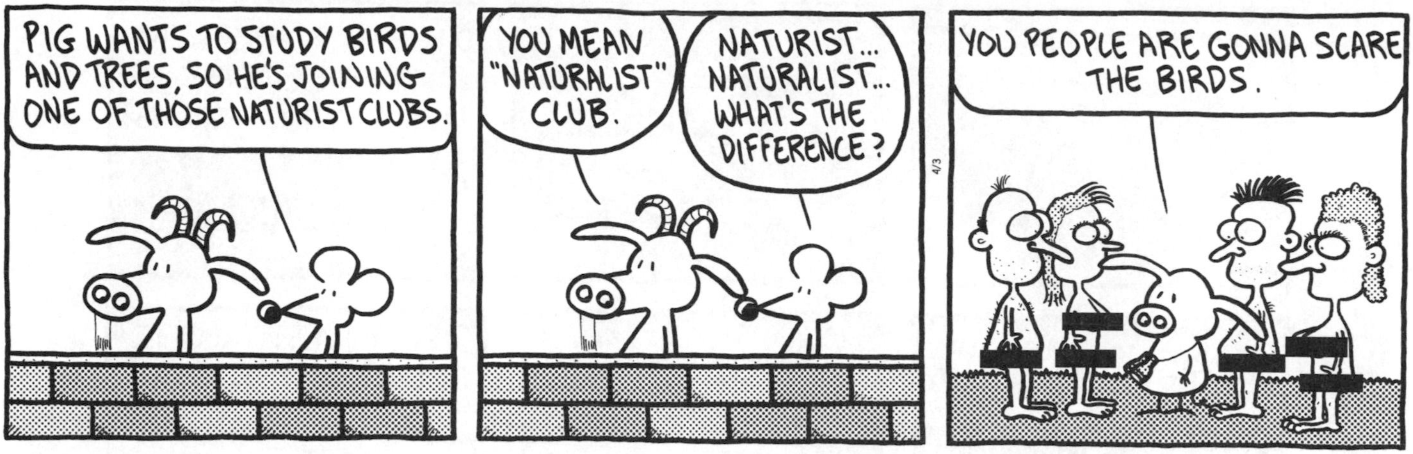
PIG WANTS TO STUDY BIRDS AND TREES, SO HE'S JOINING ONE OF THOSE NATURIST CLUBS.
YOU MEAN "NATURALIST" CLUB.
NATURIST... NATURALIST... WHAT'S THE DIFFERENCE?
4/3
YOU PEOPLE ARE GONNA SCARE THE BIRDS.

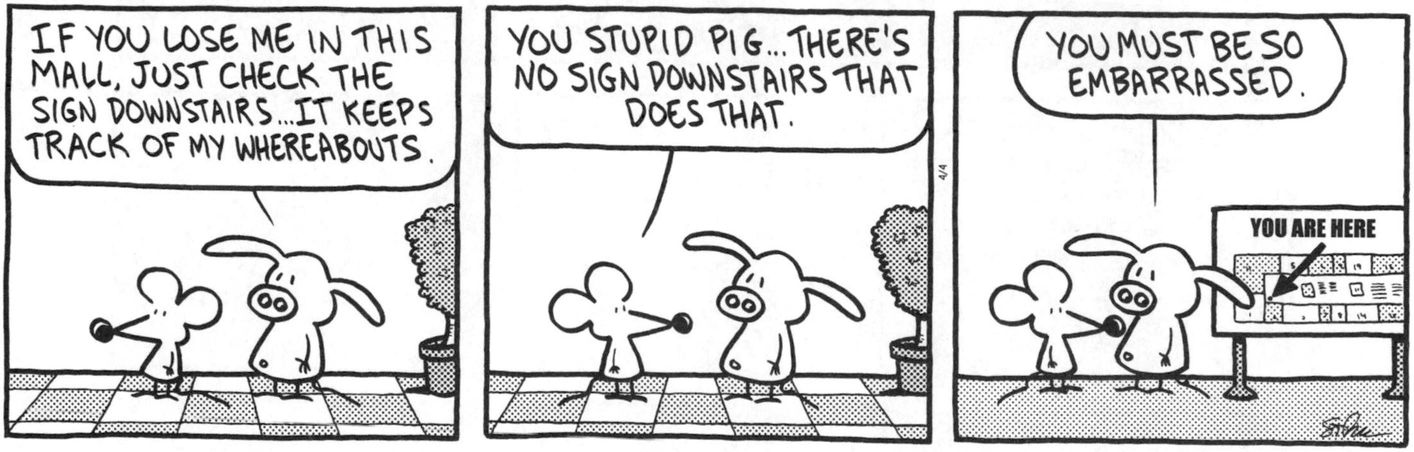
IF YOU LOSE ME IN THIS MALL, JUST CHECK THE SIGN DOWNSTAIRS...IT KEEPS TRACK OF MY WHEREABOUTS.
YOU STUPID PIG... THERE'S NO SIGN DOWNSTAIRS THAT DOES THAT.
4/4
YOU MUST BE SO EMBARRASSED.
YOU ARE HERE

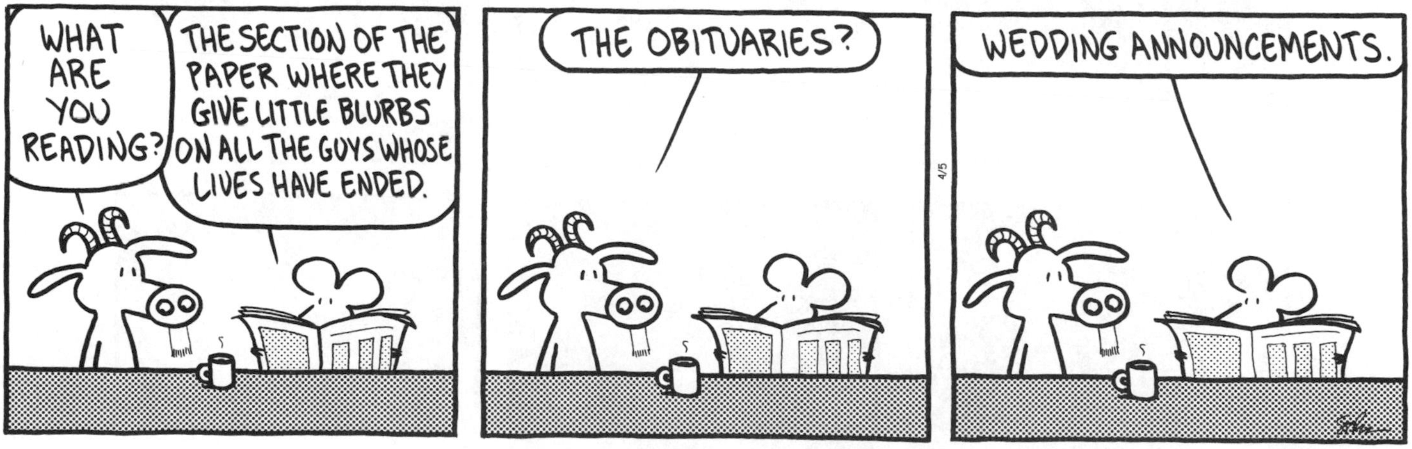
WHAT ARE YOU READING?
THE SECTION OF THE PAPER WHERE THEY GIVE LITTLE BLURBS ON ALL THE GUYS WHOSE LIVES HAVE ENDED.
THE OBITUARIES?
4/5
WEDDING ANNOUNCEMENTS.

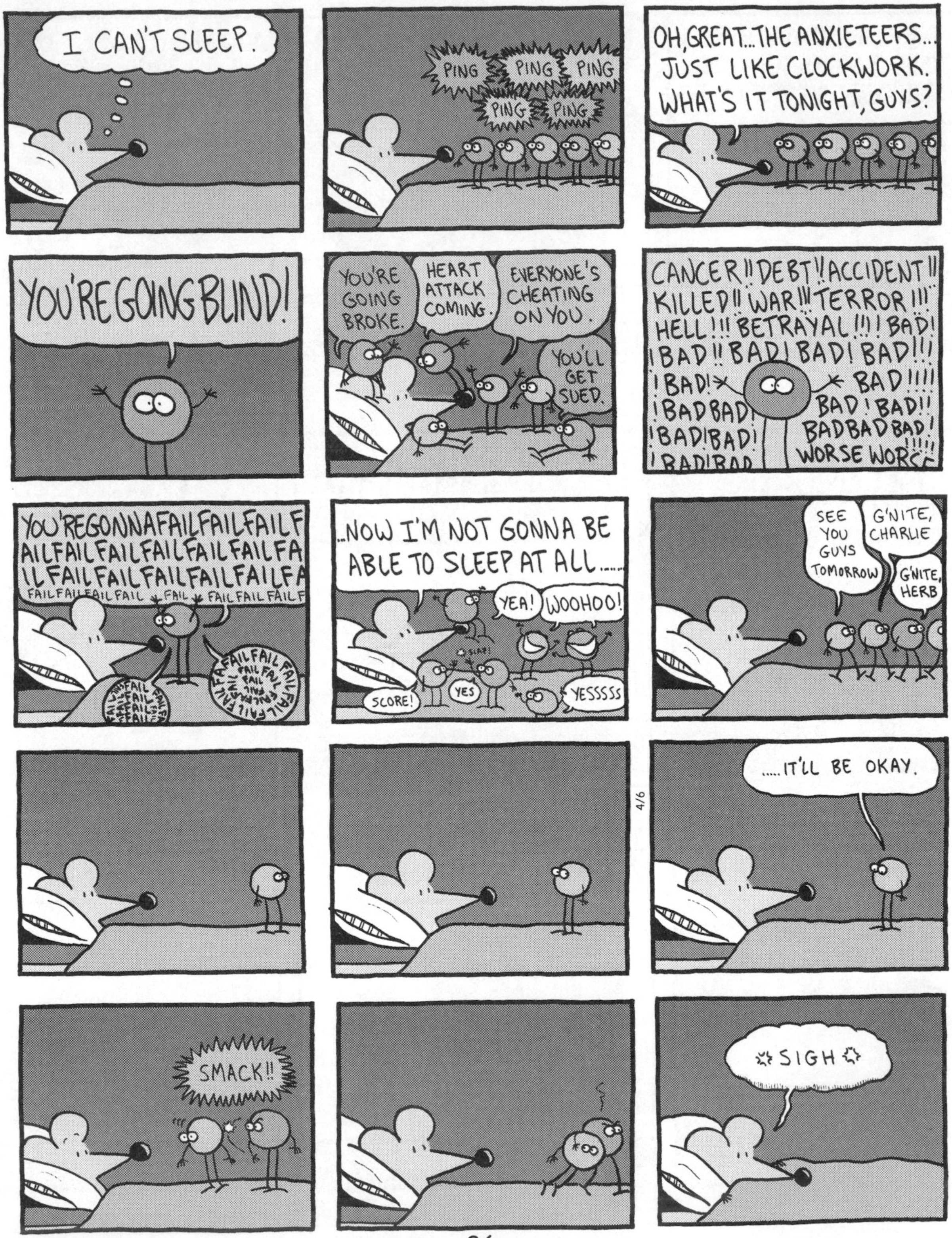

I CAN'T SLEEP.
PING PING PING
PING PING
OH, GREAT... THE ANXIETEERS... JUST LIKE CLOCKWORK. WHAT'S IT TONIGHT, GUYS?
YOU'RE GOING BLIND!
YOU'RE GOING BROKE.
HEART ATTACK COMING.
EVERYONE'S CHEATING ON YOU.
YOU'LL GET SUED.
CANCER!! DEBT!! ACCIDENT!! KILLED!! WAR!!! TERROR!!! HELL!!! BETRAYAL!!!! BAD! BAD!! BAD! BAD! BAD!!! BAD! BAD!!!! BAD BAD! BAD! BAD!! BAD! BAD! BAD BAD BAD! WORSE
YOU'RE GONNA FAIL FAIL FAIL F AIL FAIL FAIL FAIL FAIL FAIL FA IL FAIL FAIL FAIL FAIL FAIL FA
FAIL FAIL FAIL FAIL FAIL FAIL FAIL FAIL
...NOW I'M NOT GONNA BE ABLE TO SLEEP AT ALL......
YEA!
WOOHOO!
SCORE!
YES
YESSSSS
SEE YOU GUYS TOMORROW
G'NITE, CHARLIE
G'NITE, HERB
.....IT'LL BE OKAY.
SMACK!!
SIGH

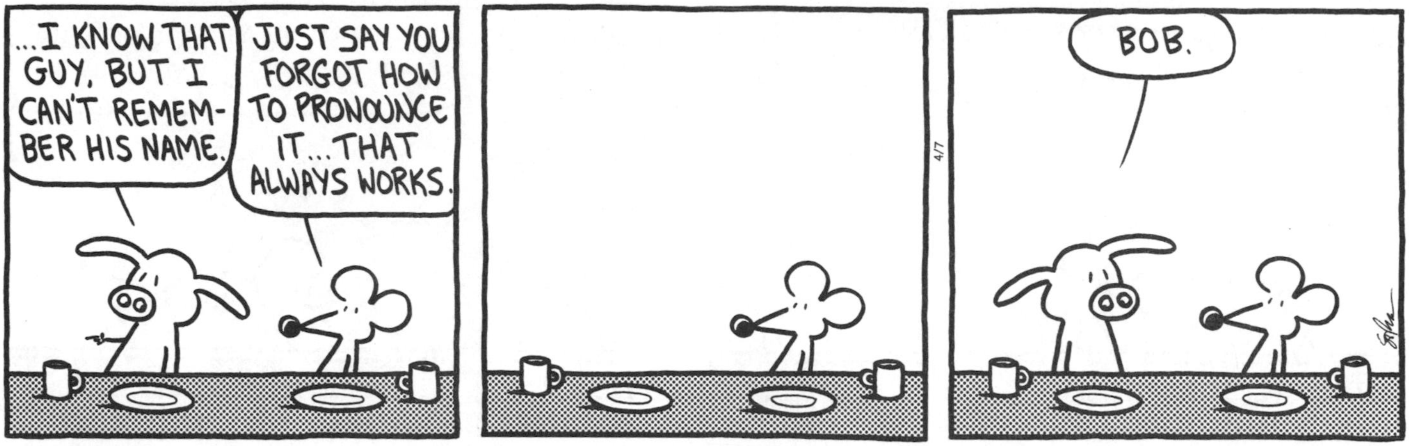
...I KNOW THAT GUY. BUT I CAN'T REMEMBER HIS NAME.
JUST SAY YOU FORGOT HOW TO PRONOUNCE IT...THAT ALWAYS WORKS.
4/7
BOB.

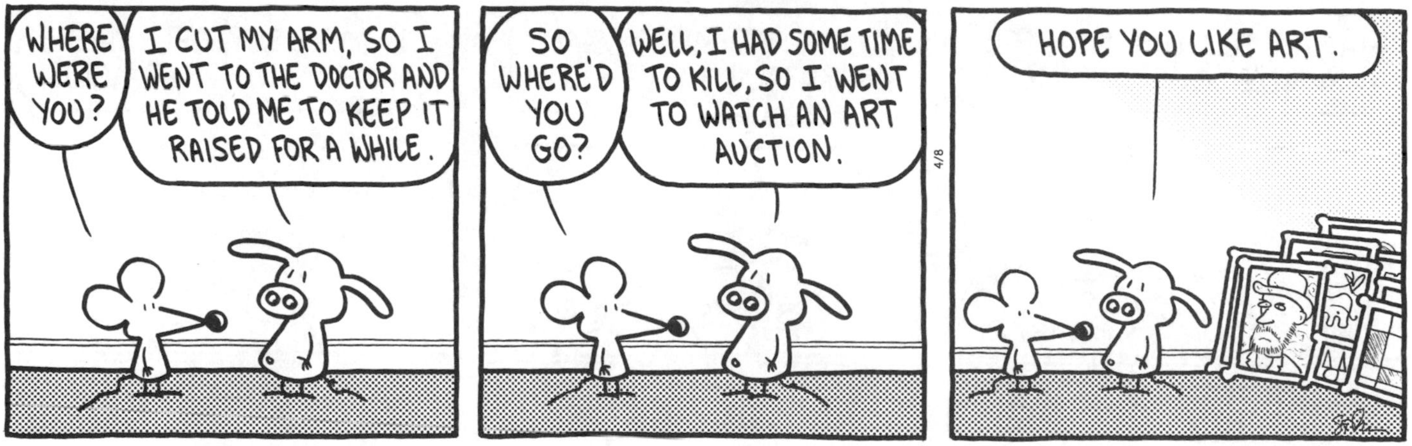
WHERE WERE YOU?
I CUT MY ARM, SO I WENT TO THE DOCTOR AND HE TOLD ME TO KEEP IT RAISED FOR A WHILE.
SO WHERE'D YOU GO?
WELL, I HAD SOME TIME TO KILL, SO I WENT TO WATCH AN ART AUCTION.
4/8
HOPE YOU LIKE ART.

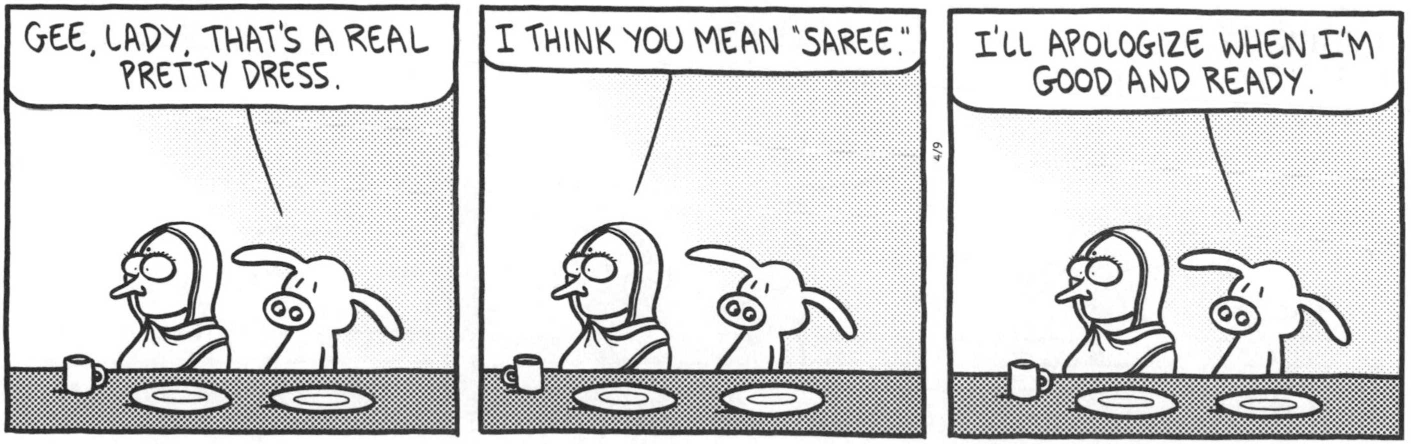
GEE, LADY, THAT'S A REAL PRETTY DRESS.
I THINK YOU MEAN "SAREE."
4/9
I'LL APOLOGIZE WHEN I'M GOOD AND READY.

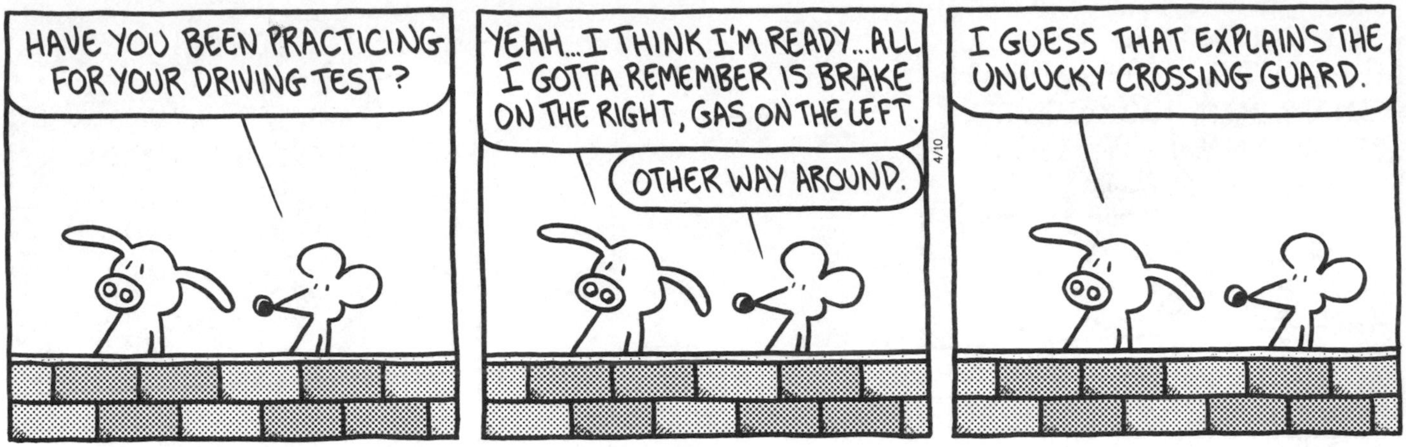
HAVE YOU BEEN PRACTICING FOR YOUR DRIVING TEST?
YEAH...I THINK I'M READY...ALL I GOTTA REMEMBER IS BRAKE ON THE RIGHT, GAS ON THE LEFT.
OTHER WAY AROUND.
4/10
I GUESS THAT EXPLAINS THE UNLUCKY CROSSING GUARD.

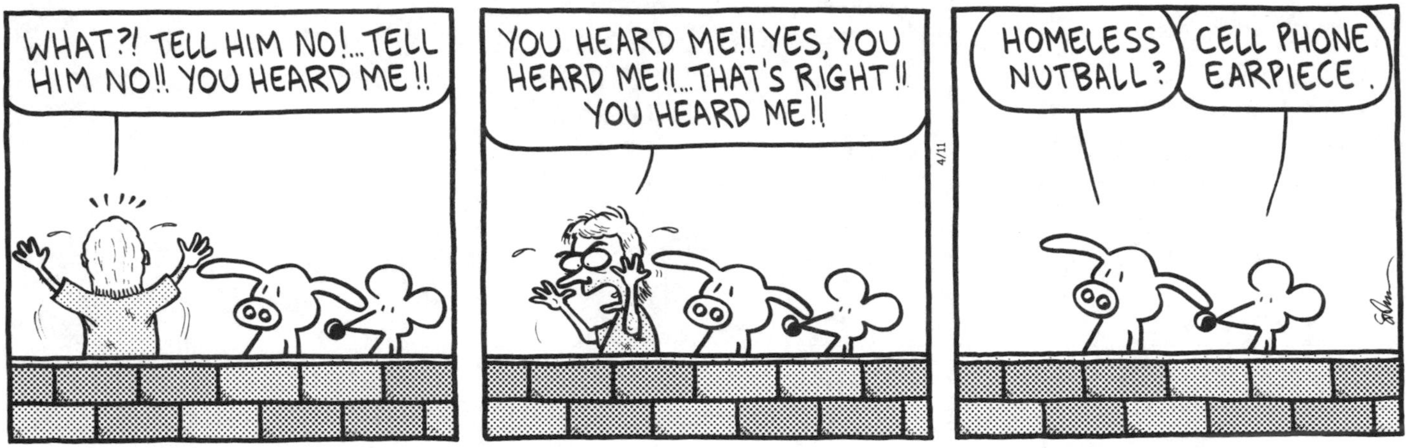
WHAT?! TELL HIM NO!...TELL HIM NO!! YOU HEARD ME!!
YOU HEARD ME!! YES, YOU HEARD ME!!...THAT'S RIGHT!! YOU HEARD ME!!
4/11
HOMELESS NUTBALL?
CELL PHONE EARPIECE.

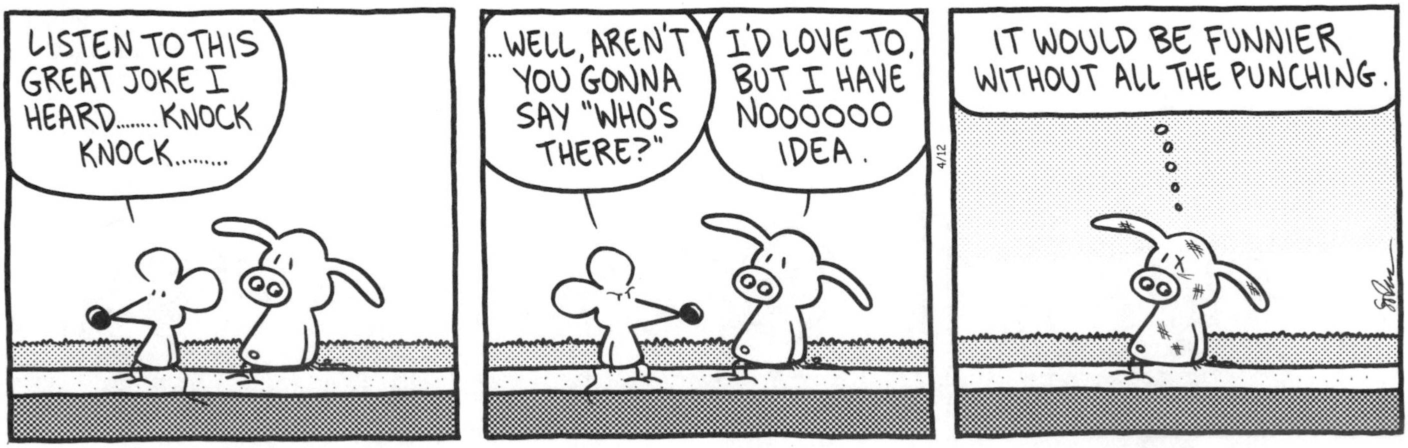
LISTEN TO THIS GREAT JOKE I HEARD........KNOCK KNOCK.........
...WELL, AREN'T YOU GONNA SAY "WHO'S THERE?"
I'D LOVE TO, BUT I HAVE NOOOOOO IDEA.
4/12
IT WOULD BE FUNNIER WITHOUT ALL THE PUNCHING.

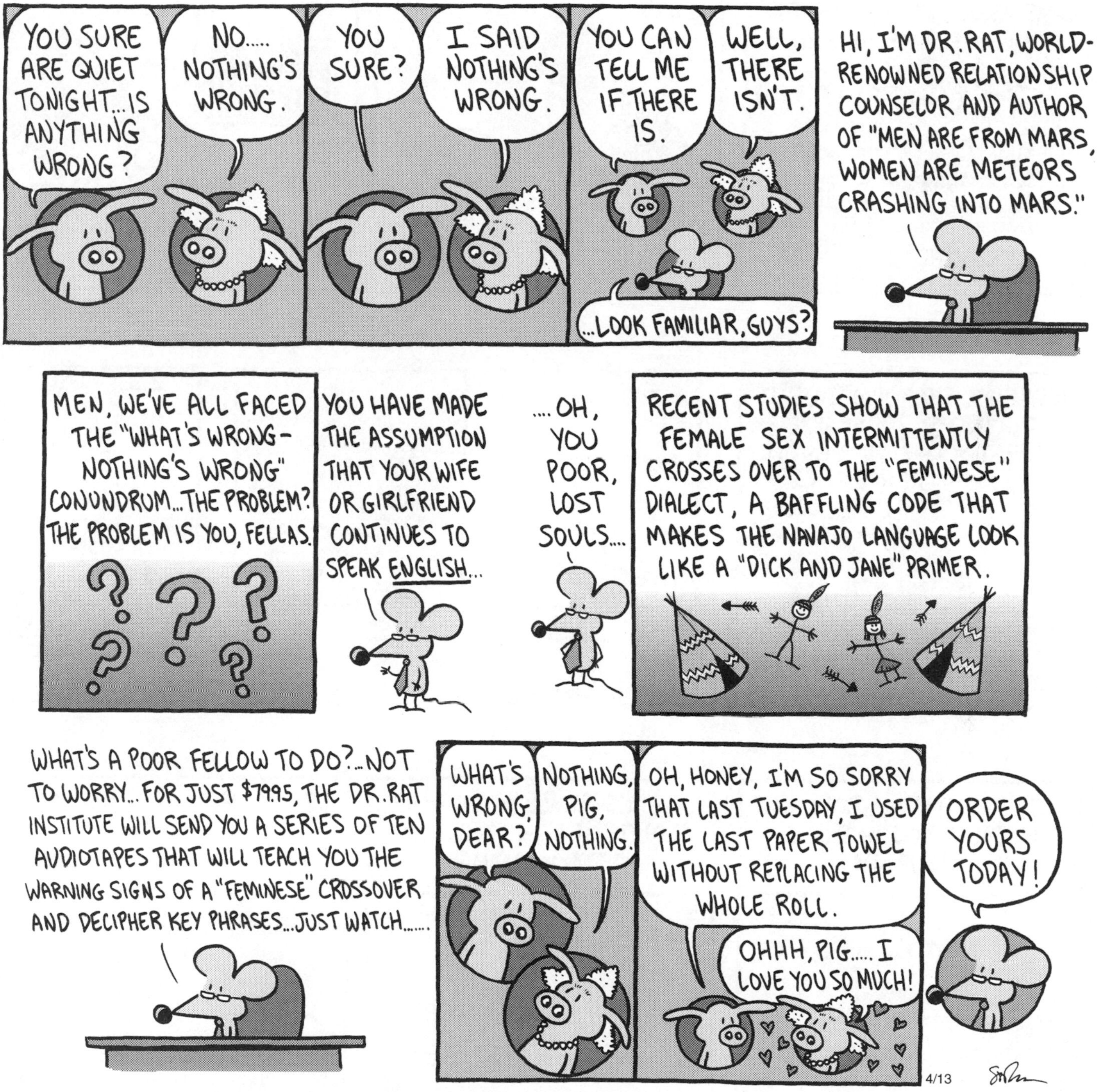
YOU SURE ARE QUIET TONIGHT...IS ANYTHING WRONG?
NO..... NOTHING'S WRONG.
YOU SURE?
I SAID NOTHING'S WRONG.
YOU CAN TELL ME IF THERE IS.
WELL, THERE ISN'T.
...LOOK FAMILIAR, GUYS?
HI, I'M DR. RAT, WORLD-RENOWNED RELATIONSHIP COUNSELOR AND AUTHOR OF "MEN ARE FROM MARS, WOMEN ARE METEORS CRASHING INTO MARS."
MEN, WE'VE ALL FACED THE "WHAT'S WRONG-NOTHING'S WRONG" CONUNDRUM...THE PROBLEM? THE PROBLEM IS YOU, FELLAS.
YOU HAVE MADE THE ASSUMPTION THAT YOUR WIFE OR GIRLFRIEND CONTINUES TO SPEAK ENGLISH...
....OH, YOU POOR, LOST SOULS....
RECENT STUDIES SHOW THAT THE FEMALE SEX INTERMITTENTLY CROSSES OVER TO THE "FEMINESE" DIALECT, A BAFFLING CODE THAT MAKES THE NAVAJO LANGUAGE LOOK LIKE A "DICK AND JANE" PRIMER.
WHAT'S A POOR FELLOW TO DO?...NOT TO WORRY... FOR JUST $79.95, THE DR. RAT INSTITUTE WILL SEND YOU A SERIES OF TEN AUDIOTAPES THAT WILL TEACH YOU THE WARNING SIGNS OF A "FEMINESE" CROSSOVER AND DECIPHER KEY PHRASES...JUST WATCH.......
WHAT'S WRONG, DEAR?
NOTHING, PIG, NOTHING.
OH, HONEY, I'M SO SORRY THAT LAST TUESDAY, I USED THE LAST PAPER TOWEL WITHOUT REPLACING THE WHOLE ROLL.
OHHH, PIG..... I LOVE YOU SO MUCH!
ORDER YOURS TODAY!
4/13

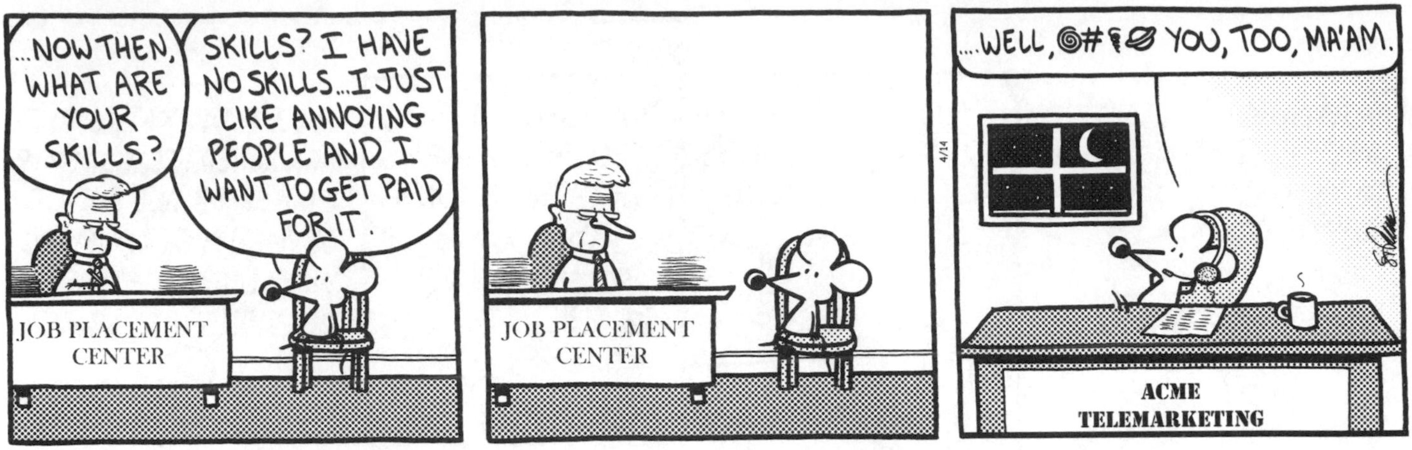
...NOW THEN, WHAT ARE YOUR SKILLS?
SKILLS? I HAVE NO SKILLS...I JUST LIKE ANNOYING PEOPLE AND I WANT TO GET PAID FOR IT.
JOB PLACEMENT CENTER
JOB PLACEMENT CENTER
4/14
....WELL, @#!@ YOU, TOO, MA'AM.
ACME TELEMARKETING

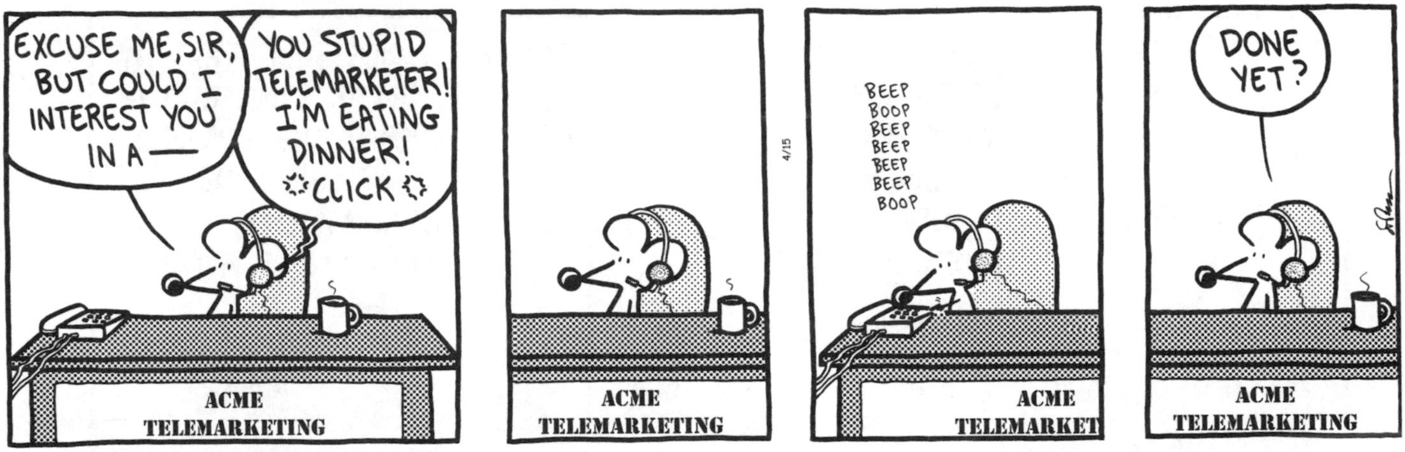
EXCUSE ME, SIR, BUT COULD I INTEREST YOU IN A—
YOU STUPID TELEMARKETER! I'M EATING DINNER! CLICK
ACME TELEMARKETING
ACME TELEMARKETING
4/15
BEEP BOOP BEEP BEEP BEEP BEEP BOOP
ACME TELEMARKET
DONE YET?
ACME TELEMARKETING

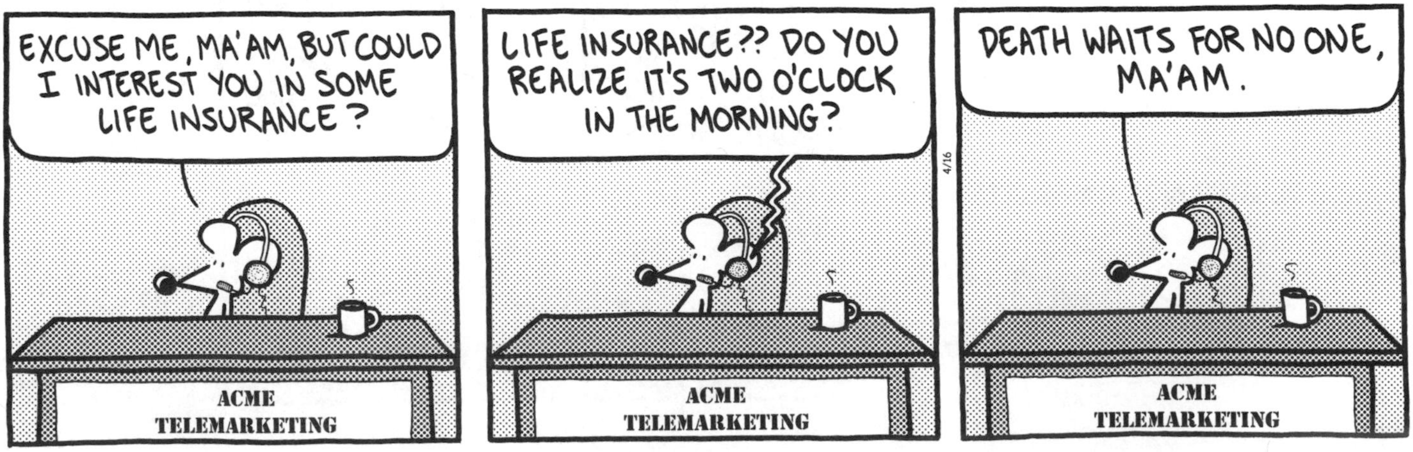
EXCUSE ME, MA'AM, BUT COULD I INTEREST YOU IN SOME LIFE INSURANCE?
ACME TELEMARKETING
LIFE INSURANCE?? DO YOU REALIZE IT'S TWO O'CLOCK IN THE MORNING?
ACME TELEMARKETING
4/16
DEATH WAITS FOR NO ONE, MA'AM.
ACME TELEMARKETING

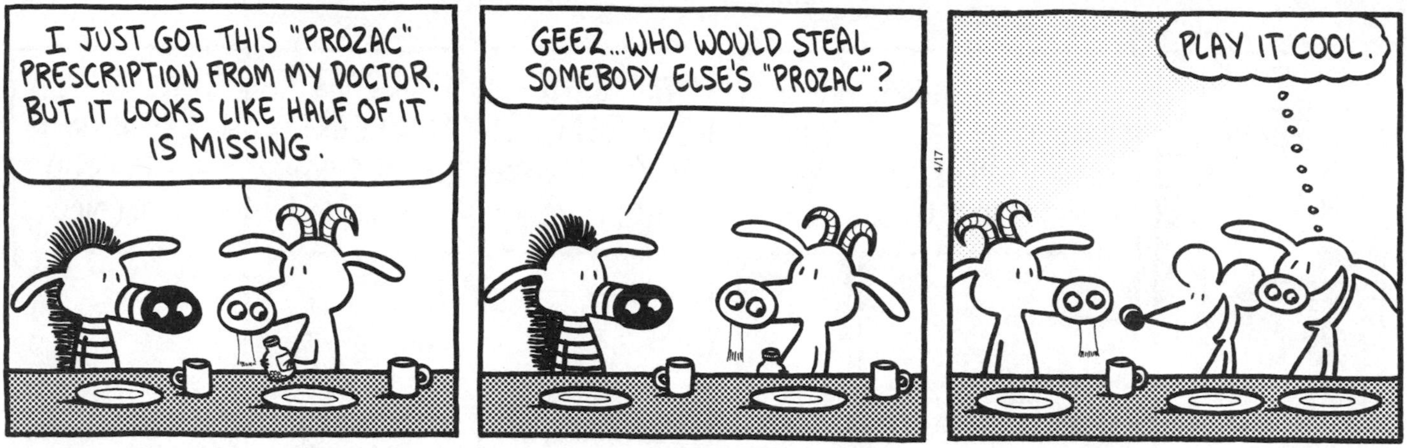
I JUST GOT THIS "PROZAC" PRESCRIPTION FROM MY DOCTOR, BUT IT LOOKS LIKE HALF OF IT IS MISSING.
GEEZ...WHO WOULD STEAL SOMEBODY ELSE'S "PROZAC"?
4/17
PLAY IT COOL.

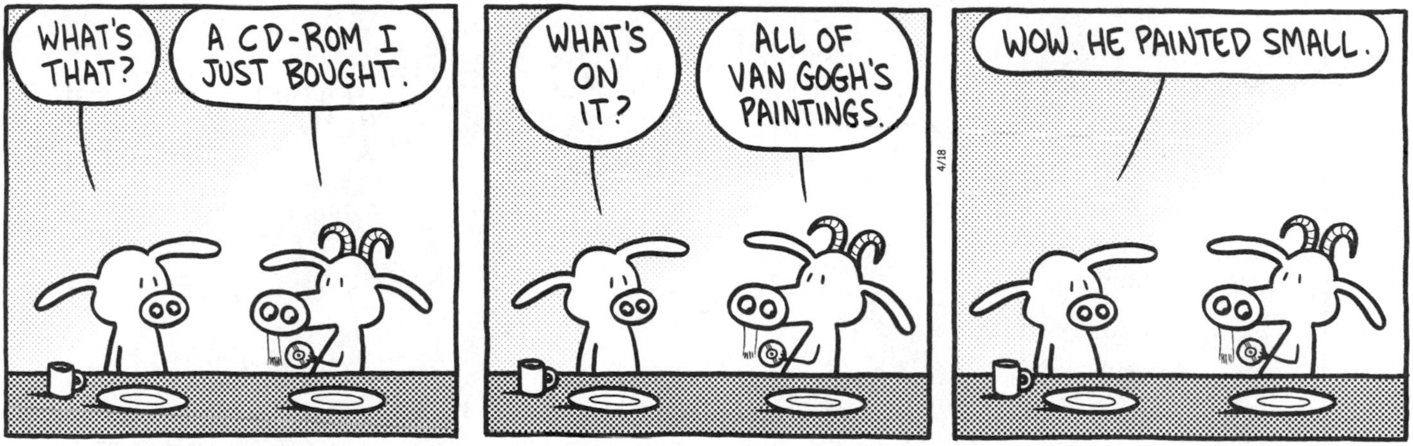
WHAT'S THAT?
A CD-ROM I JUST BOUGHT.
WHAT'S ON IT?
ALL OF VAN GOGH'S PAINTINGS.
4/18
WOW. HE PAINTED SMALL.

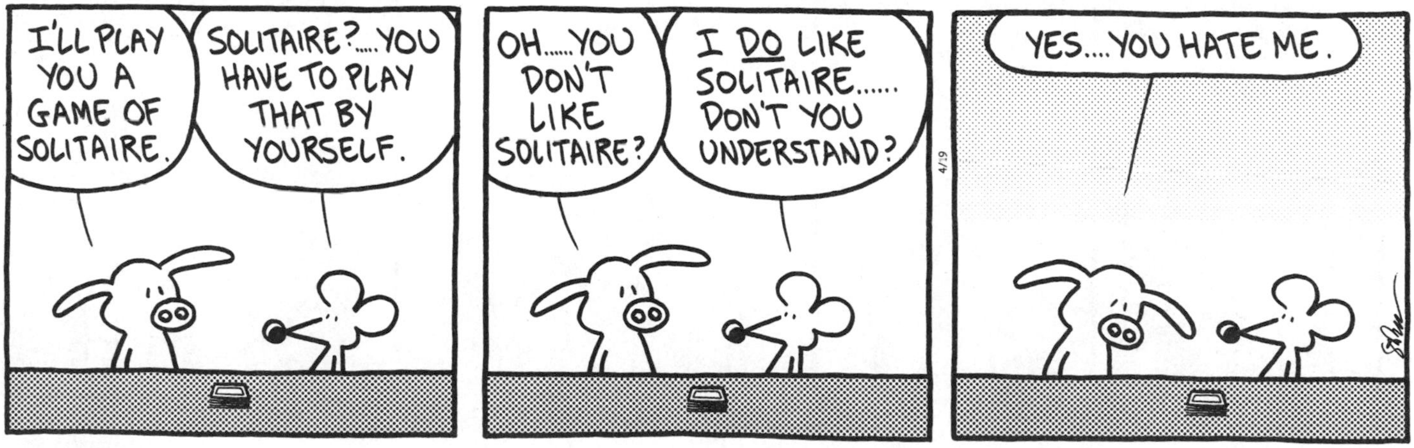
I'LL PLAY YOU A GAME OF SOLITAIRE.
SOLITAIRE?.....YOU HAVE TO PLAY THAT BY YOURSELF.
OH.....YOU DON'T LIKE SOLITAIRE?
I DO LIKE SOLITAIRE...... DON'T YOU UNDERSTAND?
4/19
YES....YOU HATE ME.

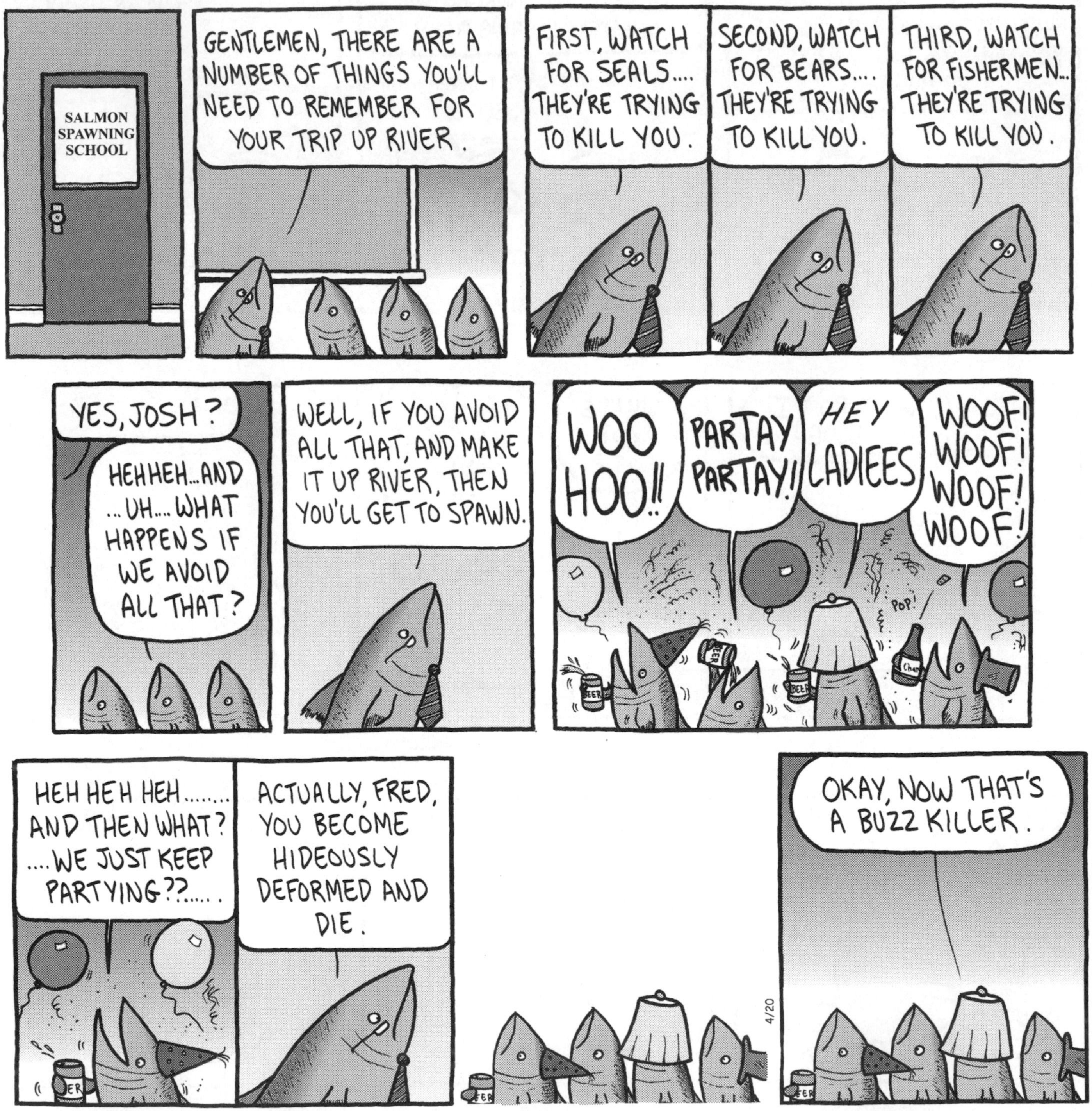
SALMON SPAWNING SCHOOL
GENTLEMEN, THERE ARE A NUMBER OF THINGS YOU'LL NEED TO REMEMBER FOR YOUR TRIP UP RIVER.
FIRST, WATCH FOR SEALS.... THEY'RE TRYING TO KILL YOU.
SECOND, WATCH FOR BEARS.... THEY'RE TRYING TO KILL YOU.
THIRD, WATCH FOR FISHERMEN... THEY'RE TRYING TO KILL YOU.
YES, JOSH?
HEHHEH...AND ...UH.... WHAT HAPPENS IF WE AVOID ALL THAT?
WELL, IF YOU AVOID ALL THAT, AND MAKE IT UP RIVER, THEN YOU'LL GET TO SPAWN.
WOO HOO!!
PARTAY PARTAY!
HEY LADIEES
WOOF! WOOF! WOOF! WOOF!
POP!
HEH HEH HEH........ AND THEN WHAT? ....WE JUST KEEP PARTYING??......
ACTUALLY, FRED, YOU BECOME HIDEOUSLY DEFORMED AND DIE.
4/20
OKAY, NOW THAT'S A BUZZ KILLER.

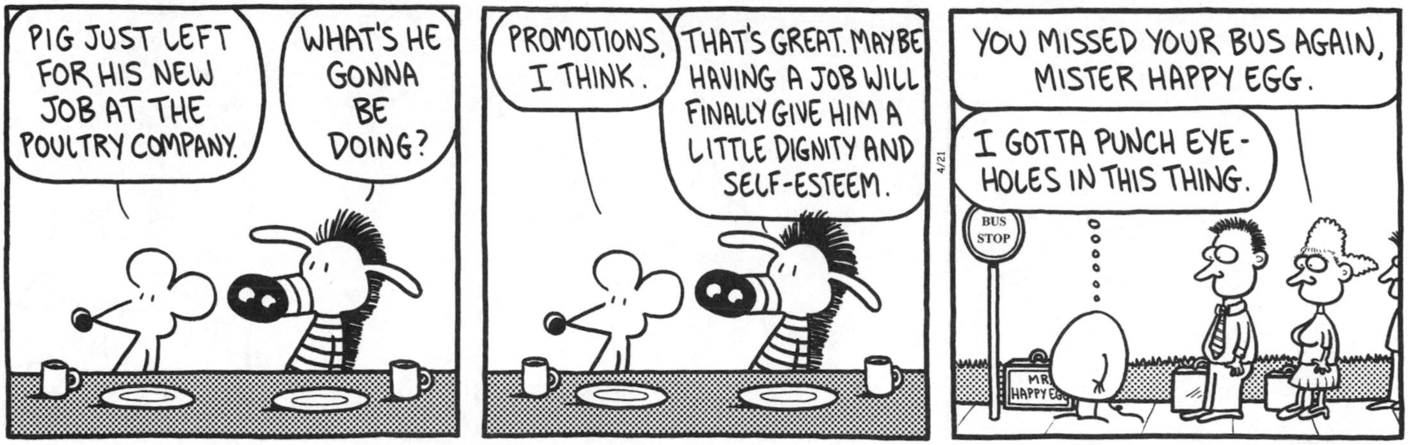
PIG JUST LEFT FOR HIS NEW JOB AT THE POULTRY COMPANY.
WHAT'S HE GONNA BE DOING?
PROMOTIONS, I THINK.
THAT'S GREAT. MAYBE HAVING A JOB WILL FINALLY GIVE HIM A LITTLE DIGNITY AND SELF-ESTEEM.
4/21
YOU MISSED YOUR BUS AGAIN, MISTER HAPPY EGG.
I GOTTA PUNCH EYE-HOLES IN THIS THING.
BUS STOP
MR HAPPY EGG

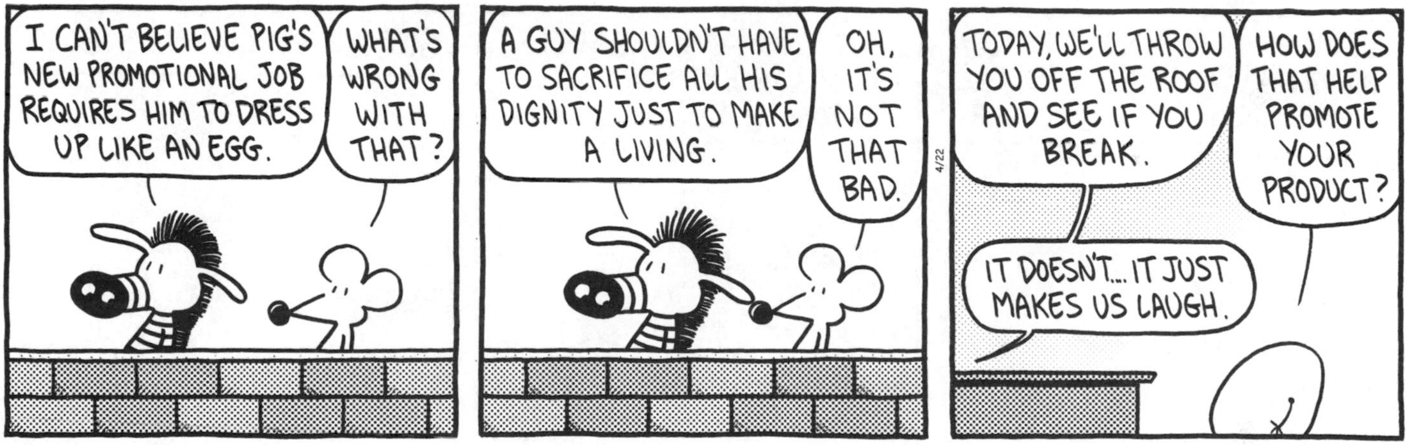
I CAN'T BELIEVE PIG'S NEW PROMOTIONAL JOB REQUIRES HIM TO DRESS UP LIKE AN EGG.
WHAT'S WRONG WITH THAT?
A GUY SHOULDN'T HAVE TO SACRIFICE ALL HIS DIGNITY JUST TO MAKE A LIVING.
OH, IT'S NOT THAT BAD.
4/22
TODAY, WE'LL THROW YOU OFF THE ROOF AND SEE IF YOU BREAK.
HOW DOES THAT HELP PROMOTE YOUR PRODUCT?
IT DOESN'T... IT JUST MAKES US LAUGH.

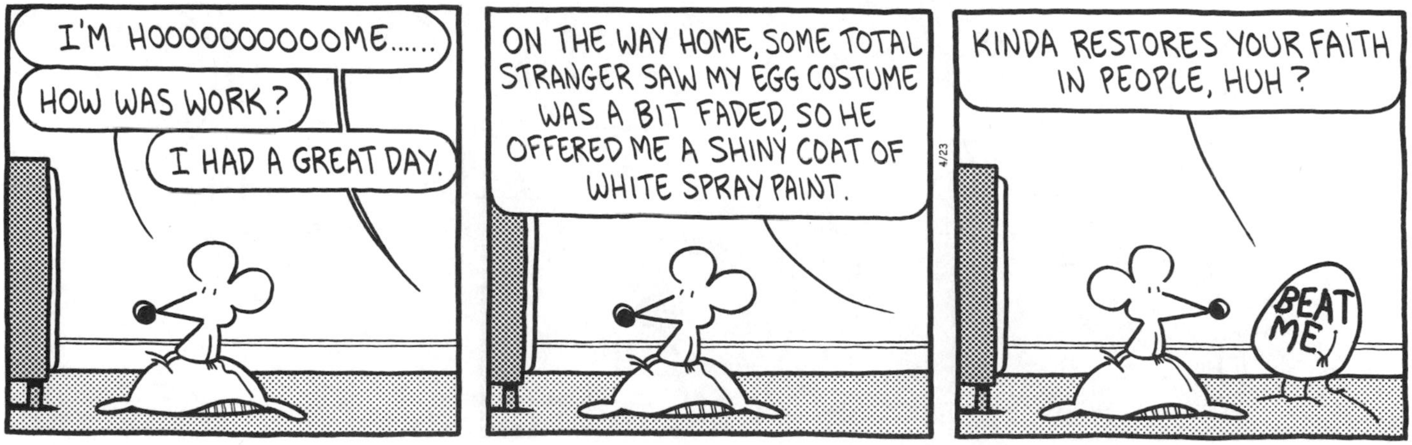
I'M HOOOOOOOOOOME......
HOW WAS WORK?
I HAD A GREAT DAY.
ON THE WAY HOME, SOME TOTAL STRANGER SAW MY EGG COSTUME WAS A BIT FADED, SO HE OFFERED ME A SHINY COAT OF WHITE SPRAY PAINT.
4/23
KINDA RESTORES YOUR FAITH IN PEOPLE, HUH?
BEAT ME

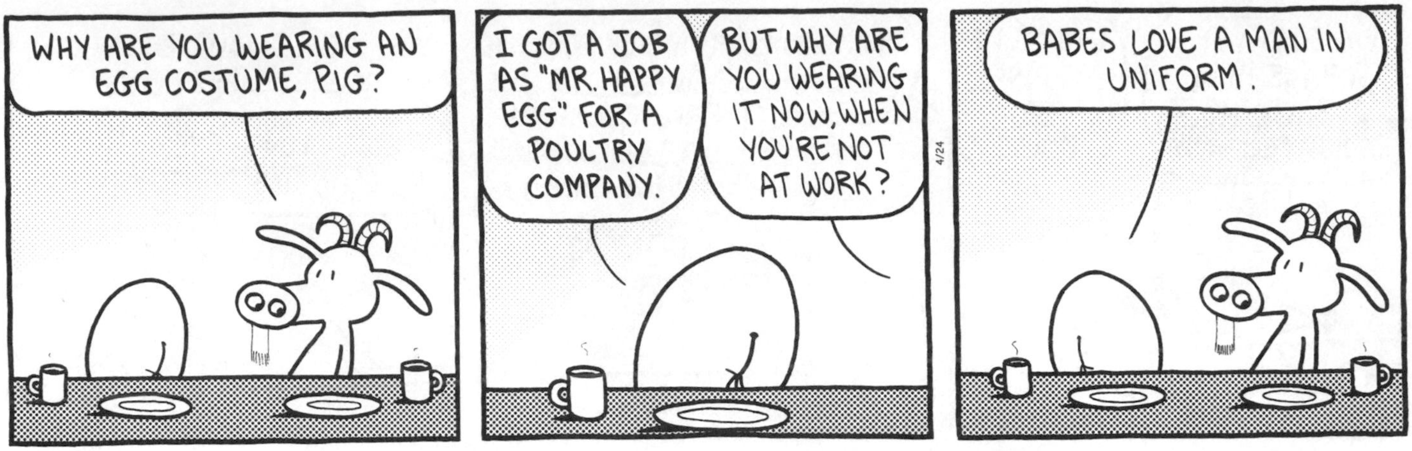
WHY ARE YOU WEARING AN EGG COSTUME, PIG?
I GOT A JOB AS "MR. HAPPY EGG" FOR A POULTRY COMPANY.
BUT WHY ARE YOU WEARING IT NOW, WHEN YOU'RE NOT AT WORK?
4/24
BABES LOVE A MAN IN UNIFORM.

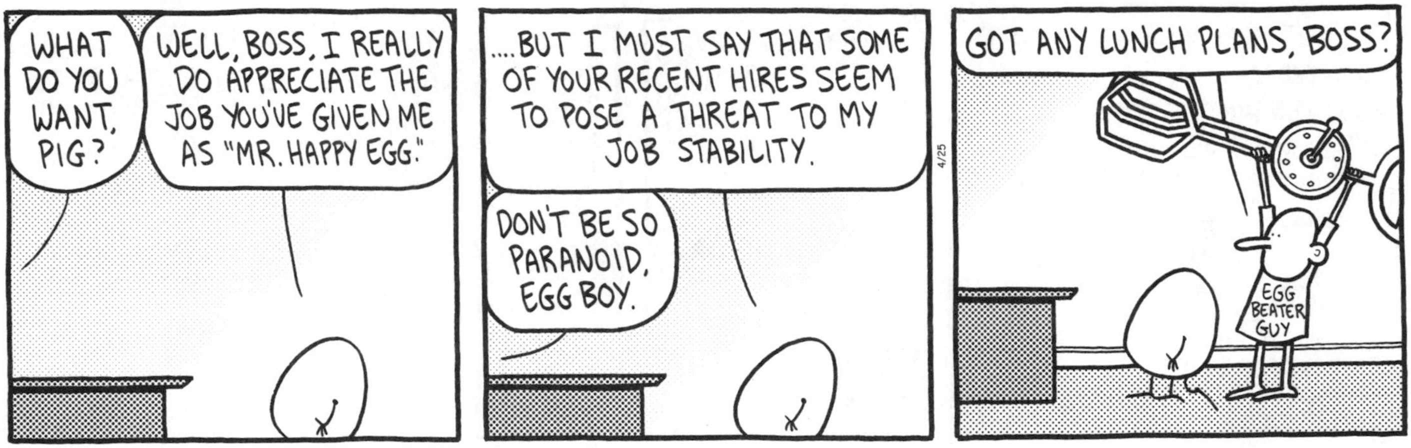
WHAT DO YOU WANT, PIG?
WELL, BOSS, I REALLY DO APPRECIATE THE JOB YOU'VE GIVEN ME AS "MR. HAPPY EGG."
....BUT I MUST SAY THAT SOME OF YOUR RECENT HIRES SEEM TO POSE A THREAT TO MY JOB STABILITY.
DON'T BE SO PARANOID, EGG BOY.
4/25
GOT ANY LUNCH PLANS, BOSS?
EGG BEATER GUY

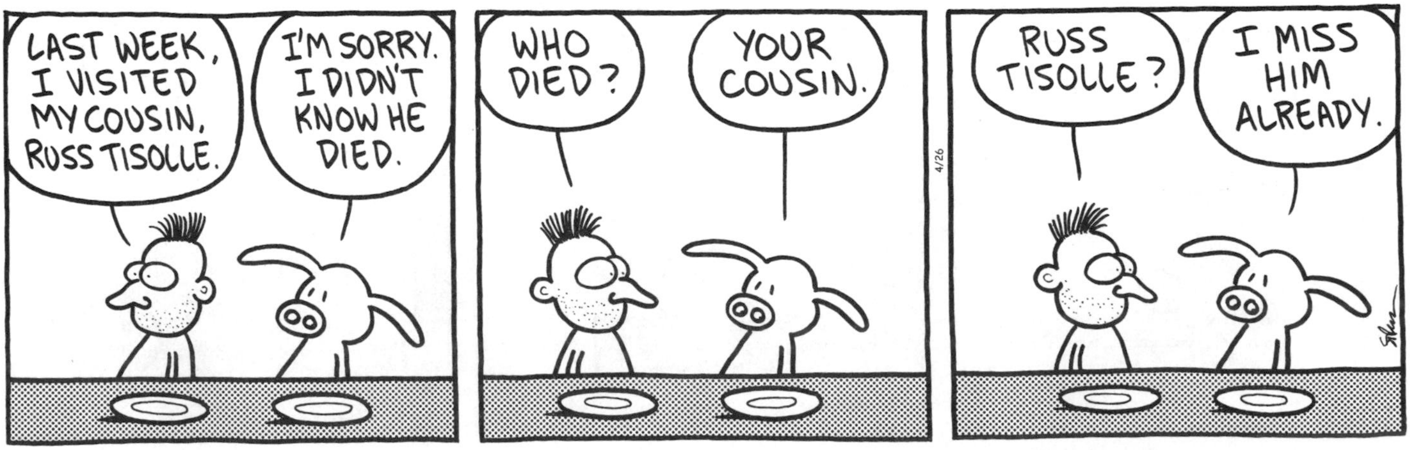
LAST WEEK, I VISITED MY COUSIN, RUSS TISOLLE.
I'M SORRY. I DIDN'T KNOW HE DIED.
WHO DIED?
YOUR COUSIN.
4/26
RUSS TISOLLE?
I MISS HIM ALREADY.

WHAT ARE YOU LOOKING AT?

MY LIST OF THE TOP TEN GREATEST INVENTIONS EVER.

WHAT ARE THEY?

WELL, FIRST IS THE GAS PUMP YOU STICK YOUR CREDIT CARD IN.... IT LETS YOU GET YOUR GAS WITHOUT TALKING TO ANYONE.

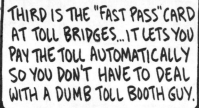

SECOND IS "PAY PER VIEW" MOVIES...IT LETS YOU ORDER MOVIES WITHOUT SEEING THE MORONS AT THE VIDEO STORE.

THIRD IS THE "FAST PASS" CARD AT TOLL BRIDGES...IT LETS YOU PAY THE TOLL AUTOMATICALLY SO YOU DON'T HAVE TO DEAL WITH A DUMB TOLL BOOTH GUY.

BUT YOU'RE JUST CALLING STUFF GREAT THAT ELIMINATES CONTACT WITH OTHER PEOPLE.... I LOVE TALKING FACE-TO-FACE WITH OTHERS...DON'T YOU?

MAYBE I'LL JUST FAX THIS TO YOU.

4/27

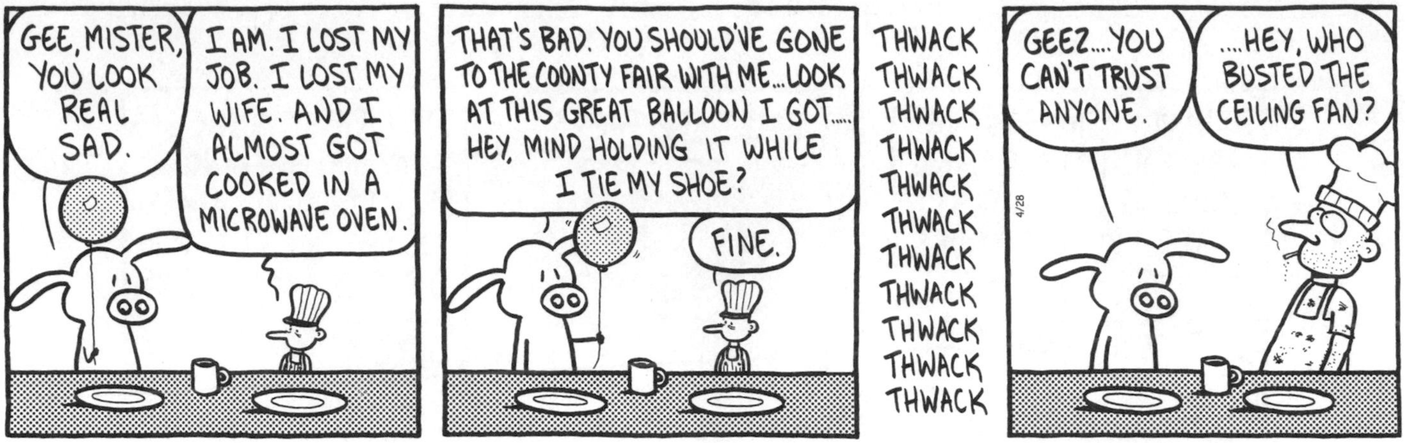
GEE, MISTER, YOU LOOK REAL SAD.
I AM. I LOST MY JOB. I LOST MY WIFE. AND I ALMOST GOT COOKED IN A MICROWAVE OVEN.
THAT'S BAD. YOU SHOULD'VE GONE TO THE COUNTY FAIR WITH ME...LOOK AT THIS GREAT BALLOON I GOT..... HEY, MIND HOLDING IT WHILE I TIE MY SHOE?
FINE.
THWACK THWACK THWACK THWACK THWACK THWACK THWACK THWACK THWACK THWACK THWACK
4/28
GEEZ....YOU CAN'T TRUST ANYONE.
....HEY, WHO BUSTED THE CEILING FAN?

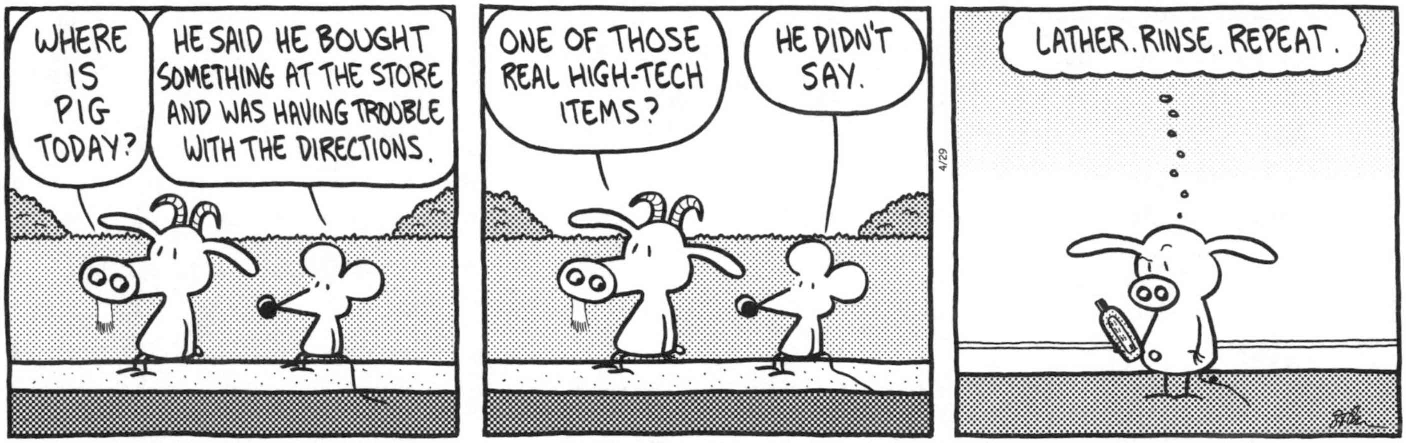
WHERE IS PIG TODAY?
HE SAID HE BOUGHT SOMETHING AT THE STORE AND WAS HAVING TROUBLE WITH THE DIRECTIONS.
ONE OF THOSE REAL HIGH-TECH ITEMS?
HE DIDN'T SAY.
4/29
LATHER. RINSE. REPEAT.

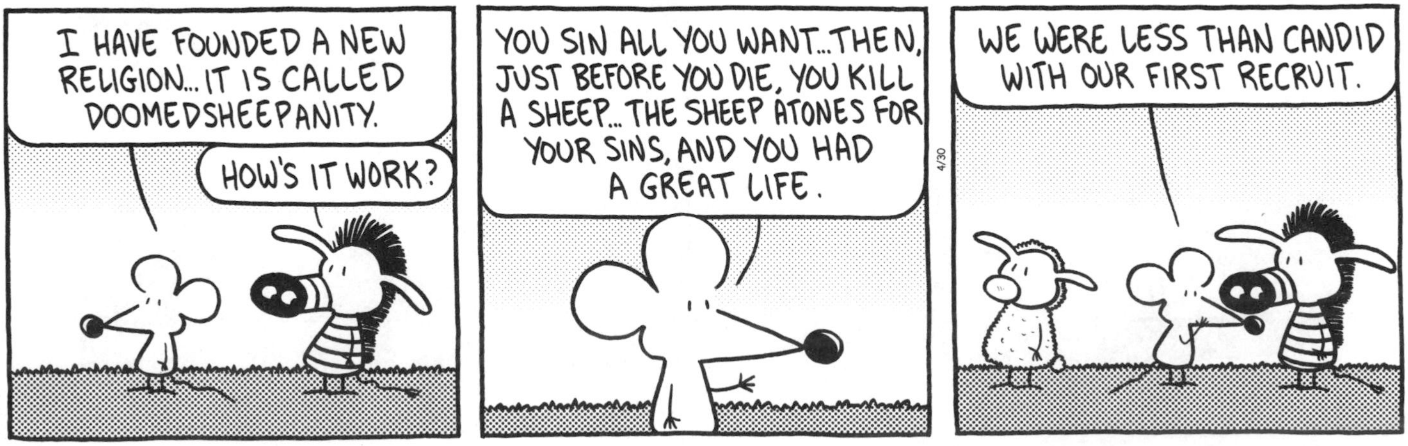
I HAVE FOUNDED A NEW RELIGION... IT IS CALLED DOOMEDSHEEPANITY.
HOW'S IT WORK?
YOU SIN ALL YOU WANT...THEN, JUST BEFORE YOU DIE, YOU KILL A SHEEP... THE SHEEP ATONES FOR YOUR SINS, AND YOU HAD A GREAT LIFE.
4/30
WE WERE LESS THAN CANDID WITH OUR FIRST RECRUIT.

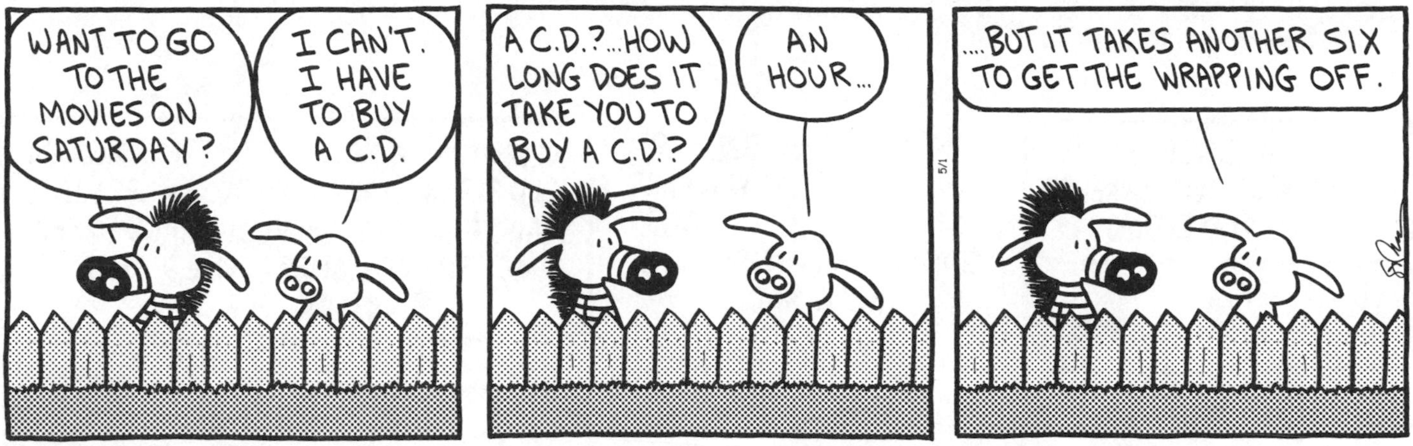
WANT TO GO TO THE MOVIES ON SATURDAY?
I CAN'T. I HAVE TO BUY A C.D.
A C.D.?...HOW LONG DOES IT TAKE YOU TO BUY A C.D.?
AN HOUR...
....BUT IT TAKES ANOTHER SIX TO GET THE WRAPPING OFF.

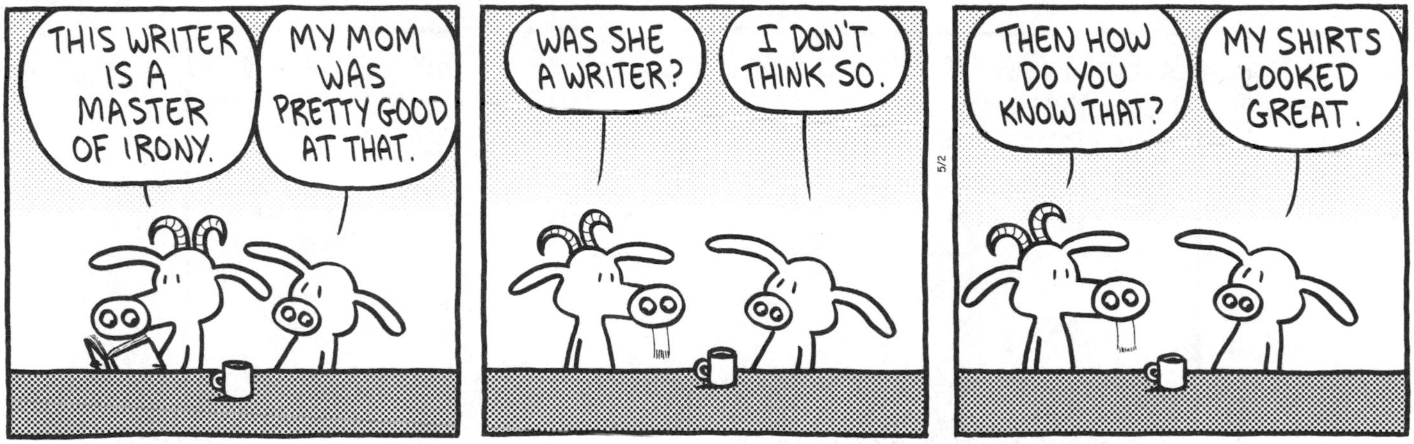
THIS WRITER IS A MASTER OF IRONY.
MY MOM WAS PRETTY GOOD AT THAT.
WAS SHE A WRITER?
I DON'T THINK SO.
THEN HOW DO YOU KNOW THAT?
MY SHIRTS LOOKED GREAT.

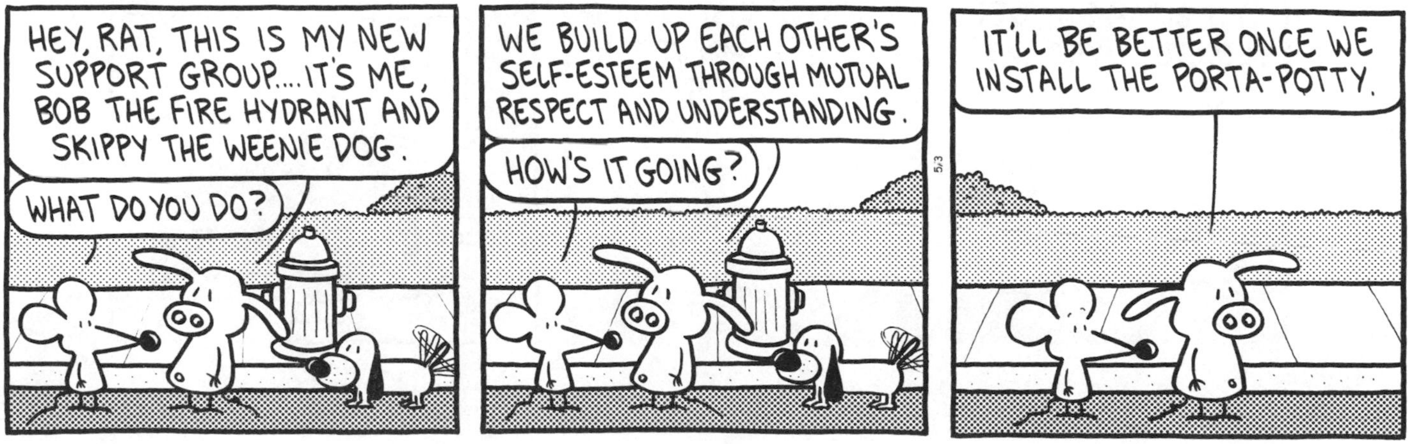
HEY, RAT, THIS IS MY NEW SUPPORT GROUP.... IT'S ME, BOB THE FIRE HYDRANT AND SKIPPY THE WEENIE DOG.
WHAT DO YOU DO?
WE BUILD UP EACH OTHER'S SELF-ESTEEM THROUGH MUTUAL RESPECT AND UNDERSTANDING.
HOW'S IT GOING?
IT'LL BE BETTER ONCE WE INSTALL THE PORTA-POTTY.

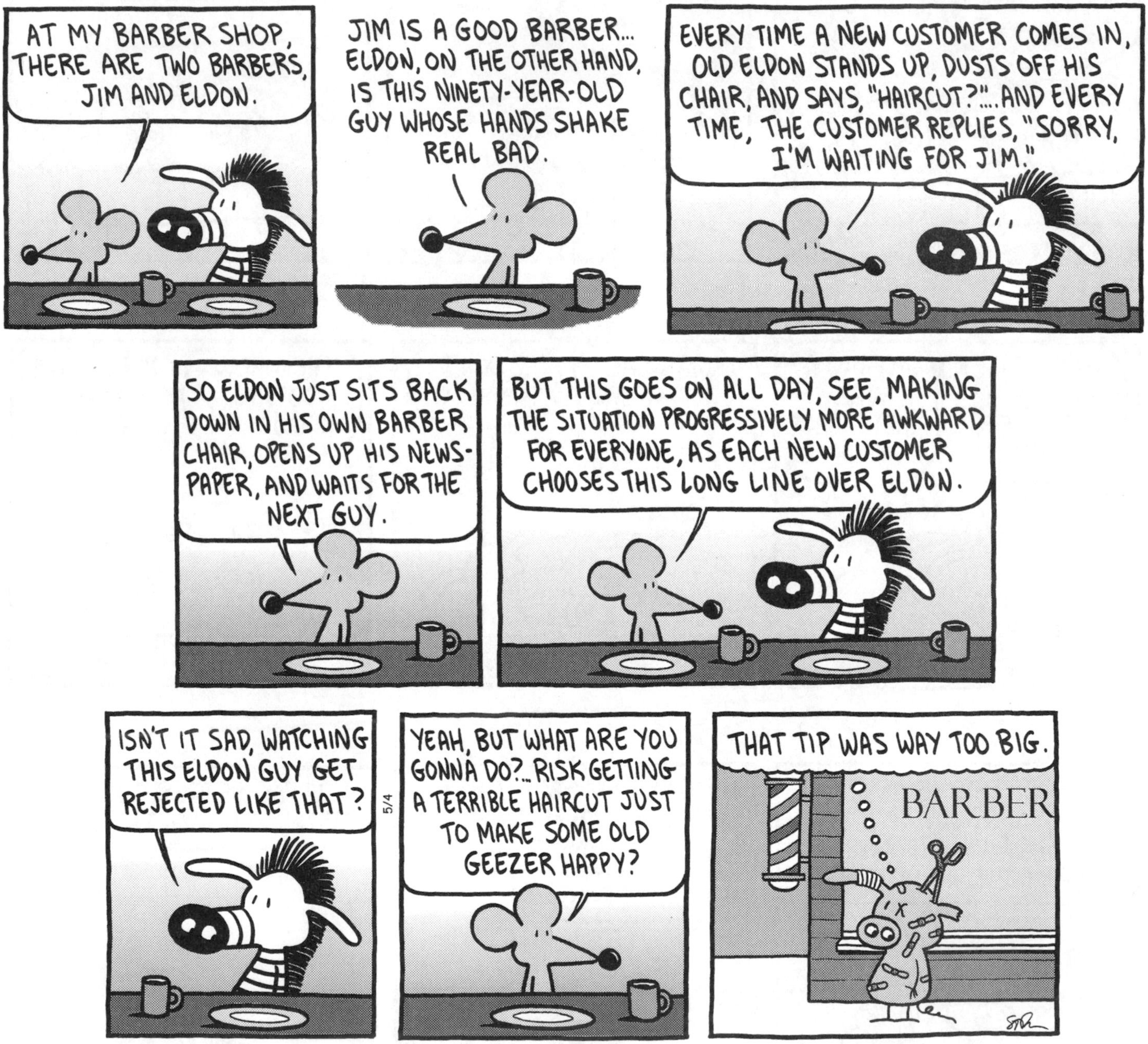
AT MY BARBER SHOP, THERE ARE TWO BARBERS, JIM AND ELDON.
JIM IS A GOOD BARBER... ELDON, ON THE OTHER HAND, IS THIS NINETY-YEAR-OLD GUY WHOSE HANDS SHAKE REAL BAD.
EVERY TIME A NEW CUSTOMER COMES IN, OLD ELDON STANDS UP, DUSTS OFF HIS CHAIR, AND SAYS, "HAIRCUT?"... AND EVERY TIME, THE CUSTOMER REPLIES, "SORRY, I'M WAITING FOR JIM."
SO ELDON JUST SITS BACK DOWN IN HIS OWN BARBER CHAIR, OPENS UP HIS NEWSPAPER, AND WAITS FOR THE NEXT GUY.
BUT THIS GOES ON ALL DAY, SEE, MAKING THE SITUATION PROGRESSIVELY MORE AWKWARD FOR EVERYONE, AS EACH NEW CUSTOMER CHOOSES THIS LONG LINE OVER ELDON.
ISN'T IT SAD, WATCHING THIS ELDON GUY GET REJECTED LIKE THAT?
5/4
YEAH, BUT WHAT ARE YOU GONNA DO?... RISK GETTING A TERRIBLE HAIRCUT JUST TO MAKE SOME OLD GEEZER HAPPY?
THAT TIP WAS WAY TOO BIG.
BARBER

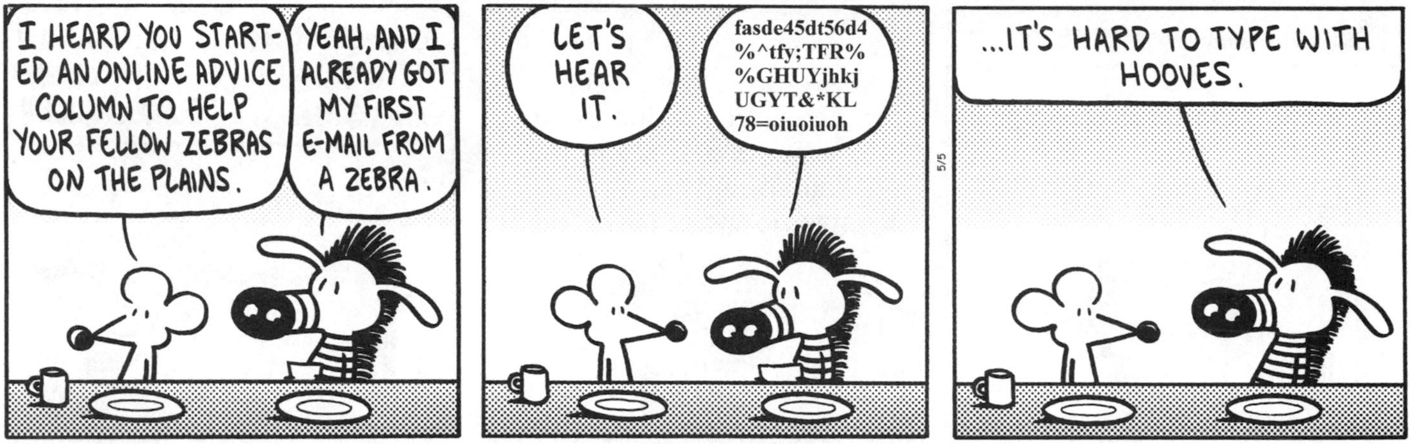
I HEARD YOU STARTED AN ONLINE ADVICE COLUMN TO HELP YOUR FELLOW ZEBRAS ON THE PLAINS.
YEAH, AND I ALREADY GOT MY FIRST E-MAIL FROM A ZEBRA.
LET'S HEAR IT.
fasde45dt56d4 %^tfy;TFR% %GHUYjhkj UGYT&*KL 78=oiuoiuoh
5/5
...IT'S HARD TO TYPE WITH HOOVES.

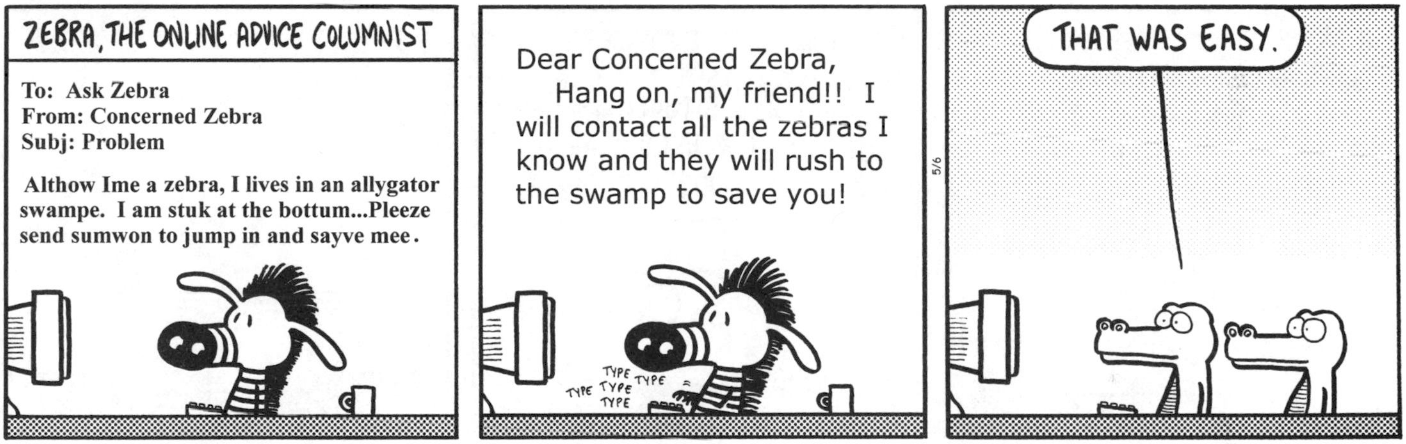
ZEBRA, THE ONLINE ADVICE COLUMNIST
To: Ask Zebra
From: Concerned Zebra
Subj: Problem
Althow Ime a zebra, I lives in an allygator swampe. I am stuk at the bottum...Pleeze send sumwon to jump in and sayve mee.
Dear Concerned Zebra,
Hang on, my friend!! I will contact all the zebras I know and they will rush to the swamp to save you!
TYPE TYPE TYPE TYPE TYPE
5/6
THAT WAS EASY.

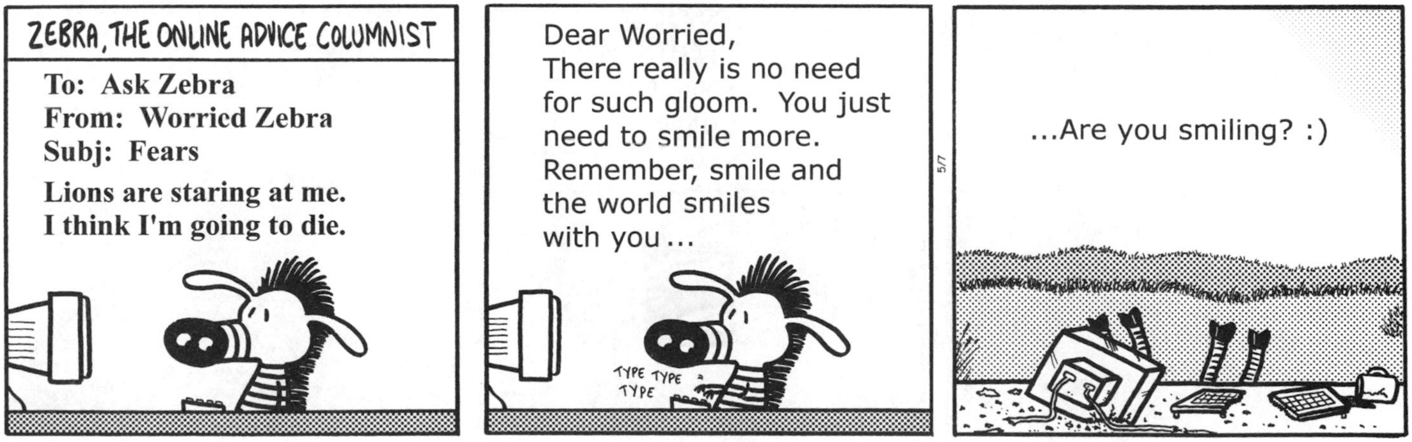
ZEBRA, THE ONLINE ADVICE COLUMNIST
To: Ask Zebra
From: Worried Zebra
Subj: Fears
Lions are staring at me.
I think I'm going to die.
Dear Worried,
There really is no need for such gloom. You just need to smile more. Remember, smile and the world smiles with you...
TYPE TYPE TYPE
5/7
...Are you smiling? :)

ZEBRA, THE ONLINE ADVICE COLUMNIST

To: Ask Zebra
From: Hert Zebra
Subj: My Feelings

When the hieenas eet us, they laff. This reely hertz my feelings. Am I noremal???

Dear Hurt,
You are not alone. Zebras are sensitive, caring beings, and it hurts to be laughed at. You should tell the hyenas how you feel.

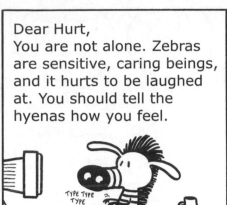

TYPE TYPE TYPE

OH, YEEEEEESS... TELL 'DEM HOW YOU FEEEEEEEEL...

HAHAHAHA!! SEND ANOTHER!! SEND ANOTHER!!

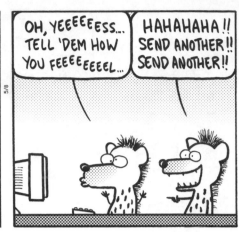

DEAR OLYMPIC COMMITTEE, LIKE ALL RIGHT-THINKING MEN, I FIND WOMEN'S FIGURE-SKATING BORING... THUS, I HAVE A SUGGESTION.

HIRE SOME N.H.L. ENFORCERS AND HIDE THEM OUTSIDE THE RINK.... AT RANDOM MOMENTS, HAVE THEM JUMP OUT AND POP SOME OF THOSE ICE QUEENS INTO THE BOARDS.

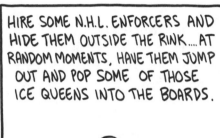

P.S. THIS MAY AFFECT SCORING.

WHAT ARE WE DOING HERE?

WE'RE TALKING ON OUR FRONT LAWN.

I'M TALKING ON A GRAND SCALE.

YOU'RE TALKING ON THE FRONT LAWN.

I'M TALKING TO AN IDIOT.

BUT NOT ON A GRAND SCALE.

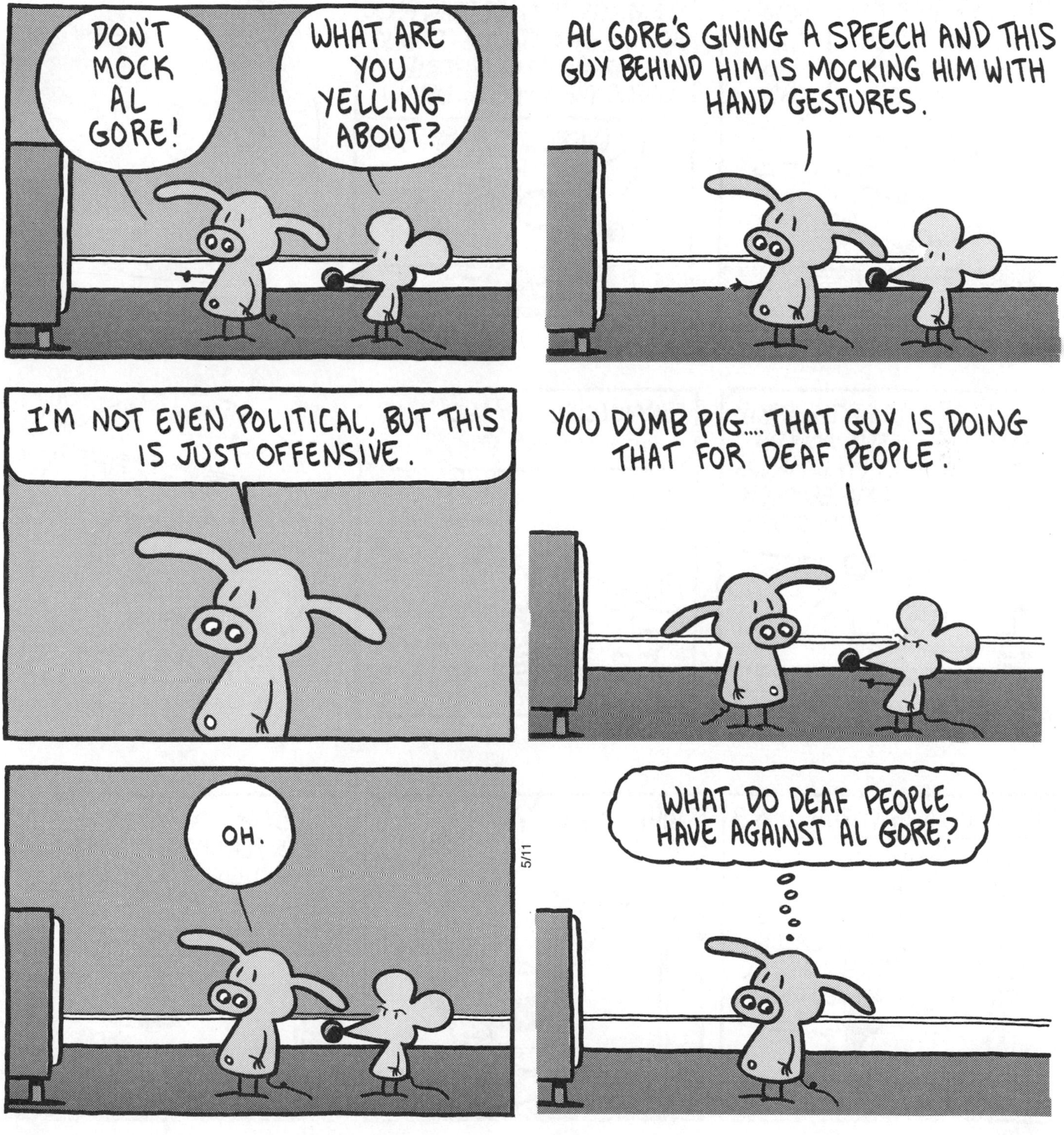
DON'T MOCK AL GORE!
WHAT ARE YOU YELLING ABOUT?
AL GORE'S GIVING A SPEECH AND THIS GUY BEHIND HIM IS MOCKING HIM WITH HAND GESTURES.
I'M NOT EVEN POLITICAL, BUT THIS IS JUST OFFENSIVE.
YOU DUMB PIG.... THAT GUY IS DOING THAT FOR DEAF PEOPLE.
OH.
WHAT DO DEAF PEOPLE HAVE AGAINST AL GORE?
5/11

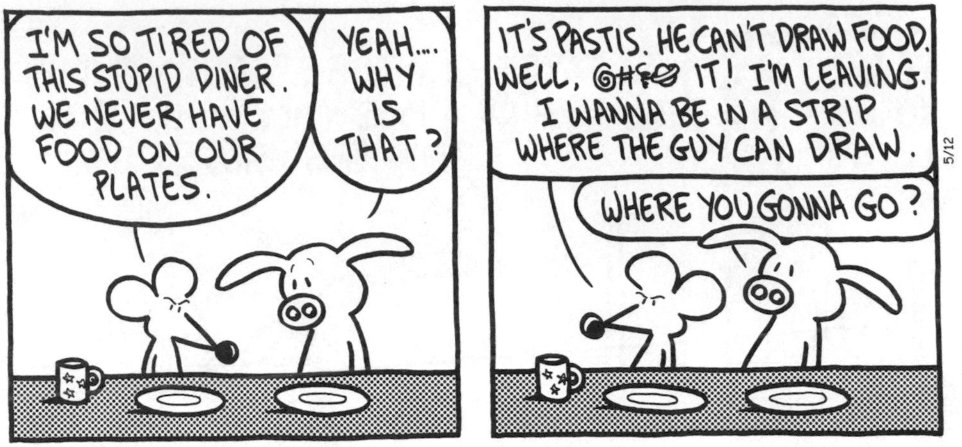
I'M SO TIRED OF THIS STUPID DINER. WE NEVER HAVE FOOD ON OUR PLATES.
YEAH.... WHY IS THAT?
IT'S PASTIS. HE CAN'T DRAW FOOD. WELL, @#!@ IT! I'M LEAVING. I WANNA BE IN A STRIP WHERE THE GUY CAN DRAW.
WHERE YOU GONNA GO?
5/12

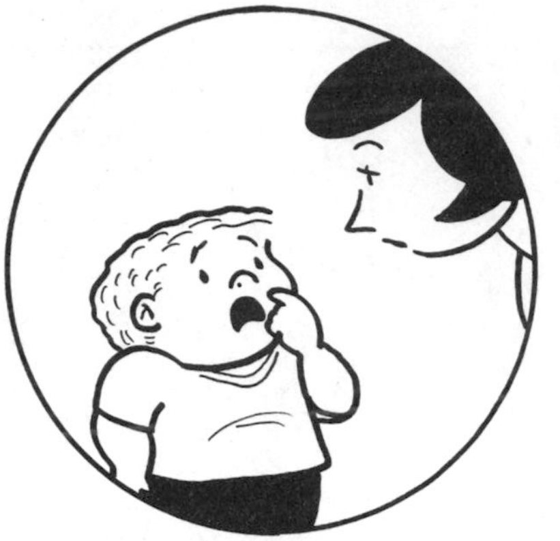

"Mommy, there's a rat in our refrigerator."

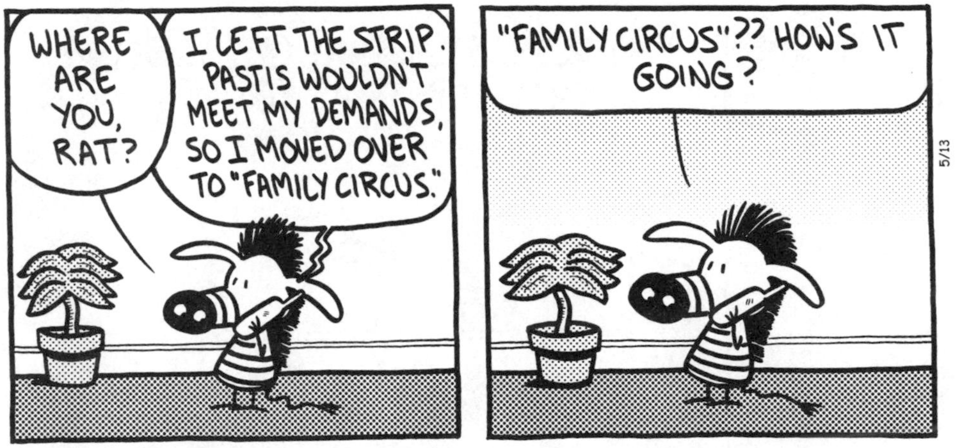
WHERE ARE YOU, RAT?
I LEFT THE STRIP. PASTIS WOULDN'T MEET MY DEMANDS, SO I MOVED OVER TO "FAMILY CIRCUS."
"FAMILY CIRCUS"?? HOW'S IT GOING?
5/13

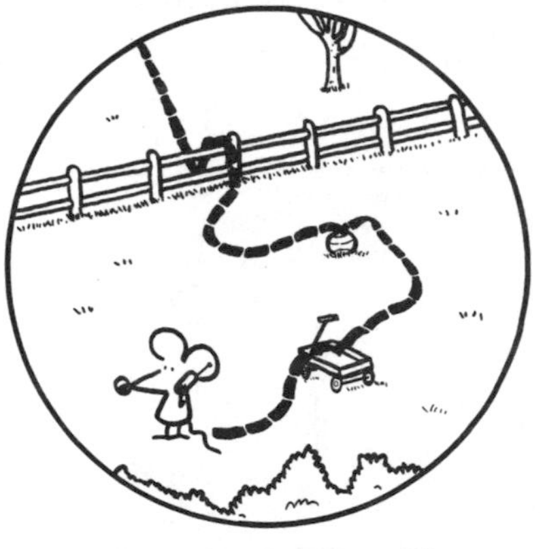

"I feel like a #%$@*# snail."

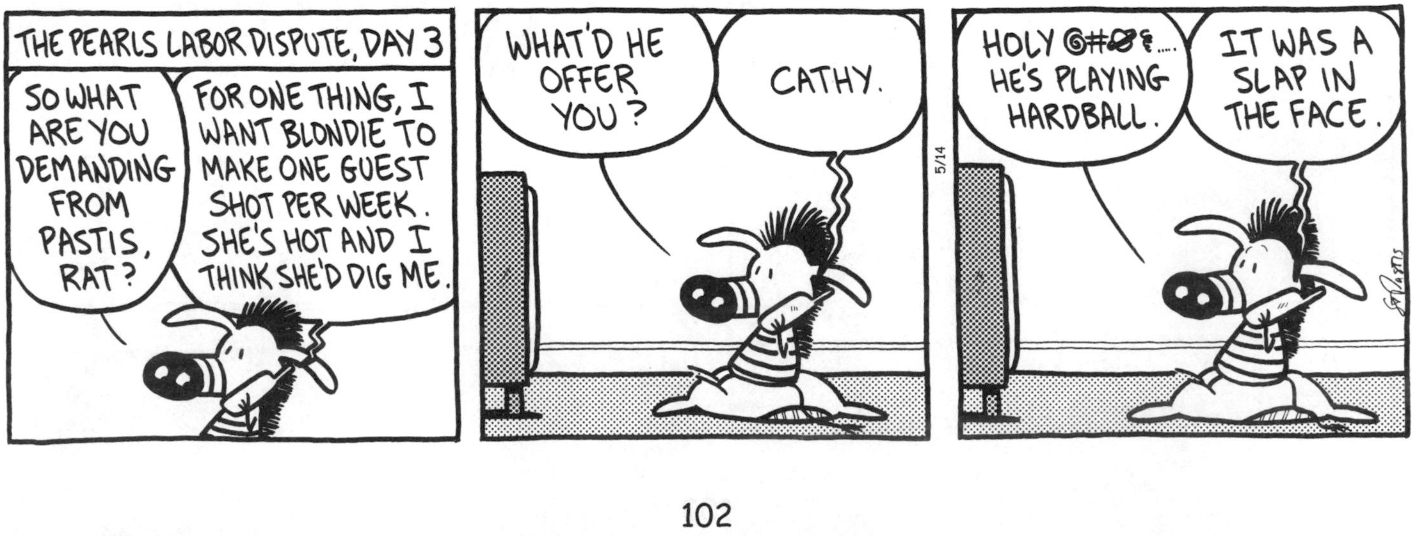
THE PEARLS LABOR DISPUTE, DAY 3
SO WHAT ARE YOU DEMANDING FROM PASTIS, RAT?
FOR ONE THING, I WANT BLONDIE TO MAKE ONE GUEST SHOT PER WEEK. SHE'S HOT AND I THINK SHE'D DIG ME.
WHAT'D HE OFFER YOU?
CATHY.
HOLY @#!@.... HE'S PLAYING HARDBALL.
IT WAS A SLAP IN THE FACE.
5/14

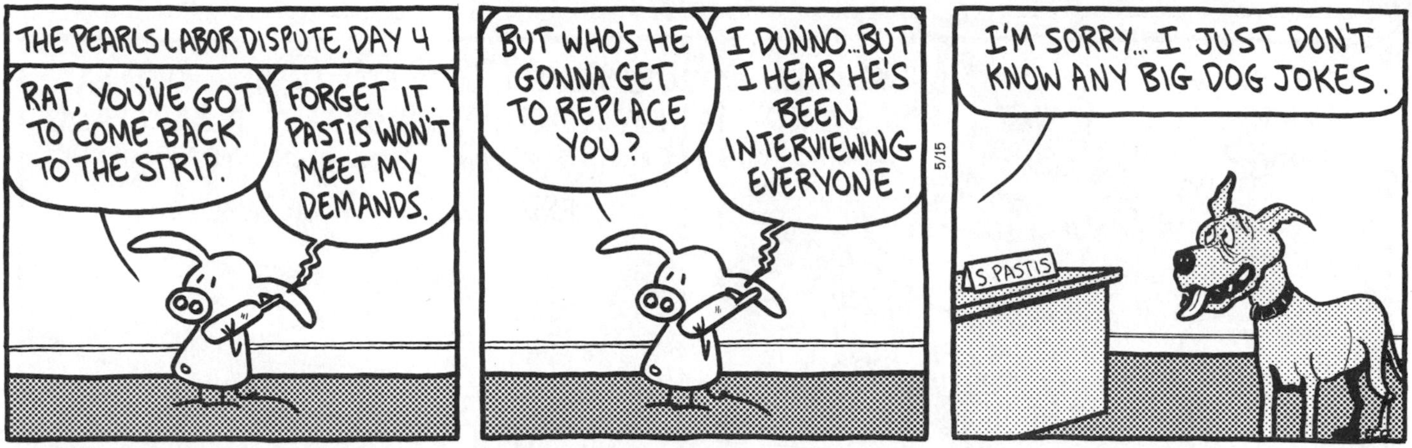
THE PEARLS LABOR DISPUTE, DAY 4
RAT, YOU'VE GOT TO COME BACK TO THE STRIP.
FORGET IT. PASTIS WON'T MEET MY DEMANDS.
BUT WHO'S HE GONNA GET TO REPLACE YOU?
I DUNNO...BUT I HEAR HE'S BEEN INTERVIEWING EVERYONE.
5/15
I'M SORRY... I JUST DON'T KNOW ANY BIG DOG JOKES.
S. PASTIS

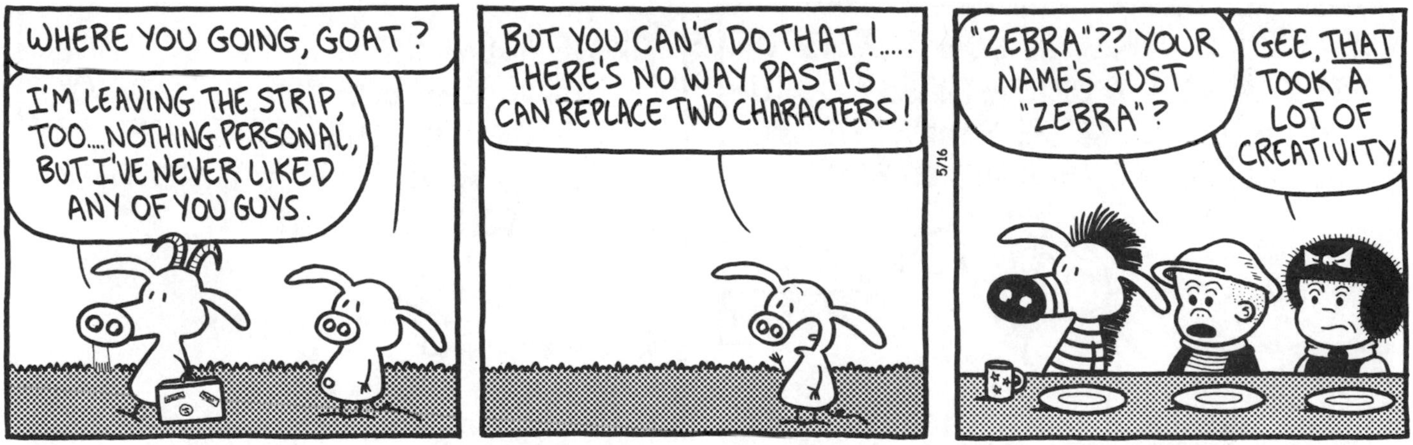
WHERE YOU GOING, GOAT?
I'M LEAVING THE STRIP, TOO....NOTHING PERSONAL, BUT I'VE NEVER LIKED ANY OF YOU GUYS.
BUT YOU CAN'T DO THAT!..... THERE'S NO WAY PASTIS CAN REPLACE TWO CHARACTERS!
5/16
"ZEBRA"?? YOUR NAME'S JUST "ZEBRA"?
GEE, THAT TOOK A LOT OF CREATIVITY.

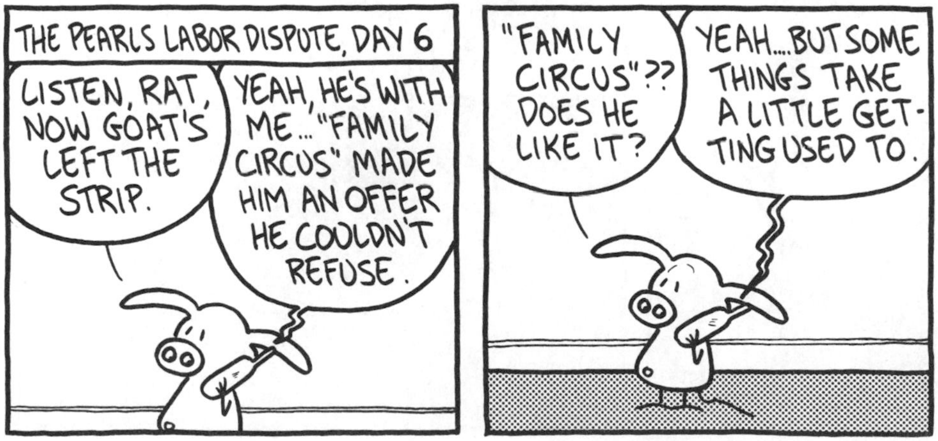
THE PEARLS LABOR DISPUTE, DAY 6
LISTEN, RAT, NOW GOAT'S LEFT THE STRIP.
YEAH, HE'S WITH ME... "FAMILY CIRCUS" MADE HIM AN OFFER HE COULDN'T REFUSE.
"FAMILY CIRCUS"?? DOES HE LIKE IT?
YEAH....BUT SOME THINGS TAKE A LITTLE GETTING USED TO.
5/17

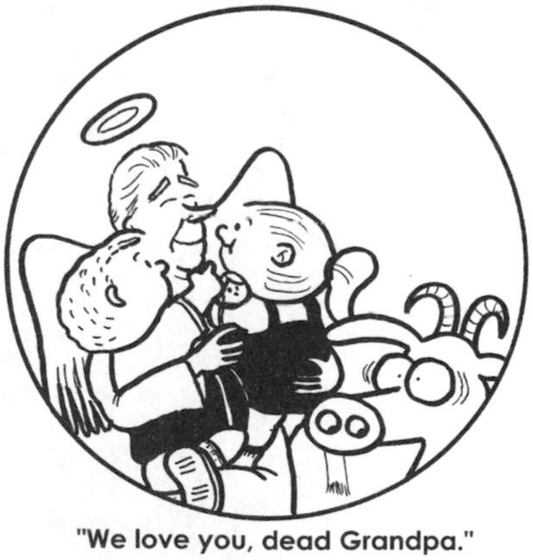

"We love you, dead Grandpa."

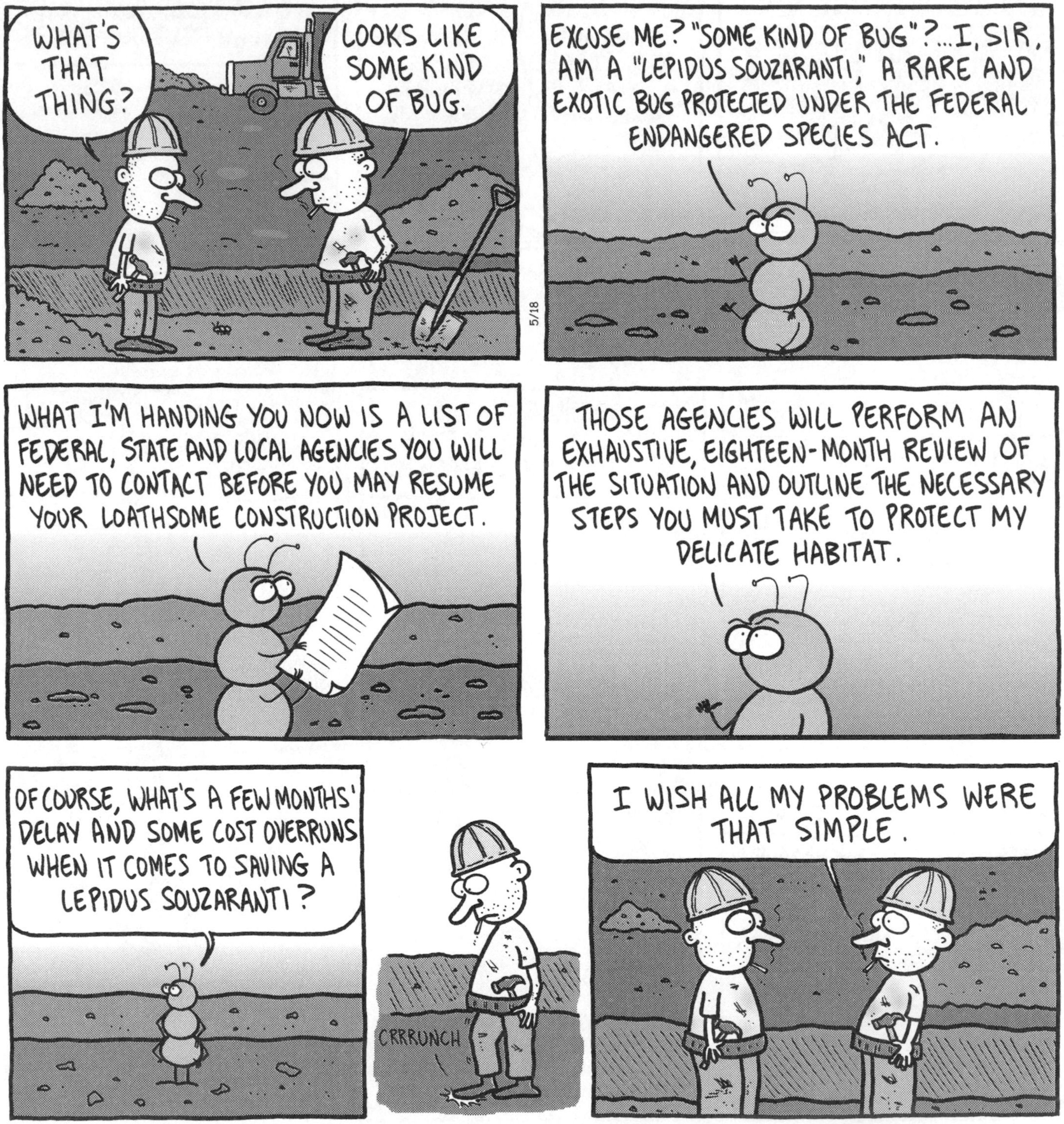
WHAT'S THAT THING?
LOOKS LIKE SOME KIND OF BUG.
5/18
EXCUSE ME? "SOME KIND OF BUG"?...I, SIR, AM A "LEPIDUS SOUZARANTI," A RARE AND EXOTIC BUG PROTECTED UNDER THE FEDERAL ENDANGERED SPECIES ACT.
WHAT I'M HANDING YOU NOW IS A LIST OF FEDERAL, STATE AND LOCAL AGENCIES YOU WILL NEED TO CONTACT BEFORE YOU MAY RESUME YOUR LOATHSOME CONSTRUCTION PROJECT.
THOSE AGENCIES WILL PERFORM AN EXHAUSTIVE, EIGHTEEN-MONTH REVIEW OF THE SITUATION AND OUTLINE THE NECESSARY STEPS YOU MUST TAKE TO PROTECT MY DELICATE HABITAT.
OF COURSE, WHAT'S A FEW MONTHS' DELAY AND SOME COST OVERRUNS WHEN IT COMES TO SAVING A LEPIDUS SOUZARANTI?
CRRRUNCH
I WISH ALL MY PROBLEMS WERE THAT SIMPLE.

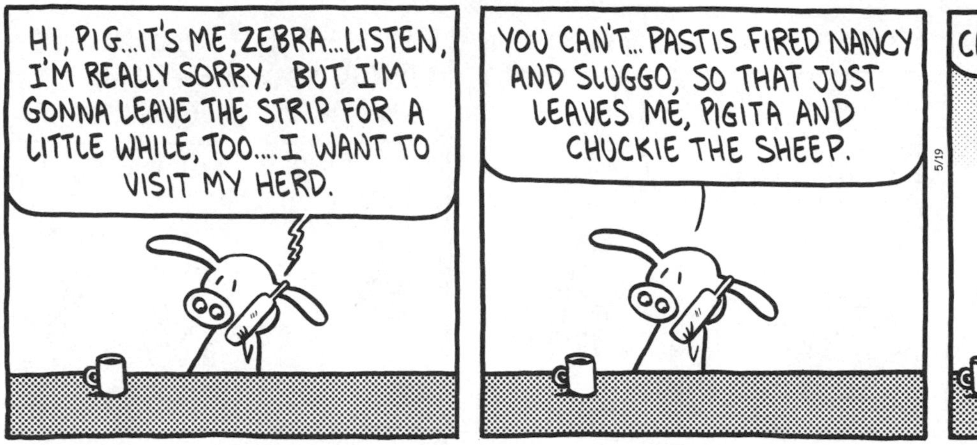
HI, PIG...IT'S ME, ZEBRA...LISTEN, I'M REALLY SORRY, BUT I'M GONNA LEAVE THE STRIP FOR A LITTLE WHILE, TOO....I WANT TO VISIT MY HERD.
YOU CAN'T... PASTIS FIRED NANCY AND SLUGGO, SO THAT JUST LEAVES ME, PIGITA AND CHUCKIE THE SHEEP.
5/19
CARE FOR SOME MUTTON, HONEY?

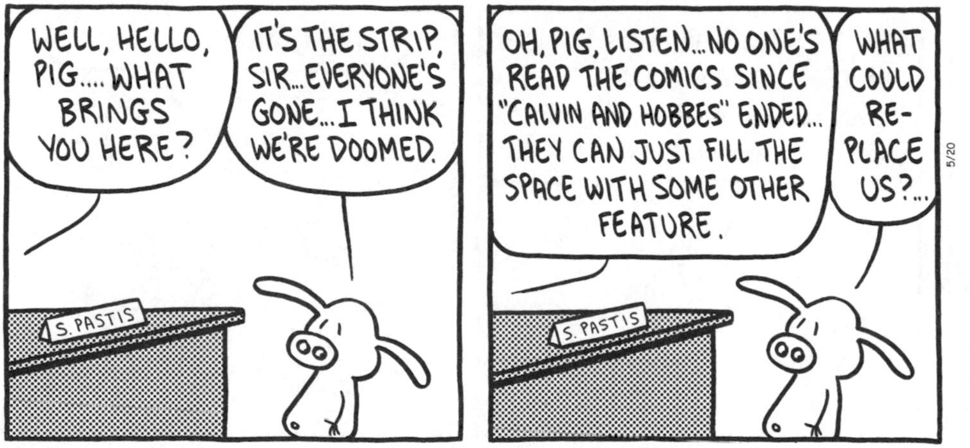
WELL, HELLO, PIG.... WHAT BRINGS YOU HERE?
IT'S THE STRIP, SIR...EVERYONE'S GONE...I THINK WE'RE DOOMED.
S. PASTIS
5/20
OH, PIG, LISTEN...NO ONE'S READ THE COMICS SINCE "CALVIN AND HOBBES" ENDED... THEY CAN JUST FILL THE SPACE WITH SOME OTHER FEATURE.
WHAT COULD RE-PLACE US?...
S. PASTIS

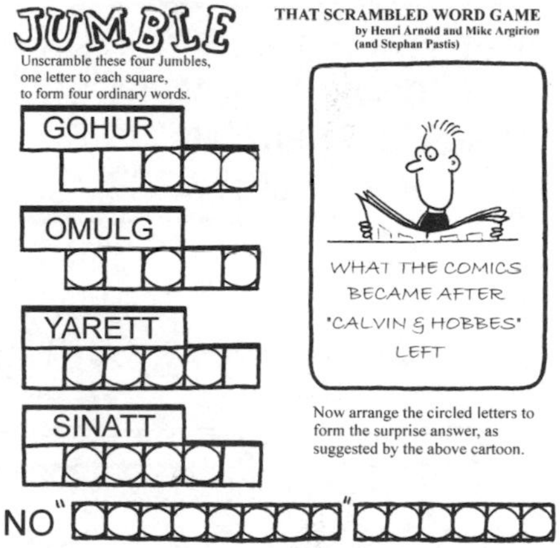
JUMBLE
THAT SCRAMBLED WORD GAME
by Henri Arnold and Mike Argirion (and Stephan Pastis)
Unscramble these four Jumbles, one letter to each square, to form four ordinary words.
GOHUR
OMULG
YARETT
SINATT
WHAT THE COMICS BECAME AFTER "CALVIN & HOBBES" LEFT
Now arrange the circled letters to form the surprise answer, as suggested by the above cartoon.
NO" "

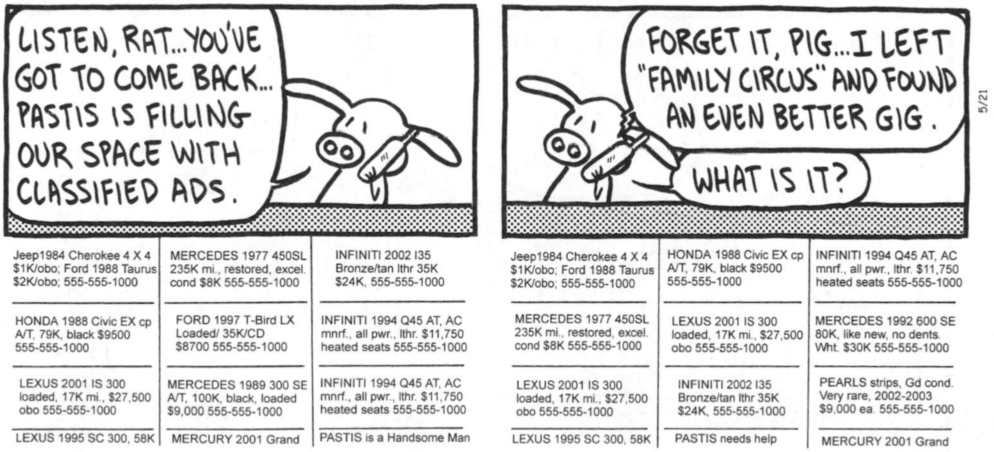
LISTEN, RAT...YOU'VE GOT TO COME BACK... PASTIS IS FILLING OUR SPACE WITH CLASSIFIED ADS.
Jeep1984 Cherokee 4 X 4 $1K/obo; Ford 1988 Taurus $2K/obo; 555-555-1000
MERCEDES 1977 450SL 235K mi., restored, excel. cond $8K 555-555-1000
INFINITI 2002 I35 Bronze/tan lthr 35K $24K, 555-555-1000
HONDA 1988 Civic EX cp A/T, 79K, black $9500 555-555-1000
FORD 1997 T-Bird LX Loaded/ 35K/CD $8700 555-555-1000
INFINITI 1994 Q45 AT, AC mnrf., all pwr., lthr. $11,750 heated seats 555-555-1000
LEXUS 2001 IS 300 loaded, 17K mi., $27,500 obo 555-555-1000
MERCEDES 1989 300 SE A/T, 100K, black, loaded $9,000 555-555-1000
INFINITI 1994 Q45 AT, AC mnrf., all pwr., lthr. $11,750 heated seats 555-555-1000
LEXUS 1995 SC 300, 58K
MERCURY 2001 Grand
PASTIS is a Handsome Man
FORGET IT, PIG...I LEFT "FAMILY CIRCUS" AND FOUND AN EVEN BETTER GIG.
WHAT IS IT?
5/21
Jeep1984 Cherokee 4 X 4 $1K/obo; Ford 1988 Taurus $2K/obo; 555-555-1000
HONDA 1988 Civic EX cp A/T, 79K, black $9500 555-555-1000
INFINITI 1994 Q45 AT, AC mnrf., all pwr., lthr. $11,750 heated seats 555-555-1000
MERCEDES 1977 450SL 235K mi., restored, excel. cond $8K 555-555-1000
LEXUS 2001 IS 300 loaded, 17K mi., $27,500 obo 555-555-1000
MERCEDES 1992 600 SE 80K, like new, no dents. Wht. $30K 555-555-1000
LEXUS 2001 IS 300 loaded, 17K mi., $27,500 obo 555-555-1000
INFINITI 2002 I35 Bronze/tan lthr 35K $24K, 555-555-1000
PEARLS strips, Gd cond. Very rare, 2002-2003 $9,000 ea. 555-555-1000
LEXUS 1995 SC 300, 58K
PASTIS needs help
MERCURY 2001 Grand

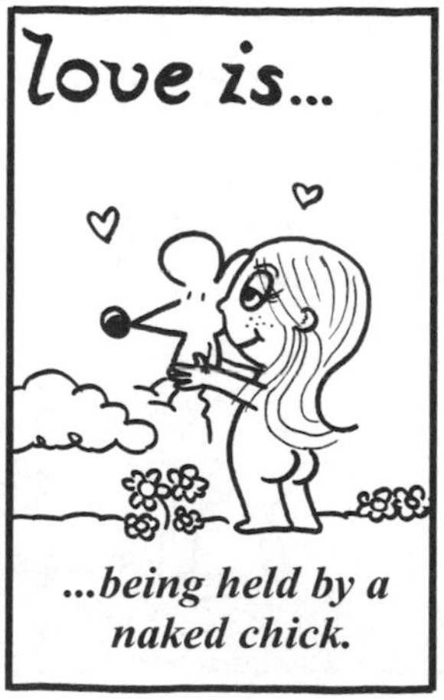
love is...
...being held by a naked chick.

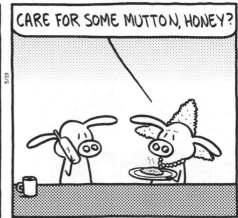

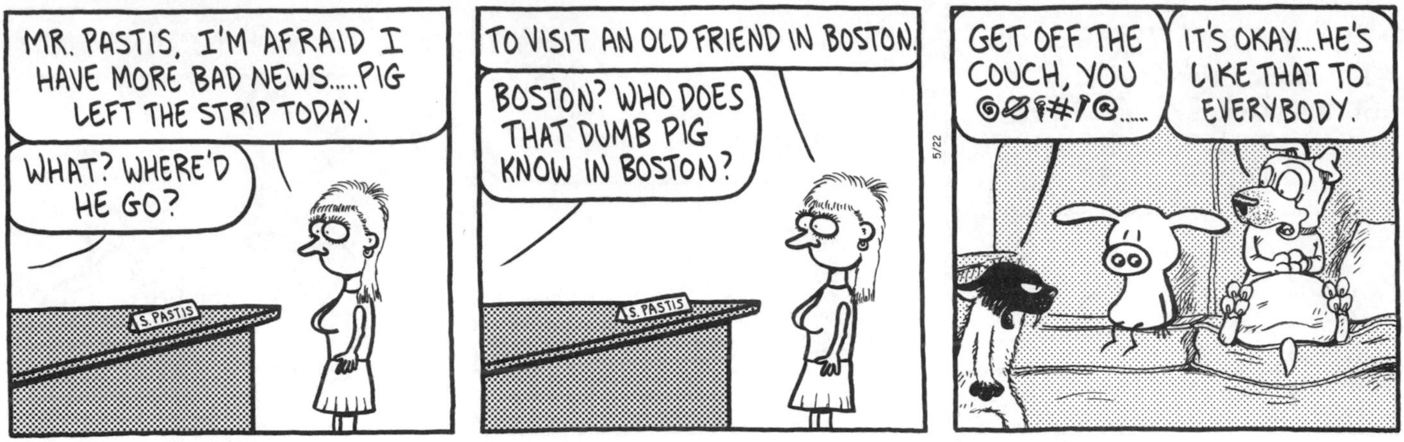
MR. PASTIS, I'M AFRAID I HAVE MORE BAD NEWS.....PIG LEFT THE STRIP TODAY.
WHAT? WHERE'D HE GO?
S. PASTIS
TO VISIT AN OLD FRIEND IN BOSTON.
BOSTON? WHO DOES THAT DUMB PIG KNOW IN BOSTON?
S. PASTIS
5/22
GET OFF THE COUCH, YOU
IT'S OKAY....HE'S LIKE THAT TO EVERYBODY.

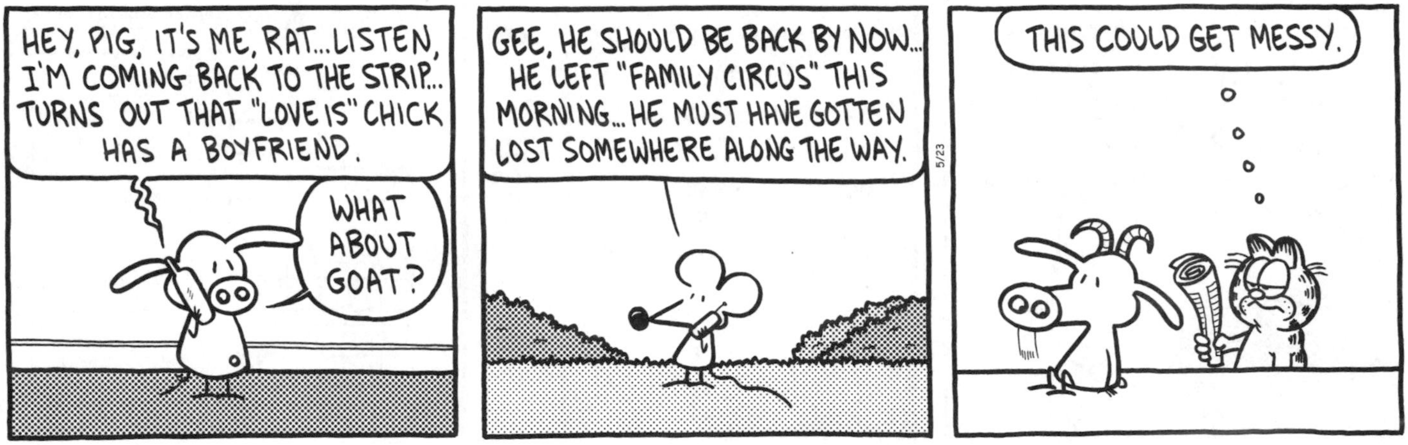
HEY, PIG, IT'S ME, RAT...LISTEN, I'M COMING BACK TO THE STRIP... TURNS OUT THAT "LOVE IS" CHICK HAS A BOYFRIEND.
WHAT ABOUT GOAT?
GEE, HE SHOULD BE BACK BY NOW... HE LEFT "FAMILY CIRCUS" THIS MORNING... HE MUST HAVE GOTTEN LOST SOMEWHERE ALONG THE WAY.
5/23
THIS COULD GET MESSY.

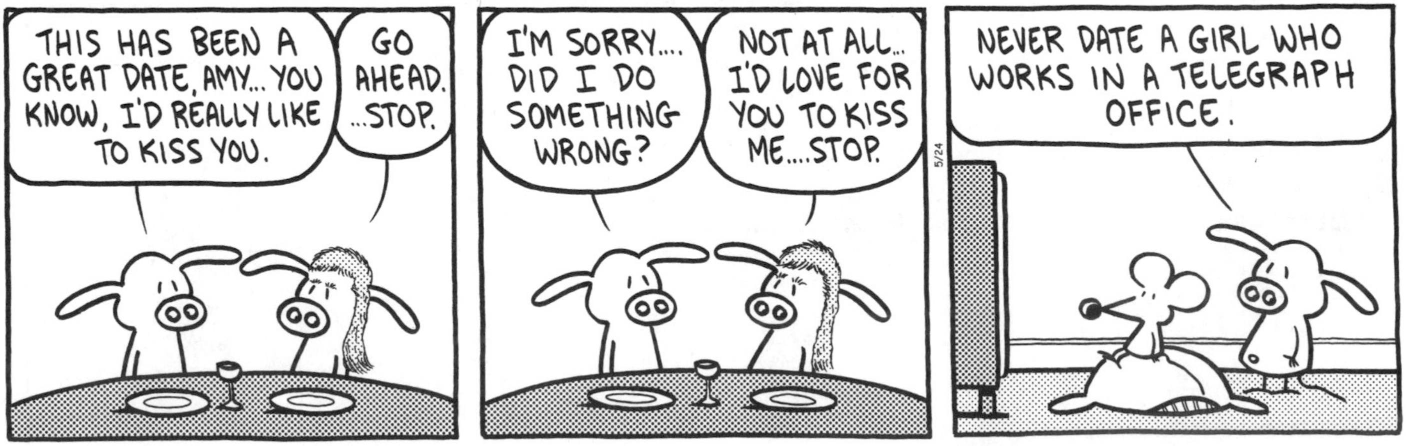
THIS HAS BEEN A GREAT DATE, AMY... YOU KNOW, I'D REALLY LIKE TO KISS YOU.
GO AHEAD. ...STOP.
I'M SORRY.... DID I DO SOMETHING WRONG?
NOT AT ALL... I'D LOVE FOR YOU TO KISS ME....STOP.
5/24
NEVER DATE A GIRL WHO WORKS IN A TELEGRAPH OFFICE.

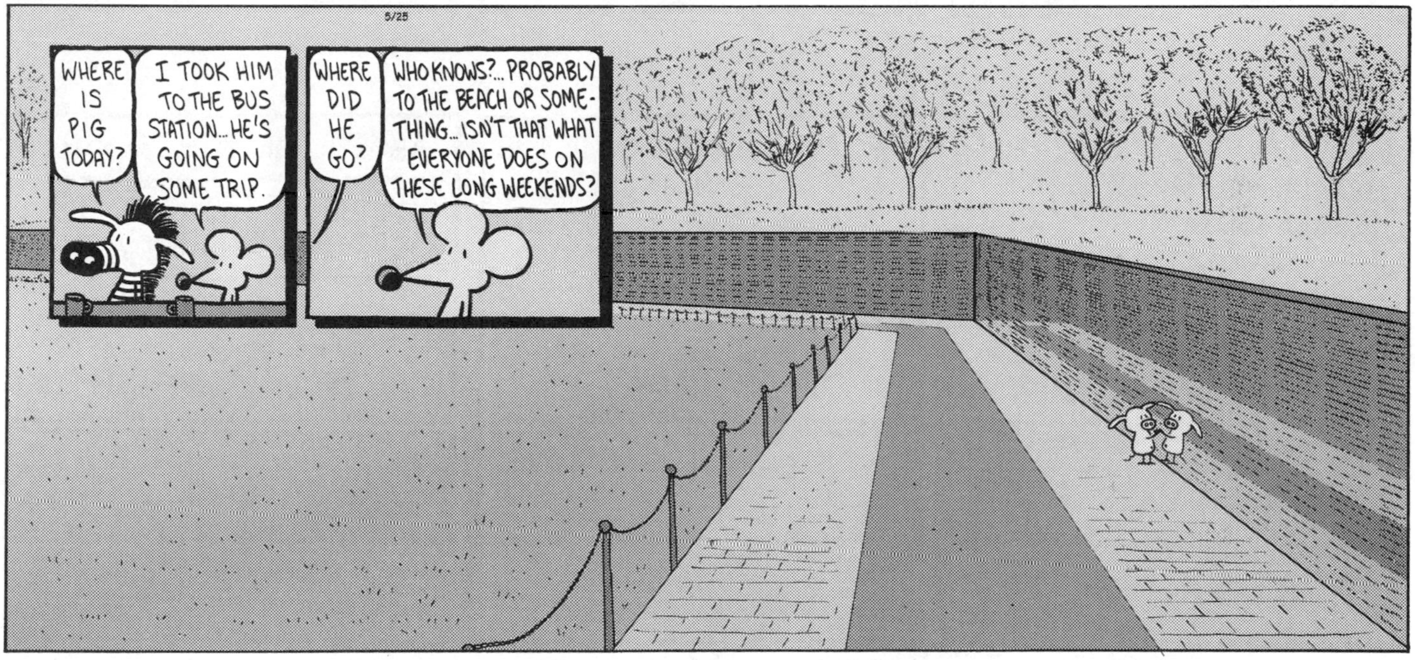
5/25
WHERE IS PIG TODAY?
I TOOK HIM TO THE BUS STATION... HE'S GOING ON SOME TRIP.
WHERE DID HE GO?
WHO KNOWS?... PROBABLY TO THE BEACH OR SOME-THING... ISN'T THAT WHAT EVERYONE DOES ON THESE LONG WEEKENDS?

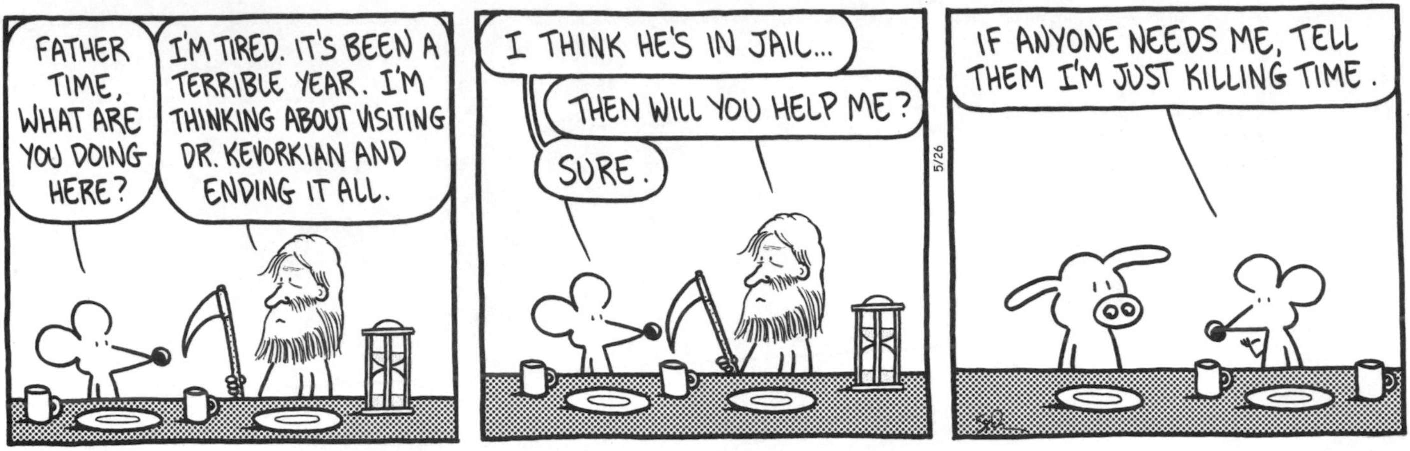
FATHER TIME, WHAT ARE YOU DOING HERE?
I'M TIRED. IT'S BEEN A TERRIBLE YEAR. I'M THINKING ABOUT VISITING DR. KEVORKIAN AND ENDING IT ALL.
I THINK HE'S IN JAIL...
THEN WILL YOU HELP ME?
SURE.
5/26
IF ANYONE NEEDS ME, TELL THEM I'M JUST KILLING TIME.

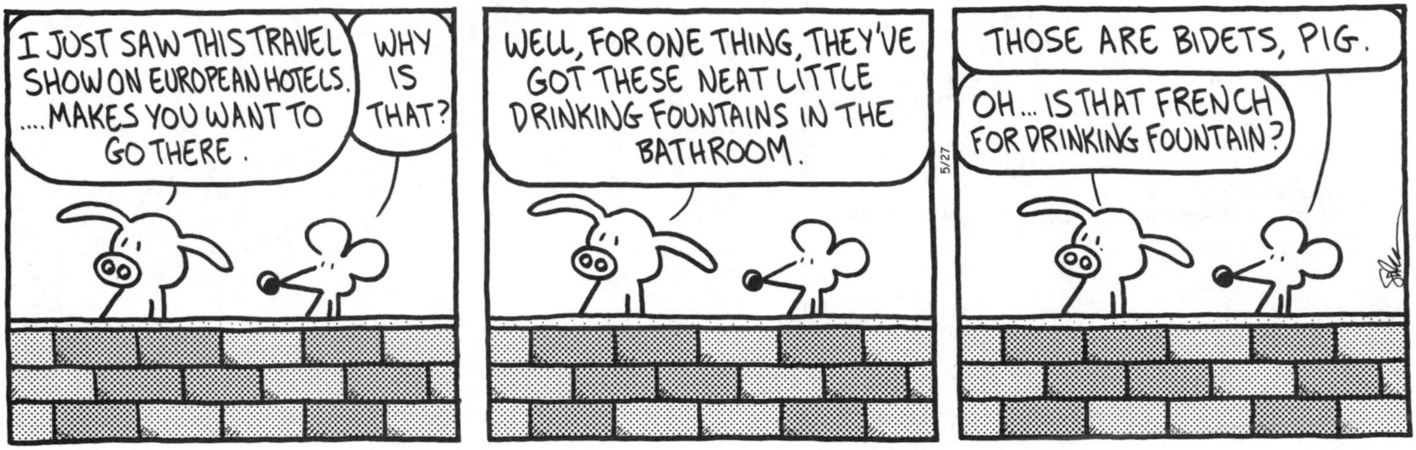
I JUST SAW THIS TRAVEL SHOW ON EUROPEAN HOTELS. ....MAKES YOU WANT TO GO THERE.
WHY IS THAT?
WELL, FOR ONE THING, THEY'VE GOT THESE NEAT LITTLE DRINKING FOUNTAINS IN THE BATHROOM.
5/27
THOSE ARE BIDETS, PIG.
OH... IS THAT FRENCH FOR DRINKING FOUNTAIN?

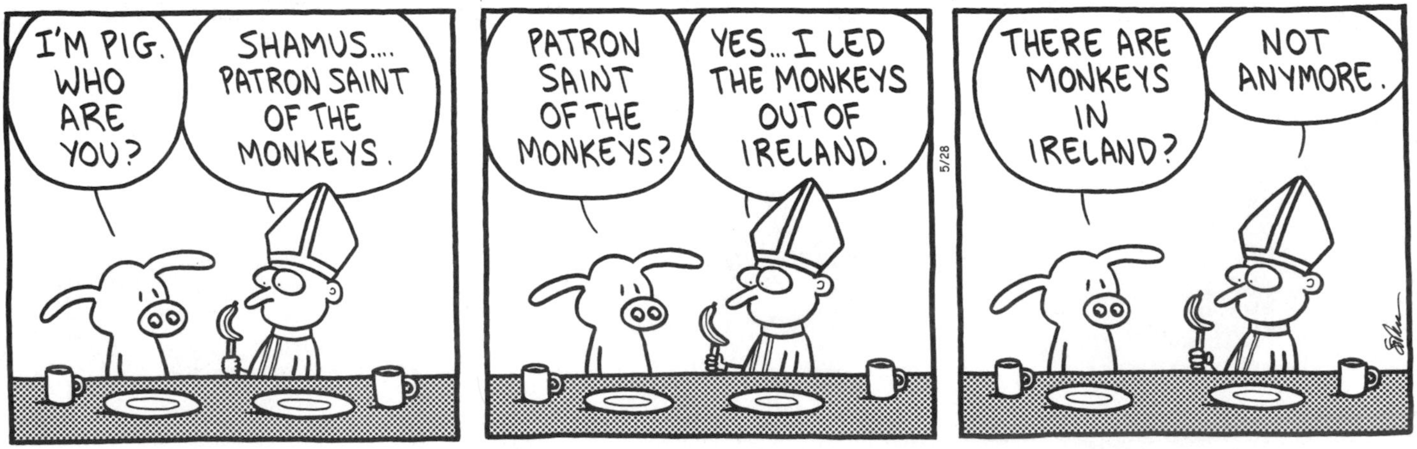
I'M PIG. WHO ARE YOU?
SHAMUS.... PATRON SAINT OF THE MONKEYS.
PATRON SAINT OF THE MONKEYS?
YES... I LED THE MONKEYS OUT OF IRELAND.
5/28
THERE ARE MONKEYS IN IRELAND?
NOT ANYMORE.

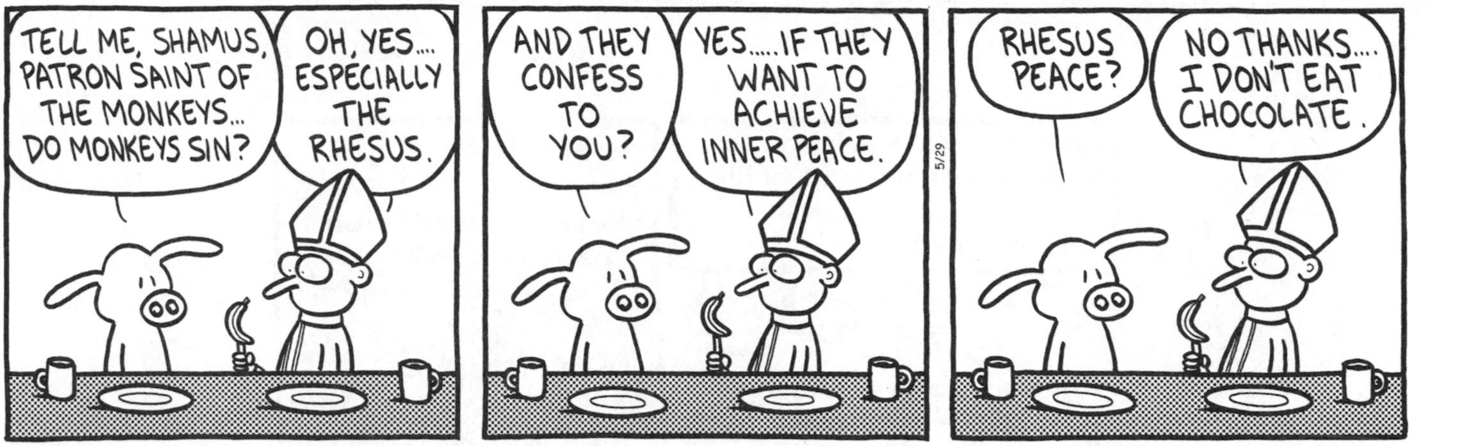
TELL ME, SHAMUS, PATRON SAINT OF THE MONKEYS... DO MONKEYS SIN?
OH, YES.... ESPECIALLY THE RHESUS.
AND THEY CONFESS TO YOU?
YES.....IF THEY WANT TO ACHIEVE INNER PEACE.
5/29
RHESUS PEACE?
NO THANKS.... I DON'T EAT CHOCOLATE.

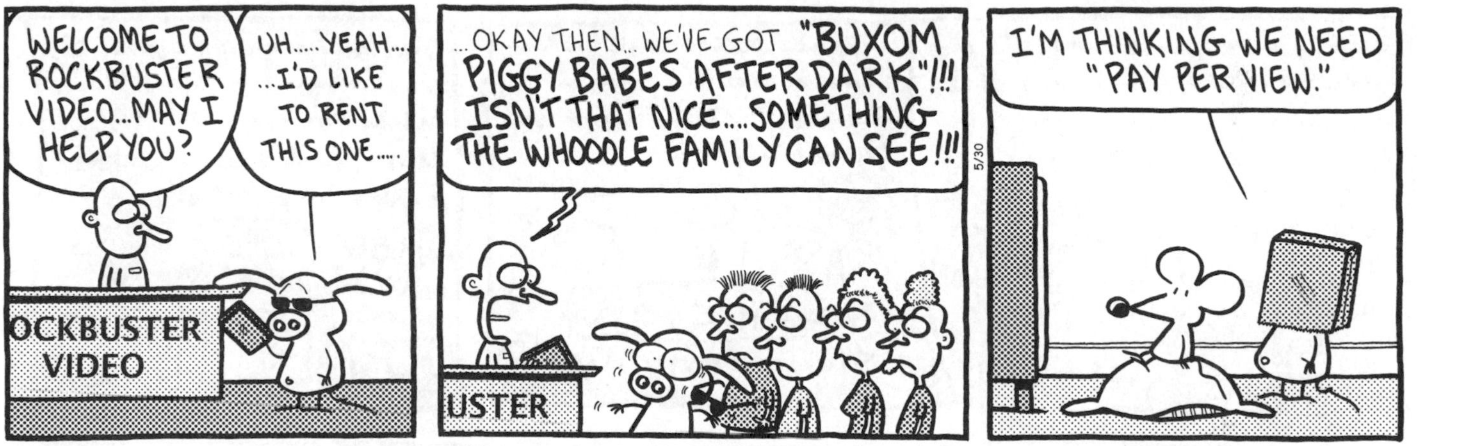
WELCOME TO ROCKBUSTER VIDEO...MAY I HELP YOU?
UH.....YEAH... ...I'D LIKE TO RENT THIS ONE.....
OCKBUSTER VIDEO
...OKAY THEN...WE'VE GOT "BUXOM PIGGY BABES AFTER DARK"!!! ISN'T THAT NICE....SOMETHING THE WHOOOLE FAMILY CAN SEE!!!
USTER
5/30
I'M THINKING WE NEED "PAY PER VIEW."

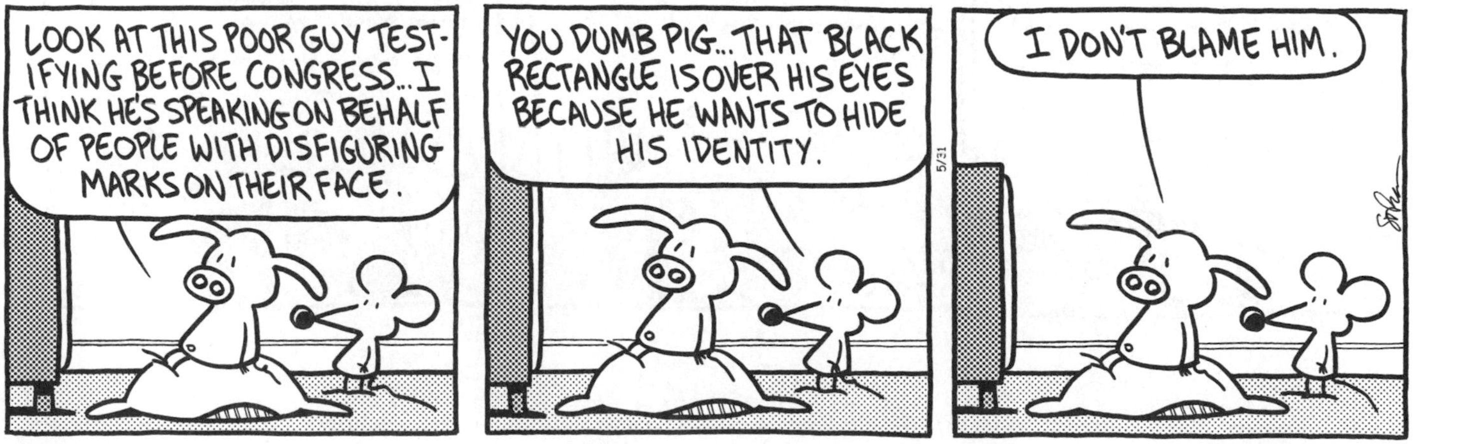
LOOK AT THIS POOR GUY TEST-IFYING BEFORE CONGRESS...I THINK HE'S SPEAKING ON BEHALF OF PEOPLE WITH DISFIGURING MARKS ON THEIR FACE.
YOU DUMB PIG...THAT BLACK RECTANGLE IS OVER HIS EYES BECAUSE HE WANTS TO HIDE HIS IDENTITY.
5/31
I DON'T BLAME HIM.

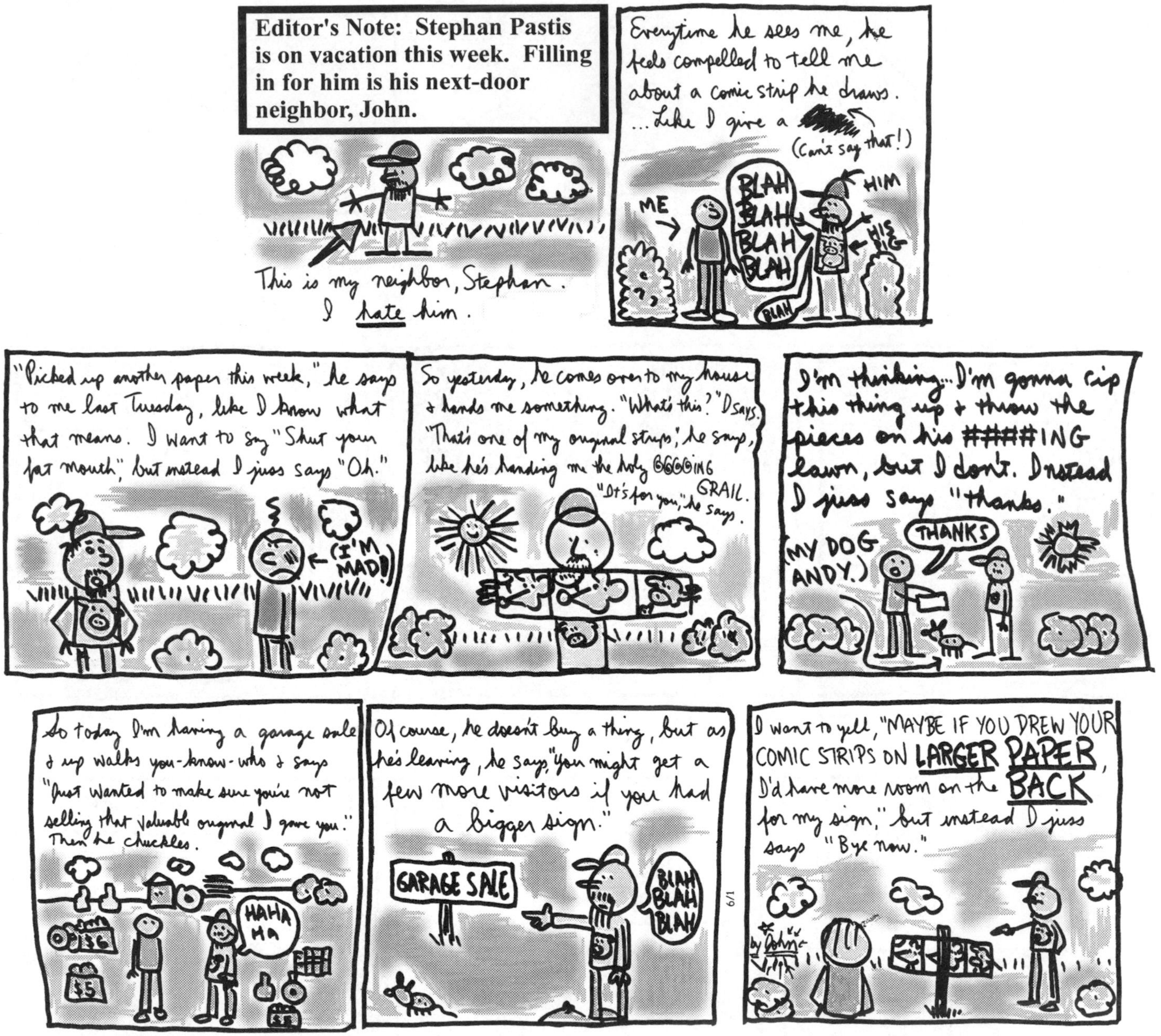
Editor's Note: Stephan Pastis is on vacation this week. Filling in for him is his next-door neighbor, John.
This is my neighbor, Stephan. I hate him.
Everytime he sees me, he feels compelled to tell me about a comic strip he draws. ...Like I give a [redacted]
(Can't say that!)
ME
HIM
BLAH BLAH BLAH BLAH
HIS PIG
BLAH
"Picked up another paper this week," he says to me last Tuesday, like I know what that means. I want to say "Shut your fat mouth," but instead I juss says "Oh."
(I'M MAD!)
So yesterday, he comes over to my house & hands me something. "What's this?" I says. "That's one of my original strips," he says, like he's handing me the holy 6666ING GRAIL.
"It's for you," he says.
I'm thinking... I'm gonna rip this thing up & throw the pieces on his ####ING lawn, but I don't. Instead I juss says "thanks."
(MY DOG ANDY.)
THANKS
So today I'm having a garage sale & up walks you-know-who & says "Just wanted to make sure you're not selling that valuable original I gave you." Then he chuckles.
$5
$5
HAHA HA
Of course, he doesn't buy a thing, but as he's leaving, he says "You might get a few more visitors if you had a bigger sign."
GARAGE SALE
BLAH BLAH BLAH
I want to yell, "MAYBE IF YOU DREW YOUR COMIC STRIPS ON LARGER PAPER, I'd have more room on the BACK for my sign," but instead I juss says "Bye now."
by John

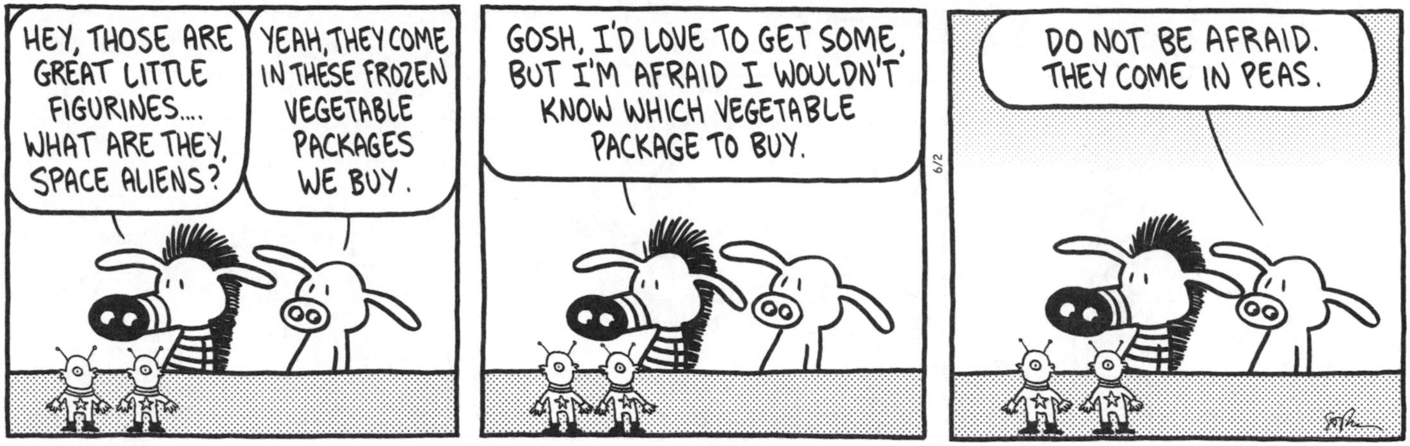
HEY, THOSE ARE GREAT LITTLE FIGURINES.... WHAT ARE THEY, SPACE ALIENS?
YEAH, THEY COME IN THESE FROZEN VEGETABLE PACKAGES WE BUY.
GOSH, I'D LOVE TO GET SOME, BUT I'M AFRAID I WOULDN'T KNOW WHICH VEGETABLE PACKAGE TO BUY.
6/2
DO NOT BE AFRAID. THEY COME IN PEAS.

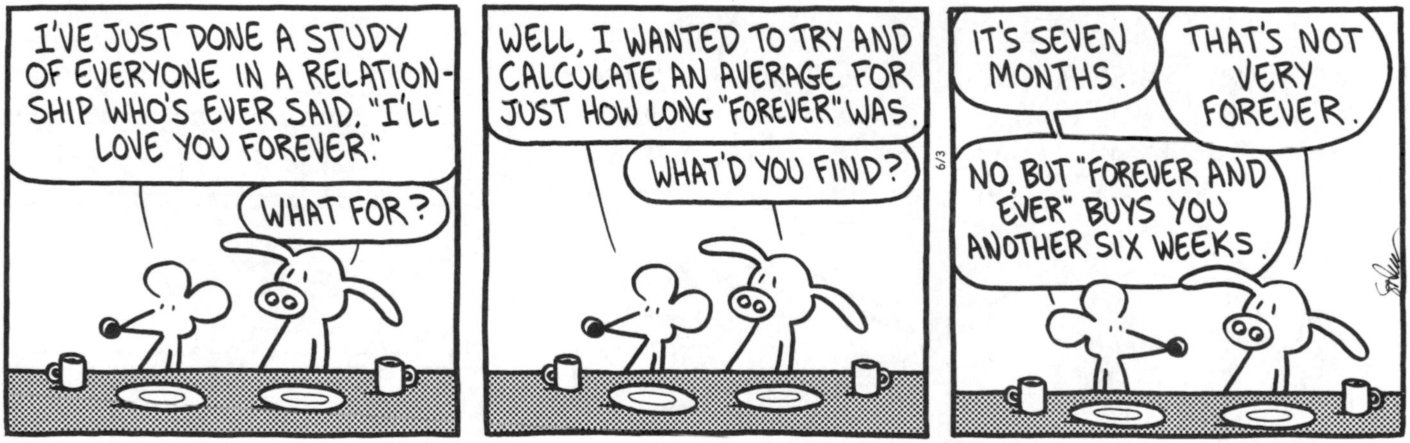
I'VE JUST DONE A STUDY OF EVERYONE IN A RELATIONSHIP WHO'S EVER SAID, "I'LL LOVE YOU FOREVER."
WHAT FOR?
WELL, I WANTED TO TRY AND CALCULATE AN AVERAGE FOR JUST HOW LONG "FOREVER" WAS.
WHAT'D YOU FIND?
6/3
IT'S SEVEN MONTHS.
THAT'S NOT VERY FOREVER.
NO, BUT "FOREVER AND EVER" BUYS YOU ANOTHER SIX WEEKS.

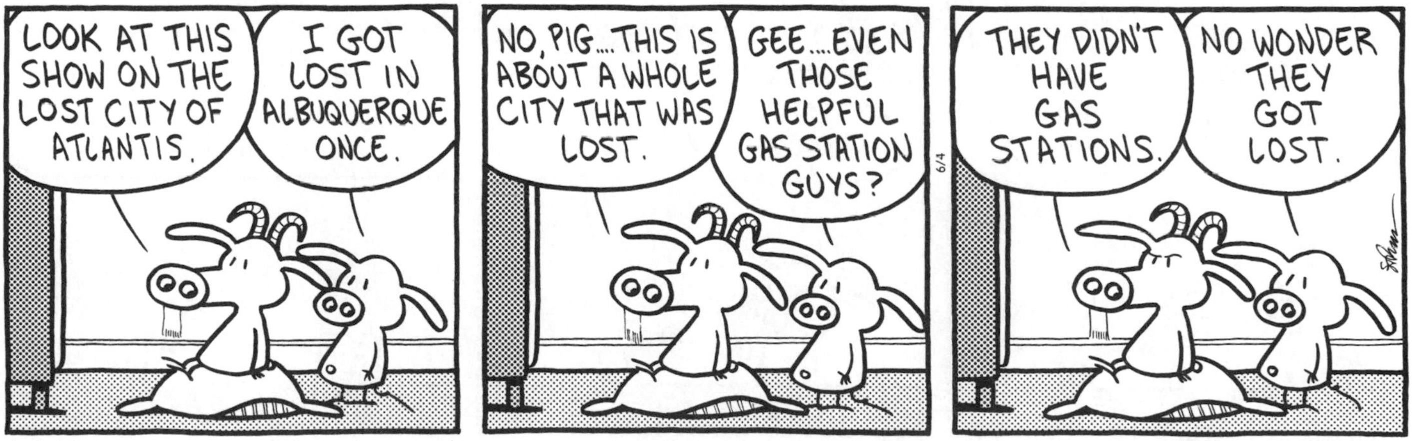
LOOK AT THIS SHOW ON THE LOST CITY OF ATLANTIS.
I GOT LOST IN ALBUQUERQUE ONCE.
NO, PIG.... THIS IS ABOUT A WHOLE CITY THAT WAS LOST.
GEE.... EVEN THOSE HELPFUL GAS STATION GUYS?
6/4
THEY DIDN'T HAVE GAS STATIONS.
NO WONDER THEY GOT LOST.

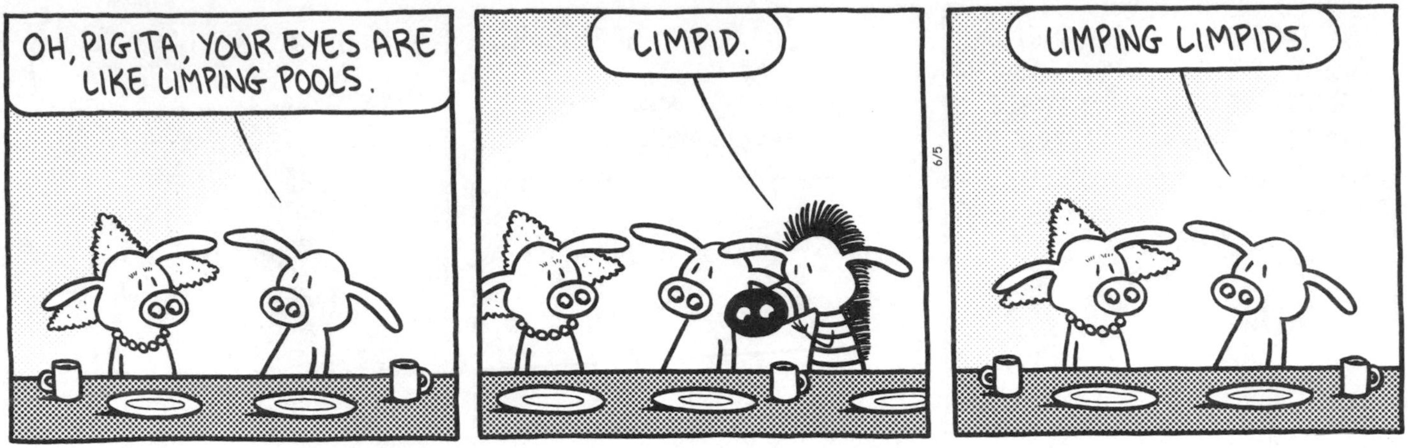
OH, PIGITA, YOUR EYES ARE LIKE LIMPING POOLS.
LIMPID.
6/5
LIMPING LIMPIDS.

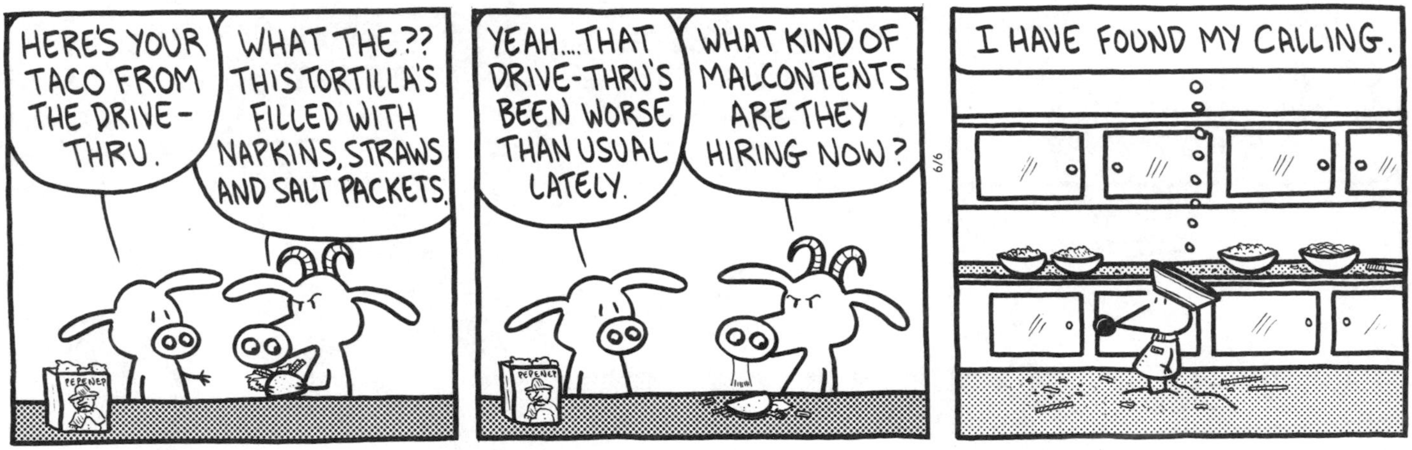
HERE'S YOUR TACO FROM THE DRIVE-THRU.
WHAT THE?? THIS TORTILLA'S FILLED WITH NAPKINS, STRAWS AND SALT PACKETS.
YEAH....THAT DRIVE-THRU'S BEEN WORSE THAN USUAL LATELY.
WHAT KIND OF MALCONTENTS ARE THEY HIRING NOW?
6/6
I HAVE FOUND MY CALLING.

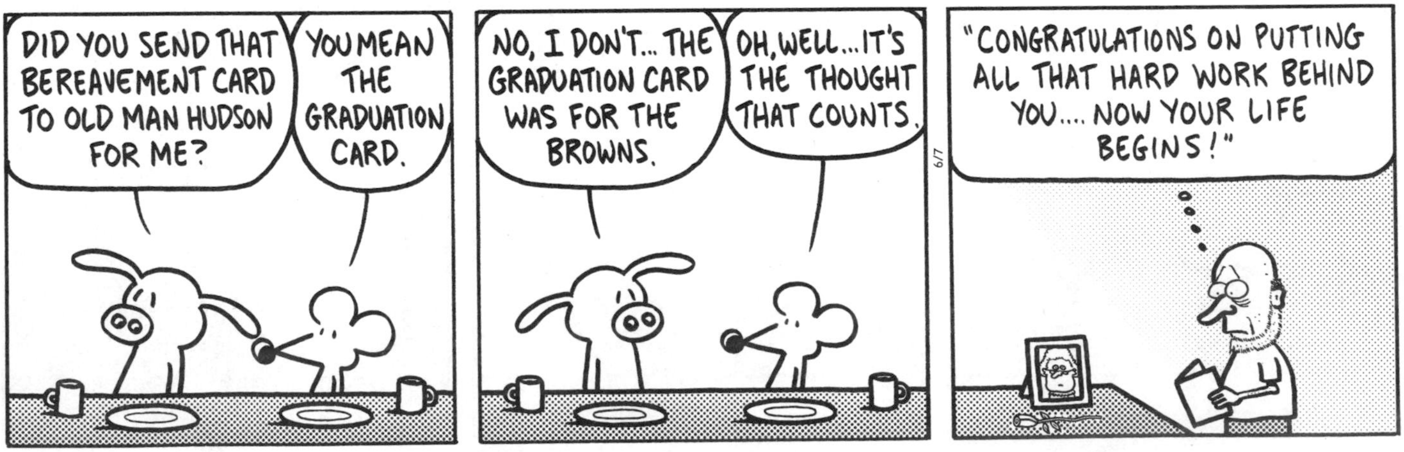
DID YOU SEND THAT BEREAVEMENT CARD TO OLD MAN HUDSON FOR ME?
YOU MEAN THE GRADUATION CARD.
NO, I DON'T... THE GRADUATION CARD WAS FOR THE BROWNS.
OH, WELL...IT'S THE THOUGHT THAT COUNTS.
6/7
"CONGRATULATIONS ON PUTTING ALL THAT HARD WORK BEHIND YOU.... NOW YOUR LIFE BEGINS!"

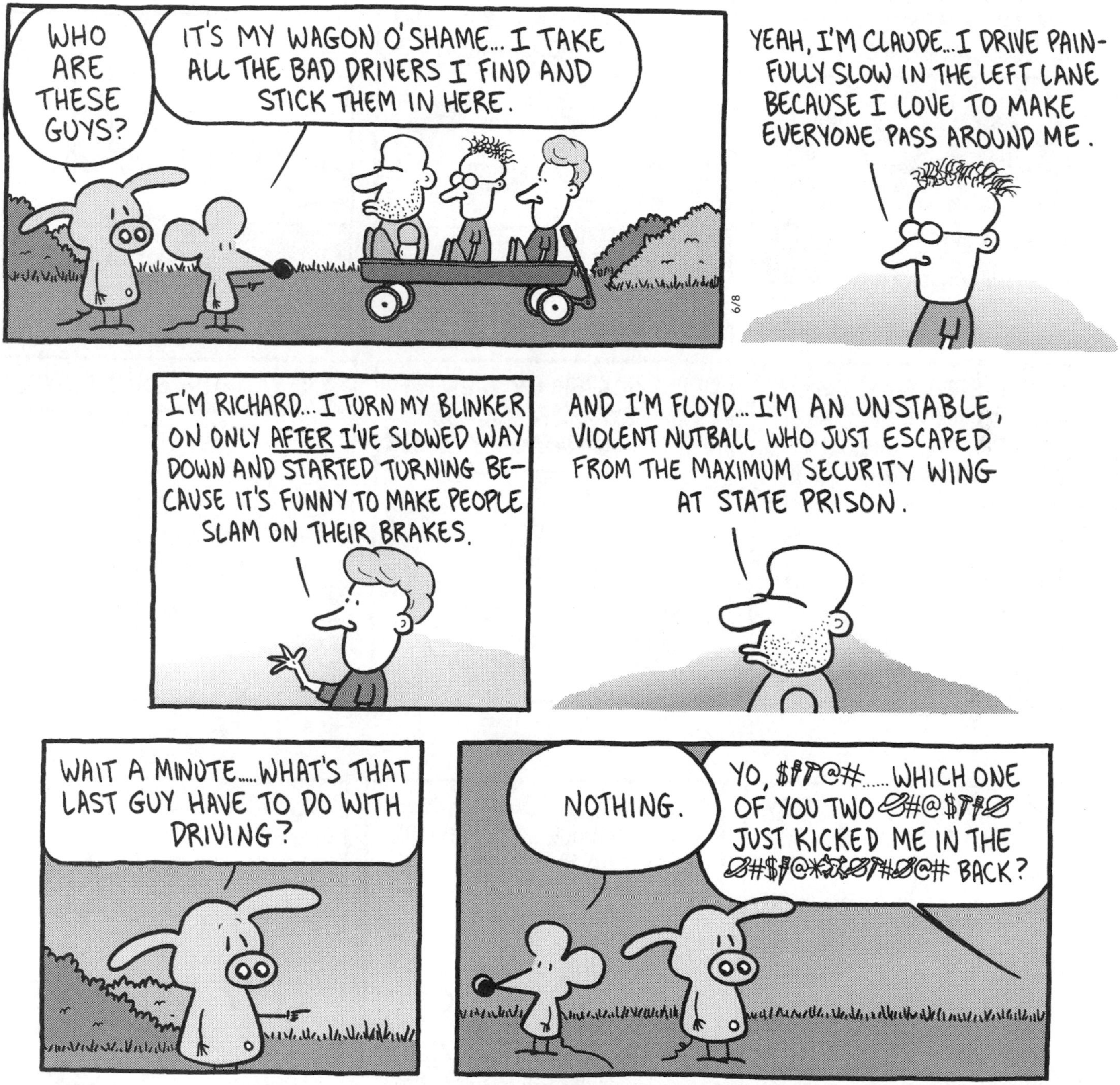

WHO ARE THESE GUYS?
IT'S MY WAGON O' SHAME... I TAKE ALL THE BAD DRIVERS I FIND AND STICK THEM IN HERE.
6/8
YEAH, I'M CLAUDE...I DRIVE PAINFULLY SLOW IN THE LEFT LANE BECAUSE I LOVE TO MAKE EVERYONE PASS AROUND ME.
I'M RICHARD...I TURN MY BLINKER ON ONLY AFTER I'VE SLOWED WAY DOWN AND STARTED TURNING BECAUSE IT'S FUNNY TO MAKE PEOPLE SLAM ON THEIR BRAKES.
AND I'M FLOYD...I'M AN UNSTABLE, VIOLENT NUTBALL WHO JUST ESCAPED FROM THE MAXIMUM SECURITY WING AT STATE PRISON.
WAIT A MINUTE.....WHAT'S THAT LAST GUY HAVE TO DO WITH DRIVING?
NOTHING.
YO, $!?@#..... WHICH ONE OF YOU TWO @#@$!?@ JUST KICKED ME IN THE @#$!@*%@!#@@# BACK?

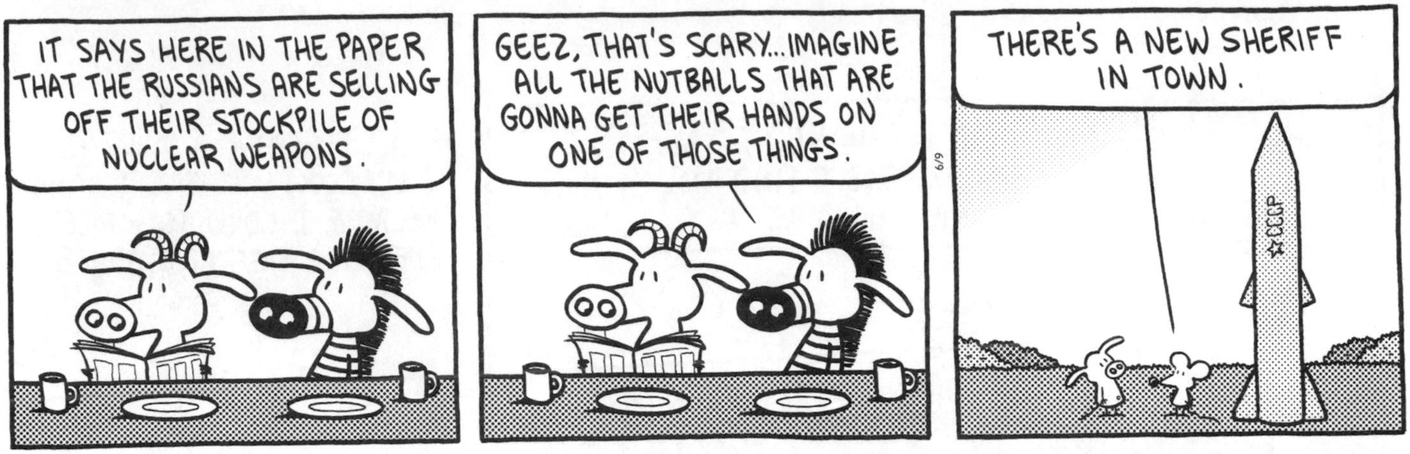
IT SAYS HERE IN THE PAPER THAT THE RUSSIANS ARE SELLING OFF THEIR STOCKPILE OF NUCLEAR WEAPONS.
GEEZ, THAT'S SCARY... IMAGINE ALL THE NUTBALLS THAT ARE GONNA GET THEIR HANDS ON ONE OF THOSE THINGS.
6/9
THERE'S A NEW SHERIFF IN TOWN.
CCCP

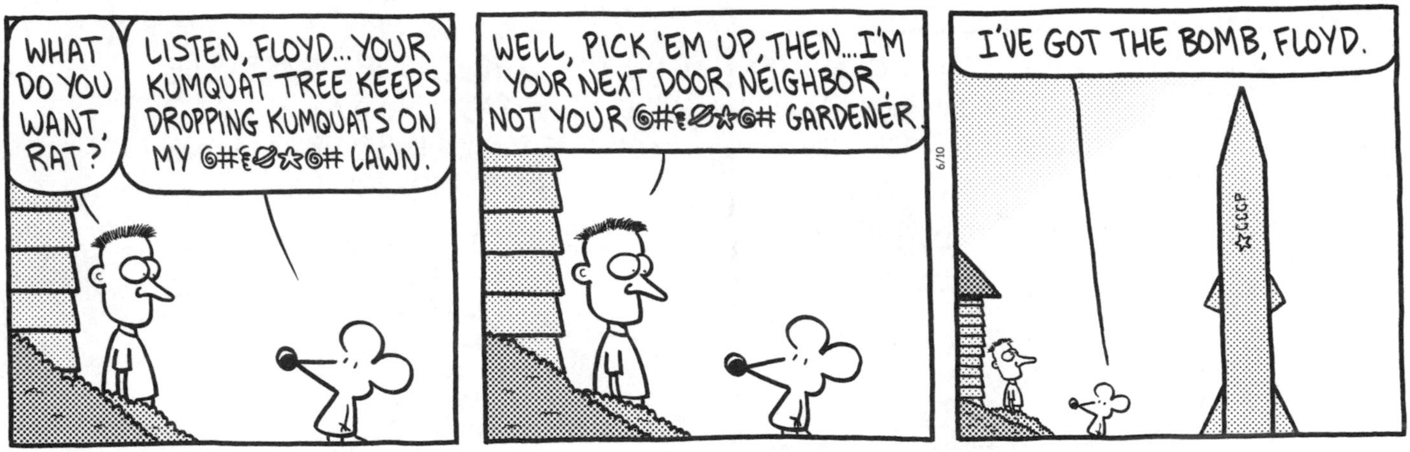
WHAT DO YOU WANT, RAT?
LISTEN, FLOYD... YOUR KUMQUAT TREE KEEPS DROPPING KUMQUATS ON MY @#$@☆@# LAWN.
WELL, PICK 'EM UP, THEN... I'M YOUR NEXT DOOR NEIGHBOR, NOT YOUR @#$@☆@# GARDENER.
6/10
I'VE GOT THE BOMB, FLOYD.
CCCP

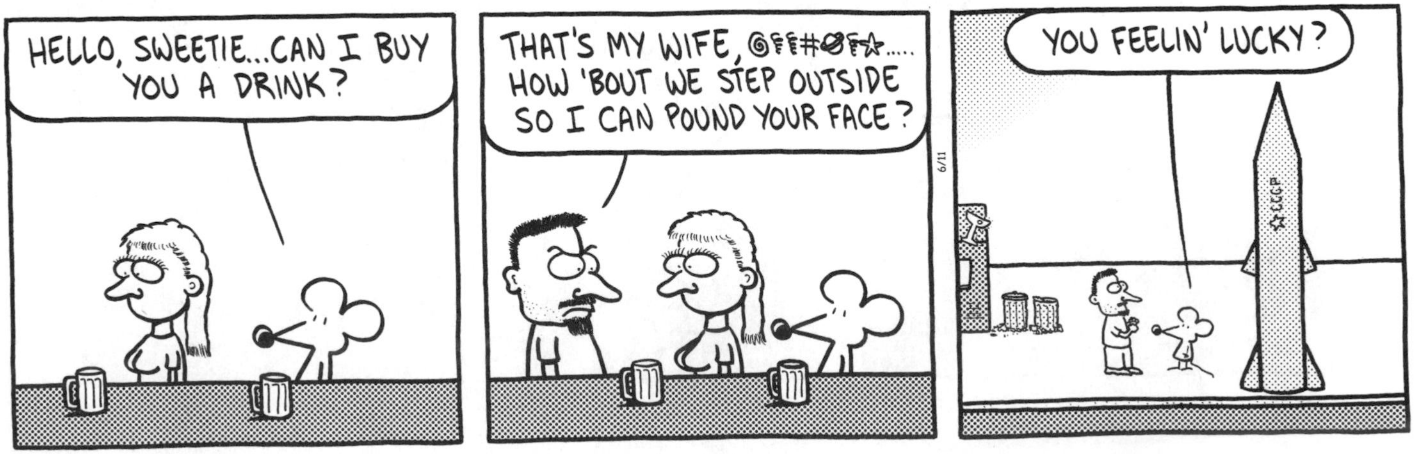
HELLO, SWEETIE... CAN I BUY YOU A DRINK?
THAT'S MY WIFE, @$$#@$☆..... HOW 'BOUT WE STEP OUTSIDE SO I CAN POUND YOUR FACE?
6/11
YOU FEELIN' LUCKY?
CCCP

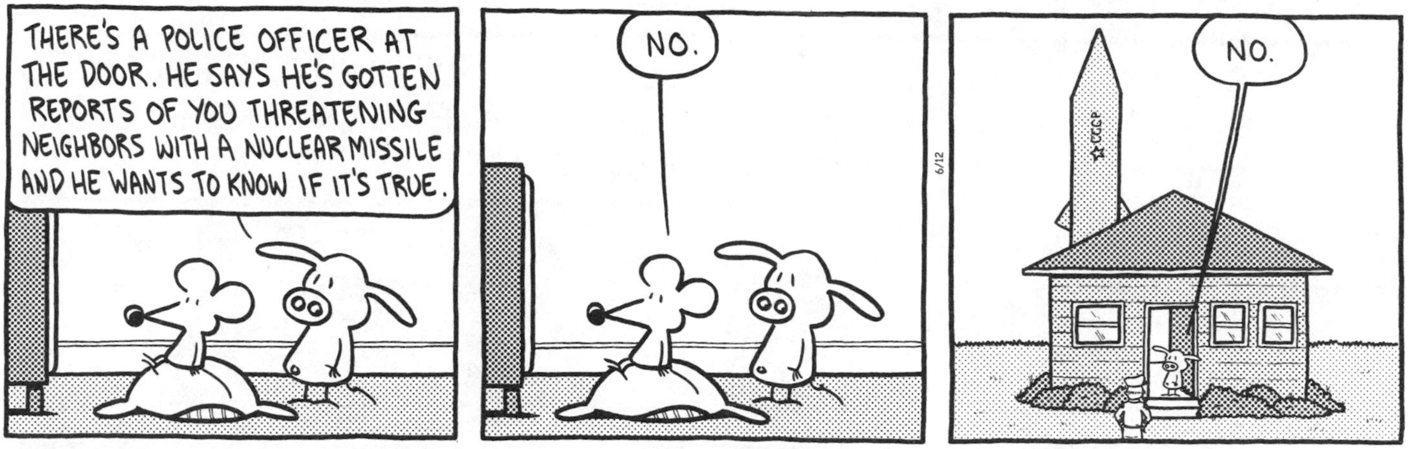
THERE'S A POLICE OFFICER AT THE DOOR. HE SAYS HE'S GOTTEN REPORTS OF YOU THREATENING NEIGHBORS WITH A NUCLEAR MISSILE AND HE WANTS TO KNOW IF IT'S TRUE.
NO.
6/12
CCCP
NO.

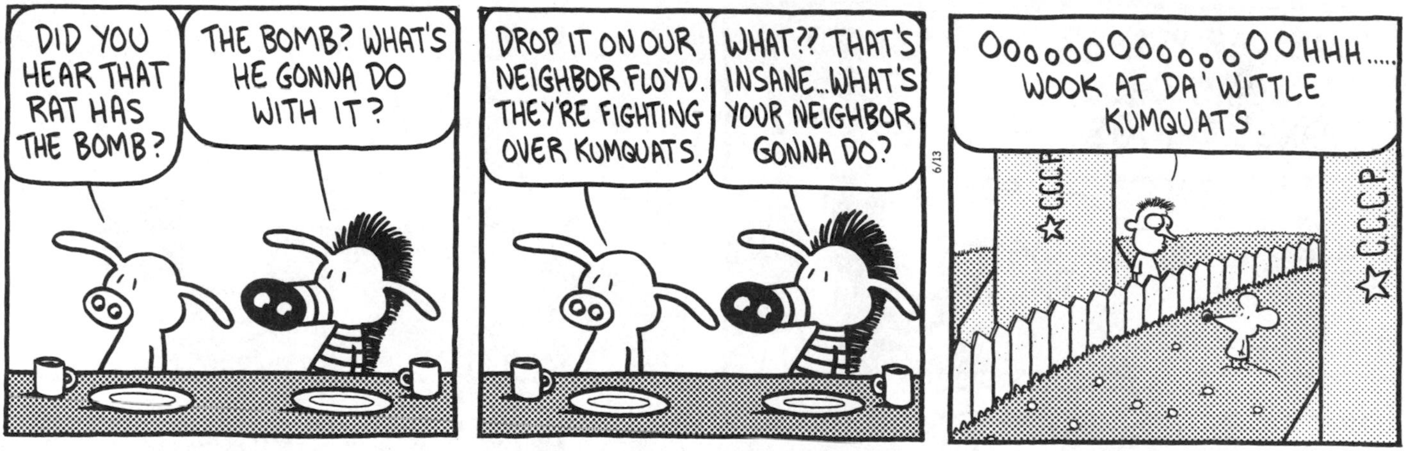
DID YOU HEAR THAT RAT HAS THE BOMB?
THE BOMB? WHAT'S HE GONNA DO WITH IT?
DROP IT ON OUR NEIGHBOR FLOYD. THEY'RE FIGHTING OVER KUMQUATS.
WHAT?? THAT'S INSANE...WHAT'S YOUR NEIGHBOR GONNA DO?
6/13
OooooOOooooOOHHH..... WOOK AT DA' WITTLE KUMQUATS.
C.C.C.P.
C.C.C.P.

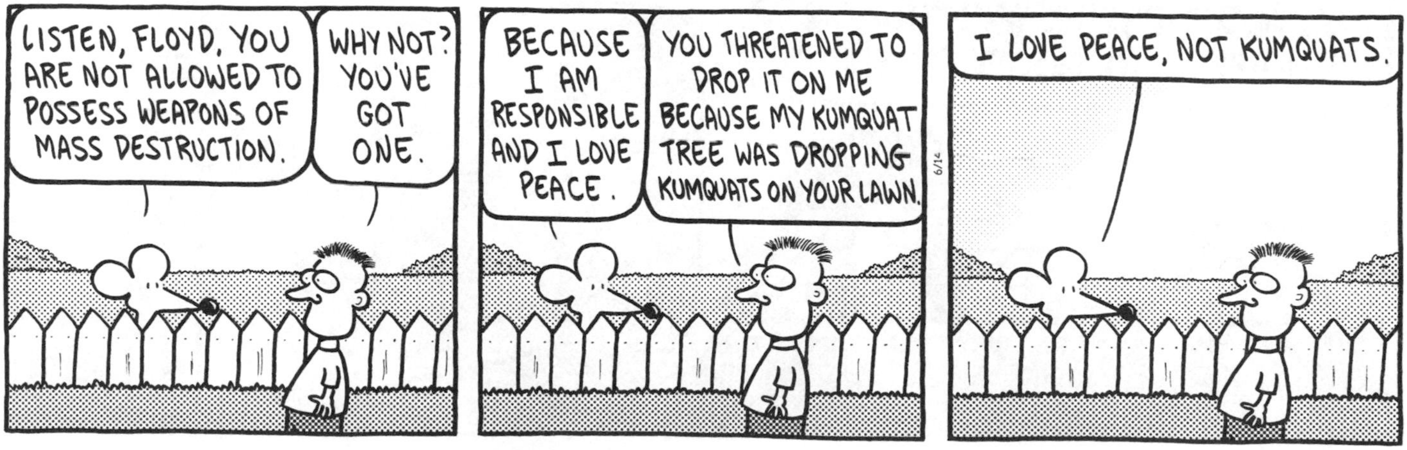
LISTEN, FLOYD, YOU ARE NOT ALLOWED TO POSSESS WEAPONS OF MASS DESTRUCTION.
WHY NOT? YOU'VE GOT ONE.
BECAUSE I AM RESPONSIBLE AND I LOVE PEACE.
YOU THREATENED TO DROP IT ON ME BECAUSE MY KUMQUAT TREE WAS DROPPING KUMQUATS ON YOUR LAWN.
6/14
I LOVE PEACE, NOT KUMQUATS.

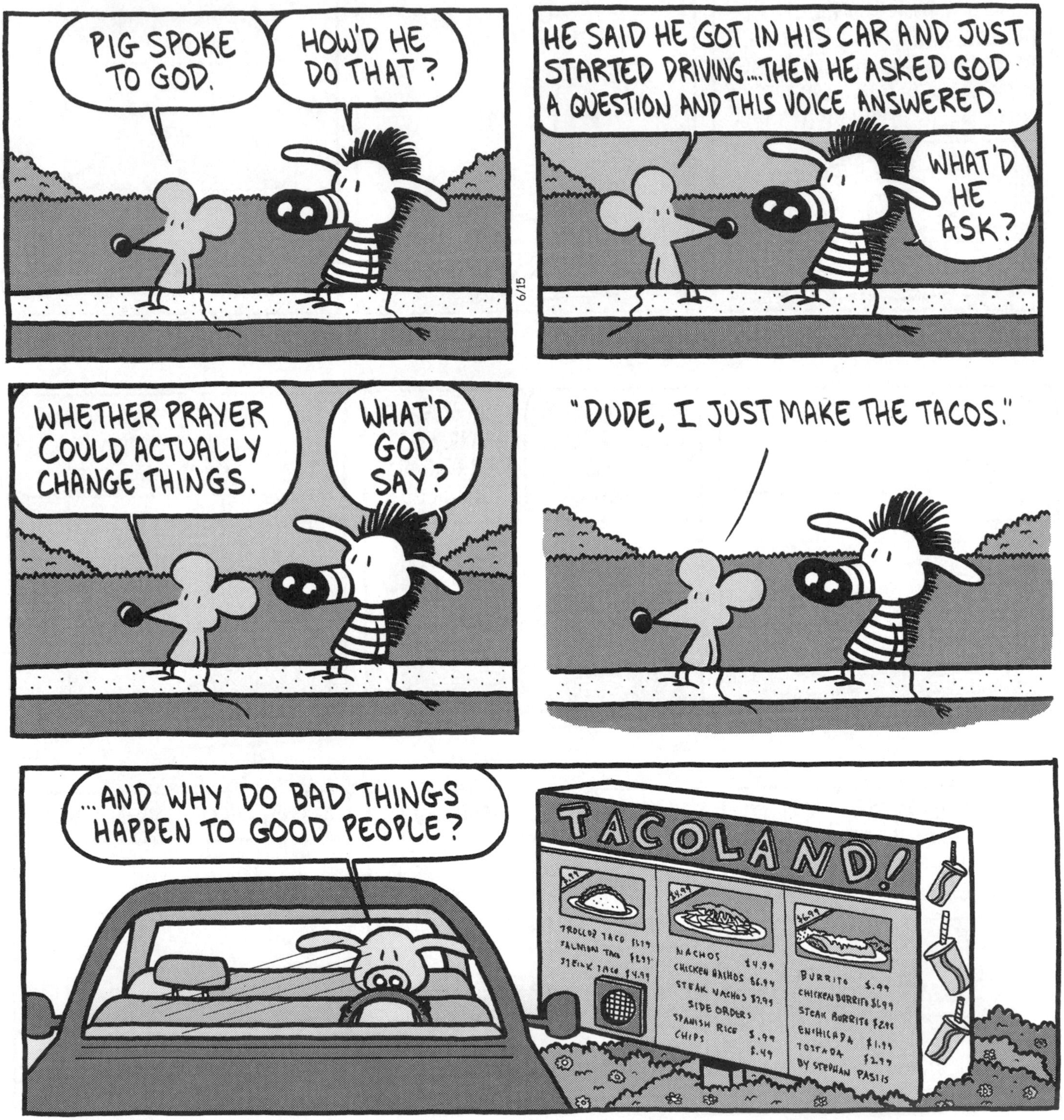
PIG SPOKE TO GOD.
HOW'D HE DO THAT?
6/15
HE SAID HE GOT IN HIS CAR AND JUST STARTED DRIVING....THEN HE ASKED GOD A QUESTION AND THIS VOICE ANSWERED.
WHAT'D HE ASK?
WHETHER PRAYER COULD ACTUALLY CHANGE THINGS.
WHAT'D GOD SAY?
"DUDE, I JUST MAKE THE TACOS."
...AND WHY DO BAD THINGS HAPPEN TO GOOD PEOPLE?
TACOLAND!
NACHOS
SIDE ORDERS
BURRITO
TOSTADA
BY STEPHAN PASTIS

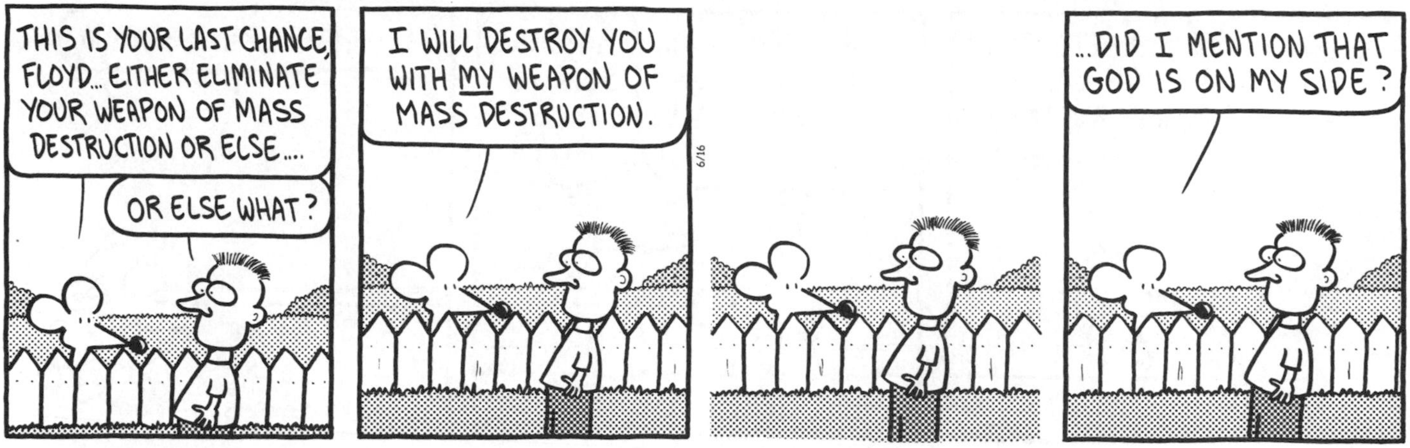
THIS IS YOUR LAST CHANCE, FLOYD... EITHER ELIMINATE YOUR WEAPON OF MASS DESTRUCTION OR ELSE....
OR ELSE WHAT?
I WILL DESTROY YOU WITH MY WEAPON OF MASS DESTRUCTION.
6/16
...DID I MENTION THAT GOD IS ON MY SIDE?

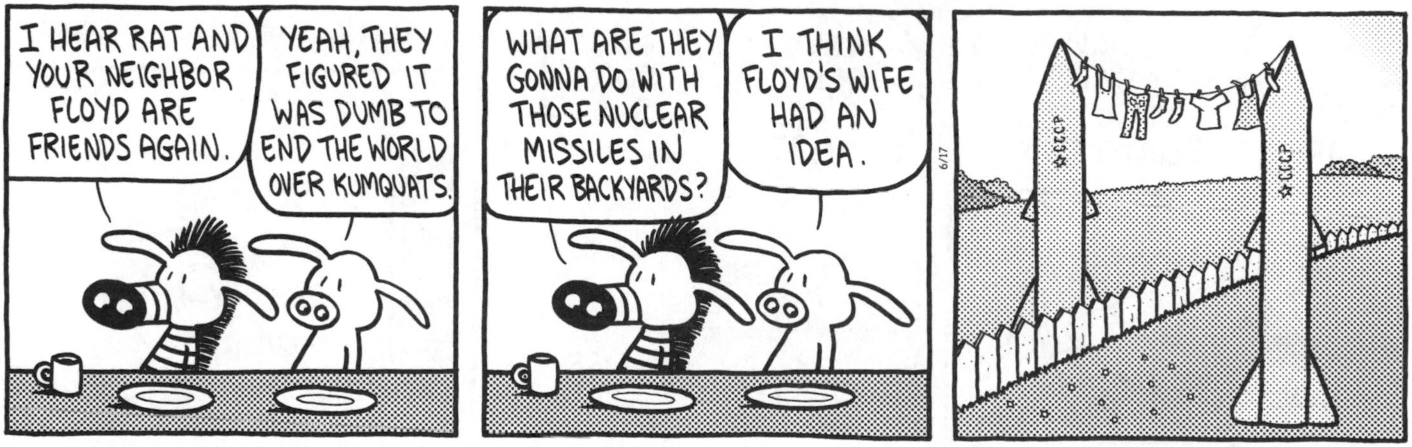
I HEAR RAT AND YOUR NEIGHBOR FLOYD ARE FRIENDS AGAIN.
YEAH, THEY FIGURED IT WAS DUMB TO END THE WORLD OVER KUMQUATS.
WHAT ARE THEY GONNA DO WITH THOSE NUCLEAR MISSILES IN THEIR BACKYARDS?
I THINK FLOYD'S WIFE HAD AN IDEA.
6/17
CCCP
CCCP

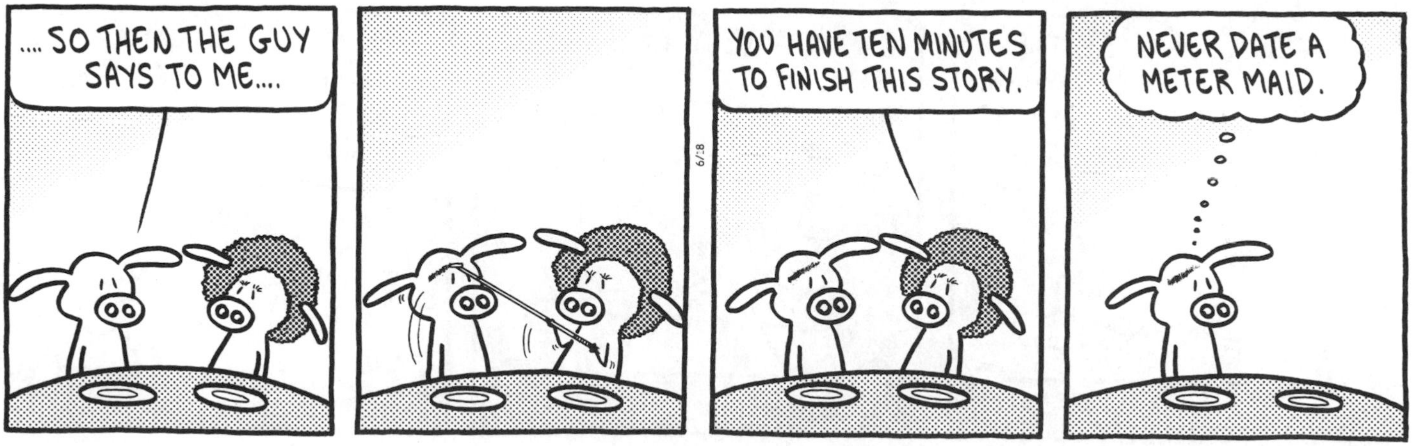
.... SO THEN THE GUY SAYS TO ME....
YOU HAVE TEN MINUTES TO FINISH THIS STORY.
NEVER DATE A METER MAID.

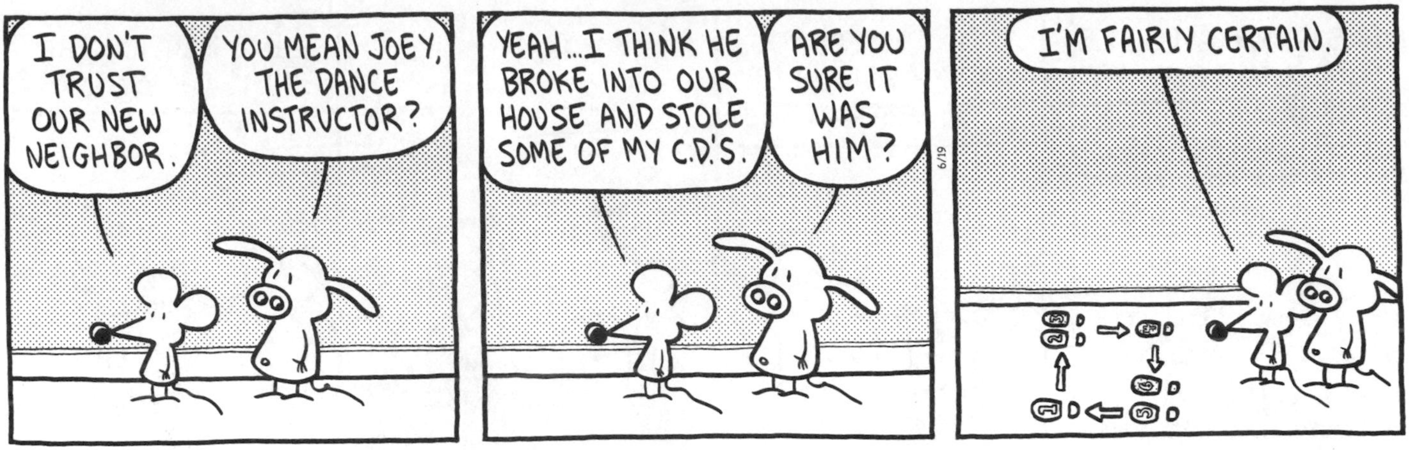
I DON'T TRUST OUR NEW NEIGHBOR.
YOU MEAN JOEY, THE DANCE INSTRUCTOR?
YEAH...I THINK HE BROKE INTO OUR HOUSE AND STOLE SOME OF MY C.D.'S.
ARE YOU SURE IT WAS HIM?
6/19
I'M FAIRLY CERTAIN.

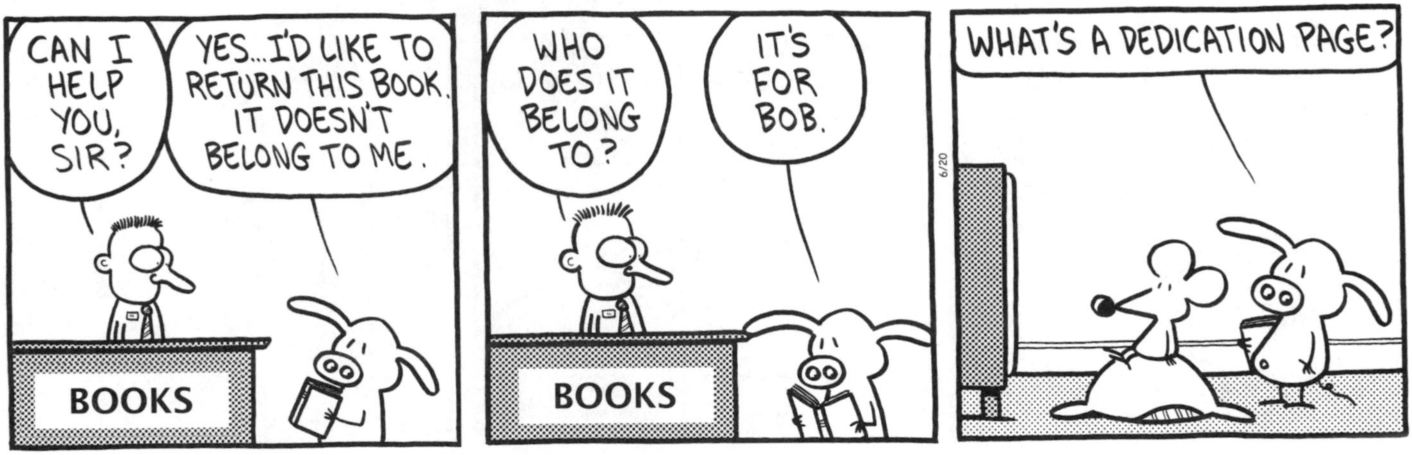
CAN I HELP YOU, SIR?
YES...I'D LIKE TO RETURN THIS BOOK. IT DOESN'T BELONG TO ME.
BOOKS
WHO DOES IT BELONG TO?
IT'S FOR BOB.
BOOKS
6/20
WHAT'S A DEDICATION PAGE?

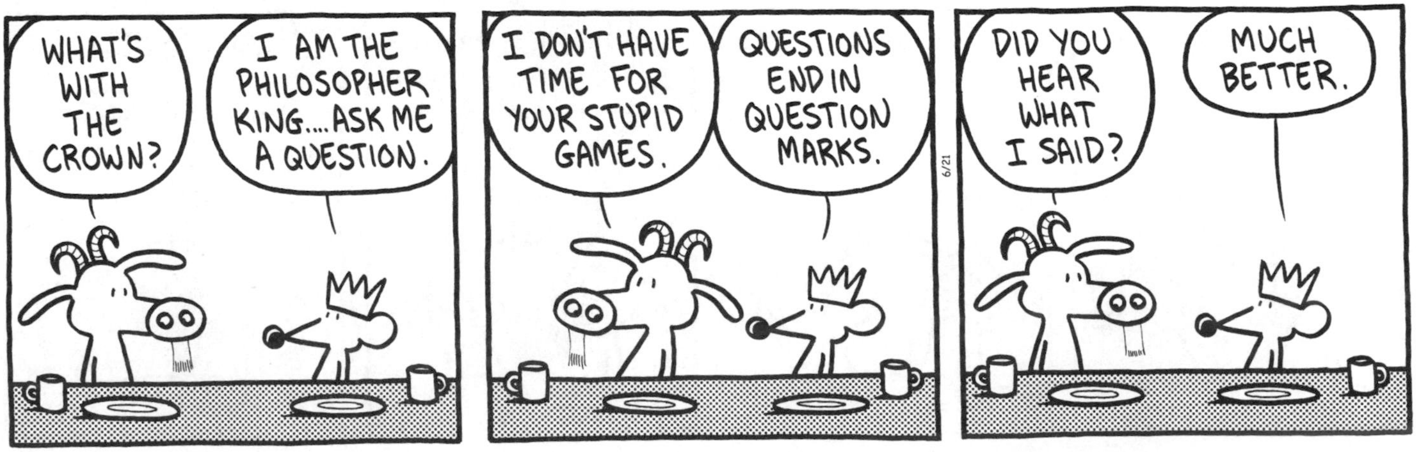
WHAT'S WITH THE CROWN?
I AM THE PHILOSOPHER KING....ASK ME A QUESTION.
I DON'T HAVE TIME FOR YOUR STUPID GAMES.
QUESTIONS END IN QUESTION MARKS.
6/21
DID YOU HEAR WHAT I SAID?
MUCH BETTER.

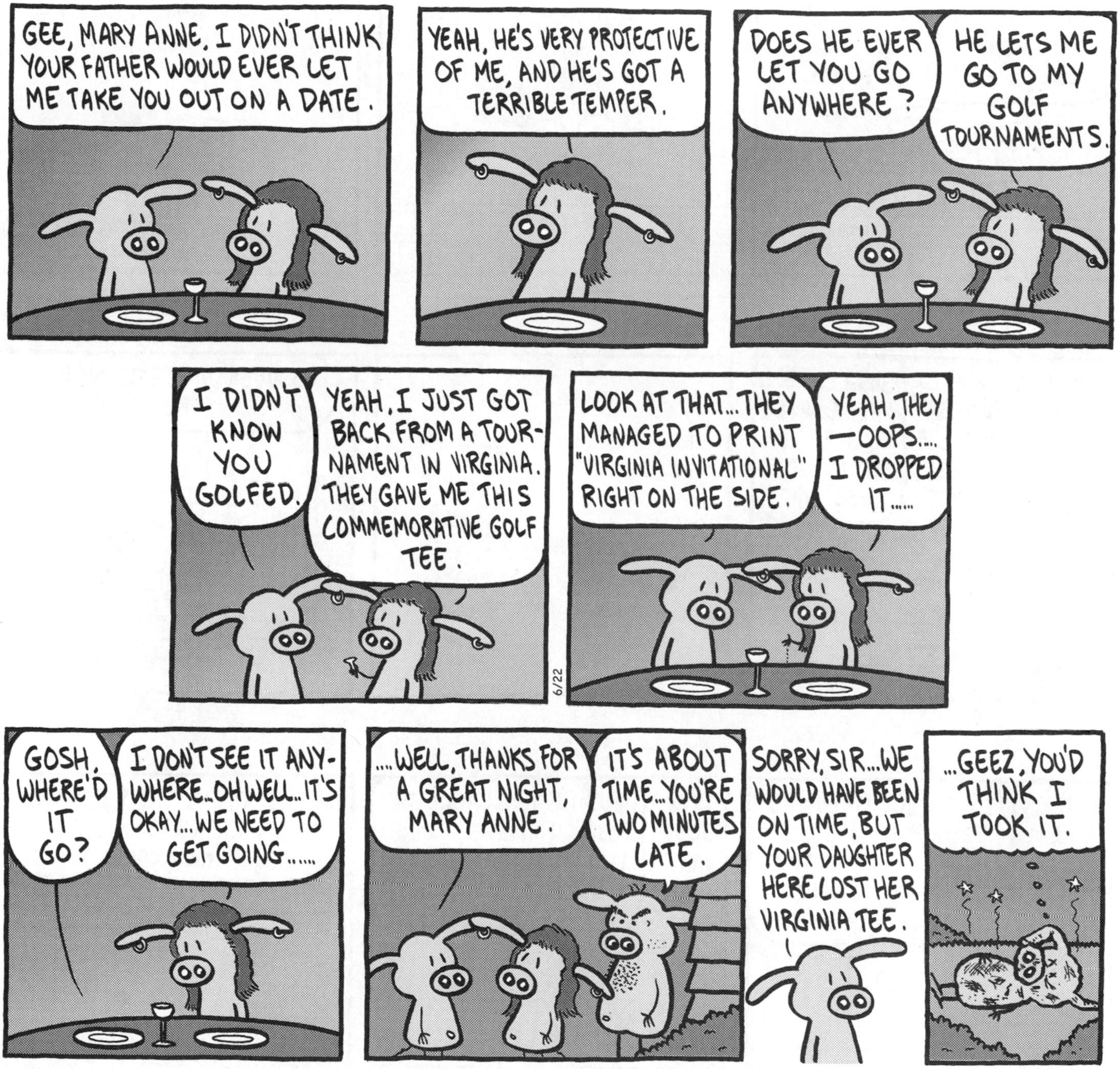
GEE, MARY ANNE. I DIDN'T THINK YOUR FATHER WOULD EVER LET ME TAKE YOU OUT ON A DATE.
YEAH, HE'S VERY PROTECTIVE OF ME, AND HE'S GOT A TERRIBLE TEMPER.
DOES HE EVER LET YOU GO ANYWHERE?
HE LETS ME GO TO MY GOLF TOURNAMENTS.
I DIDN'T KNOW YOU GOLFED.
YEAH, I JUST GOT BACK FROM A TOURNAMENT IN VIRGINIA. THEY GAVE ME THIS COMMEMORATIVE GOLF TEE.
6/22
LOOK AT THAT... THEY MANAGED TO PRINT "VIRGINIA INVITATIONAL" RIGHT ON THE SIDE.
YEAH, THEY —OOPS.... I DROPPED IT.....
GOSH, WHERE'D IT GO?
I DON'T SEE IT ANYWHERE.. OH WELL.. IT'S OKAY... WE NEED TO GET GOING......
....WELL, THANKS FOR A GREAT NIGHT, MARY ANNE.
IT'S ABOUT TIME... YOU'RE TWO MINUTES LATE.
SORRY, SIR... WE WOULD HAVE BEEN ON TIME, BUT YOUR DAUGHTER HERE LOST HER VIRGINIA TEE.
...GEEZ, YOU'D THINK I TOOK IT.

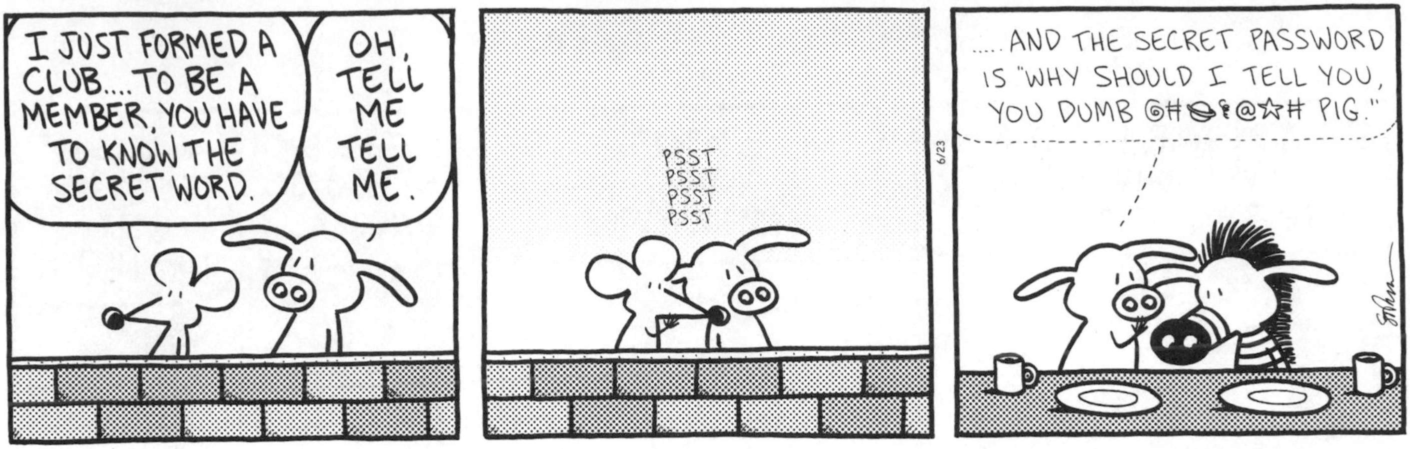
I JUST FORMED A CLUB.... TO BE A MEMBER, YOU HAVE TO KNOW THE SECRET WORD.
OH, TELL ME TELL ME.
PSST PSST PSST PSST
6/23
..... AND THE SECRET PASSWORD IS "WHY SHOULD I TELL YOU, YOU DUMB @#⊜!@☆# PIG."

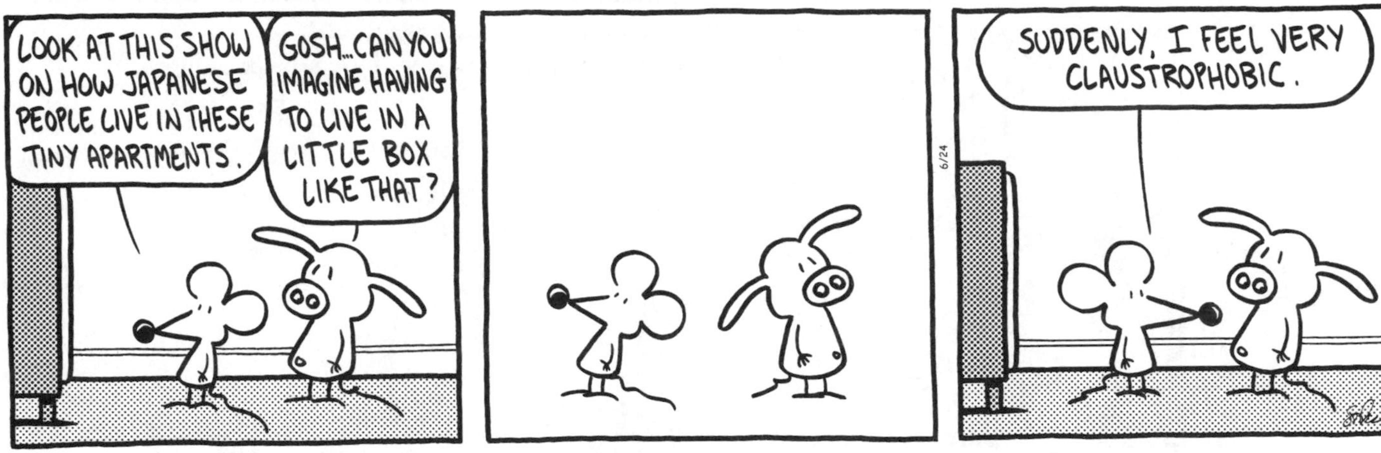
LOOK AT THIS SHOW ON HOW JAPANESE PEOPLE LIVE IN THESE TINY APARTMENTS.
GOSH... CAN YOU IMAGINE HAVING TO LIVE IN A LITTLE BOX LIKE THAT?
6/24
SUDDENLY, I FEEL VERY CLAUSTROPHOBIC.

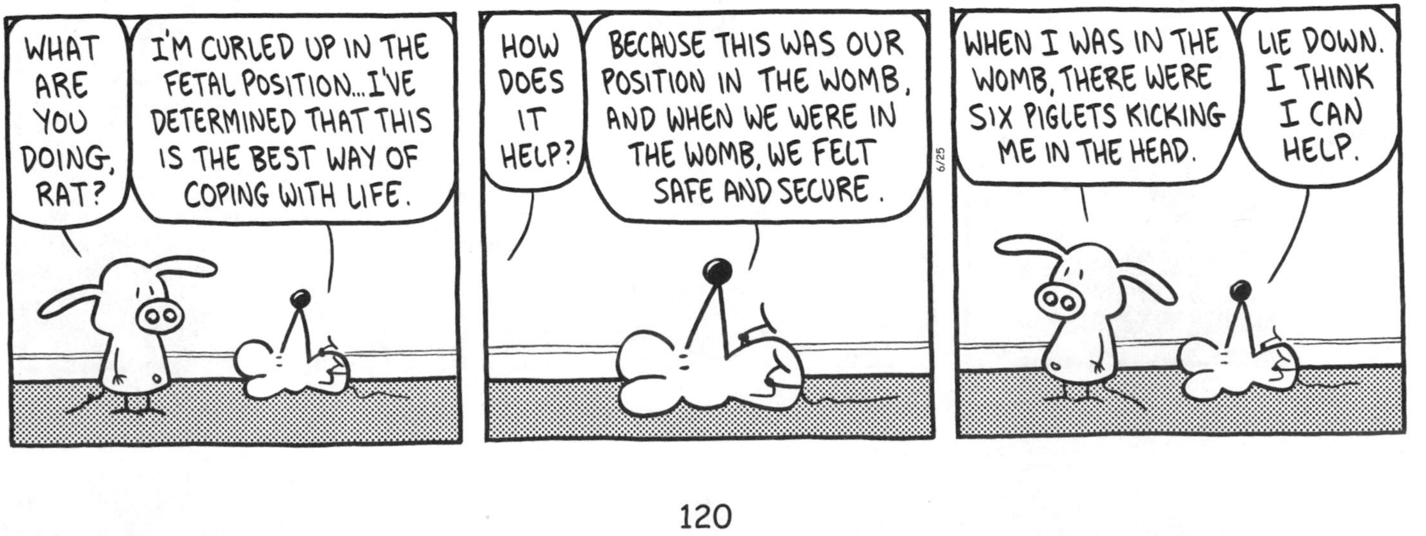
WHAT ARE YOU DOING, RAT?
I'M CURLED UP IN THE FETAL POSITION... I'VE DETERMINED THAT THIS IS THE BEST WAY OF COPING WITH LIFE.
HOW DOES IT HELP?
BECAUSE THIS WAS OUR POSITION IN THE WOMB, AND WHEN WE WERE IN THE WOMB, WE FELT SAFE AND SECURE.
6/25
WHEN I WAS IN THE WOMB, THERE WERE SIX PIGLETS KICKING ME IN THE HEAD.
LIE DOWN. I THINK I CAN HELP.

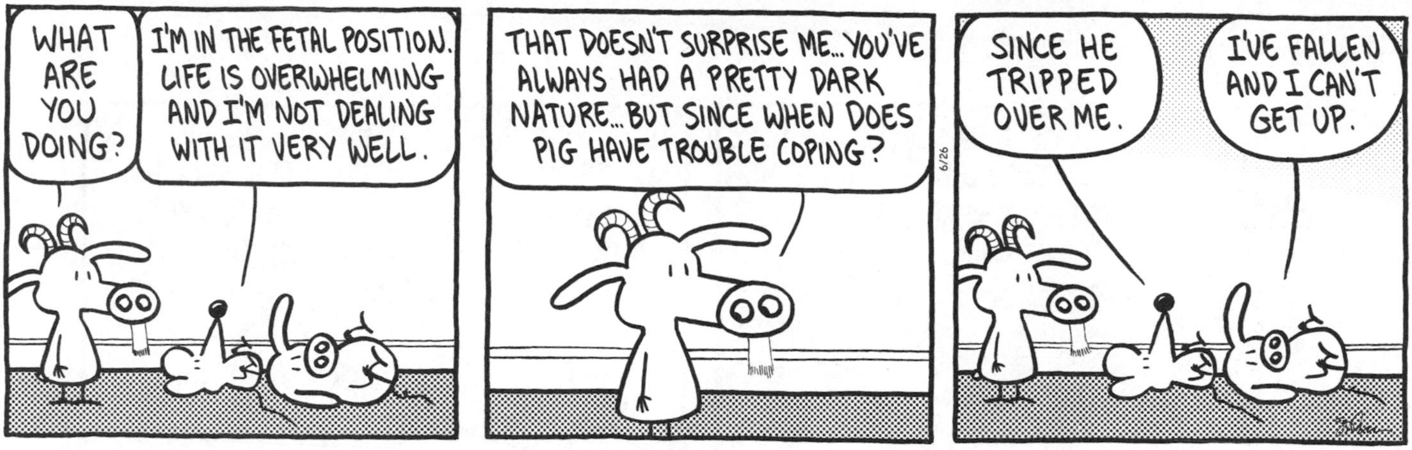
WHAT ARE YOU DOING?
I'M IN THE FETAL POSITION. LIFE IS OVERWHELMING AND I'M NOT DEALING WITH IT VERY WELL.
THAT DOESN'T SURPRISE ME... YOU'VE ALWAYS HAD A PRETTY DARK NATURE... BUT SINCE WHEN DOES PIG HAVE TROUBLE COPING?
6/26
SINCE HE TRIPPED OVER ME.
I'VE FALLEN AND I CAN'T GET UP.

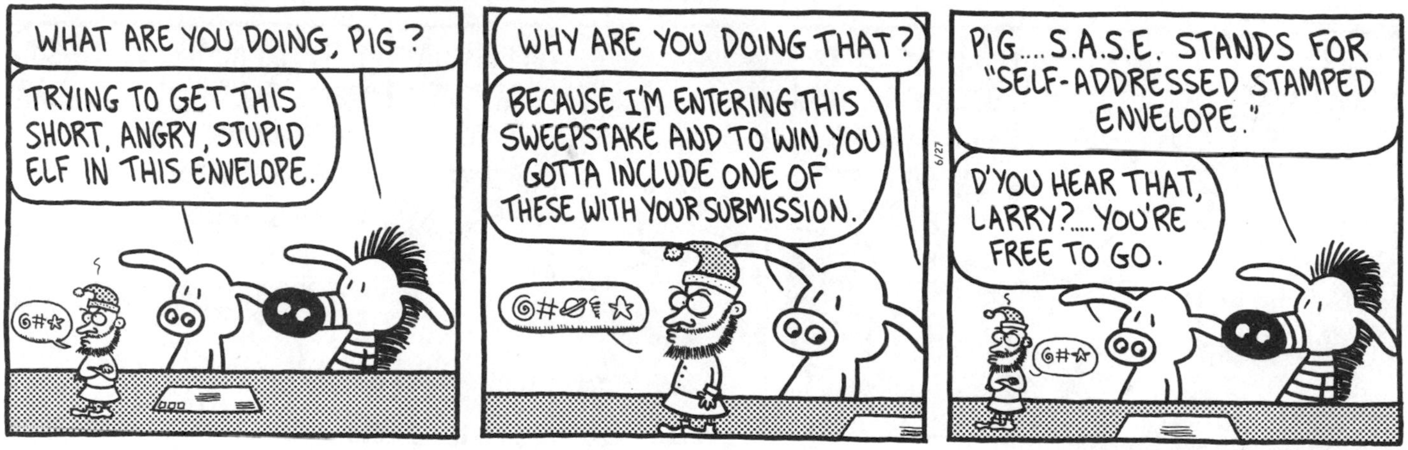
WHAT ARE YOU DOING, PIG?
TRYING TO GET THIS SHORT, ANGRY, STUPID ELF IN THIS ENVELOPE.
WHY ARE YOU DOING THAT?
BECAUSE I'M ENTERING THIS SWEEPSTAKE AND TO WIN, YOU GOTTA INCLUDE ONE OF THESE WITH YOUR SUBMISSION.
6/27
PIG.... S.A.S.E. STANDS FOR "SELF-ADDRESSED STAMPED ENVELOPE."
D'YOU HEAR THAT, LARRY?..... YOU'RE FREE TO GO.

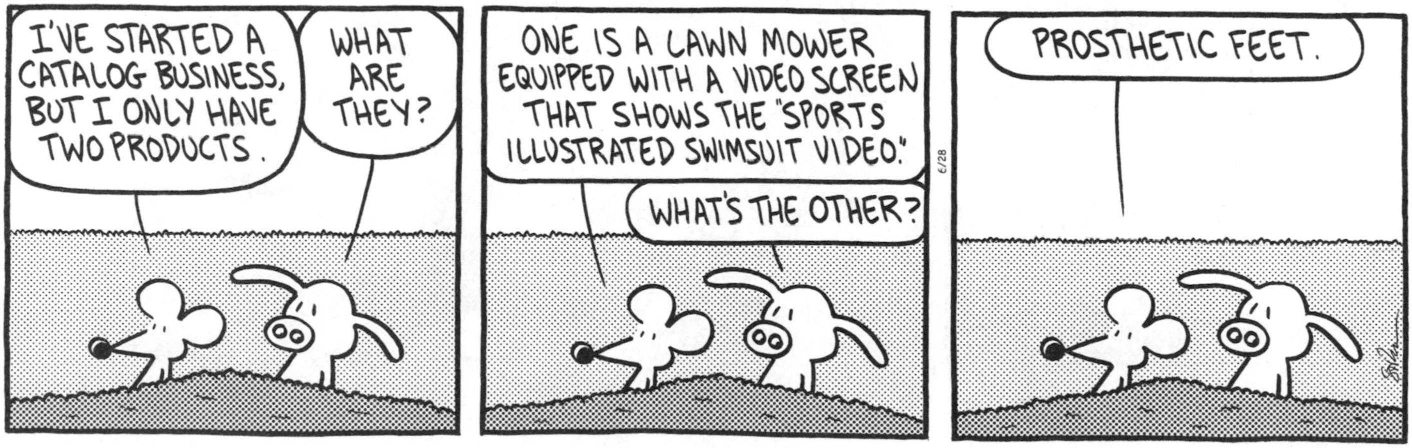
I'VE STARTED A CATALOG BUSINESS, BUT I ONLY HAVE TWO PRODUCTS.
WHAT ARE THEY?
ONE IS A LAWN MOWER EQUIPPED WITH A VIDEO SCREEN THAT SHOWS THE "SPORTS ILLUSTRATED SWIMSUIT VIDEO."
WHAT'S THE OTHER?
6/28
PROSTHETIC FEET.

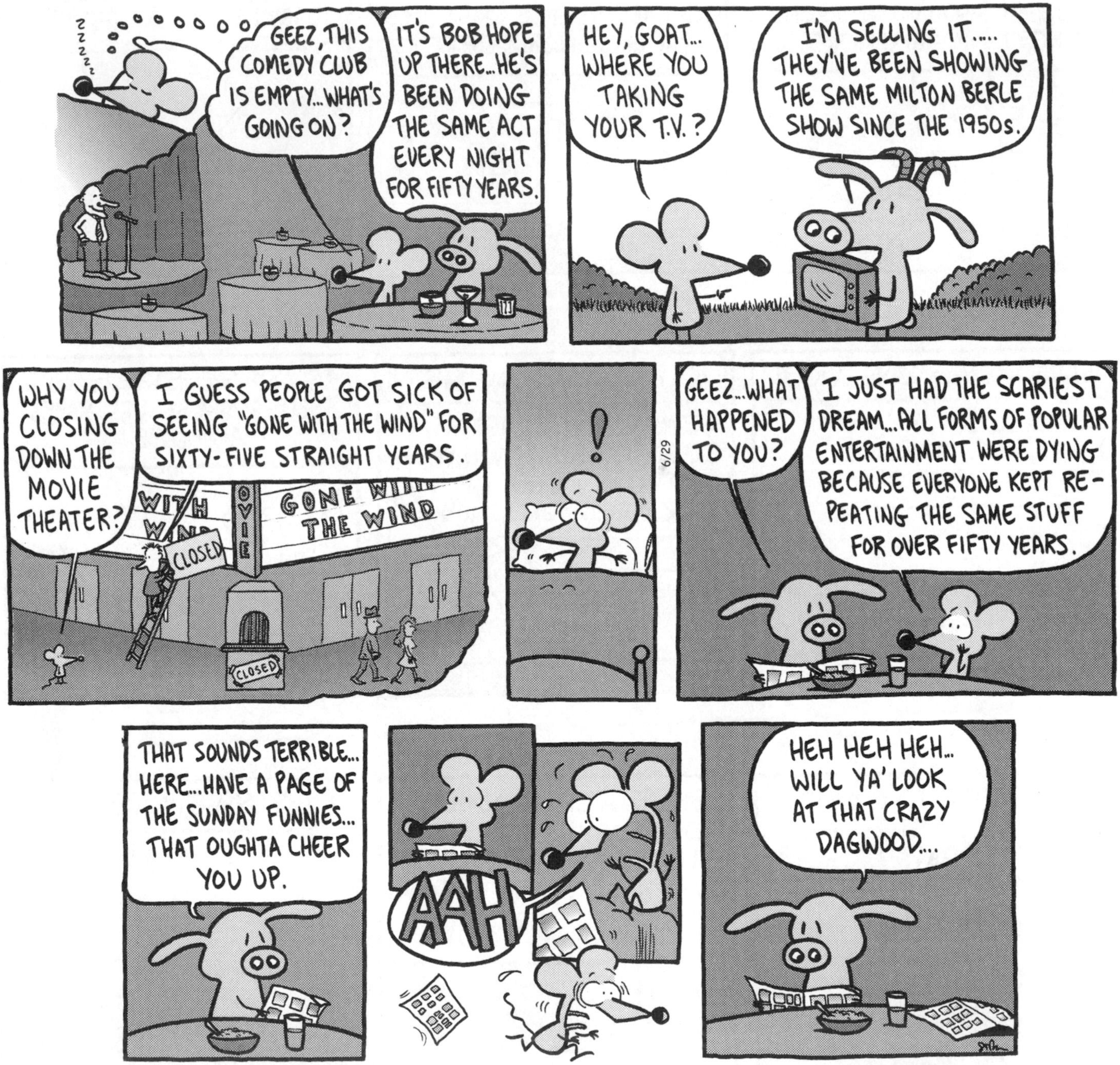
GEEZ, THIS COMEDY CLUB IS EMPTY...WHAT'S GOING ON?
IT'S BOB HOPE UP THERE...HE'S BEEN DOING THE SAME ACT EVERY NIGHT FOR FIFTY YEARS.
HEY, GOAT... WHERE YOU TAKING YOUR T.V.?
I'M SELLING IT..... THEY'VE BEEN SHOWING THE SAME MILTON BERLE SHOW SINCE THE 1950s.
WHY YOU CLOSING DOWN THE MOVIE THEATER?
I GUESS PEOPLE GOT SICK OF SEEING "GONE WITH THE WIND" FOR SIXTY-FIVE STRAIGHT YEARS.
GONE WITH THE WIND
CLOSED
CLOSED
!
6/29
GEEZ...WHAT HAPPENED TO YOU?
I JUST HAD THE SCARIEST DREAM...ALL FORMS OF POPULAR ENTERTAINMENT WERE DYING BECAUSE EVERYONE KEPT RE-PEATING THE SAME STUFF FOR OVER FIFTY YEARS.
THAT SOUNDS TERRIBLE... HERE...HAVE A PAGE OF THE SUNDAY FUNNIES... THAT OUGHTA CHEER YOU UP.
AAH
HEH HEH HEH... WILL YA' LOOK AT THAT CRAZY DAGWOOD....

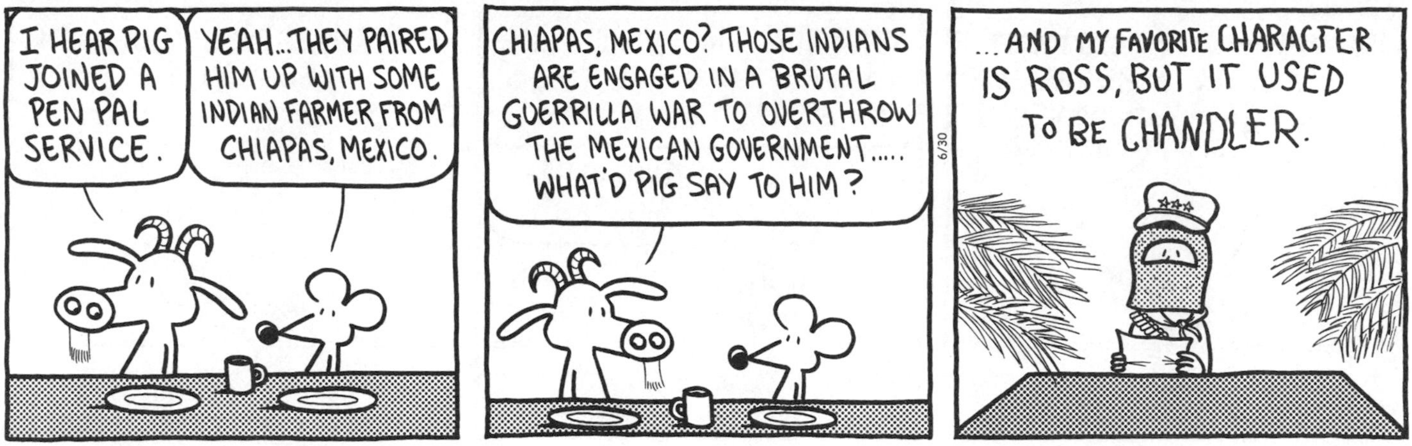
I HEAR PIG JOINED A PEN PAL SERVICE.
YEAH...THEY PAIRED HIM UP WITH SOME INDIAN FARMER FROM CHIAPAS, MEXICO.
CHIAPAS, MEXICO? THOSE INDIANS ARE ENGAGED IN A BRUTAL GUERRILLA WAR TO OVERTHROW THE MEXICAN GOVERNMENT..... WHAT'D PIG SAY TO HIM?
6/30
...AND MY FAVORITE CHARACTER IS ROSS, BUT IT USED TO BE CHANDLER.

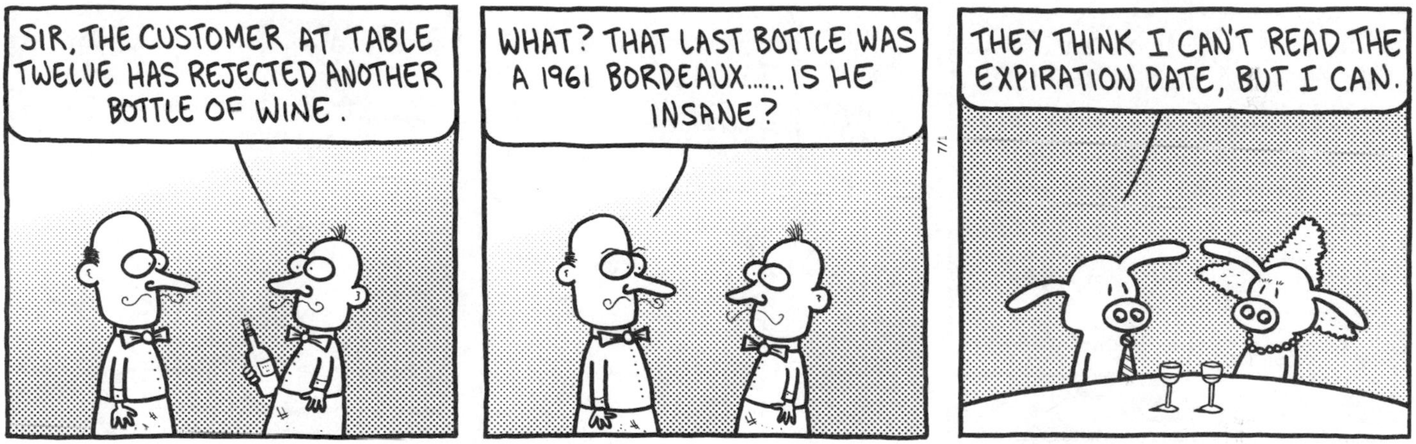
SIR, THE CUSTOMER AT TABLE TWELVE HAS REJECTED ANOTHER BOTTLE OF WINE.
WHAT? THAT LAST BOTTLE WAS A 1961 BORDEAUX...... IS HE INSANE?
7/1
THEY THINK I CAN'T READ THE EXPIRATION DATE, BUT I CAN.

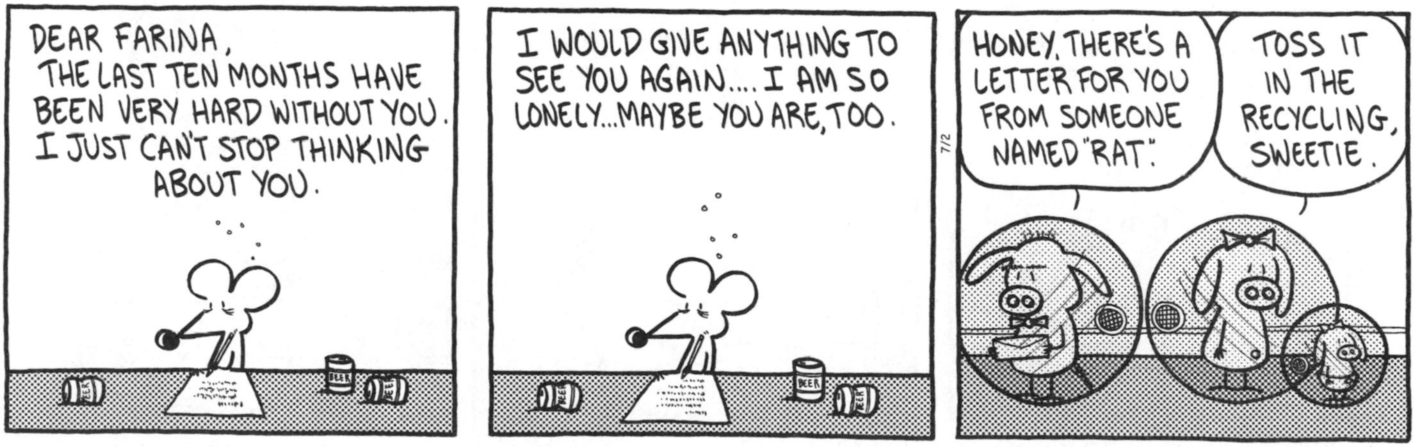
DEAR FARINA, THE LAST TEN MONTHS HAVE BEEN VERY HARD WITHOUT YOU. I JUST CAN'T STOP THINKING ABOUT YOU.
I WOULD GIVE ANYTHING TO SEE YOU AGAIN.... I AM SO LONELY...MAYBE YOU ARE, TOO.
7/2
HONEY, THERE'S A LETTER FOR YOU FROM SOMEONE NAMED "RAT".
TOSS IT IN THE RECYCLING, SWEETIE.

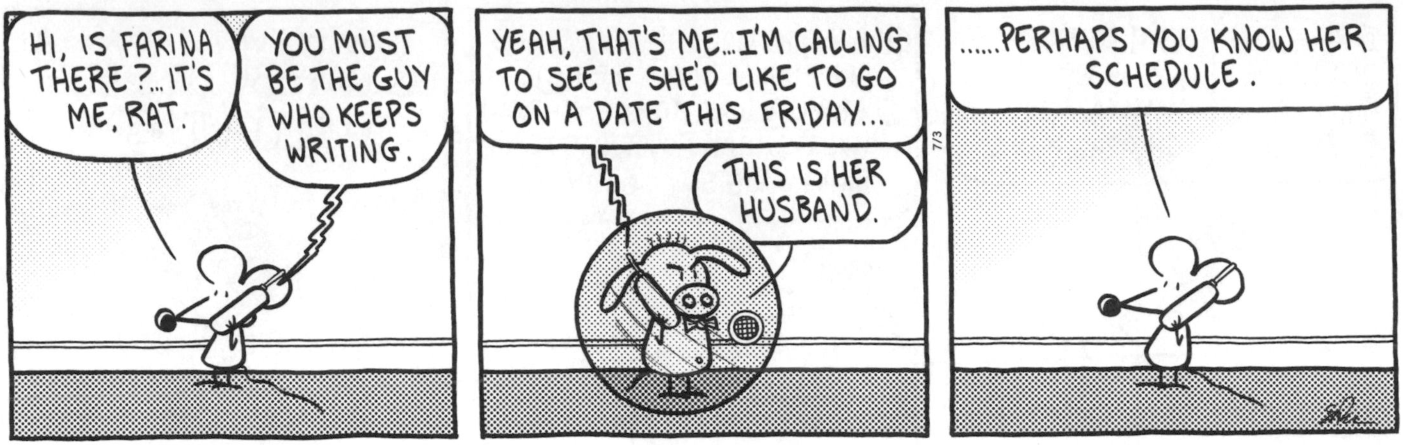
HI, IS FARINA THERE ?... IT'S ME, RAT.
YOU MUST BE THE GUY WHO KEEPS WRITING.
YEAH, THAT'S ME... I'M CALLING TO SEE IF SHE'D LIKE TO GO ON A DATE THIS FRIDAY...
THIS IS HER HUSBAND.
7/3
......PERHAPS YOU KNOW HER SCHEDULE.

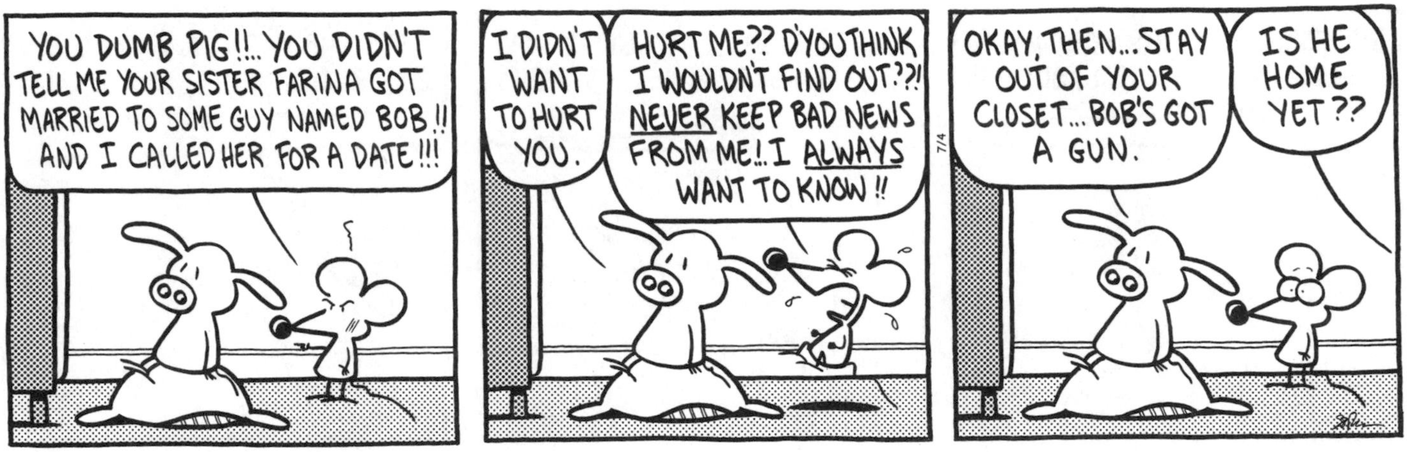
YOU DUMB PIG!!... YOU DIDN'T TELL ME YOUR SISTER FARINA GOT MARRIED TO SOME GUY NAMED BOB!! AND I CALLED HER FOR A DATE!!!
I DIDN'T WANT TO HURT YOU.
HURT ME?? D'YOUTHINK I WOULDN'T FIND OUT??! NEVER KEEP BAD NEWS FROM ME!.. I ALWAYS WANT TO KNOW!!
7/4
OKAY, THEN... STAY OUT OF YOUR CLOSET... BOB'S GOT A GUN.
IS HE HOME YET??

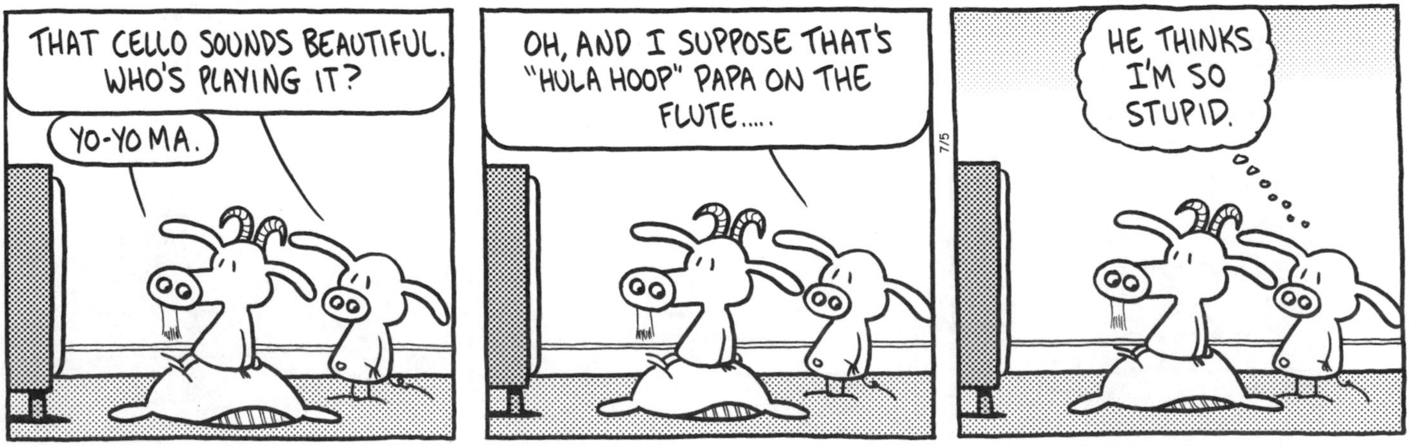
THAT CELLO SOUNDS BEAUTIFUL. WHO'S PLAYING IT?
YO-YO MA.
OH, AND I SUPPOSE THAT'S "HULA HOOP" PAPA ON THE FLUTE.....
7/5
HE THINKS I'M SO STUPID.

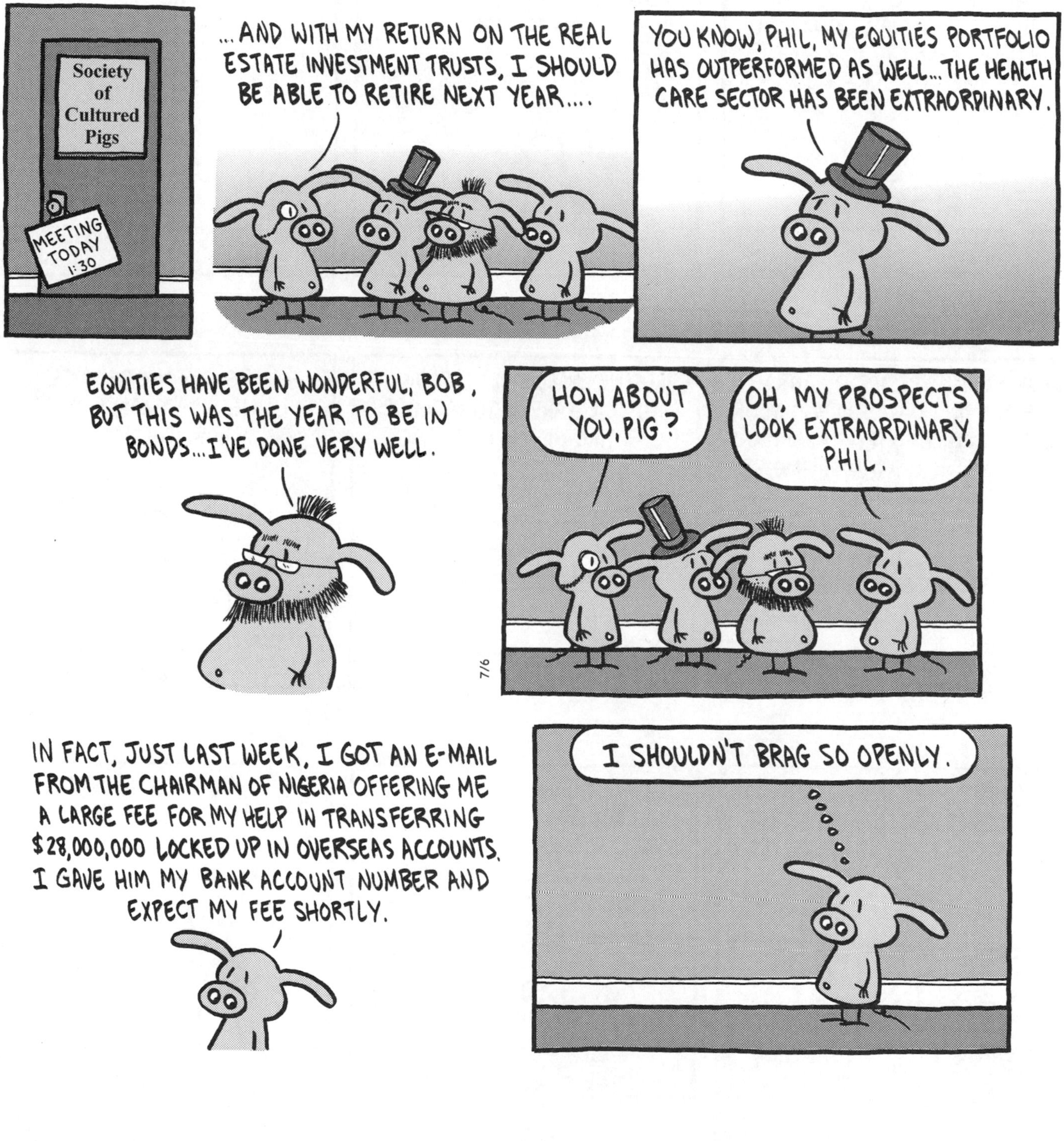
Society of Cultured Pigs
MEETING TODAY 1:30
...AND WITH MY RETURN ON THE REAL ESTATE INVESTMENT TRUSTS, I SHOULD BE ABLE TO RETIRE NEXT YEAR....
YOU KNOW, PHIL, MY EQUITIES PORTFOLIO HAS OUTPERFORMED AS WELL...THE HEALTH CARE SECTOR HAS BEEN EXTRAORDINARY.
EQUITIES HAVE BEEN WONDERFUL, BOB, BUT THIS WAS THE YEAR TO BE IN BONDS...I'VE DONE VERY WELL.
HOW ABOUT YOU, PIG?
OH, MY PROSPECTS LOOK EXTRAORDINARY, PHIL.
7/6
IN FACT, JUST LAST WEEK, I GOT AN E-MAIL FROM THE CHAIRMAN OF NIGERIA OFFERING ME A LARGE FEE FOR MY HELP IN TRANSFERRING $28,000,000 LOCKED UP IN OVERSEAS ACCOUNTS. I GAVE HIM MY BANK ACCOUNT NUMBER AND EXPECT MY FEE SHORTLY.
I SHOULDN'T BRAG SO OPENLY.

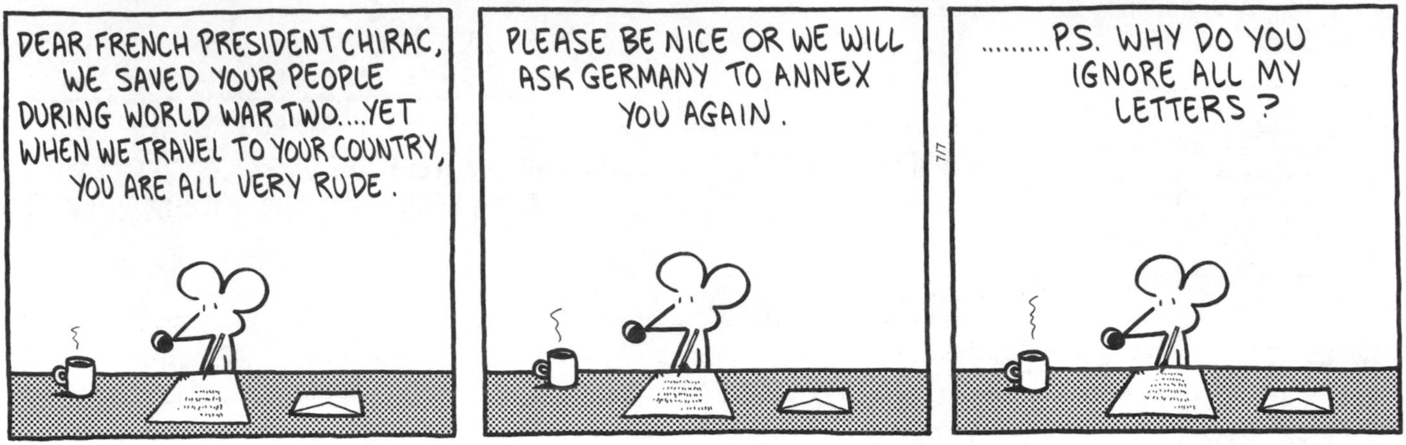
DEAR FRENCH PRESIDENT CHIRAC, WE SAVED YOUR PEOPLE DURING WORLD WAR TWO....YET WHEN WE TRAVEL TO YOUR COUNTRY, YOU ARE ALL VERY RUDE.
PLEASE BE NICE OR WE WILL ASK GERMANY TO ANNEX YOU AGAIN.
7/7
.........P.S. WHY DO YOU IGNORE ALL MY LETTERS?

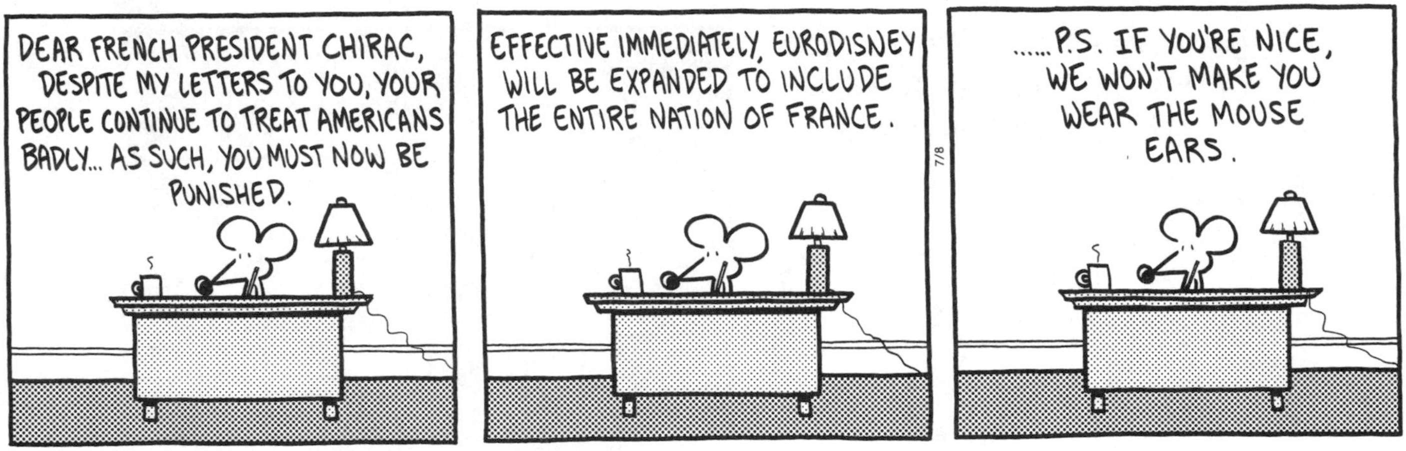
DEAR FRENCH PRESIDENT CHIRAC, DESPITE MY LETTERS TO YOU, YOUR PEOPLE CONTINUE TO TREAT AMERICANS BADLY... AS SUCH, YOU MUST NOW BE PUNISHED.
EFFECTIVE IMMEDIATELY, EURODISNEY WILL BE EXPANDED TO INCLUDE THE ENTIRE NATION OF FRANCE.
7/8
......P.S. IF YOU'RE NICE, WE WON'T MAKE YOU WEAR THE MOUSE EARS.

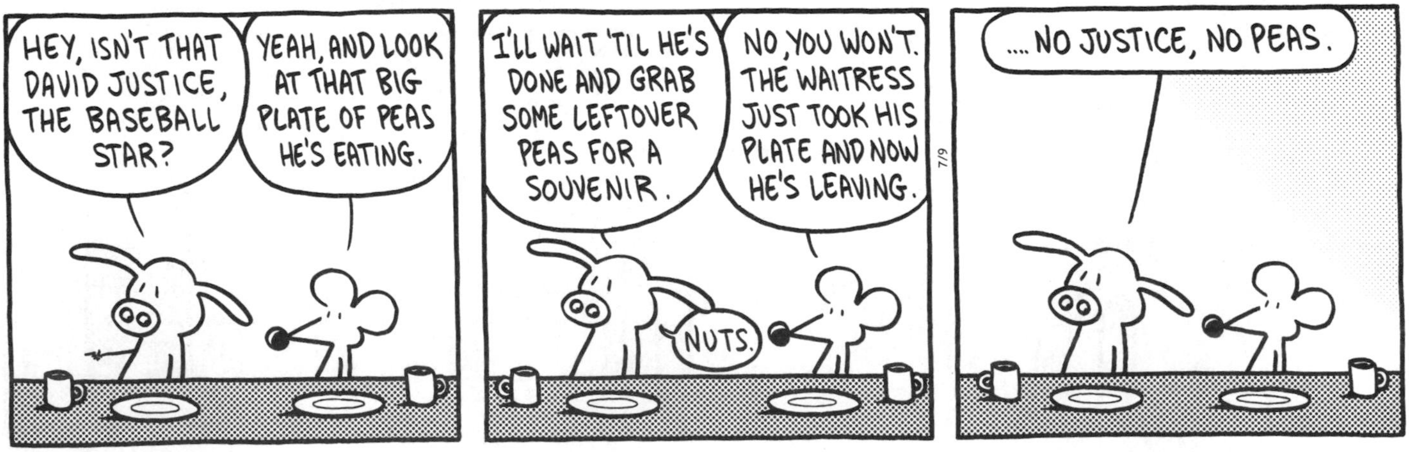
HEY, ISN'T THAT DAVID JUSTICE, THE BASEBALL STAR?
YEAH, AND LOOK AT THAT BIG PLATE OF PEAS HE'S EATING.
I'LL WAIT 'TIL HE'S DONE AND GRAB SOME LEFTOVER PEAS FOR A SOUVENIR.
NO, YOU WON'T. THE WAITRESS JUST TOOK HIS PLATE AND NOW HE'S LEAVING.
NUTS.
7/9
....NO JUSTICE, NO PEAS.

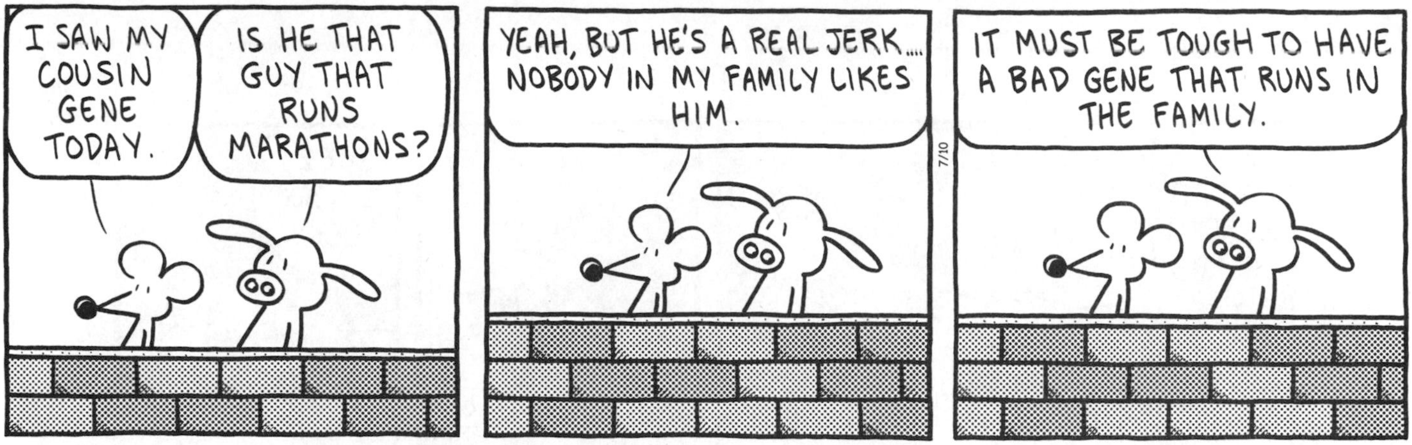
I SAW MY COUSIN GENE TODAY.
IS HE THAT GUY THAT RUNS MARATHONS?
7/10
YEAH, BUT HE'S A REAL JERK.... NOBODY IN MY FAMILY LIKES HIM.
IT MUST BE TOUGH TO HAVE A BAD GENE THAT RUNS IN THE FAMILY.

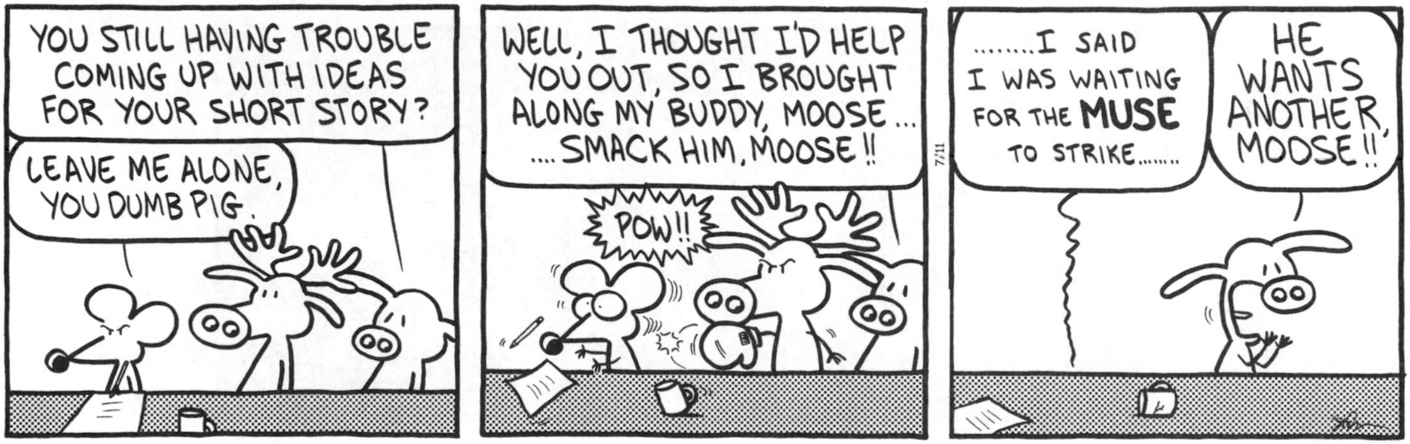
YOU STILL HAVING TROUBLE COMING UP WITH IDEAS FOR YOUR SHORT STORY?
LEAVE ME ALONE, YOU DUMB PIG.
7/11
WELL, I THOUGHT I'D HELP YOU OUT, SO I BROUGHT ALONG MY BUDDY, MOOSE... ....SMACK HIM, MOOSE!!
POW!!
........I SAID I WAS WAITING FOR THE **MUSE** TO STRIKE........
HE WANTS ANOTHER, MOOSE!!

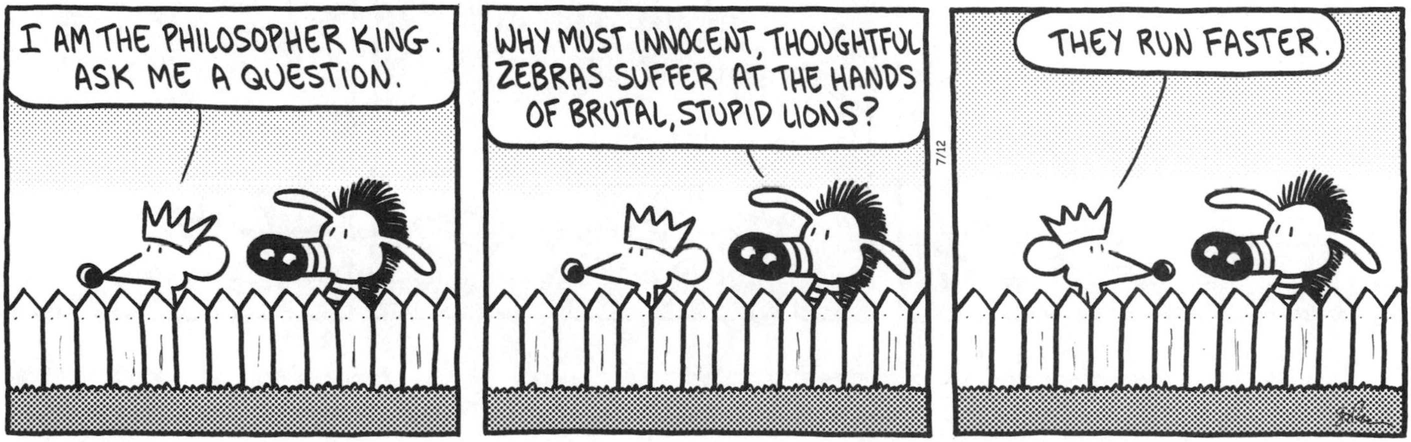
I AM THE PHILOSOPHER KING. ASK ME A QUESTION.
7/12
WHY MUST INNOCENT, THOUGHTFUL ZEBRAS SUFFER AT THE HANDS OF BRUTAL, STUPID LIONS?
THEY RUN FASTER.

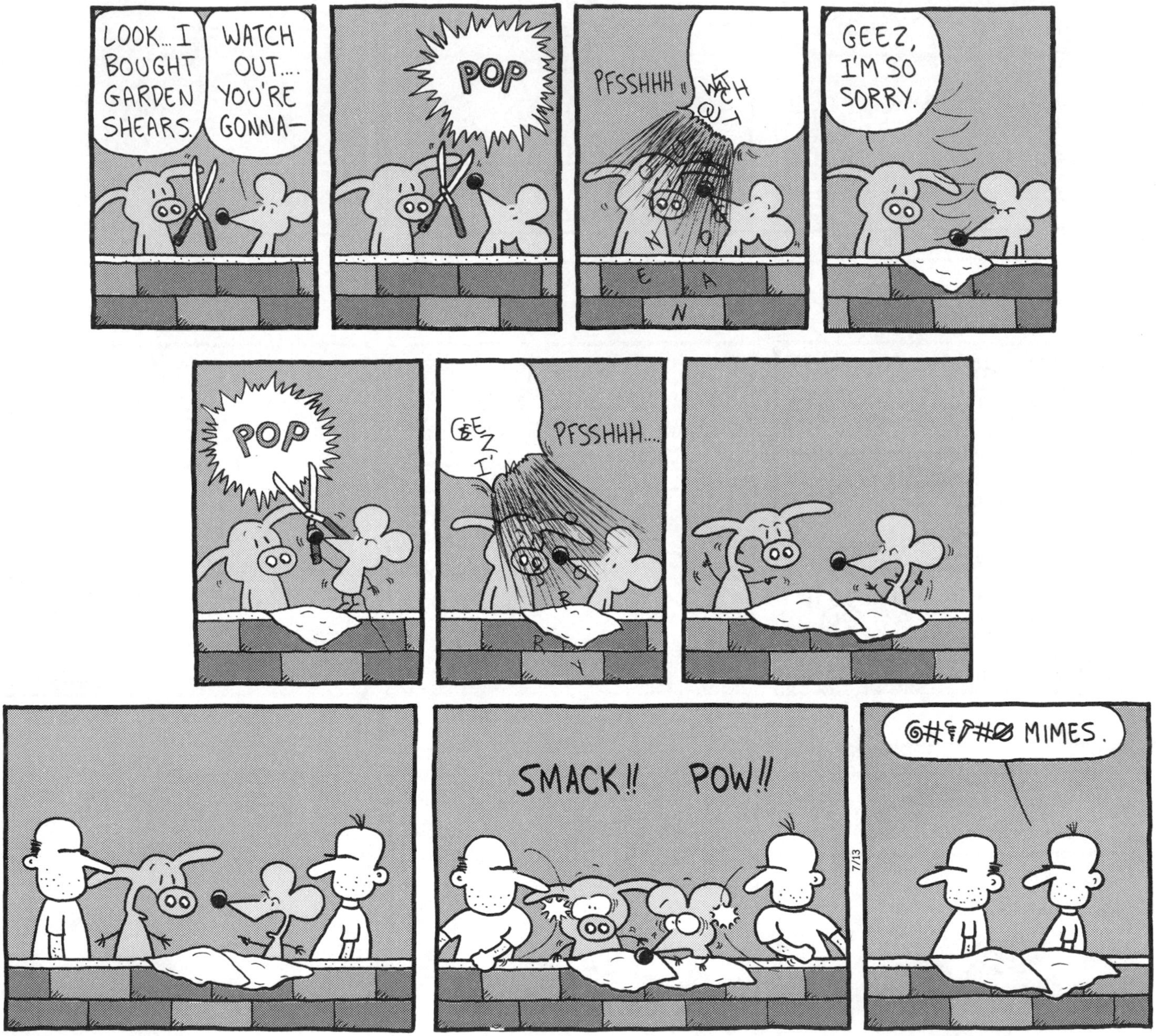
LOOK... I BOUGHT GARDEN SHEARS.
WATCH OUT.... YOU'RE GONNA—
POP
PFSSHHH
GEEZ, I'M SO SORRY.
POP
PFSSHHH...
SMACK!! POW!!
7/13
MIMES.